Forensic Accounting FOR DUMMIES®

by Frimette Kass-Shraibman
and Vijay S. Sampath

WILEY

John Wiley & Sons, Inc.

Forensic Accounting For Dummies®

Published by
Wiley Publishing, Inc.
111 River St.
Hoboken, NJ 07030-5774
www.wiley.com

Copyright © 2011 by Wiley Publishing, Inc., Indianapolis, Indiana

Published by Wiley Publishing, Inc., Indianapolis, Indiana

Published simultaneously in Canada

For general information on our other products and services, please contact our Customer Care Department within the U.S. at 877-762-2974, outside the U.S. at 317-572-3993, or fax 317-572-4002.

For technical support, please visit www.wiley.com/techsupport.

Wiley also publishes its books in a variety of electronic formats. Some content that appears in print may not be available in electronic books.

Library of Congress Control Number: 2010943056

ISBN: 978-0-470-88928-2

Manufactured in the United States of America

10 9 8 7

WILEY

About the Authors

Frimette Kass-Shraibman, PhD, CPA, is an associate professor of accounting at Brooklyn College-CUNY. She is also the editor of the *Journal of the CPA Practitioner,* a publication of the National Conference of CPA Practitioners News and Views. She is also a member of their Board of Directors. She spent over 20 years in public practice accounting where she practiced tax, audit, and forensics. She is formerly director of education for the Foundation for Accounting Education and a professional development manager at the American Institute of Certified Public Accountants. She has been awarded several medals for national tai chi competition. She is a life-long resident of Brooklyn, New York.

Vijay S. Sampath, CPA, CFE, MBA, is a managing director in the forensic accounting and litigation consulting practice at FTI Consulting Inc. He has more than 22 years of experience providing forensic accounting, litigation consulting, financial statement auditing, and business consulting services. He specializes in complex financial investigations involving generally accepted accounting principles and generally accepted auditing standards matters. Vijay also manages Foreign Corrupt Practices Act investigations, post-closing purchase price disputes, and other litigation matters involving white collar crime, bankruptcy, and contract proceedings. He is an adjunct professor at the Rutgers Business School, where he teaches financial accounting courses.

The views expressed in this book are those of the authors and not necessarily those of FTI Consulting Inc.

Dedications

My love and appreciation go to my wife, Ameesha, and my son, Karthik, for their unwavering support, understanding, and encouragement during this endeavor. — Vijay

I'd like to dedicate this to my husband Henry S. Shraibman for helping me pass the audit part of the CPA examination and for his endless help with the stories of frauds from his long auditing career. Also to my children Joseph, Sara, and Avi for being patient while I spent endless hours writing. — Frimette

Authors' Acknowledgments

The authors would like to acknowledge the following for their help with this book:

Toby Birnbaum, Esq., assistant professor of business law at Brooklyn College-CUNY

Susan Gross, CPA, JD, Feldman, Meinberg & Co

Clair Greifer & Assoc LLP, Feldman, Meinberg & Co

Carol Markman, CPA

Many students at Brooklyn College who contributed to Chapter 24; special thanks go to Arthur Nazarov, Winnie Yuen, and Nick Zavanov

For sharing their many experiences and war stories over their many years as auditors, we would like to thank:

Henry Shraibman, Bank Examiner, NYS Dept. of Banking

Prof. Sy Jones, CPA, New York University

Prof. Julius Cherney, CPA, Baruch College-CUNY

Authors would also like to thank the following people for their help and expertise:

Jamal Ahmad	Veeral Gosalia	Stephen O'Malley
Lisa Dane	Salahuddin Kamran	Dhruv Phopalia
Joseph Foy	Peter Kyviakidis	Roger Siefert

Publisher's Acknowledgments

We're proud of this book; please send us your comments at http://dummies.custhelp.com. For other comments, please contact our Customer Care Department within the U.S. at 877-762-2974, outside the U.S. at 317-572-3993, or fax 317-572-4002.

Some of the people who helped bring this book to market include the following:

Acquisitions, Editorial, and Media Development

Project Editor: Susan Hobbs

Acquisitions Editor: Stacy Kennedy

Copy Editor: Susan Hobbs

Assistant Editor: Erin Calligan Mooney

Editorial Program Coordinator: Joe Niesen

Technical Editor: Brian Muncy, CPA, CFE

Editorial Manager: Jennifer Ehrlich

Editorial Supervisor and Reprint Editor: Carmen Krikorian

Editorial Assistants: David Lutton, Jennette ElNaggar

Art Coordinator: Alicia B. South

Cover Photos: ©iStockphoto.com / Feng Yu

Cartoons: Rich Tennant (www.the5thwave.com)

Composition Services

Project Coordinator: Katie Crocker

Layout and Graphics: Carl Byers, Vida Noffsinger, Lavonne Roberts, Laura Westhius

Proofreader: ConText Editorial Services, Inc.

Indexer: Estalita Slivoskey

Publishing and Editorial for Consumer Dummies

Diane Graves Steele, Vice President and Publisher, Consumer Dummies

Kristin Ferguson-Wagstaffe, Product Development Director, Consumer Dummies

Ensley Eikenburg, Associate Publisher, Travel

Kelly Regan, Editorial Director, Travel

Publishing for Technology Dummies

Andy Cummings, Vice President and Publisher, Dummies Technology/General User

Composition Services

Debbie Stailey, Director of Composition Services

Contents at a Glance

Table of Contents

Introduction

So, what exactly is forensic accounting? If you're signed up to take a course on the subject or are considering where you'd like your accounting career to take you, you may be reading this page because you're looking for clarity about what the field of forensic accounting entails.

The word *forensic* usually inspires visions of *Law and Order* or *CSI* scenarios: a crime was committed, and detectives are gathering forensic evidence to try and figure out the cause and manner of death. But *accounting* inspires visions of debits, credits, and financial statements. How could these two words possibly fit together?

When you realize that *forensic* means applying scientific knowledge to legal issues, the phrase becomes easier to figure out. *Forensic accounting* is the study and interpretation of accounting evidence for presentation in a legal forum.

Most of the time, forensic accounting is used when someone commits fraud. For this reason, forensic accountants are often referred to as *fraud investigators* or *fraud examiners*. Fraud takes many forms, but at its heart, fraud is theft. Fraud is profiting by deceit or trickery; it involves the theft of funds or information or the use of someone's assets without permission. Many fraud cases are small, but some are downright catastrophic, which is why names such as Enron and Bernie Madoff are now part of our cultural literacy. The latest statistics show that $2.9 trillion (trillion with a *t*) is lost every year due to fraud, so as a forensic accountant, you have the chance to be a bit of a superhero — at least to the stockholders and employees whose life savings may be preserved if you can nip a business fraud in the bud.

Not every forensic accounting engagement centers around fraud. Forensic accountants are also involved in commercial litigation, calculating damages that can literally run into the billions of dollars. (BP oil spill, anybody?)

And forensic accountants don't always work on cases involving businesses. Sometimes, they're hired to search for hidden assets during a divorce, to help a homeowner whose property has been stolen with the stroke of a fraudulent signature, or to protect the estate of an elderly person who's been targeted by someone looking to make a quick fortune.

As we show you, the field of forensic accounting is new and growing explosively. If you think it may be the right path for you, we hope to help you better understand how exciting and challenging it can be.

About This Book

Most books about forensic accounting focus on one or two aspects of the field. This book is different — we wanted to give you a taste of every aspect of forensic accounting in a single book. We don't provide as much detail about each aspect as a forensic accounting textbook might (we can hear you shouting for joy!), but that's because our goal is different than a textbook's goal. First, we want you to actually understand what you read! Second, we want you to walk away from each chapter understanding why that subject matters — how the information comes into play when you're actually on the job.

We organized this book so that you can open up any chapter and start reading. If you're looking for something in a jiffy — whether it's information about inventory fraud or applying technology to prevent fraud — you can put your finger on it easily and read just that chapter or section without feeling lost.

We're also big believers in the importance of rooting academic discussions in real life. For that reason, we provide lots of stories in this book about real fraudsters and their get-rich schemes (which often result in them getting arrested and getting imprisoned).

Conventions Used in This Book

This isn't a book about financial accounting, so you don't have to memorize loads of picky conventions. Just keep a couple things in mind as you read:

- ✔ When we introduce a term that we think may be new to you, we put that word in italic and then define it for you.

- ✔ When this book was printed, some Web addresses may have needed to break across two lines of text. If that happened, rest assured that we haven't put in any extra characters (such as hyphens) to indicate the break. When using one of these Web addresses, just type in exactly what you see in this book, pretending as though the line break doesn't exist.

What You're Not to Read

We spent a lot of time creating this book, so we'd really like to believe that you're going to savor every word! But we're not that naïve. So here's the scoop: If you're in a rush and need to focus on the true nitty gritty, feel free to skip past the *sidebars* in this book: the gray boxes that are set apart from the rest of the text. (See how this whole italic/definition thing works?) We've included some really juicy stories in some of those sidebars, but they are truly asides. If time is short, read around them and know that you're not missing any information that is crucial to your forensic accounting education.

Foolish Assumptions

We wrote this book believing that you're either an accounting student or a fairly new accountant still feeling your way around the field. For that reason, we assume that you know very little about how to identify, investigate, and prevent fraud.

However, we do assume that you bring a certain level of accounting knowledge with you:

- ✔ We trust that you have had a grounding in financial accounting. We don't explain the basics of debits and credits, trial balances, and the mechanics of preparing balance sheets and income statements. If you haven't yet taken an introductory accounting course, you need to do so for parts of this book to make sense.

- ✔ We also assume that, courtesy of your introductory accounting course(s), you know something about auditing as well. For that reason, we don't discuss the particulars of how an audit works. (We'd run out of pages in no time if we did so!)

Finally, we assume that you're truly interested in learning new and exciting stuff, and that you picked this particular book because you want to have fun reading it. We had a great time writing it, and we tried to make it enjoyable. We can just about guarantee it's more fun than any accounting textbook sitting on your shelf!

How This Book Is Organized

This book is divided into seven parts, each of which contains several chapters. Here, we run down what you find in each part.

Part I: Investigating Forensic Accounting

In Part I we provide an overview of forensic accounting, including what fraud is, who the buyers of forensic accounting services are, and what you should do when embarking on a career in forensic accounting. We discuss the most common types of fraud in the business and public sectors. And because not every forensic accounting engagement deals with fraud, we explain other types of engagements you will encounter during your career as a forensic accountant.

Part II: The Anatomy of Occupational Fraud

Occupational fraud is any type of fraud taking place within a business or institution (whether large or small). Part II starts out by discussing financial statement fraud, known as *cooking the books*. We then tell you about inventory fraud and revenue recognition issues. If you want to learn how businesses manipulate their own stock values and steer investor decisions that benefit the business (and often harm the investor), we give you that information as well.

Part III: It's All in the Family: Fraud against Individuals

Many forensic accountants work on cases that don't involve businesses or institutions. These chapters focus on the most common types of forensic accounting engagements that involve frauds perpetrated against friends, family members, and neighbors. You learn about what forensic accountants do when they're hired by individuals who suspect their soon-to-be ex-spouses aren't playing fair during divorce proceedings; when they investigate crimes that involve the elderly, estates, trusts, and life insurance; and when they're called on to help people defrauded by real estate schemes.

Part IV: Meeting Your Methods of Investigation

This part details the methods most commonly used by forensic accountants to discover and investigate occupational fraud, as well as fraud against individuals. We walk you through the investigation process, getting information about subjects, and using technology in finding fraud. We then discuss the crucial role played by the forensic accountant prior to and possibly during litigation. This part outlines those responsibilities and offers insights into the specific requirements for litigation involving government and business entities.

Part V: Preventing Occupational Fraud

Deterring fraud is as important as investigating it, and accountants often counsel their clients on fraud prevention. The goal of this part is to teach you internal controls and fraud-deterrence techniques that reduce the probability of fraud. Small and large businesses have their own unique issues that we explore in this part. We also discuss the types of technology available to keep a business secure from fraud.

Part VI: The Part of Tens

This part is probably the most fun of all. We give you three short chapters to whet your whistle for the forensic accounting field. We start with a list of ten portrayals of fraud in TV and in the movies that you may want to add to your "must-watch" list. We continue with a chapter about ten frauds that are fairly common but often unsuspected. And we conclude with ten truly strange fraud stories that may leave you shaking your head.

Also, assuming that you want to know more about forensic accounting after getting initiated, we provide a short appendix that lists valuable online resources to check out.

Icons Used in This Book

In the left margins of this book, you find the following icons, each of which alerts you to specific types of text:

The Case File icon sits next to real-life stories that relate to the topic at hand. Fortunately for us, the world is full of fraudsters who supplied ample fodder for this book. Read all about them where you see this icon.

The Tip icon alerts you to actions you can take to improve your chances of discovering, investigating, and following up on fraud.

When you see this icon, you know the information in that paragraph is worth tucking into your mental filing cabinet for future use.

On rare occasions, we delve a bit deeper into the subject matter than you may need to go. This icon lets you know that the paragraph contains in-depth information that may offer more details than a student or beginning forensic accountant needs.

Where to Go from Here

The beauty about this book is that you can jump in anywhere: We've designed it so you can start in the middle or at the end and easily understand everything we're saying. So spend a few minutes with the table of contents or index, locate a subject that's particularly interesting to you, and jump in! Or, if your mind is just too linear for that approach, feel free to turn the page and head to Chapter 1. Either way, we're confident you're going to enjoy the time you spend with us, so let's begin!

Part I
Investigating Forensic Accounting

The 5th Wave   By Rich Tennant

FORENSIC ACCOUNTANTS

"Sweet. I didn't know Smith and Wesson made a calculator."

In this part . . .

We start at the very beginning, by explaining what forensic accountants do, how their work differs from the work done by other accountants and auditors, and how you can steer your career toward forensic accounting by taking the right courses and looking for the right types of jobs.

We then get deeper into the discussion of why forensic accountants are necessary (and becoming more in demand every day). The reason for this is because lots and lots of people commit fraud. We devote a whole chapter to outlining the most common types of fraud, focusing largely on those committed within businesses. Forensic accountants don't always deal with fraud, however, so we also offer a chapter explaining other types of work you may do as a forensic accountant.

Chapter 1

Why the World Needs
Forensic Accountants

. . . .

. . . .

*E*nron, WorldCom, Tyco, Bernie Madoff — their names are infamous, and they're all known to us for the same reason: fraud. Recent estimates indicate that almost $3 trillion is lost globally to occupational fraud and abuse (the kind that occurs within a business) each year. That number would seem hard to believe if we hadn't all heard about the massive scale of fraud that has occurred at businesses such as Enron.

Investigating fraud can be complex. In a larger engagement, forensic accountants assist in performing various procedures that include reviewing millions and millions of documents, decoding financial information, interviewing scores of people, and gathering background information about key company players. Using technology is critical to the investigative process, and at the end of the investigation forensic accountants report their findings and sometimes provide testimony in a litigation context.

Forensic accounting as a profession has evolved in the past two decades. Recently, some universities and colleges have included it in their curricula. Organizations such as the Association of Certified Fraud Examiners (ACFE) and the American Institute of Certified Public Accountants (AICPA) now offer designations in fraud examination and forensics.

What motivates people to commit fraud? What are common types of fraud schemes? How can frauds be detected or prevented? How should they be investigated? These are some of the questions we explore in this book. To get you started, we offer an overview in this chapter of what forensic accounting is and why the proliferation of fraud has created such a strong need for it.

Accounting versus Auditing: Defining Our Terms

Accounting and auditing are substantially interrelated. In brief, *accounting* is the preparation of financial statements, and *auditing* is the examination of those financial statements. Every collegiate accounting program also offers auditing. Auditors have traditionally been certified public accountants (CPAs).

In this section, we examine accounting and auditing more closely to illustrate what they are and how they interrelate.

Working as an accountant

What is accounting? When Frimette teaches introductory accounting classes, she defines accounting as the gathering, analyzing, recording, summarizing, reporting, and interpretation of financial transactions for an entity. Wow, what a mouthful! What does it mean? Accountants gather information about transactions, record that information, and then massage it so that the end product is a set of financial statements that various types of users can use to make rational financial decisions about the entity.

The recipe that accountants use to do all this gathering, recording, and massaging is called *generally accepted accounting principles* or GAAP. Way back in 1494, a Franciscan monk in Venice named Friar Luca Pacioli published a book called *Summa de Arithmetica, Geometria, Proportioni et Proportionalita* (Everything about Arithmetic, Geometry, and Proportion). In it, Fr. Pacioli described the double-entry method of accounting — the method we still use today. *Double-entry accounting* reflects the fact that businesses have two sides:

✔ They have assets.

✔ They have claims on those assets, as well as sources that create the assets.

Although the basics of double-entry accounting have been around a while, business transactions have become much more complicated than they were in 1494. To refine how accounting should be used in today's complex world, we have guidelines. In the United States, these guidelines — GAAP — are determined by the Financial Accounting Standards Board (FASB), an accounting think tank in Norwich, Connecticut. Most developed countries have their own version of the FASB and GAAP. There is even an International Accounting Standards Board (IASB) that sets International Financial Reporting Standards (IFRS). All these systems of standards have a lot of similarities because they are all based on Fr. Pacioli's work.

In the United States, financial accountants may work inside industry (working for one company) or in public accounting (having many clients). They help companies prepare their financial information and present it in the form of financial statements.

For detailed information about working as an accountant in the United States, check out *Accounting For Dummies,* 4th edition, by John A. Tracy, CPA (Wiley).

Working as an auditor

An audit is an independent, objective, and systematic examination of underlying data in order to form an opinion about someone else's assertions. Wow, another big definition! Let's pull it apart a bit.

First, let's focus on what *independent* and *objective* mean. An auditor must be independent of the entity he audits, which means he cannot have any relationship with that entity other than the audit itself. He has to be objective, meaning he may not enter the engagement with any preconceived notions about the client or the work he is to perform.

Next, consider what *systematic* means, or what it means for an auditor to perform his work systematically. Every auditor has to prepare an audit plan before she begins the actual audit. The audit plan explains what types of evidence the auditor will analyze and the tests she plans to perform. The auditor develops the plan based on substantial preliminary risk assessment about the client. After the plan is developed, the auditor may change the preliminary risk assessment if additional information is discovered during the planned audit procedures. If the preliminary risk assessment is modified, the auditor must document the reason for modifying the preliminary risk assessment.

After the auditor has gathered enough information, she gives an opinion about whether someone else's statements are true or not. In most cases, audits focus on a company's financial statements. Company management is making a variety of assertions in those statements:

✔ That the financial statements are inclusive of all transactions

✔ That all transactions have really occurred

✔ That assets and liabilities exist and are recorded at the proper value

✔ That the company has rights to all its assets

✔ That all the necessary *disclosures* (notes to the financial statements) have been made

Management also asserts which set of standards (such as GAAP) the company is using as its guideline. The auditor's job is to test all these assertions thoroughly enough to form an opinion about their validity.

Whereas most audits are financial statements audits, other kinds of audits exist as well. *Compliance audits* check to see if an entity is in compliance with certain rules. For example, if the IRS knocks on your door, it wants to check whether your tax returns were prepared in accordance with the Internal Revenue Code. *Operational audits* are used to determine if an entity is operating efficiently.

To perform a financial statement audit, most jurisdictions require that the auditor be a CPA in that jurisdiction. The CPA license is certainly required when performing financial statement audits of companies whose securities trade in the public markets.

Generally, the ethics for auditors are embodied in the Code of Ethics of the American Institute of Certified Public Accountants (AICPA). Every CPA licensing board (there are 54 of them) has its own code of conduct for accountants. However, for the most part, they are all similar to the AICPA's code of conduct.

To get the nitty-gritty details about life as an auditor, pick up a copy of *Auditing For Dummies* by Maire Loughran (Wiley).

Adding "Forensic" to the Mix

Forensic means having to do with the court or with public debate. *Forensic accounting* happens when special accounting and auditing techniques are used to gather and present information for the courts or other legal matters.

Taking accounting and auditing to the courtroom

Sometimes the courts, or lawyers, need a deeper understanding of financial transactions. Rather than wade through the transactions themselves, they retain a forensic accountant.

In the case of a criminal act, lawyers may need help figuring out if a financial fraud has occurred. Who better to determine this than an accountant, who already has a deep knowledge of how to follow transactions through the maze of books and records? The forensic accountant may not only help determine if a fraud has occurred but also determine how much money was taken and where it went. This information may be crucial if victims are trying to get back any of their stolen funds.

Accountants are often part of a team that may be defending a taxpayer in a tax fraud case or a company accused of financial statement fraud. The defense may call upon an accountant to explain to the courts why certain transactions or financial statements are not fraudulent. An accountant may practice tax forensics even when it's not a direct tax case. Every white-collar crime attorney knows that the U.S. Attorney's office will look at a suspect's tax returns. If they can't get the suspect on the original criminal accusation, they will try to get him on tax fraud. That's how Al Capone was finally convicted! Attorneys weren't able to get him for all the suspected murders he was involved in, but they did put him away for tax evasion. We've reviewed and/or prepared many a suspect's tax return at the request of that person's criminal defense attorney.

Accountants are also involved in *business valuation*, which means determining the value of a small business. Business valuation comes into play in many situations, including:

- ✔ Disputes between partners
- ✔ Buy-sell agreements
- ✔ Mergers and acquisitions
- ✔ Estate planning and gifting
- ✔ Divorce
- ✔ Eminent domain cases
- ✔ Torts

Getting special training and licenses — or not

As of this writing, you don't need any specific licenses or training to call yourself a forensic accountant. (That situation is subject to change as the field grows.) Many forensic accountants get on-the-job training. They are thrust into a situation that requires forensic techniques, and they need to catch on fast. Fortunately, most accountants adapt easily to the demands of this field. Our skills as auditors, knowledge of transactions, and natural skepticism make it easy for us to adapt. And when on-the-job training involves working alongside a more seasoned forensic accountant, you often pick up the necessary skills even faster.

Many of the large accounting firms have in-house forensic accounting training programs. The various state CPA societies also offer training and education in many areas of interest to accountants, including forensics.

Two of the most prominent organizations that offer training in forensic accounting also offer certification. These are the Association of Certified Fraud Examiners (ACFE) and the National Association of Certified Valuation Analysts (NACVA). Both organizations offer many education programs as well as certification. ACFE is probably the better-known organization. Its former president, Joseph T. Wells, CFE, CPA, is a prolific writer on the subject of forensic financial examination and is often quoted by the press. ACFE also issues the Certified Fraud Examiner (CFE) designation, which requires documented experience in the field, education, and testing. The CFE does not require that you have an accounting background. We talk more about the CFE and other certifications in Chapter 2.

Why bother with training and certification if it isn't required? First, getting additional education is never a bad thing — especially if you know that forensic accounting is going to be your niche. Second, being recognized as having the knowledge and skills sets to perform investigations will give you an edge over those who don't have these skills. Finally, consider the fact that forensic accountants often have to testify in court. A jury may be more likely to accept that you're an expert if you have specialty certifications.

Creating the Need for Forensic Accountants: Fraud

Investigating fraud is a growing industry. The more fraud that occurs, the more the need for forensic accountants expands. In its annual report, the ACFE estimated the cost of fraud in 2009 to be $2.9 trillion and reported that nearly a quarter of those fraud cases involved losses of $1 million or more.

In this section, we touch on what fraud is, who the perpetrators and victims of fraud may be, and why fraud happens. We also discuss in more detail how much fraud is happening in the business world today.

What is fraud, anyway?

Fraud is theft. Fraud is stealing. Fraud is profiting by deceit or trickery. Fraud involves the theft of funds or information or possibly the use of another's assets without permission.

Fraud may be done directly or indirectly: Someone can steal something outright or can encourage stealing. Fraud can also take the form of not caring when you know someone else is doing the stealing. Fraud requires at least some degree of intent to commit the wrong or to go along with the wrong. Therefore, errors in judgment are not a fraud.

Unlike a lot of other types of theft, fraud does not usually involve physical violence. Therefore, fraud is considered *white-collar* crime. Some people hold the belief that fraud is a "clean" form of crime, but fraud can have a devastating effect on its victims. Many victims of Enron and Bernie Madoff, for example, lost their entire savings and had to drastically alter their lifestyles.

Frauds can be small, big, or gargantuan. A thief who steals a credit card and charges a few hundred dollars to it is committing a small fraud. Madoff made off with an estimated $65 billion.

Who commits fraud, and who are the victims?

Frauds are committed by businesses, big and small, and by individuals. And those same entities can all become victims of fraud. Here, we introduce several scenarios to show how business and individuals may commit or be victimized by fraud.

Businesses committing fraud on individuals

Businesses often commit frauds against their individual customers. It's not hard. You may even have been a victim.

Do you have a credit card? How do you know that your credit card company is computing your finance charge correctly? Imagine if the card company performed the interest computation so that you got charged just one penny more. A penny isn't a big deal; you wouldn't know about the overcharge or miss the money. But if you multiply the number of credit cards issued by that bank by one cent, the result can be a tidy sum.

Now, take this scenario a step farther. Because you have a small balance on your credit card, you get charged only a penny more. However, finance charges are usually computed using multiplication. You get charged a penny, but the guy down the street happens to be carrying a large balance so he gets charged 20 cents more. If you don't pay your full balance, next month you're paying interest on the remainder. If part of your balance is a fraud and you don't catch it, you get to pay interest on the fraudulent interest, which gets computed fraudulently as well. A one-cent fraud on each account can turn into millions of dollars for the credit card company very quickly.

Banks and bank employees have been known to commit frauds like this. Unless someone such as a forensic accountant recomputes the interest, no one knows.

In Frimette's neighborhood, there was a small beauty salon that did not have the cash register electronically compute sales tax. Every time someone got a haircut, the sales tax was computed differently. Customers long suspected that this situation was a ploy to raise revenue. To this day, we still can't figure out if the cashier was pocketing the difference between the collections and the true amount or if she was following the owner's instructions. Or it may not have been a fraud at all. Maybe the cashier just couldn't do arithmetic and didn't fully understand the importance of getting the sales tax right.

Individuals committing fraud on businesses

Obviously, individuals commit frauds on businesses, too. You may know someone who has perpetrated such a fraud, or you may have done it yourself. Some of these frauds are small: Have you ever used the office copy machine or postage meter for personal reasons? Have you ever taken home some office supplies? C'mon now, come clean!

Here's another common fraud that department stores complain about all the time: A woman is invited to a special event and needs an appropriate dress. She buys a dress for the event but doesn't take off the tags; she somehow manages to stick the tags inside the garment. (They may scratch a little, but it's worth the discomfort.) The day after the event, she takes the dress back to the store for a refund. Is this fraud? Yes. You may be wondering "What's the harm? The store has the dress back!" The problem is that the store now has a *worn* dress. Maybe the dress has a little stain that you didn't even notice, and as a result the dress has to go on a clearance rack. Even if the dress is returned in perfect condition, the store has to deal with the cost of having salespeople around to sell, take returns, and restock garments. Not to mention that the store may have lost the opportunity for a real sale while the dress was out partying with the fraudster.

Other types of fraud perpetrated by individuals against businesses can be much larger. These may include (but are definitely not limited to) insurance fraud and mortgage fraud. *Insurance fraud* is the filing of false insurance claims or lying on an insurance application. *Mortgage fraud* could be lying about the applicant's income on an application or inflating the value of the property being mortgaged.

The key to preventing frauds that individuals commit against businesses is for those businesses to maintain strong *internal controls*: paperwork and procedures that govern the way the business is run. For much more on this subject, be sure to check out Part VI.

Individuals committing fraud on individuals

Individuals defrauding individuals is very common. It happens in more ways than we can count, and we're accountants! We could write a whole book on this topic alone, but in this book Part III is where you can find the goods.

Do you know anyone who has been sold an unnecessary life insurance policy by a slick salesman? Do you know anyone who had an unnecessary repair done on his or her home? Then you know someone who has been defrauded by another individual.

Why does fraud occur?

In the beginning, there was the *fraud triangle*. Experts have long considered the three components of fraud to be motivation, rationalization, and opportunity. These days, we've created a fraud quadrangle because the component of expertise has been added to the mix. Keep reading to find out what the four sides of the quadrangle represent.

Motivation

There are a few principal motivators for fraud. One is need. Often fraud starts out as a response to a need. Bob is getting a low salary, Aunt Hilda needs surgery, and Bob "borrows" from the company to pay Aunt Hilda's bills. He has every intention of paying off the hidden debt. However, after the doctors get done with Aunt Hilda, the amount she owes is much higher than originally expected. Bob keeps trying to pay the debt back, but spends all his energy just trying to keep his "borrowing" from becoming known.

In Chapter 7, we tell the story of Barry Minkow of ZZZZ Best Company. The fraud he committed was motivated by need. Minkow needed to borrow money to keep his small carpet cleaning business running. Then he needed more, and then even more. The legitimate part of his business couldn't support the amount of funds he was borrowing, so he made up sales just to be able to look better to the banks and borrow more money. Before he knew it, the whole thing got out of hand. By the end, about 85 percent of the reported ZZZZ Best sales volume was fictional.

Is need the only motivator for fraud? No. Another biggie is adrenaline. Some people just get off on the high they feel from getting away with something. Their only need is to experience the rush on an ongoing basis.

Rationalization

The most common rationalization for fraud that we've heard is this: "They owe me. I work hard, and they pay me very little for my work, so I'm just going to take." We see this rationalization when employees perceive that management treats them poorly.

Another common rationalization is "They won't miss it." We tend to see this rationalization when the victim is blessed with riches and the perpetrator much less so.

Executives committing financial fraud have their own rationalizations for their behaviors. For instance, they may tell themselves that falsifying financial reports is acceptable because doing so maintains the company stock price and saves jobs. In essence, anything goes as long as the stock price increases and shareholders are happy. (Some of them may also assume that the public is ignorant and will never know what's going on.) Executives may also rationalize that if a fraud occurs only once, and they plan to correct it in the future, no real harm is done. Or, they may tell themselves, "This is the way business gets done — some of our competitors are doing it, so we have to do it as well."

Opportunity

Sometimes fraud is just easy to commit. For example, if you don't have a firewall on your computer system, you're essentially inviting a hacker to steal your personal information. Often people (and businesses) lack the foresight to see the holes that criminals see. Therefore, forensic accountants have to be ever vigilant and try to think like thieves. This way, we can outsmart the thieves before the opportunity is found.

A large membership organization with about 650 employees and offices in New Jersey announced that it was merging one division with an organization in Texas. Most of the jobs in New Jersey would be eliminated in about six months as a result of the merger. Employees rationalized that the employer owed them because they had worked hard all these years and were being rewarded with pink slips. They also needed computers at home to work on their résumés for their upcoming job searches. They started taking computers home. Because the organization didn't have security, employees literally walked the computers out the front door.

Management got wind of the disappearing computers so it posted security guards at the elevators. The employees were not deterred. They started boxing up the computers and mailing them home. An alert mailroom clerk realized something was fishy with all these heavy, large boxes being mailed to employees and blew the whistle. An edict was issued that all parcels not being mailed to a known customer had to be approved by a manager. The organization finally got some internal controls in place, but by that time the losses had already added up.

Expertise

In the old days, criminals valued the skill of safe cracking. If you were going to rob a bank or a diva's jewels you had to know how to get into the safe. Today, many frauds are committed using computers and computer networks. It's essential to have a certain level of computer expertise, therefore, to commit fraud. Have you received a spam e-mail lately? We don't even know how to send an e-mail to "undisclosed-recipient@yahoo.com," but a lot of fraudsters out there sure know how.

For many frauds, you don't have to have high-level skills; your expertise comes from having figured out how to manipulate the system at hand. If you know how to trick your boss into signing a check without looking, for example, you can commit a fraud.

The incidence of fraud

In its *2010 Report to the Nations on Occupational Fraud and Abuse,* the Association of Certified Fraud Examiners (ACFE) indicates that organizations around the world lose an estimated 5 percent of their annual revenues to fraud. When you consider how hard most businesses work to eek out every dollar of revenue possible, you realize that a 5 percent loss is enormous.

Here are some other key findings from the ACFE report that offer some perspective on what occupational fraud looks like:

- ✔ **Fraud schemes are costly:** The median loss caused by the occupational fraud cases in the study was $160,000. Nearly one-quarter of the frauds involved losses of at least $1 million.

- ✔ **Fraudsters leave footprints behind:** Fraud perpetrators often display warning signs that they are engaging in illicit activity. The most common behavioral red flags include living beyond their means and experiencing financial difficulties.

- ✔ **Frauds have a long incubation period:** The frauds in the study lasted a median of 18 months before being discovered.

- ✔ **Frauds are similar globally:** Most of the trends in fraud schemes, perpetrator characteristics, and antifraud controls are similar regardless of where the fraud occurred.

- ✔ **Tips are key in detecting fraud:** Occupational frauds are much more likely to be detected by tip than by any other means.

- ✔ **Executive-level fraud is most damaging:** Frauds committed by owners and executives are more than three times as costly as frauds committed by managers and more than nine times as costly as employee frauds. Executive-level frauds also take much longer to detect.

- ✔ **Small businesses are especially vulnerable to occupational fraud:** These companies typically lack the resources for instituting antifraud controls.

You can read the ACFE's *2010 Report to the Nations on Occupation Fraud and Abuse* yourself by visiting www.acfe.com/rttn/2010-rttn.asp.

Identifying Potential Employers: Who Hires Forensic Accountants?

Considering your options as a forensic accountant? We offer lots of career talk in Chapter 2. For now, keep in mind that many types of entities hire forensic accountants. Here are the biggies:

✔ **Government:** The federal government is probably the largest organization hiring forensic accountants. Traditionally, the Federal Bureau of Investigation (FBI) investigated frauds. Now, in addition to the FBI, many federal agencies have their own Office of the Inspector General (OIG) that investigates financial crimes and frauds particular to that agency's mission. Often crimes are committed that cross the thresholds of several agencies. In these cases the agencies tend to form task forces that bring in agents from many agencies to work together.

✔ **CPA firms:** Many accounting firms have divisions that employ forensic accountants. They are hired by attorneys, companies, and individuals who have a problem and need the services of a forensic accountant to help uncover the truth.

✔ **Attorneys:** Some large law firms have their own forensic accountants on their investigative staff. These forensic accountants are used to support cases involving financial frauds, asset division and child support in divorce cases, mergers and acquisitions, securities frauds, and other types of cases.

✔ **Consulting firms:** Some consulting firms have forensic accountants on staff and work on cases just like CPA firms do.

✔ **Insurance and companies:** Insurance companies hire forensic accountants to investigate fraud on applications for life insurance as well as false claims on workers' compensation and death benefits.

✔ **Retail companies:** Retail companies hire forensic accountants to reduce product theft from consumers and employees by developing and auditing policies and procedures.

Chapter 2

Steering Your Career toward Forensic Accounting

In This Chapter

▶ Focusing on education and certification

▶ Looking at potential employers

▶ Considering a computer fraud specialty

*A*s we note in Chapter 1, fraud is a big business, and it's growing. The FBI reported that from 2001 to 2007, white-collar crime increased 39 percent. In its *2010 Report to the Nations on Occupational Fraud and Abuse*, the Association of Certified Fraud Examiners (ACFE) estimated that a typical organization loses 5 percent of its annual revenue to fraud, which means about $2.9 trillion is lost worldwide to business (*occupational*) fraud.

Someone needs to investigate all these frauds. Because most of these frauds involve financial matters, who better to investigate them than an accountant? Accountants already know how to critically examine a company's books and transactions; we do that when we perform an audit. Performing a financial forensic examination is a logical next step.

In this chapter, we guide you through some steps you want to consider taking if you think forensic accounting is your thing. If you work hard up front and prove that you're serious about fraud investigation and prevention, this career field is ripe for the picking.

Setting Yourself Apart from the Accounting Pack

Forensic accounting is different from other types of accounting and auditing. In this section, we review some of the education, training, and certifications related to being a forensic accountant.

Taking the right courses

If you are (or were) an accounting major in college, you're on your way. Accounting curricula are generally the same across the United States. Your program probably includes (or included) a variety of courses in financial and advanced accounting, as well as one or two courses in auditing. These are the basic and essential education requirements to get started in forensic accounting, but we strongly encourage you to add a few other courses to your schedule. Here, we offer our recommendations.

Computer courses

First and foremost, take some computer courses. You need to be absolutely proficient in such common programs as Word, Excel, Access, and PowerPoint. When you investigate fraud, you use these programs to perform your analysis, write reports, and present your findings. Also, your *targets* (individuals and companies that you investigate) will be using these programs to do their work. You need to use them, too, so you can navigate through complex files and find the frauds. Plus, you often need to do some statistical analysis when investigating fraud, and many types of statistical analyses can be done in Excel.

You also need to know about accounting software. Many colleges teach the use of QuickBooks and/or Peachtree. Because your targets will most likely use software packages to keep their accounting records using, you need to know your way around.

If your school offers them, you may want to take some computer courses related to programming or computer operations. Doing so will allow you to understand the code that programmers write to determine if there are weaknesses or loopholes in the programs that allow frauds to occur. Understanding best practices in computer operations will help you understand proper internal controls in a computerized environment.

If you know these two software packages well but don't know others, don't fret. Remember that all accounting is the same at its core (assets = liabilities + owners' equity). The differences between different accounting packages are the interface and the bells and whistles. When faced with a program you're not familiar with, go back to basics and review the program in terms of the accounting equation.

If you're having trouble with a particular accounting package, look for the function that exports data to Excel. Export the data and use Excel to hunt for the fraud.

If you want to purchase QuickBooks or Peachtree at little or no cost so that you have a copy you can use to learn from, watch the ads from large office supply stores carefully. Once a year, there is usually a sale on one or both of these packages with a 100 percent rebate.

Forensic accounting courses

This goes without saying, but we'll say it anyway: If your school has a forensic accounting course, *take it!* Forensic accounting is an increasingly popular college course, and it's usually an elective (not a requirement). A forensic accounting course will teach you all the things we talk about in this book and then some. You'll learn forensic techniques, internal controls, and legal issues, and you'll review some of the biggest and most interesting fraud cases.

Many master's programs in forensic accounting are springing up around the country as well. If you plan to become a CPA, in most states you need to accumulate 150 credit hours before you can sit for the CPA exam. If you're in that boat, consider entering a master's program in forensic accounting. If such a program isn't available in your area, check out Utica College (www.onlineuticacollege.com), which offers a fully online master's in Economic Crime and Fraud Management.

Law courses

If you're an accounting or business major, you'll probably be required to take a business law course, and that's good. Knowing the law is invaluable for a forensic accountant. For example, you may see a strange transaction during an audit and wonder if it's legal or not. And you need to know the *Uniform Commercial Code* (a federal act that governs sales and other commercial transactions throughout the United States) and how it applies to the transactions that your target has engaged in.

Try to take additional law courses if you can. A fair amount of forensic accounting relates to matrimonial cases. It helps to understand matrimonial law in your state so you can make better judgments about the finances you are reviewing.

As a forensic accountant, you don't make legal judgments. Doing so is practicing law, which you are not permitted to do unless you are a lawyer. You need to know enough to know when you have to ask a lawyer.

Statistics courses

Understanding the use of statistics is invaluable for auditors and forensic accountants. That's why this topic is taught in every auditing course. Knowing statistics and the principles of *chance* or *odds* will help you determine the true rate of errors and *defalcations* (the amount of money that has been misappropriated) in the transactions you examine.

Go a step farther and take a course in correlation analysis. If you can perform correlation analysis on transactions, you can better pinpoint who is committing fraud, where it's occurring, and how frauds are being committed.

Psychology courses

We've long believed that every accounting major should have a minor in psychology. If you think accounting, auditing, and forensic accounting are just about numbers, you're very much mistaken. Accounting is as much about people as it is about numbers. Accountants are trusted professionals. Clients come to us with their problems with employees, customers, spouses, children, landlords . . . They expect us to help them with the human side of their businesses and lives. We become their personal advisors, confidants, and confessors. You need to learn how to handle these situations.

Forensic accounting requires additional people skills because you have to know how to read people. Have you ever played poker? To be successful, you need to understand the statistics related to the game. (What are the odds of the next card being the card you need?) But the most successful poker players are also experts in reading people. They recognize how their opponents react when they have a good hand or a bad hand, or when they're trying to bluff. You need these same skills when interviewing suspects and witnesses to the crimes you are investigating. You'll also be a better forensic investigator if you understand the human side of fraud motivators and how people react under pressure.

Criminology courses

Criminology is the study of crime, criminals, corrections, and how they affect society. A course in criminology will help you understand how the fraudsters you are up against work, why they do what they do, and how they interact with the people around them.

Here's an interesting tidbit that shows how psychology and criminology play into fraud investigations: Reports indicate that massive fraudster Bernie Madoff has become the big man on campus in prison. His fellow prisoners ask him for financial advice. He is revered within the prison population for the size of his crime and for his financial acumen. Go figure!

Ethics courses

As a forensic accountant, you'll come across many situations where someone's actions are within the limits of the law but are still wrong. How will you know the action was wrong? What framework will you use for guidance? A study of ethics can help.

Ethics may be divided into two distinct types:

- According to dictionary.com, *axiological ethics* is the branch of ethics dealing primarily with the relative goodness or value of the motives and end of any action.

- *Deontological ethics* deals with rules of behavior. The American Institute of Certified Public Accountants (AICPA) Code of Conduct is a good example of deontological ethics. The code is a set of rules of behavior for CPAs who are AICPA members.

Understanding the study of axiological ethics can help you make decisions in gray areas — those times when something is wrong, but no law has been broken.

Language courses

Never underestimate the value of speaking a second (or third or fourth) language. If a criminal speaks a language other than English, the investigator should as well. Many times we've uncovered information during the course of an investigation because we had language skills that the criminals didn't know we had.

We can't tell you that any specific language is more important than any other; you never know which language you'll need. But if you took a foreign language in high school or learned a little bit of a foreign language by listening to Grandma and Grandpa, take some courses to maintain and improve your language skills.

Getting certified: The CFE and other certifications

To become a CPA, you take an exam to get licensed by a state or by one of four other jurisdictions. To become a forensic accountant, no government-issued license is required (as of this writing, at least).

However, certifications related to forensic accounting and fraud investigation are issued by several professional associations. In this section, we present some of the more common certifications and the associations that convey them. We also let you know about some organizations that support forensic accountants without any particular certification.

Certified Public Accountant (CPA)

You don't have to be a CPA to be a forensic accountant (or any other type of accountant, for that matter). However, having those magical three letters after your name is very valuable. They say that you are an accountant who has had a rigorous accounting education and passed one of the toughest licensing examinations in the nation. The CPA credential is recognized worldwide.

The requirements for becoming a CPA vary from jurisdiction to jurisdiction (54 jurisdictions have the CPA designation), but all are similar. In most jurisdictions, you need 150 hours of college education, and some jurisdictions require a master's degree. Most jurisdictions require that you have some experience (one or two years) working under a CPA. All the jurisdictions require that you pass all four parts of the Uniform CPA Examination. All jurisdictions also have a continuing education requirement in order to maintain your license.

The largest national professional association is the American Institute of Certified Public Accountants (AICPA). Membership in the AICPA includes a subscription to the *Journal of Accountancy,* which often features fraud-related articles. Members can also buy books and attend conferences at reduced rates. Check out www.aicpa.org for details. The AICPA also offers a designation called Certified in Financial Forensics (CFF).

Each of the licensing jurisdictions also has a local CPA society. You can find links to their various Web sites at the site for the National Conference of CPA Practitioners, www.nccpap.org. Look under the Resources button.

Certified Fraud Examiner (CFE)

The CFE is arguably the most recognized credential related to forensic accounting. The Association of Certified Fraud Examiners (ACFE) issues the CFE designation. Requirements to achieve the CFE designation include:

- ✔ Being an Associate Member of the ACFE in good standing.

- ✔ Meeting minimum academic requirements. Generally, applicants for CFE certification have a minimum of a bachelor's degree (or equivalent) from an institution of higher learning. No specific field of study is required. If you do not have a bachelor's degree, you may substitute two years of fraud-related professional experience for each year of academic study.

- ✔ Meeting minimum professional requirements, which include two years of professional experience in a field either directly or indirectly related to the detection or deterrence of fraud. Professional experience includes:
  - Accounting or auditing, including fraud detection or prevention
  - Being an educator or researcher in the criminology or sociology of fraud or white-collar crime
  - Investigating fraud, including working in law enforcement and insurance fraud
  - Working in loss prevention (but not as a security guard)

- ✔ Practicing law, as long as it includes the consideration of fraud.

- ✔ Demonstrating high moral character.

- ✔ Agreeing to abide by ACFE Bylaws and Code of Professional Ethics.

- ✔ Having three letters of recommendation.

- ✔ Passing the CFE examination. The examination tests four major areas:
  - Fraudulent financial transactions
  - Legal elements of fraud
  - Investigation methods
  - Fraud prevention and deterrence

- ✔ Gaining final approval from the certification committee.

Maintaining the CFE designation requires 20 hours of continuing education (at least ten of these must relate directly to the detection and deterrence of fraud) in a 12-month period. Membership in the ACFE allows you to partake of many resources related to being a fraud investigator, including a subscription to the journal *Fraud Magazine,* various books, conferences, and seminars. There are many local and international ACFE chapters that offer ways to meet local CFEs. More information is available at www.acfe.com.

Certified Forensic Financial Analyst (CFFA)

The CFFA designation is sponsored by the National Association of Certified Valuation Analysts (NACVA). NACVA is best known for its Certified Valuation Analyst (CVA) certification: a certification in the valuation of businesses.

Business valuations are often performed for forensic purposes: matrimonial disputes, torts, and litigation with the IRS related to estate and gift taxes. That's where the CFFA comes in. The CFFA designation has five subspecialties:

- ✔ Financial litigation
- ✔ Forensic accounting
- ✔ Business and intellectual property damages
- ✔ Business fraud: deterrence, detection, prevention
- ✔ Matrimonial litigation support

The requirements for becoming a CFFA include:

- ✔ Being a CPA, CVA, or CFE; or having another acceptable credential from NACVA's list (which is available at www.nacva.com/CTI/ CFFAprerequisites.asp).
- ✔ Showing proof of experience in the area you wish to specialize in. The proof and amount of experience required vary by specialty.
- ✔ Attending a training program, which includes general forensics and issues related to the specialty.
- ✔ Passing two examinations: one in the specialty area and one in general financial forensics.
- ✔ Being a member of NACVA.

The recertification process includes a mixture of continuing education (including specific courses), professional experience, authorship, and course development. More detailed information is available at www.nacva.com.

National Association of Forensic Accountants (NAFA)

NAFA is an association of forensic accountants doing business with the property and casualty insurance industry. It offers a certification as well. If this specific field interests you, find details at www.nafanet.com.

Forensic Accountants Society of North America (FASNA)

FASNA is also an association of forensic accountants doing business with the insurance industry. Each member firm is carefully screened and trained. The organization serves as a clearinghouse for firms seeking engagements with insurance companies. More information is available at www.fasna.org.

Forensic CPA (FCPA)

The FCPA is sponsored by the Forensic CPA Society. Requirements for certification include being a CPA or having an equivalent designation from another country and passing a five-part examination. The examination requirement is waived for applicants who already hold the CFE or CFFA designations. There is a continuing education requirement of 20 hours per year. More information is available at http://shopsite.fcpas.org.

Finding Work

You can find many ways to make money as a forensic accountant. Many types of entities hire forensic accountants, or you can go into business by yourself. Here, we list some of your potential employers and outline the types of forensic accounting jobs that exist.

Considering public sector options

Government hires the most forensic accountants in all agencies in all kinds of work. The two agencies with the most forensic accountants are the Federal Bureau of Investigation (FBI) and the Internal Revenue Service (IRS).

The FBI

The FBI investigates all sorts of crimes including terrorism, bank frauds, physical crimes (such as murder), and any crime that is committed by crossing state lines. FBI investigators get the title *special agent.* There are five programs for entry-level special agents: accounting, law, computer technology, languages, or a general diversified program. (Our list of recommended college courses really comes in handy here.)

The FBI has other requirements for hiring. As with any federal agency, you must be a U.S. citizen. Because it's a law enforcement position, you must be between the ages of 23 and 37. You also have to pass the background check and meet certain physical requirements. If you are hired, you go through a rigorous job training program at the FBI's training center called FBI College in Quantico, Virginia. More information can be found at www.fbi.gov.

The IRS

The IRS also hires many accountants. IRS Revenue Agents are the dreaded auditors. To become a Revenue Agent, generally you must be a college graduate with at least 30 credits in accounting. When we last checked, these jobs were paying up to $125,000. Revenue Agents audit tax returns of all sorts to determine if the taxpayer has complied with all laws and regulations when preparing and filing the return. If agents find errors, they make corrections and adjust the tax bill. If they believe that a criminal issue exists, they refer the case for criminal investigation.

IRS Special Agents are the criminal investigators for the agency. They work cases that are referred by Revenue Agents, come in from tips provided by citizens, or are part of task forces with other government agencies. They follow the money trail and use other financial forensic and investigative techniques to uproot crime. Because of the expertise required to conduct these complex financial investigations, IRS Special Agents are considered the premier financial investigators for the federal government.

The requirements for hire are similar to those for FBI jobs because this is also a law enforcement job. Salaries are high and carry a 25 percent premium over other federal jobs at the same grade level. IRS Special Agents receive their specialized training at one of several Federal Law Enforcement Training Centers (FLETC) throughout the country. More information about jobs with the IRS is available at www.jobs.irs.gov.

Offices of the Inspector General

Many federal departments and agencies have investigators who focus on frauds and crimes related to the mission of that agency. The investigative arm of these agencies is usually called the Office of the Inspector General (OIG). To find jobs at these agencies go to www.usajobs.gov.

State and local agencies

All state governments and many local governments have agencies that investigate fraud and white-collar crimes. Usually these investigations are done under the aegis of the attorney general (AG) of that state. The New York State Attorney General's Office is particularly active in investigating financial frauds. The major stock exchanges are in New York, which gives New York the jurisdiction to investigate frauds related to securities transactions. Check the Web site for your state or local government to find job openings.

Considering private sector options

The two principal groups of firms hiring forensic accountants in the private sector are CPA firms and investigative firms, but other options exist as well.

CPA firms

To our knowledge, all large CPA firms have forensic accounting divisions, but they usually don't hire entry-level staff for the forensic division. The common practice is to hire entry-level staff for the audit and tax divisions. As junior staff members become more seasoned, they can ask for a transfer into forensics. Often the large CPA firms recruit their entry-level staff on college campuses. Check with the career services office on your campus about recruiting efforts by accounting firms.

Many small ("boutique") accounting firms specialize in forensic accounting. You may be able to find these firms using an Internet search engine. Your state CPA society may also have a feature on its Web site to search for firms and members based on specialty practices.

Investigative firms

The large investigative firms also have forensic accounting divisions. You can find a list of many investigative firms at www.nalionline.org, the Web site for the National Association of Legal Investigators.

Other options

Some large law firms also have their own investigative divisions. You can search for law firms in your area at www.lawyers.com.

Sometimes insurance companies also have forensic investigators. For example, the State Insurance Fund of New York, the largest Workman's Compensation carrier in the state, routinely sends out investigators to insured entities to determine if the premium being paid is correct.

Some online sources for jobs or freelance work in forensic accounting include www.forensicaccountingjobs.com and www.frauddetectives.com.

CASE FILE

Under the microscope

Frimette once worked for a small, local accounting firm whose largest client suddenly went belly up. Allegedly, senior management colluded to commit a fraud against the firm's lenders. Because the firm's financial statements had been audited, everyone wanted to know why the auditors did not find the fraud during the audit. (It is *very* difficult to find a fraud when there is collusion at the highest levels of management.)

Various courts, government agencies, and insurance companies all sent forensic accountants to look over the audit work papers. The investigators came from accounting firms (small and large), insurance companies, government agencies, and investigation firms. For a while it seemed that we had new investigators in the office every other day. In the end, they did not have any findings to report. That's because we did the audit right and had pristine work papers.

Internal auditors: Preventing fraud before it can occur

It's nearly impossible to stop all fraud before it happens. However, it is possible to reduce the risk of fraud through strong internal controls and risk management programs. We discuss how to do so in Part VI of this book. Here, we focus on who takes on the job of fraud prevention within a business.

The Sarbanes-Oxley Act of 2002 requires publicly traded companies to have an internal control system. The people behind internal controls are the *internal auditors*. Internal auditors are charged with making sure a company's internal control systems are working properly and recommending ways to make internal controls stronger.

An internal auditor must have an accounting background and is often a CPA (although that certification is not required by law). The Institute of Internal Auditors (IIA) sponsors the Certified Internal Auditor (CIA) designation. The requirements to become a CIA include:

✔ A bachelor's or higher degree.

✔ Twenty-four months of experience in internal auditing. A masters' degree may be substituted for 12 months of experience.

✔ A character reference from someone who is IIA-certified.

✔ Successful passage of a four-part examination.

Another way to work on fraud prevention within a company is to become an expert on Enterprise Risk Management (ERM): a system that helps businesses reduce their risks. ERM should be a comprehensive system, meaning it reduces all kinds of risks, including the risk of the business being a victim of fraud. More information on ERM can be found at the Web site of the Committee of Sponsoring Organizations of the Treadway Commission (www. coso.org/Publications/ERM/COSO_ERM_ExecutiveSummary.pdf) or at the Casualty Actuarial Society Web site (www.casact.org/research/ erm/overview.pdf).

Specializing in Finding Computer Crimes

Computers have become more important to criminals than lock picks. Within a company, a fraudster can use the computer system to steal money and cover up the crime. When using the Internet, the fraudster has an infinite supply of potential victims. Internet crimes can include:

✔ Placing viruses and *Trojans* (programs that sneak onto a computer and do nasty things like delete data, tie up the computer, and steal information)

✔ Selling phony goods, including pharmaceuticals

✔ *Hacking* (gaining unauthorized entry to a computer network) to steal information or funds

✔ Marketing phony investments

✔ Scamming people by convincing them they have won or inherited money

✔ Using phony Web sites to convince users to enter sensitive information like passwords, birthdates, or Social Security numbers

To investigate and prevent fraud-related computer crimes requires specialized training and knowledge. One group that has this knowledge is the Information Systems Audit and Control Association (ISACA), which offers several certifications related to computer security, governance, and audit. More information can be found at www.isaca.org.

Chapter 3

Getting to Know the Most Common Fraud Schemes

*W*e are all affected by fraud, whether directly or indirectly. Even if you haven't been a victim of fraud, you pay for it. Think about it: Does your credit card company really need to charge you 24 percent interest and all those big fees? It does so to make up for all the costs associated with phony credit cards, stolen credit cards, and customers who just don't pay because they just don't pay.

In this chapter, we introduce some of the most common types of fraud committed by businesses, against businesses, and against the government. Our goal here isn't to give you all the details about every type of fraud imaginable; we'd need a much bigger book to accomplish that task. Instead, we want to simply get you thinking about what fraud often looks like so you have a sense of the scope of work a forensic accountant may encounter.

Frauds Committed by Businesses

Businesses are driven to keep profits up so that Wall Street and the shareholders are happy. Part II of this book details some of the most common questionable practices that businesses engage in. Here, we briefly introduce those practices and explain why they so often occur.

Preying on vulnerable populations

Some businesses thrive by taking advantage of people who are weak or unknowledgeable. Here are just a few examples:

✔ **Robbing the poor:** The recent financial meltdown in the United States was largely driven by the unethical practice of convincing people who couldn't really afford mortgage loans that they could (and offering mortgage products with adjustable rates that started out low but ballooned over time). Some of the same companies engaging in these shady practices also encouraged mortgage applicants to falsify information in order to qualify for loans, which is straight-up fraud.

See the upcoming section "Dealing in subprime and predatory lending" for more detailed information about fraudulent mortgage practices.

✔ **Scamming the sick:** Another common (and horrible) fraud scheme involves offering phony cures for deadly diseases. Many innocuous foods and chemicals, and even some dangerous items, have been hawked as cures for cancer and other diseases.

✔ **Taking advantage of the elderly:** People who are constantly concerned about their health and finances and worried about being a burden to their children can be especially vulnerable to fraudsters who spin tales of how they can make money and regain their health. Throw in the possibility that the elderly person's sight and hearing may not be perfect, and that he may be suffering from dementia, and you've got lots of layers of vulnerability.

Many elderly are easily talked into signing documents they can't read or understand. The next thing you know, their savings are gone. The American Association of Retired Persons (www.aarp.org) maintains a section on its Web site with the latest scams and frauds targeting the elderly. AARP also provides information on how not to become a victim of these frauds.

✔ **Circling surviving spouses:** Widows and widowers are also very vulnerable, whether elderly or not. They are in a very emotional state and may be overwhelmed by financial and other concerns. Someone who seems to offer comfort during such a stressful time can easily take advantage of that vulnerability.

CASE FILE

We once knew a real estate agent who found prospects by reading the obituary column. When someone died in her area, and the obituary mentioned a surviving spouse, she would knock on the door a few days after the funeral. She sounded very friendly and offered sincere condolences. Then she would convince the survivor that because they were now single, they didn't need such a big house anymore. And they were lucky that she just happened by and could help them unload the house.

Picking investors' pockets

Would you like to make millions with only a small investment? Of course, you would! Unfortunately, it rarely happens that way. Yet, Frimette gets at least three pieces in the mail *every day* promising riches from investing in gold, penny stocks, foreign stocks, systems for investing when the market is going up, systems for investing when the market is going down, distressed real estate, yada, yada, yada. There are also invitations to free seminars or luncheons where someone will expound on the *only* proven system for getting rich. Besides the mailers, there are also advertisements on the radio and in newspapers. The only ones getting rich from these schemes are the promoters.

Although the investment schemes advertised in mailers and newspapers may seem easy to spot, other types of investment fraud are much less obvious to the general public. We devote Chapter 8 to a discussion of various securities frauds that some businesses use to manipulate their own stock values (or the values of stocks they have invested in) and steer investor decisions in ways that benefit the business rather than the investor.

Doing business with bribes

We all know what a bribe is, right? If you've ever watched TV or read a newspaper in your life, you're familiar with the concept of greasing someone's palm in order to get special consideration.

Why would a company resort to bribes to conduct business? Some bribes are relatively minor, such as when a company offers a bribe in order to speed up the processing of an application that would have been approved, anyway. Other bribes are much more serious, such as when a company offers a bribe to be allowed to create dangerous conditions for its employees or the public. For example, after several deadly crane collapses in New York City, the city's Department of Investigation launched probes into the crane business. It found indications that a large crane company had bribed inspectors from the Department of Buildings to falsify inspection reports. This bribery had deadly results.

In some foreign countries, bribing government officials is not illegal and is considered a normal business practice. But U.S. companies doing business abroad are not allowed to engage in bribery, even in countries where the practice is legal. Giving bribes in these circumstances would be a violation of the Foreign Corrupt Practices Act (FCPA). The FCPA prohibits paying bribes to foreign government officials for obtaining or retaining business.

Breakfast bribery

Frimette once represented a large, popular catering establishment during an IRS audit. One morning, the client had a breakfast event and there was a lot of leftover food. The catering staff was well trained. Anyone on the premises was to be fed! They brought large platters of lox, bagels, cheeses, and salads into the room where Frimette was working with the IRS agent. The staff certainly didn't intend to offer a bribe; feeding people is just what they did. However, later that day the IRS agent's supervisor showed up to do a surprise inspection. He declared the food an attempt to bribe a government official, which was a felony. He ordered the food to be taken away and warned the agent, Frimette, and the client that if he ever saw this type of activity again on a visit we would all go to jail!

Laundering money

When money that is earned by illegal means is made to look like it has come from a legal source, we call the process *laundering money.* Organized crime and drug traffickers often have a lot of cash money to launder by using methods such as these:

- ✓ **Around the world in 80 days:** The cash is taken out of the United States and deposited in banks in foreign countries. The best countries to go to are those with bank secrecy laws because investigators can't get any information about the accounts. The money is often moved from country to country. After traveling the world for a while, the money is transferred to the U.S. entity in the guise of a loan from a foreign contact.

- ✓ **The shell company:** A company is set up that does no actual business. The "dirty" money is put into the business as sales. Taxes are paid on the revenue, after which the money is "clean" and available for any use.

- ✓ **The blender:** A criminal may control a small legitimate business. The "dirty" money is deposited into that business and reported as sales. Taxes are paid, after which the money can be used.

The U.S. government has enacted several laws to try to combat money laundering. For starters, any cash transaction over $10,000 must be reported to the Internal Revenue Service. If you get lucky in Las Vegas and cash in chips for $10,000 or more, the casino will ask you for your Social Security number and report the transaction. If you then walk over to a car dealer and pay for a car with $10,000 in cash, the car dealer will likewise ask for your Social Security number and prepare a report to the IRS.

If a bank suspects that someone's transactions are being broken up into amounts smaller than $10,000 to avoid the reporting, the bank will still make a report to the IRS. (However, if a business has routine bank deposits of $10,000 or more, it may request an exemption from the required filing.)

Also, it is illegal to transport more than $10,000 in cash in or out of the United States without a customs declaration. Reporting requirements also exist for money transfers; money transfer agencies are required to report any money transfer of $3,000 or more.

Perpetrating construction fraud

Construction fraud happens when a contractor does not complete a project according to the specifications of the contract, does not build the project according to the relevant building codes, or bills inappropriately.

The cleanup of the World Trade Center site after 9/11 offers a perfect example of what can go wrong. Not surprisingly, the cleanup effort was somewhat disorganized. Several building and demolition contractors were each assigned areas to clean up, but there were no clear lines of demarcation. Workers would arrive for their shifts, go to an onsite office (in a trailer) of the contractor they wanted to work for that day, sign in, and go to work. At the end of each week the contractors would present their bills to the city. Accompanying each bill would be "proof" of the expenses in the form of a payroll journal that identified workers and listed the hours they worked.

A city worker, during his examination of the contractors' bills, found that one worker had supposedly worked for two contractors at the same time. The managers of the contracting companies were interviewed as part of a fraud investigation. As it turns out, the companies did not commit the fraud; the worker did. He figured that because the site was so large and disorganized, he could sign in with two contractors and neither would realize that he was working for the other one, too.

The fruits of his labor? A legal nightmare

Total Lawyers (www.totallawyers.com) reports the case of Pedro Zapeta, an illegal alien from Guatemala. Pedro worked hard for 11 years at jobs that paid $5.25 to $5.75 per hour. He saved $59,000. One day he put all the money in a duffle bag and headed to the airport. He was going to use the money to give his impoverished family a better life. Pedro, who speaks no English, did not know about the customs law and failed to fill out the customs declaration that he was taking more than $10,000 out of the United States. Customs officers stopped him at the airport and seized the money. Pedro was turned over to immigration authorities who want to deport him. Pedro wants his money to take home, but it has not been released yet. The IRS wants his money to pay for 11 years of taxes that Pedro did not pay. Several lawyers, working pro bono, are trying to straighten out Pedro's mess.

Dealing in subprime and predatory lending

These two problems, related to mortgages, often go hand-in-hand:

- *Subprime lending* occurs when a mortgage is given to a homeowner who shouldn't be eligible for that mortgage. Maybe the homeowner doesn't make sufficient income or cannot make a sufficient down payment. Or perhaps the home is appraised for more than it is worth.

- *Predatory lending* is when a homeowner is talked into taking out a mortgage he doesn't need or can't afford. Also considered predatory are interest rates and fees that are substantially higher than the homeowner could have received from a reputable lender.

Usually, the victims of subprime and predatory lending are desperate and/or lack financial sophistication. And usually, they don't have accountants in the wings waiting to offer advice on whether a deal seems legitimate or not. The U.S. financial crisis that began in 2008 certainly shined a spotlight on these despicable practices, but that doesn't mean they're certain to end.

Taking advantage of employees

Many employers play by the rules, but some want to write their own rulebooks when it comes to what they expect from employees. How can they get away with treating employees unfairly? Especially when the economy is fragile, people earning paychecks don't want to rock the boat; they're too concerned about feeding their families.

Here are some of the most common rackets run by bad employers:

- **Violations of wage and hour laws:** An employee who works more than 40 hours a week is entitled to 1½ times her hourly rate for any time in excess of 40 hours. This goes for employees who earn a weekly salary (depending on their level of responsibility within the company), as well as those who earn an hourly wage. Many employers who violate this law tell employees that they are not eligible because they are on salary.

- **The 1099 versus W-2:** When an employer pays an employee, the employer assumes a whole host of tax and insurance obligations including Social Security tax, Medicare tax, unemployment insurance (state and federal), workers' compensation insurance, and disability insurance. All these obligations can add up to a tidy sum. To save money, the employer may treat the employee like an *independent contractor,* meaning the employee gets a fee and the employer has no tax obligations. At the end of the year, instead of getting an employee's W-2 form with wages and tax deductions listed, the independent contractor gets a form 1099 just listing the gross amount of "fees."

✔ **Discriminatory benefits:** An employer that has a benefits package, such as health insurance and pensions, must make the benefits available to any employee who works more than 1,000 hours per year (about 20 hours per week). The employer also must notify all employees about benefit plans and eligibility rules. We've seen many small businesses that have a plan for the owners and leave the employees out. We've also seen cases where employers have pension plans that get more expensive as employees get older. To save money, these companies fire employees whose plans are getting too expensive.

✔ **Safety violations:** The federal and state governments have many rules for safety in the workplace, but we've seen employers flout those rules, which can have deadly consequences. Depending on the nature of the job and job site, employers are supposed to provide rest breaks, rest areas, first-aid supplies, and safety equipment. Many localities also require emergency exits, emergency lighting, and regular fire drills.

We've touched on only a few of the rules of responsibility for employers to their employees. There are many rules for employers to follow, and they are complex. The leading source for information in this area is the U.S. Department of Labor (www.dol.gov). Safety issues fall under the aegis of the Occupational Safety and Hazards division of the Department of Labor (www.osha.gov). There is also information about many employment issues at the Internal Revenue Service Web site (www.irs.gov). Your state's Department of Revenue and Secretary of State's Web sites are two more resources for information about employment issues.

Watching Walmart

Walmart is one of the largest employers in the United States. Over the years, it has been accused of violating various laws relating to employment. Some of the cases against Walmart have gone to court, and Walmart was found guilty of these violations. Some of the allegations include:

✔ Locking workers in the store overnight without an emergency exit

✔ Making employees work *off the clock* (work overtime without compensation)

✔ Discriminating against women in promotions and raises

✔ Discriminating against disabled and minority employees

✔ Providing inadequate and/or expensive health coverage

✔ Opposing and interfering with unionization

If this subject tickles your fancy, you can read more at www.walmartwatch.com.

Frauds Committed against Businesses

Despite what you may be thinking, businesses are not always on the giving end of fraud; sometimes they're also on the receiving end. And they can get it from all sides: employees, customers, vendors, and the public. This all adds to the cost of doing business, and we explain some of those costs in this section.

Employee theft

At some point, an employee has to be trusted. The trust may be as simple as access to the premises and a desk with supplies. It may be as important and complex as access to cash receipts, valuable inventory, formulas and trade secrets, or customers. An employee in a position of trust can easily commit *asset misappropriation* or *embezzlement*: the appropriation of entrusted assets for one's own use.

Asset misappropriation can be as simple as the employee using the copy machine for a personal copy or taking office supplies home. But it may also be as serious as diverting cash.

In Part VI of this book, we devote a lot of space to the discussion of how to prevent employee theft in small and larger businesses. In particular, Chapter 22 tackles the subject of employee theft in depth.

Vendor and customer fraud

A company's customers and vendors can also be sources of fraudulent activity. A customer may open up a credit line with no intention of paying. A vendor may take a deposit for an order and disappear.

To prevent being a victim, a company must check out who it's doing business with to make sure potential customers and vendors have a history of delivering as promised and making timely payments.

Many sources of information about businesses exist, including rating agencies such as Dun & Bradstreet and information services such as Mergent. If a company is too small to afford subscriptions to these services, some public libraries make them available. And some banks that subscribe to these databases may allow a business customer to look up a certain name.

A company can't rely on online information to make decisions about which customers and vendors to trust. It doesn't take much for a fraudster to set up a pretty Web site.

Insurance fraud

Insurance fraud occurs when someone files a claim with an insurance company to get benefits that she's not entitled to — or when someone otherwise intentionally causes an insurance company to pay out money that shouldn't be paid out. The Coalition Against Insurance Fraud (`www.insurancefraud.org`) estimates that insurance fraud costs about $80 billion per year. And guess what? To stay in business, the insurance companies that face such daunting amounts of fraud spread the joy to all their customers in the form of higher rates. (Lucky us!)

Here are just a few examples of what insurance fraud can look like:

- ✔ A doctor bills an insurance company for procedures he didn't perform.

- ✔ Someone stages a car accident in order to file an injury claim against the other driver's insurance company.

- ✔ To collect cash from her insurance company, someone reports a car or boat stolen when it's not, or reports a phony fire or robbery.

It's a criminal offense to file a phony insurance claim, and filing a false police report is also a crime, so people perpetrating insurance fraud are taking a whole lot of risk.

Bilking the Government

The government is always a convenient target for fraud. Because government is big, bulky, and subject to political pressures, it has a very hard time controlling frauds despite its many efforts. There are more ways to commit fraud against the government than we can count, but in this section we talk about some of the most common frauds — and how the government's forensic accountants try to uncover them.

Tax fraud

The more taxes that are imposed, the more people try to wiggle out of paying them. But the wiggling counts as tax fraud, and the consequences of getting caught can be severe. Title 26 of the Internal Revenue Code says that tax fraud is a felony, and anyone committing it may be subject to imprisonment, fines, or both.

Title 26 also provides some examples of tax fraud: Evading paying taxes (including estimated taxes), refusing to remit any taxes collected from other parties (such as withholding tax), signing a tax return that you know contains untrue information, intimidating a government employee who is enforcing the tax law . . . the list goes on.

For a while now, the U.S. Congress has not given the IRS sufficient funds to investigate and stop tax fraud. As a result, there is a huge amount of money that the IRS should be collecting but is not. The difference between what is collected and what should be collected is called the *tax gap*. For fiscal year 2005 (the most recent year for which this figure is available), the IRS estimated the gross tax gap at $345 billion. If the IRS were able to collect 100 percent of the tax due under the tax law, we could see a rewrite of tax law to lower the rates substantially.

There are more schemes to evade taxes than we can count. Someone is always coming up with something new. We've seen and heard about deceptively simple schemes and some really complex ones. The IRS tries to stay one step ahead of the tax cheats, but usually is a few steps behind.

However, the IRS has several tactics in its war against the cheats. Perhaps the most powerful is the dreaded tax audit. IRS auditors are, in essence, forensic accountants, and they do compliance auditing. The absolute best defense for an audit is to do the tax return correctly in the first place. If the return is correct, the audit is a mild pain that will go away. If the return is wrong, the IRS will collect the unpaid taxes and, in extreme cases, refer the case to the criminal investigation division.

How does the IRS choose which returns to audit? Every few years, the IRS runs programs to determine where taxpayers are cheating the most. To do so, the IRS pulls returns randomly, conducts audits, and determines which kinds of errors and omissions are being seen the most. After completing this process, it has its computer system flag any returns that come in bearing the same signs as the faulty returns in the audit. The signs may include your occupation, the relationship of your mortgage interest deduction to your income, the number of children you are claiming, the relationship of your charitable giving to your income, and so on.

Of course, the IRS also audits returns based on information from whistleblowers, other auditors, and criminal investigations. If you know that someone is committing a tax fraud, you can file form 3949-A with the IRS. The IRS will analyze your information, and if it conducts an audit and manages to collect money, you may be eligible for a cash reward (which is taxable income — what the IRS giveth, the IRS taketh away).

Income tax

In the United States, the income of individuals and entities such as corporations is subject to tax (unless an exception applies to that individual or entity). That's why April 15 is such a banner day for accountants (and why, in our opinion, April 16 should be a national holiday). For individuals, tax is computed based on gross income less certain adjustments and itemized deductions. For a business, tax is computed on revenues less ordinary and necessary expenses.

There are two ways to commit income tax fraud:

- ✔ Not reporting all your income
- ✔ Deducting too many expenses

How can you avoid reporting income? If you have a business that collects cash from its customers, the cash can go directly in your pocket, and you just don't report the income. If you get checks, you could cash them at a compliant check-cashing agency or send them to a bank overseas.

What about deducting too many expenses? Often, in closely held businesses, the owners charge personal expenses to the business. By doing so, they reduce the net income of the business and reduce their tax obligation. Ferreting out this type of fraud is rather easy: You examine the invoices for company expenses to determine who the recipient of the goods or services really is. For example, look at all the utility bills and find the address being serviced (which is shown right on the bill). Determine if the address is a business site or the business owner's home. We once caught a small business owner who was charging her toddler's daycare provider as a business consultant. As soon as we saw the bills, we knew we were looking at tax fraud.

Sales tax

Sales tax is imposed on the purchase of certain goods and services. Sales tax exists in most states, but not all. Many local governments (counties and municipalities) also impose a sales tax. As of this writing, the Tax Foundation (www.taxfoundation.org) reports that the highest state sales tax rate is in California at 8.25 percent, but the highest overall sales tax rate is in Chicago at 10.25 percent.

Generally, the way sales tax works is that at the time of purchase the retailer collects the tax from the purchaser. Then, at a specified due date, the retailer remits the tax to the government. When sales tax is not collected at the time of sale, in most cases the purchaser is responsible for paying the equivalent amount (to their state) in *use tax*.

Where does fraud come into play with sales tax? Sometimes a retailer will collect the tax from its customers and not remit it to the government. When this happens, usually the retailer is also not reporting all its income.

Trying to tax interstate sales

Because of constitutional issues, the government cannot impose sales tax on interstate sales. For a long while, in order to avoid the sales tax, consumers would order from catalogs of companies that were based in different states. But the states got wise to this trick. They wrote laws that said if a catalog house had *nexus* (a connection) to the purchaser's state, it was subject to the laws of that state and, therefore, had to collect sales tax. The states interpreted nexus very broadly. They tried to claim that if the company sent a purchasing agent to their state, there was nexus, if the catalog house's Internet provider housed its Web site on a server in their state there was nexus, and certainly if it had a satellite store or office in the state there was nexus. In 1992, the U.S. Supreme Court decided that the catalog company had to have substantial presence in a state for nexus to exist. This argument is far from over. The more the states try to hook businesses for taxes, the more businesses will fight it.

How can a business get caught skipping out on sales tax? We've seen cases where state auditors have stood outside businesses and watched how many people go in and out and used this number to estimate sales. We've also seen auditors use the gross percentage profit (GPP) method to estimate a company's sales amount, which involves comparing a company's percentage of profit to that same percentage in other companies in the same industry. (If the GPP of one company is much higher than the industry average, you may be smelling something rotten.) State and local governments are continually finding new and creative ways to pick up the underreporting of sales tax.

You can also use this method of estimating sales if you're representing a client who is buying a business.

Remember, sales tax is a *fiduciary* tax: The business collects and holds the government's money. If the business does not remit the tax to the government, the government can and will go after the responsible parties personally. These people do not have the protection of a corporation for fiduciary taxes.

Employment taxes

In the section "Taking advantage of employees" earlier in the chapter, we explain that some employers like to have employees accounted for as independent contractors. A principal reason for doing so is to save on the many employment taxes and other levies that an employer must pay, which can add up to quite a bit of money. These taxes and levies include:

- ✓ Employer's portion of Social Security: 6.2 percent of the employee's salary (the maximum limitation for Social Security taxes)

- ✓ Employer's portion of Medicare: 1.45 percent of the employee's salary

- ✓ Federal unemployment insurance

✔ State unemployment insurance

✔ Disability insurance

✔ Worker's compensation insurance

✔ Voluntary pension plans

✔ Voluntary health plans (which will become mandatory health plans in the near future as a result of federal legislation passed in 2010)

Employment taxes can add up and put a significant dent in the bottom line of a business. But trying to pass off employees as individual contractors is risky business. Besides the IRS, other federal and state agencies (as well as private insurance companies) send auditors and forensic accountants to businesses to determine if they are classifying their employees correctly. If these auditors and forensic accountants determine that individual contractors should be classified as employees, the employers are on the hook for taxes and insurance premiums.

Transfer pricing

Transfer pricing is the price at which goods are exchanged between two separate accounting systems within the same holding company. Here's an example: Conglomerate, Inc.'s U.S. division buys widgets from Conglomerate's Martian division to put into a machine it assembles and sells in the United States. The transfer price is the price the U.S. division pays the Mars division.

Jersey stores

To avoid paying sales tax on clothing, some New Yorkers would get into their cars and go to New Jersey, where there is no sales tax on clothing. The State of New York started sending tax agents to New Jersey malls to write down the license plate numbers of New York cars in the parking lots. The state would then send the owners of those cars audit notices. To conduct these audits, it would get copies of credit card statements and compute the use tax on charges from out of state. (The *use tax* can be levied on goods and services when sales tax isn't paid.)

When New Yorkers found out about this situation, the state took a big hit in the media. The public was incensed that New York State would sneak around New Jersey this way. Now the state has added a line to its personal income tax form for the use tax. As a taxpayer, you'd better write something down on that line, even if it's $0. If you leave it blank, the state just may decide to audit you to determine if you've failed to pay any sales tax.

Here's where the fraud comes in. Let's say the corporate tax rate on Mars is 15 percent, and the rate in the United States is 35 percent. If the transfer price is high, the Martian division makes more money and the U.S. division makes less money. For every dollar of profit that is transferred to Mars, Conglomerate saves 20 cents in tax. Artificially increasing the Martian price is a fraud. The IRS and the international conglomerates have forensic economists working to determine what a fair price is for the transfer of goods. For more information, take a look at `www.transferpricing.com`.

Contract fraud

Earlier in the chapter, we discuss the potential for fraud related to construction work (see the section "Perpetrating construction fraud"). But the potential for contract fraud against the government extends way beyond construction because the government hires contractors for just about everything: military research, medical research, hospital management, school management, prison management, and on and on. In any of these contract situations, the potential for fraud exists:

- ✔ Contractors may deliver substandard goods.
- ✔ Contractors may overbill.
- ✔ Contractors may charge items to these contracts that aren't used for the contracted work.

Here's just one example: Stanford University was accused of charging flowers, for the home of the university president, to a defense contract. The instant this accusation hit the news, every university in the country that had a defense contract initiated examinations to see if anything was charged to government contracts that should not have been. After a thorough forensic examination by the Office of Naval Research, Stanford paid the government $1.2 million for improper expensing from 1981-1992.

Any entity with government grants or contracts is subject to being audited by government examiners. These examiners look at accounting records as well as production or usage records.

Medicare and Medicaid fraud

Medicare is a federally sponsored and managed program (funded partially by the federal government and partially by the states) that provides medical care for the elderly and recipients of Social Security disability payments. *Medicaid* provides medical care for the poor. Both programs are riddled with fraud.

Healthcare provider fraud

Many of the frauds occur when so-called healthcare providers bill for services they have not rendered. For example, there are ongoing investigations in Florida of sham providers of healthcare supplies. Here's how it works: A sham operation opens up in a storefront and somehow gets lists of seniors and their Medicare billing information. Then the fraudsters bill the Medicare program for wheelchairs, walkers, and other items that were never ordered by the patients' doctors and were never provided to the patients. Unfortunately, many times these guys close up shop and move on before the investigators arrive at their door.

Sometimes doctors and clinics bill for procedures that were never performed. To combat this type of fraud, Medicare and Medicaid computers are programmed to look for excessive billing by providers. If the average clinic doctor sees 25 to 40 patients during an eight-hour day, and a certain doctor bills for 80 to 120 patients per day, alarm bells ring.

The Medicare and Medicaid computer programs also look for hysterectomies performed on men (yes, fraudsters are stupid enough to bill for this) and treatments for organs that have previously been removed (it's very rare to have more than one appendix).

Tales from the nursing home

Phil, a longtime friend of ours, is a controller at a nursing home. Here are some of the tales he has told us about Medicare fraud in that environment:

✔ One nursing home had a psychotherapist on staff to see patients. Medicare requires that psychotherapy be billed in one-hour increments. Allegedly, the therapist would walk into a patient's room, say "Hi! How are you doing?" and walk out. The nursing home billed Medicare for 48 one-hour visits per day.

✔ Medicare regulations require that patients receiving physical therapy be seen individually. The Health Insurance Portability and Accountability Act (HIPAA) requires that patients be seen in private. At one nursing home, the physical therapists allegedly treat two to four patients at a time, in a hallway.

(Medicare fraud and HIPAA violations in one neat package!)

✔ The nursing home Phil works in received a transfer patient from another facility in a nearby city. The patient had been in the first facility for two years, sedated and with a feeding tube. The tube had to be removed from the patient during the transport to the new facility. At the new place, before replacing the tube, the staff decided to see if the patient could eat anything by mouth. Within two days, the patient was eating a normal diet. Why would the other facility insert an unnecessary feeding tube? Because sedated patients are easier to handle, and the nursing home gets to bill Medicare for monitoring the feeding tube. (Wow! Medical malpractice and Medicare fraud all rolled into one!)

Recipient fraud

On the recipient side, we hear a lot of stories of fraud in the Medicaid program. For example, someone may not qualify for Medicaid but "rents" a Medicaid card when she needs to go to the doctor. She may pay a certain amount to use the card for a single doctor's visit or a higher amount to keep the card for a whole day.

We also hear stories of people lying about their financial condition so they can get Medicaid benefits. Unfortunately, many local Medicaid offices are underfunded and too swamped to check out applicants thoroughly.

Social Security fraud

Social Security is a federal benefits program started during the Great Depression that provides benefits for retirees, widows and widowers, orphans, and people unable to work because of permanent disability. Eligibility and benefit amounts are complicated, and you can find more information at www.ssa.gov. The Social Security Administration (SSA) also administrates the Medicare program.

Whenever the government gives away money, fraudsters line up to collect their share. Some of the common types of Social Security fraud are:

- Concealing work activity while receiving disability benefits
- Receiving Social Security benefits for a child not under that person's care
- Failing to notify SSA of the death of a beneficiary and continuing to receive and cash the checks of the deceased
- Concealing a marriage or assets from the Social Security Administration while receiving Supplemental Security Income payments
- Residing overseas and receiving Supplemental Security Income payments

The fraudsters accomplish their deceits in a wide variety of ways, including:

- Making false statements on claims
- Concealing material facts or events that affect eligibility for benefits
- Misusing benefits (for example, a surviving parent receives the orphan benefits for his or her children but uses the money for some other purpose)
- Buying or selling Social Security cards or SSA information
- Bribing SSA employees

The SSA relies on IRS agents to report possible frauds they find while they are performing audits. It also relies heavily on the public to report suspected frauds.

A Social Security number (SSN) is one of the critical pieces of information needed by an identity thief to create a new set of papers and commit all sorts of crime. No one should *ever* give out their SSN unless they are in a situation where it is required to do so by law. If a doctor's office asks for your SSN, ask why that information is necessary to practice medicine. Last time we looked, the American Medical Association was advising their members not to ask for SSNs. Yet, many doctors continue to do so.

Introducing the Ponzi Scheme

This type of fraud deserves a section all its own. In a *Ponzi scheme,* a fraudster steals money to create the illusion of being legitimate so he can continue to steal money. The Bernie Madoff fraud that shocked the world in 2008 is probably the best-known example.

Here's how a simple Ponzi scheme works: Mr. Fraud needs money. He approaches Allison and says that he can invest her money and earn her an interest rate of 10 percent. Allison believes him and gives him $100. Mr. Fraud doesn't really invest Allison's money; he spends it. But he needs to give Allison her interest, so he approaches Billy with the same deal. Billy believes him and gives him $200. Mr. Fraud puts $110 in Allison's account and $90 in his pocket.

When the time comes for Mr. Fraud to give both Allison and Billy their interest, he approaches Charlie with the same deal. Mr. Fraud convinces Charlie to invest $300. He puts $10 in Allison's account and $20 in Billy's account to cover the interest. He puts $270 in his own pocket.

Uh oh, now Billy wants to withdraw money. Mr. Fraud finds Diana and convinces her to invest money. Diana gives him $400, part of which Mr. Fraud uses to put Billy's principal back in his account.

You get the picture. The Ponzi schemer keeps up an elaborate scheme of borrowing from Peter to pay Paul. At some point it gets too big to handle; the schemer just can't find enough new investors to pay off the old. When that happens, the house of cards comes tumbling down.

Early reports on the Madoff scheme indicated that Bernie actually started off as an honest financial advisor. When the market got a little bit soft, he started doing the Ponzi thing so that his investors would continue to get high returns. However, even when the market rebounded he couldn't make enough money to make up for the money he had borrowed, so he kept the Ponzi going. When the market took big hits in 2008 and investors needed to get their money out to cover their cash shortfalls, Madoff couldn't keep up anymore, and it all fell apart.

Charles Ponzi

The story of Carlo Pietro Giovanni Guglielmo Tebaldo (Charlie) Ponzi is a fascinating one. He was born in Italy in 1882 and immigrated to the United States in 1903 with $2.50 in his pocket.

In 1907, Ponzi moved to Montreal where he was employed at the Banco Zarossi, which served Italian immigrants. Zarossi was offering 6 percent interest: double the going rate at the time. This attracted a lot of funds. When Mr. Zarossi did not make enough to pay the interest, he used deposits to new accounts to cover it. Eventually, the bank failed, and Mr. Zarossi fled to Mexico. Ponzi stayed in Montreal, living in Mr. Zarossi's house and helping the abandoned family. One day while visiting an old Zarossi client, he stole a check, made it out to himself, and forged the signature. When caught he immediately confessed and was imprisoned for three years. He then got involved in a ring that was illegally smuggling Italian immigrants into the United States. He again was caught and spent two years in prison in Atlanta.

After his release, he returned to Boston. He decided to publish a business directory that would be funded by the sale of advertising to the businesses. The business failed quickly. Several weeks after he closed this business he got an inquiry about it from a company in Spain. With their letter the company enclosed an International Reply Coupon (IRC) that would allow him to exchange the coupon at a U.S. post office for postage to send a reply letter. Based on differences in foreign exchange rates, it was possible to make money on cashing the coupon. Ponzi realized that he could make money arbitraging IRCs.

Ponzi borrowed every penny he could, sent it to his family in Italy, and asked that they purchase IRCs and send them to him. Then he borrowed $750 from some friends, promising a 50 percent return within 90 days. When he made good on that promise, word got out about Ponzi's ability to get large returns. He started the Old Colony Foreign Exchange Company, and money poured in. By July 1920, he had made millions — enough to buy a controlling interest in the Hanover Trust Bank. The truth, however, was that he did not make *any* money. He had long stopped trying to buy IRCs. He was using the money from new investors to pay off old investors.

The house of cards tumbled when Charles Barron (the founder of Barron's magazine) began to investigate. Barron's findings caused a panic and ensuing run (demand for cash) on Old Colony, after which the Massachusetts Banking Commissioner launched an investigation. Ponzi was arrested for mail fraud and pleaded guilty. The scandal brought down Hanover Trust and five other banks. Ponzi's investors got back about 30 cents on the dollar.

Ponzi served three years in federal prison and then was indicted by the state of Massachusetts on 22 larceny charges. Despite his protests about double jeopardy, Ponzi was eventually found guilty and sentenced to seven to nine years. He appealed this conviction and, while out on bail, took a boat to New Orleans and changed his appearance and name. He started selling land tracts in Florida, but the land he sold was actually swamp land. Ponzi was indicted, convicted, and sentenced to a year in prison, but he posted bond and was released while the appealing the case. While out on bail, he changed his appearance again and boarded a ship for Italy. The ship made one last port call in New Orleans, where Ponzi was caught and sent to Massachusetts. He served seven years in prison and was then deported to Italy. He jumped from scheme to scheme but never made it big again.

Ponzi spent his last years in poverty and died in a charity hospital in Brazil in 1949. To read more about his life, check out *Ponzi: The Incredible True Story of the King of Financial Cons* by Donald Dunn (Library of Larceny).

Chapter 4

Forensic Accounting Minus the Fraud

A perception exists that forensic accountants are one-dimensional: They only detect and investigate fraud. The truth is that forensic accountants are also involved in commercial disputes, calculating damages that can literally run into billions of dollars. This work is sometimes referred to as "litigation support." In these situations, you provide accounting assistance in matters involving existing or pending litigation. A typical litigation support assignment results in calculating damages resulting from a breach of contract.

As a forensic accountant, you play three roles in commercial litigation:

▸ **Consultant:** You advise the client on technical accounting or financial issues. This involves providing discovery assistance, gathering and proving business facts, and calculating damages.

▸ **Expert witness:** You formulate an expert opinion based on your area of expertise.

▸ **Arbitrator:** As an arbitrator or *trier of facts,* you play the role of judge and jury in rendering your decision.

In this chapter, we delve into some of the tasks you may encounter when working on commercial litigation.

Business Valuation: Estimating Value

Forensic accountants may be asked to value a firm, its securities, its business divisions, or even specific transactions. Whereas *public accountants* (those who have many clients rather than working for a single business) must meet specific licensing requirements (see Chapter 2), no formal licensing requirements exist for valuation professionals. But if business valuation interests you, consider seeking membership in professional organizations such as The National Association of Certified Valuation Analysts, the American Society of Appraisers, and the Institute of Business Appraisers.

You should also consider the following accreditations that are offered by various professional organizations:

- ✔ Accredited in Business Valuation (ABV) conferred on CPAs by the AICPA

- ✔ Certified Valuation Analyst (CVA) offered by the National Association of Certified Valuation Analysts (NACVA)

- ✔ Accredited Valuation Analyst (AVA) granted by NACVA

- ✔ Accredited Senior Appraiser and the Accredited Senior Appraiser in Appraisal Review and Management (ASA) conferred by the American Society of Appraisers

- ✔ Certified Business Appraiser (CBA) designation awarded by the Institute of Business Appraisers (IBA)

When might you be asked to provide valuation services? Here are a few common scenarios:

- ✔ You may be asked to value a business whose stock is either not traded or barely traded in the stock markets. This information may be required by a potential purchaser of the business, for example.

- ✔ If the value of a company's assets and liabilities is in dispute, your services may be needed. For example, two parties involved in a lawsuit may have differing opinions of the value of certain assets.

- ✔ You may be asked to value a company's stock if disgruntled stockholders initiate litigation disputing the stock's value or purchase price.

- ✔ Your services may be needed in determining the value of a private business during divorce proceedings; total value of the estate for estate tax purposes after death; and gifts for gift tax purposes when shares in a privately owned company are passed from one generation to the next.

In this section, we walk you through just the basics of business valuation. If this subject interests you, you may want to pick up *Business Valuation For Dummies* by Lisa Holton and Jim Bates (Wiley).

Standards of value

One of the first questions you will be asked when valuing a business is related to the *standards of value* you will use. That phrase refers to standard measures of how much a business or asset is worth. The standard used in a business valuation scenario depends upon the specific circumstances you're looking at or the party for whom the valuation is performed. Using different standards of value may lead to different conclusions about the worth of a business. Several standards of value exist, but these three are the most common:

- ✔ **Fair market value:** The amount of money that a buyer may reasonably offer, and a seller accepts, in exchange for the asset. The primary requirement here is that both the buyer and seller should have reasonable knowledge of the facts surrounding the company or asset being valued. Both parties should also be acting in their best self-interest and be under no compulsion to buy or sell.

- ✔ **Investment value:** Refers to the value of the investment to a particular investor, which means that this number reflects the specific attributes of that investor. If three bidders in an auction wanted to buy a company, each of the three would likely offer a different price because the prices reflect their individual outlooks regarding what the company is worth.

- ✔ **Intrinsic value:** Refers to the *true* worth of the business based on the evaluation of available facts. Also called the *fundamental value* of the business, this amount is calculated by estimating the future income the business will generate and then discounting it to what the business is worth today.

Premise of value

A *premise of value* is the assumption that is made regarding the most likely set of circumstances affecting the asset or transaction being valued. Here are the two main premises of value in a business valuation:

- ✔ **Going concern value:** This term refers to the value of the company as an ongoing entity into the future. In other words, you expect that the company has a strong chance of survival, and you value it accordingly. In this situation, you assign value to the *intangible* assets (those that don't have a physical existence) used in running a business, such as goodwill and intellectual property.

✔ **Liquidation value:** Some companies are worth more dead than alive. *Liquidation value* refers to the estimated amount of money that a company could be sold for if it were going out of business. In other words, it's the net amount that could be gained if the business shut its doors and the assets were sold piecemeal. Liquidation can be either orderly or forced:

- *Orderly liquidation* means the assets are sold over a reasonable period of time to maximize the proceeds received.

- *Forced liquidation* means the assets are sold as quickly as possible, such as at an auction.

When you calculate liquidation value, you need to know whether you're assuming an orderly or forced liquidation.

Valuation approaches

After determining the standard and premise of value to be used, you next determine the valuation approach. You may use one approach or a combination of them to estimate value. In almost every case, the value you calculate will vary depending on the approach(es) you use. Here are the commonly used approaches to value a firm that you believe is a *going concern* (meaning you think it's going to stay in business):

✔ **Market approach:** The market approach is based on finding prices paid for comparable businesses or transactions in the public or private markets and using them to infer the value of a business or transaction. You can use several methods to determine the market value of a business, business ownership interest, security (debt or stock), or intangible asset:

- *Current market value approach:* This method is applicable to firms whose stock is actively traded in the stock market. You figure out the value by calculating the sum of the fair market value of the firm's equity and debt. The value of equity is calculated as the number of outstanding shares times the share price of the company's stock. The value of debt is calculated by aggregating the future cash flows arising from the debt, both principal and interest, and then determining what it is worth today (also known as *present value*).

- *Comparable firms approach:* This method is helpful for valuing firms whose stock is not actively traded in the stock exchange. In this situation, you first identify a comparable publicly traded firm with characteristics similar to that of the subject firm being valued. Then, you calculate *multiples* (the value of the company's stock or capital invested in the business divided by the appropriate financial statement measure, such as sales or net income) based on the performance of the comparable publicly traded firm. The challenge in this approach is to identify a good comparable firm that meets most of the characteristics of the firm being valued.

- *Comparable transactions approach:* This method is useful during mergers and acquisitions when a firm, its business divisions, or certain assets or products are being bought or sold. Here, you base the pricing multiple of the firm being purchased or sold on the value of a comparable transaction. In other words, you have to identify a similar firm that was previously purchased or sold.

✔ **Income approach:** The income approach is based on determining future earnings and then calculating its present value. The two common income approaches are as follows:

- *Discounted cash flow method (DCF):* This approach involves projecting future cash flows relating to business operations such as sales, expenses, taxes, leases, capital expenditures, and investments in working capital. Even if you think that the business you're valuing could go on forever, you can't reasonably project cash flows beyond a certain number of years. For that reason, cash flows are typically projected for a period of anywhere from five to ten years. After that, a terminal value is calculated: the value of the business after the forecast period. After you've done these calculations, you assign a total value to the business by discounting the projected cash flows for each year and the terminal value to the present using a discount rate. The discount rate is a rate of return used to convert a future sum of money into its present value.

- *Capitalized cash flow method (CCF):* The CCF is an abbreviated version of the DCF where both the growth and the discount rates are assumed to remain constant into perpetuity. This model also goes by the names "dividend discount model" and the "Gordon Growth Model." For more information about these models and valuation approaches, read the Wiley publication, *Financial Valuation Applications and Models*, by James Hitchner.

✔ **Asset approach:** This method is based on the theory that the value of a business is equal to the sum of its parts. In other words, you adjust the book value of each individual asset to an estimate of fair market value and subtracting the value of liabilities. The values of certain assets, such as long-lived assets (land, plants, equipment, and machinery) and intangible assets (patents, trademarks, and licensing agreements), typically differ from the assets' book values. You want to convert their book values to fair market values whenever possible.

So, which of these valuation approaches should you use? The answer depends on the specific situation of the firm being valued. For example, the market approach may not be suitable if transactions for comparable companies don't exist or cannot be found. Based on the results you get from the relevant approaches you use, you may present the range of values identified and then provide a final number that you believe is the firm's best estimated value.

Investigating Intellectual Property

Intellectual property refers to creations of the mind whose owners are granted exclusive rights to a variety of intangible assets, such as inventions; literary and artistic works; and symbols, names, images, and designs. Companies greatly rely on knowledge, innovation, and intellectual capital to grow and succeed. These intangible assets are increasingly becoming the factor that determines a company's success or failure. Intellectual property assets sometimes contribute more to companies' market capitalization than tangible assets.

Common types of intellectual property include copyrights, trademarks, trade secrets, and patents. The use of these critical sources of value creates disagreements and disputes among players in the market. Intellectual property litigation is common these days, especially within industries that rely on technology, innovation, and copyrights. (The information technology, life sciences, and media industries are prime examples.) Damages claims are also brought by individuals who may be patent holders, have copyrighted works, or hold other properties that they believe have been infringed.

Because intellectual property has unique characteristics, determining damages in such cases may require complex analysis. For instance, in an intellectual property infringement case, there may be claims of damages based on lost profits. That is, the plaintiff claims it lost profits on sales it would have made if not for the defendant's wrongful actions. A forensic accountant working on behalf of the plaintiff in such a case will often go beyond the calculation of lost sales and find additional losses associated with the effects of price erosion, reduced economies of scale, and the presence of competition.

Another area where disputes arise is related to infringement of licensing agreements. Licensors of intellectual property, disputing the ways in which licensees utilize their rights, may claim damages as well as lost profits. In these situations, you may act as a consultant to help establish the damages sustained by the licensor, as well as the lost profits resulting from actions taken by the licensee.

Estimating Environmental Damages

As we write this chapter, the United States is experiencing its largest offshore oil spill in history, with hundreds of millions of gallons spilling into the Gulf of Mexico as a result of the 2010 BP oil disaster. The resulting oil slick covers at least an estimated 2,500 square miles and has caused severe damage to marine and wildlife habitats. This disaster has also crippled the fishing and tourism industries and has caused environmental risks to hundreds of miles of beaches, estuaries, and wetlands.

This environmental disaster will result in a multitude of environment damages claims. Various media reports are estimating the total cost to BP in the range of $3 billion to $20 billion. Forensic accountants will play a crucial role in the adjudication of these claims.

Why are companies such as BP on the hook when they cause environmental messes? A number of federal statutes relate to environmental law, including the Comprehensive Environmental Response, Compensation and Liability Act (CERCLA), the Oil Pollution Act, and the Resource Conservation and Recovery Act. Many states have similar laws on the books. These statutes include provisions that enable federal or state agencies to recover damages from private parties for any harm to natural resources and associated clean-up activities. Liability for environmental damages can extend to subsequent owners and management, even if the subsequent owners and management were not at the scene at the time of the event that resulted in an environmental liability.

When a company finds itself entangled in an environmental damages case, it may hire forensic accountants to help with the following tasks:

- ✔ Analyzing the total present and future costs associated with the environmental damage, penalties, and insurance-related calculations.
- ✔ Calculating damages arising from bodily injury, death, property damage, business interruption claims, and other claims.
- ✔ Negotiating settlements and identifying costs already incurred by the company to meet the compliance requirements. In some cases, such costs can offset a portion of the penalties assessed by government agencies.
- ✔ Filing insurance claims.
- ✔ Providing expert testimony (see Chapter 18).

Forensic accountants may also get involved when a merger or acquisition is being considered. The companies involved must do due diligence to make sure investors understand the environmental issues and potential costs involved.

Examining Auditor Malpractice Complaints

Accountants offer myriad services to clients that extend beyond traditional auditing, tax consulting, and bookkeeping services. These services include business process consulting, management consulting, financial advisory services, and bankruptcy consulting. But when accountants face professional malpractice litigation, most often the claims relate to traditional services they provide, such as auditing financial statements.

The most common scenario that leads to an accountant being sued is that a user of the financial statement discovers a misstatement in that statement after it has been audited and released to the public. If the misstatement is *material,* meaning that it's significant enough to cause investors and other statement users to make decisions they wouldn't have otherwise made, the user is going to look for someone to blame.

In this scenario, the claim alleges that the audit firm was negligent: It failed to conform to the accepted standards of the profession (generally accepted auditing standards, or GAAS) or failed to discover misstatements in the company's financials, resulting in harm to the report users. To file a claim of negligence, the financial statement user must prove that a misrepresentation of a material fact exists and that the user was relying on the auditor to perform the duty that would have prevented the harm.

Claims for fraud are also sometimes brought against accountants under federal laws. These laws require proof that there was intent to deceive, manipulate, or defraud.

Plaintiff strategies

Here is the most common string of events in an auditor malpractice complaint:

- ✓ The *plaintiff* (the person or business filing the claim) argues that the financial statements on which the auditor rendered an opinion failed to report that the company's financial condition and results of operations were in accordance with generally accepted accounting principles (GAAP).
- ✓ Then the plaintiff contends that the auditor failed to meet its professional responsibilities by not following GAAS.
- ✓ The plaintiff alleges that the auditor ignored warning signs or red flags and that, if the auditor *had* paid attention to the red flags, it would have discovered and prevented financial misstatements.
- ✓ The plaintiff claims that it suffered damages as a result of the financial misreporting.

Defense strategies

The auditor's defense against the plaintiff's claim will center around four contentions:

- ✓ The numbers in the financial statements that the auditor opined on were correct.
- ✓ There is an absence of *justifiable reliance.* This means that the plaintiff must prove not just that the numbers were incorrect but also that the

end user of the financial reports justifiably relied on the incorrect numbers such that it was harmed.

✔ Other people, not the auditor, are primarily at fault. Remember, the company's management bears primary responsibility for preparing the financial statements. The auditor issues an opinion on them based on testing transactions.

✔ The accountant's report was correct, and it conformed to professional standards.

The forensic accountant's role

In auditor malpractice cases, the forensic accountant may be asked to provide expert testimony. He may be called to testify in these capacities:

✔ **Accounting expert:** The forensic accountant addresses whether the financial statements complied with GAAP. He quantifies the amount of the alleged misstatements and opines as to the time periods when the misstatements occurred. A plaintiff's accounting expert may testify that the misstatements were detectible by the auditor, who saw or should have seen the company accounting records that contained the misstatements.

✔ **Audit expert:** The forensic accountant addresses the requirements of GAAS and whether the auditor followed GAAS in the audit of the financial statements. By reviewing audit work papers and the testimony of the auditors, the expert forms an opinion about whether appropriate procedures were used during the audit.

✔ **Damages expert:** The determination of damages depends on the plaintiff's relation to the financial statements. A creditor of a company, for example, may seek to recover amounts owed to it by the company. A shareholder may seek to recover damages based on excess price paid for his shares. The forensic accountant can help calculate such damages.

Calculating Business Interruption Costs for Insurance Purposes

Firms are exposed to a number of risks that may lead to business interruption losses. Those risks range from machinery breakdowns to terrorist attacks to hurricanes or earthquakes. During the interruption period, a firm may lose its ability to do business and earn revenues while still incurring fixed costs such as payroll. A firm may incur additional costs relating to restarting its operations and getting things back to where they were before the interruption.

Typically, companies carry business interruption insurance policies to protect themselves from such interruption loss. The purpose of a business interruption insurance policy is to put the insured in the same financial condition as if the incident and related loss had not occurred.

In such situations, the insurance company and the insured may engage forensic accountants, engineers, attorneys, or other specialists to assess the damages incurred by the insured. The insured then puts together a claim for its losses in line with the terms and conditions of the insurance policy. The forensic accountant or other specialist should be a qualified accountant with appropriate experience in claims management and in the industry in which the insured operates.

The various steps of the claims process are as follows:

- **Understanding the insurance policy:** The insured and/or its specialist should carefully study the insurance policy in order to understand what is covered and what isn't. It's also important to understand the terms and conditions surrounding the coverage.

- **Setting up a recovery plan:** The insured should put together a recovery plan and estimate the time and costs required to get the business up and running. While setting up a recovery plan, the insured should consider various permutations and combinations of time and costs. For instance, a quick recovery may cost more in the short term than a slower recovery, but the additional revenue possible with a quick recovery may exceed the additional costs.

- **Curtailing losses:** During the business interruption period, insurance policies typically require the insured to take some steps in order to curtail losses. Insurance policies cover the costs associated with curtailing losses if those costs don't exceed the reduction in losses. Those repairs must be carried out diligently and efficiently so that excessive costs are not incurred.

- **Reaching out to the adjuster:** *Claims adjusters* investigate insurance claims to determine the insured's liability. The insured and its specialists should meet the claims adjuster as soon as possible after the incident. During this meeting, the insured may show the damaged property, discuss the recovery plan, and share action steps to be taken to curtail losses. The adjuster may request that the insured provide him all relevant information in order to calculate the claim. During the entire claims process, it is important to maintain open channels of communication, conduct additional meetings, and share appropriate information with the adjuster in order to build mutual trust and confidence.

✔ **Submitting the claim:** There is no single correct method to prepare a business interruption claim. An experienced forensic accountant or specialist can evaluate all applicable methods and identify the approach best suited for the specific situation. Generally, depending on the terms of the policy, a business interruption claim may be based on lost profits, which are calculated on lost production or lost sales. Continuing expenses such as the payroll of key employees, depreciation, rent, contractual obligations, advertising, some utilities, and other fixed costs are covered by the insurance policy. Noncontinuing expenses such as direct materials, maintenance, rental equipment, sales commissions, and most utilities are not covered.

✔ **Negotiating a settlement:** If settlement negotiations are required, the insured's team (including the forensic accountant) should be physically present to negotiate the claim. The insured should insist that a representative from the insurer with sufficient authority to settle the claim (someone other than the adjuster) be present. If the settlement negotiations are not conclusive, the matter may be determined by arbitration or appraisal rather than traditional litigation. In this situation, the forensic accountant acts as a consultant or as an expert witness.

Immediately following the 9/11 attacks, business activities in New York City were significantly affected. Most of the businesses in the immediate vicinity of the World Trade Center could not open for weeks or months due to rescue efforts and environmental hazards. The New York Stock Exchange was closed for several days. Tourism and entertainment businesses saw a significant drop in revenues. Flights in and out of New York airports were temporarily suspended. The City of New York, Office of the Comptroller, put together a preliminary estimate of $21 billion relating to business interruption losses covering a period of approximately ten months following the attacks.

Tallying Construction-Related Damages

Large construction projects, such as those that involve the construction of buildings, plants, bridges, and dams, involve a number of parties including the owners of the company paying for the construction (or the government entity footing the bill if it's a public works project), contractors, subcontractors, engineers, architects, and construction managers. The large number of involved parties exposes the company (or the government) to cost overruns, billing errors, and fraud.

Typically, such large projects go through several changes during the course of the construction period. These changes — such as the acceleration or disruption of work; changes in scope; delays; or changes in prices of labor, materials, or equipment — may result in additional costs. Because each player in the project depends on the other players to do their part (on time and on budget), costs that arise from changes may have a ripple effect and may undermine the project's profitability. The impact of such changes may also result in disputes and litigation.

Construction litigation involves a variety of claims related to delays, extra work, disruption, and contractor termination. In addition, some common construction fraud schemes (which we also discuss in Chapter 3) include:

- ✔ Claiming fees for time and material costs not incurred
- ✔ Overstating progress on construction
- ✔ Billing for work not started or yet to be completed
- ✔ Using unapproved materials
- ✔ Stealing materials and/or equipment
- ✔ Manipulating change orders and contingency accounts
- ✔ Hiding conflicts of interest or making false representations

Forensic accountants and other specialists (such as project management professionals, civil engineers, certified cost engineers, and architects) may be involved in overseeing the construction process, the quality of work, and the total expenditure. They may also be asked to investigate fraud. With large projects, forensic accountants and specialists should ideally be involved as early as during the planning phases.

In litigation, forensic accountants and other specialists may be asked to calculate damages and to serve as expert witnesses. The calculation of damages may involve tallying costs related to additional work, delays, disruption, inefficiency, unplanned costs, consequential or *liquidated* damages (monetary compensation for a loss or injury to a person that is awarded by court judgment or a contract stipulation regarding breach of contract), *soft costs* (any expenses not considered direct construction costs, such as architectural, engineering, and legal fees), indirect costs, overhead, and/or misuse of resources.

The "Big Dig" is the unofficial name of the Central Artery/Tunnel Project (CA/T) in Boston that rerouted Interstate 93, the chief highway through the heart of the city, into a 3.5-mile tunnel. Completed in December 2007, the Big Dig was the most expensive highway project in the United States. Although the project was estimated in 1985 to cost $2.8 billion, it cost over $14.6 billion. Construction companies working on the Big Dig filed claims amounting to $1.3 billion in additional contract payments primarily due to delays and cost overruns. In January 2008, Bechtel/Parsons Brinckerhoff, the consortium that oversaw the project, agreed to pay $407 million in restitution for its poor oversight of subcontractors.

Focusing on Avoidance Actions in Bankruptcy

When times get tough, some companies and individuals have to file for bankruptcy. *Bankruptcy* indicates that the sum of a company's debts is greater than the fair value of its assets. (Simply put, it can't pay its bills.) The Bankruptcy Code is the federal law that is applicable to bankruptcy situations. Generally speaking, bankrupt companies either reorganize themselves under a Chapter 11 filing or *liquidate* themselves (meaning they sell off their assets) in a Chapter 7 filing. (Individuals file for Chapter 13 when they declare bankruptcy.)

The bankrupt entity is referred to as a *debtor.* Bankruptcy courts often appoint trustees to manage the affairs of debtors. A trustee can take steps to help the estate or the creditors recover assets from the debtor if the debtor has taken what are called *avoidance actions.* There are two types of avoidance actions — fraudulent conveyances and preferential transfers — and we explain both in this section.

Fraudulent conveyance

A *fraudulent conveyance* occurs when the debtor transfers property to a third party in order to hinder, delay, or defraud creditors. In this type of transfer, the debtor gives something of value and receives substantially less in return. The trustee or creditors have to prove that the debtor intentionally transferred the property to put it out of reach of specific creditors.

A trustee or a creditor may contract a forensic accountant to help make the case against the debtor. (Or the debtor may hire a forensic accountant to defend itself when it's being investigated for fraudulent conveyances.) A *fraudulent conveyance proceeding* is a court proceeding that examines business transactions between the debtor and the affected creditor(s).

If you're working on a fraudulent conveyance proceeding, you need to carefully study the nature and underlying economic substance of the suspect transactions. If the debtor is a business, you need to review all its financial and accounting records, its legal agreements and documents, minutes of the board of directors' meetings, and any deposition testimony. You may need to conduct additional research as well.

You may also be asked to assess the insolvency of the debtor as a result of the fraudulent conveyance. A business is *insolvent* if its debts are greater than its assets at a fair valuation. Your goal in this situation is to value the debtor immediately before and after the suspect transaction. Generally, you would use the income approach and the market approach to valuation that we discuss earlier in this chapter.

Preferential payments

Certain payments made by a debtor prior to filing for bankruptcy may be deemed *preferential payments* that favor one creditor over another. If the trustee can prove this suspicion is correct, those payments can be recovered through a *preference avoidance action.* The idea in play here is that all creditors should receive equal treatment. A forensic accountant may be hired by a trustee trying to prove its case or by a creditor trying to hold on to a payment it has received from a debtor.

According to the Bankruptcy Code, a transfer to a creditor may be preferential if it meets one or more of these criteria:

- ✔ A transfer of an interest in the debtor's property was made to (or for the benefit of) a creditor.

- ✔ The debtor owed a prior debt before this transfer was made.

- ✔ The debtor made the transfer while it was *insolvent* (unable to pay its debts when they become due).

- ✔ The transfer was made within 90 days of the bankruptcy filing or within one year if the creditor was an insider. (An *insider* is an individual, partner, or corporation that is controlled by the debtor.)

- ✔ The transfer gave the creditor more than it would have received in a hypothetical Chapter 7 distribution (upon liquidation).

If a creditor has received a payment that is under investigation for being preferential, it can take several defenses. Here are two of the most important:

- ✔ **New value defense:** This defense is used in situations where a creditor was providing goods to a debtor on credit on a periodic basis, and the debtor made a series of payments to the creditor during the preference period. The value of the goods or services provided by the creditor subsequent to receiving payments will be deducted from the payments as *new value provided.* The balance represents the preference payment that may be reclaimed by the debtor's trustee.

- ✔ **Ordinary course of business defense:** In this situation, a creditor makes the case that the payment it received from the debtor was not a payment for an outstanding debt but rather a payment made in the ordinary course of business between the parties. The creditor has to prove that the payment was in accordance with the normal way the creditor and debtor did business. The other prong for this defense relates to ordinary business terms of the industry. That is, the payment was made in conformity with industry business standards.

Forensic accountants are typically asked to put together analyses that address potential preference payments. In disputes of this nature, the forensic accountant may be asked to issue an opinion about whether the debtor was insolvent during the preference period. The accountant also obtains evidence supporting or negating the preferential transfer and provides testimony on the matter. To identify whether payments are subject to the defenses listed here, a forensic accountant may need to investigate past payment practices and the normal course of dealings between the parties.

The bankruptcy court may hold hearings to determine the status of the payments. If such payments are ultimately determined to be preferential, creditors have to return the payments to the debtor.

Dealing in Divorce

Obviously, divorce is fraught with emotion, and the people involved often challenge each other on issues of what they're entitled to and how much certain assets are worth. When prenuptial agreements are involved, the parties may dispute what the living expenses of each spouse are.

Forensic accountants may be hired to assign value to assets and to estimate living expenses by looking at the historical spending patterns of each spouse. They may also be asked to value *professional goodwill*: an intangible asset that applies when one or both spouses are professionals (such as lawyers, doctors, or accountants) and own their own practices. And if the parties disagree about which assets each person brought into the marriage, forensic accountants may be asked to trace those assets and determine how they were acquired.

Divvying up assets is an essential part of the divorce agreement. In the United States, two different divorce standards are used depending on the state where the divorce occurs:

- ✔ **Equitable distribution:** The court decides what constitutes a fair, reasonable, and equitable division of assets. The court considers many factors including how long the marriage lasted, what assets each person brought into the marriage, how much compensation each person earns, and each person's responsibilities for children.

- ✔ **Community property:** Any property acquired by the couple during marriage is divided 50/50. Issues such as financial need and the ability to earn income are not taken into account.

The following assets come into play during a divorce proceeding:

- **Marital home:** This is one of the largest assets in a divorce. State law is the best source of information as to how the court will divide the marital home. The spouses must decide how to divide this asset based on what makes best sense for them. For example, if they have debts from the marriage that they have to pay off, they may decide to sell the home. Tax and other financial implications come into play, so a lawyer or a tax professional can help.

- **Retirement plans:** Pensions, 401(k) plans, individual retirement accounts, and other employment benefits such as bonuses, vacation days, and stock options all come into play. The primary issue to consider here is whether the spouses want to retain their individual retirement benefits. If the answer is no, a valuation specialist must determine the current value of these benefits.

- **Investments:** These include securities such as stocks, bonds, mutual funds, money market accounts, and certificates of deposit. Considerations include the date on which the investments will be valued and the date of separation and/or divorce. Issues such as capital gains and brokerages fees come into play, so a tax advisor should help.

- **Cash and life insurance policies:** Cash is cash and should present no problems when figuring out its value. Life insurance policies are slightly more complicated. *Term* life insurance has no market value, but a *whole life* policy may have a cash surrender value. This information is generally available from the insurance agent.

- **Vehicles and other household items:** Vehicles include automobiles, motorcycles, boats, and motor homes. For automobiles, the easiest way to get the current value is by checking *Kelly Blue Book,* which is a resource for prices, values, and reviews of new and used cars. Other household items may include jewelry, furniture, electronics, pots, pans, and antiques. The forensic accountant may be asked to value some of these items; the techniques we outline earlier in this chapter come in handy.

- **Business:** Valuing a family-owned business can be a complicated exercise and must take into account how much each spouse contributed to the business, who started the business, whether the other spouse helped in the business, and other factors. To value the business, consider the value of goodwill or reputation of the business; how much that reputation is dependent upon each spouse's contributions to the business; the value of the equipment, land, and building; and the value of other assets such as inventory and accounts receivable. Rules for determining and defining the appropriate standard of value vary by state, as does the inclusion of goodwill or professional goodwill in the marital estate.

Part II
The Anatomy of Occupational Fraud

The 5th Wave   By Rich Tennant

"Our goal is to maximize your upside and minimize your downside while we protect our own backside."

In this part . . .

*O*ccupational fraud is the name given to fraud that occurs within a business or another institution. It includes fraud committed by individuals against a business (such as when managers embezzle money or employees steal inventory), and it includes fraud committed by the business against its investors and creditors (such as falsifying information on financial reports and manipulating its own stock values).

The sums of money lost each year to occupational fraud are staggering, and the forensic accounting field is growing by leaps and bounds as a result. We show you the types of situations you're likely to encounter when you're hired to investigate occupational fraud.

Chapter 5

Cooked Books: Finding Financial Statement Fraud

. . . .

In This Chapter

▶ Understanding the basics of financial statement analysis

▶ Identifying motives behind financial statement frauds

▶ Realizing how such frauds are committed

▶ Playing sleuth: Finding the fraud

. . . .

A company records all its business transactions, culminating in the preparation of financial reports that provide information about the company's financial position and performance. Financial reports consist of the following: *principal statements* (the income statement, balance sheet, statement of cash flows, and statement of changes in owners' equity), notes to these statements, and management discussion and analysis (MD&A) of results. Financial statements provide a snapshot of the business at a given point in time: the results of its financial performance and its generation of cash flows during a given period.

Auditors conduct financial statement analysis, which involves evaluating a company's financial position and its ability to generate profits and cash flow both now and in the future. Such analysis may also include valuing the company itself. Financial statements provide the information to do so.

Financial statement fraud, commonly referred to as "cooking the books" or "fudging the numbers," usually involves manipulating one of more elements of the financial statements. Assets, revenues, and profits could be overstated, and liabilities, expenses, and losses could be understated. This type of fraud involves the deliberate misrepresentation or manipulation of the financial condition of a business, and it's accomplished through the intentional misstatement or omission of amounts or disclosures in the financial statements to deceive the people who use those statements.

According to the 2008 Association of Certified Fraud Examiners (ACFE) *Report to the Nation on Occupational Fraud and Abuse,* the median loss of a fraudulent statement incident was $2 million, far greater than any other type of fraud. When penalties and fines, legal costs, the loss of investor confidence, and reputational damage are taken into account, the total costs of this type of fraud can be enormous.

Reviewing the Basics of Financial Statements

"Show me the money!" You probably remember those words from the movie *Jerry Maguire*, and that's what financial statements do. They show you where a company's money came from, where it went, and where it currently resides. In this section, we review the basics of these statements.

There are two common types of accounting methods: the cash method and the accrual method. Under the cash method, transactions are recorded only when cash is received or expended. Under the accrual method, revenue is recorded when it's earned, and expenses are recorded when they are incurred, no matter when cash is received or expended. The main purpose of accrual accounting is to record revenue and expense in the proper accounting period. Accrual accounting accounts for the timing difference between when a transaction occurs and when cash is exchanged. Public companies are required to prepare their financial statements under the accrual method.

The big three

The three principal financial statements are the income statement, the balance sheet, and the statement of cash flows. A fourth type — the statement of changes in owners' equity — reports changes in the owners' investment in the business over time. Here, we examine just the three principal financial statements.

Income statement

The income statement portrays the financial results of a company's business activities for a period of time. It displays the amount of revenue generated by the company and the costs incurred by it to generate the revenue. The residual between revenue and costs is called *net income* (when revenue exceeds costs) or *net loss* (when costs exceed revenue). Therefore, the basic equation underlying the income statement is this:

Revenue minus Expenses = Net income (or Expenses minus Revenue = Net loss)

Three other important measures are depicted in the income statement:

- ✔ **Gross profit or margin:** The amount of revenue available after deducting the costs incurred in producing or delivering goods or services. The two main types of such costs are material and labor.

- ✔ **Operating income:** A company's earnings or profits from its business activities before deducting interest expense or taxes.

- ✔ **Earnings per share (EPS):** The net income earned per outstanding share of the company. EPS is calculated by dividing the net income by the number of shares outstanding during the period.

Balance sheet

The balance sheet (also referred to as the *statement of financial position* or *statement of financial condition*) presents a company's current financial position. It is divided into three parts:

- ✔ **Assets:** Resources or things owned by a company that have value.

- ✔ **Liabilities:** Amounts of money a company owes at a given point in time.

- ✔ **Owners' or shareholders' equity:** Also referred to as *capital* or *net worth,* it is the amount of money left over if a company were to sell off all its assets and pay off all its liabilities. The money left over would belong to the owners.

The balance sheet is set up in terms of the accounting equation:

Assets = Liabilities + Owners' Equity

On the left side of the balance sheet, companies list their assets. On the right side, they list their liabilities and owners' equity. (Balance sheets sometimes show assets at the top, followed by liabilities and owners' equity.)

Statement of cash flows

Cash or cash flow is very important for a business — it represents the life blood vital for its well-being and survival. Cash is needed to pay employees and suppliers, for investments, and to return capital to investors. The cash flow statement discloses the sources and uses of cash and helps a company's financial statement users to evaluate its liquidity, solvency, and financial flexibility. *Liquidity* and *solvency* refer to an entity's ability to meet its short-term and long-term obligations, respectively; *financial flexibility* is the ability to react to contingencies and/or opportunities.

The cash flow statement classifies the sources and uses of cash under operating, investing, and financing activities. *Operating activities* consist of activities that an entity engages in daily. *Investing activities* are those concerned with the acquisition and disposition of long-term assets. *Financing activities* relate to obtaining or repaying capital used in the business.

Who uses financial statements, and how?

People inside and outside the company use its financial statements. Users of financial statements include the following:

- ✔ Investors and lenders, to monitor their investments

- ✔ Customers and suppliers, to evaluate the financial strength of the company

- ✔ Boards of directors, to review the performance of management

- ✔ Management, to assess its own performance

- ✔ Competitors, to benchmark their financial results with other market participants

- ✔ Government agencies, responsible for taxing or regulating the company

- ✔ Potential business partners, to know about the company and its financial situation

- ✔ Labor unions, to gauge a company's strength in labor negotiations

Two types of financial statement analyses are generally performed: *cross-sectional analysis,* where a company is compared with other companies in the same industry; and *trend analysis,* where a company is analyzed over time. To facilitate these two types of analyses, users conduct ratio analysis and common-size financial statement analysis:

- ✔ **Ratio analysis:** Ratios are a useful way of expressing relationships between financial accounts over different points in time. A *ratio* expresses one quantity in relation to another and is an indicator of some aspect of a company's performance. By performing ratio analysis, you can evaluate a company's past performance, assess its current financial position, and project future results.

  The broad categories of ratios (which we discuss further in the upcoming section "Uncovering Financial Statement Fraud") are as follows:

  - *Activity ratios* measure the efficiency with which a company performs its day-to-day operations, including management of inventory or collection of receivables. For instance, the inventory turnover ratio measures the effectiveness of inventory management. A high inventory turnover ratio indicates one of two things: either highly effective inventory management or the possibility that the company is not carrying adequate inventory, which could hurt the company when shortages of inventory occur.

  - *Liquidity ratios* measure the company's ability to meet its short-term obligations. Liquidity measures how soon assets can be converted into cash. The current ratio, a common liquidity ratio, measures the amount of current assets (assets that can be converted into cash within one year) available to meet current liabilities (liabilities that fall due either on demand or within one year). A higher current ratio indicates a greater ability to meet short-term obligations.

- *Solvency ratios* measure the company's ability to meet its long-term obligations. Solvency ratios provide information regarding the amount of debt a company has as part of its capital (debt ratios) and the adequacy of earnings and cash flow to pay interest expenses on debt and other charges (coverage ratios). For example, the debt-to-equity ratio measures the amount of debt a company has relative to its equity. A higher ratio would indicate that the company is highly leveraged, which indicates weaker solvency.

- *Profitability ratios* measure the company's ability to generate profits from the use of its assets. An example of a profitability ratio is the return on assets (ROA), which measures the return earned by a company on the use of its assets. The higher the income generated on a given level of assets, the higher the ROA.

✓ **Common-size financial statement analysis:** Common-size analysis involves expressing the entire financial statements in relation to a single financial statement item. Items most commonly used as bases are total revenue or assets. The point of conducting a common-size analysis is to create a ratio between every financial statement item and the base item.

Studying What Prompts Financial Statement Fraud

In 1999, the Committee of Sponsoring Organizations (COSO) of the Treadway Commission released a study of approximately 200 financial statement frauds committed between 1987 and 1997. The study showed that senior management is the most likely group to commit financial statement fraud. The CEO was involved in 72 percent of the frauds, whereas the CFO was involved in 43 percent. Either the CEO or the CFO was involved in 83 percent of the cases.

Management has many incentives to perpetrate financial statement fraud. Managers trying to meet any number of legitimate corporate goals (such as sales targets, cost targets, analysts' earnings expectations, and bonus plan targets) or who are trying to make critical investment and financing decisions to achieve these targets can find accounting rules and systems a hindrance. Therefore, they may be tempted to compromise the fundamental informational role of accounting to manage the company's earnings.

One of the main reasons to manage earnings is to keep Wall Street happy, at least in the short run. Information about a company's current status and prospects affect its share values. The company can get punished if it does not meet its earnings targets. Sometimes the drop in share value may be large.

In Chapter 1, we explain that the *fraud triangle* represents three conditions that are always present for fraud to occur: motivation, rationalization, and opportunity. Here, we examine the fraud triangle as it relates to financial statement fraud.

The following risk factors related to motivation or incentive can lead to financial statement fraud:

- The company is facing tough economic conditions, such as a high degree of competition, rapid technological changes, the threat of bankruptcy, declines in consumer demand, or new regulatory changes that threaten profitability.

- Management is faced with pressure to meet the expectations of third parties, including analysts, investors, or creditors, in terms of raising financing. Pending merger or acquisition activity can also create third-party pressure.

- Management and the board members' personal financial situation is affected by the prospects of lower compensation or by holding shares in the company, which are tied to the company's financial performance.

Here's how a company can create the opportunity for financial statement fraud:

- Internal control deficiencies exist as a result of inadequate accounting systems or the inadequate monitoring of controls.

- There is a complex organizational structure with multiple lines of reporting for managers and/or unusual legal entities, or there is high turnover of senior management.

- Management and board oversight is deficient as evidenced by the domination by a small group of people.

- The company operates within an industry that uses significant related-party transactions or operates in foreign jurisdictions. (A related risk is that the company wants to dominate its industry sector.)

- The company may have entered into complex transactions (e.g., derivatives) that could present risks. Only a few people truly understand the mechanics of the transactions.

Risk factors associated with the rationalization of financial statement fraud include the following:

- The company has violated securities laws in the past or has been accused of fraud.

- The company suffers from ineffective communication or poor enforcement of ethical values and standards.

- Management fails to correct internal control weaknesses in a timely manner.

- The relationship between management and the auditor is strained.

Spotting the Common Methods of Fraud

A forensic accountant's role in investigating financial fraud is to look for red flags or accounting warning signs. It's akin to a doctor who initially looks at a patient's condition in terms of checking blood pressure and other vital signs, or examining blood reports. Accounting red flags include:

- Aggressive revenue recognition practices, such as recognizing revenue in earlier periods than when the product was sold or the service was delivered

- Unusually high revenues and low expenses at period end that cannot be attributed to seasonality

- Growth in inventory that does not match growth in sales

- Improper capitalization of expenses in excess of industry norms

- Reported earnings that are positive and growing, but operating cash flow that is declining

- Growth in revenues that is far greater than growth in other companies in the same industry or peer group

- Gross margin or operating margins out of line with peer companies

- Extensive use of off-balance sheet entities based on relationships that are not normal in the industry

In this section, we explain four of the most common methods used to commit financial statement fraud: hidden liabilities, cookie jar reserves, off-balance sheet transactions, and notes that no one can comprehend.

Hidden liabilities

In the accrual method of accounting (which is required for all public companies), expenses must be recorded in the period when they are incurred, irrespective of when they are paid. *Capitalization* refers to recording expenditures as assets rather than expenses because the expenditures add to the value of an asset, which provides benefits into the future. Improper capitalization occurs when companies capitalize current costs that do not benefit future periods. Improperly capitalizing or deferring expenses generally causes a company to understate reported expenses and overstate net income in the period of capitalization or deferral.

Take the case of WorldCom in the early 2000s. WorldCom was alleged to have overstated its cash flow by booking $3.8 billion of operating expenses as capital expenses. This transfer resulted in WorldCom materially understating expenses and overstating net income. It also enabled the company to report earnings that met analyst estimates. WorldCom's CEO, Bernard Ebbers, was sentenced to 25 years in prison for orchestrating the fraud.

Cookie jar reserves

Reserves are provisions for liabilities that are set up for a wide variety of future expenditures, including restructuring charges, environmental cleanup costs, or expected litigation costs. Recording a reserve on a company's books generally involves recognizing an expense and a related liability. From a fraud perspective, this may be done in good years when the company makes profits so that it is able to incur larger expenses. These provisions are called *cookie jar reserves* because management can reach into the jar and reverse it in future years when the company deems it necessary to boost earnings.

Lehman Brothers: The Repo 105 Fiasco

On March 11, 2010, the bankruptcy court-appointed examiner of Lehman Brothers issued a 2,200-page report detailing the facts and circumstances that contributed to Lehman's demise. The report talks about an accounting practice, "Repo 105," that is at the center of the storm that brought down one of our gloried institutions.

In a standard repurchase and resale transaction, called a *repo,* a firm borrows money from another firm for short periods of time by pledging assets as collateral; the firm is obliged to repurchase the assets at a later date. In this scenario, the firm's liabilities still reside on its balance sheet.

Lehman's objective was to temporarily remove securities inventory from its balance sheet. Lehman accounted for the Repo 105 transactions as sales, and accordingly, the respective securities came off its balance sheet. As with an ordinary repo, Lehman was obligated to repurchase these securities within a short period of time after the balance sheet date.

Next, with the cash proceeds from the Repo 105 transactions, Lehman paid down other existing debt, thereby reducing the assets (by reducing cash) and the corresponding liabilities (by reducing debt) on its balance sheet. Thus, it artificially lowered its debt levels to make it look financially healthier than it actually was. Upon maturity of the transaction, typically seven to ten days after the end of a reporting period, Lehman borrowed money to fund the repurchase of the securities, putting them back on the balance sheet along with the newly assumed loan liabilities. This put Lehman right back where it started prior to transacting Repo 105.

Lehman's usage of the Repo 105 transactions peaked during three quarters spanning 2007 and 2008. In the fourth quarter of 2007, $39 billion of assets were temporarily removed from the balance sheet. The amounts increased to $49 billion and over $50 billion in the first two quarters of 2008, respectively.

Symbol Technologies is a case in point. From 1998 until early 2003, Symbol engaged in numerous fraudulent accounting practices and other misconduct that had a cumulative net impact of over $230 million on Symbol's reported revenue and over $530 million on its pretax earnings. Symbol created cookie jar reserves by fabricating restructuring and other charges to artificially reduce operating expenses in order to manage earnings.

Off-balance sheet transactions

Off-balance sheet arrangements are used to raise additional financing and liquidity. These arrangements may involve the use of complex structures, including special purpose entities (SPEs), to facilitate a company's transfer of, or access to, assets. In many cases, the transferor of assets has some liability or continuing involvement with the transferred assets.

Depending on the nature of the obligations and the related accounting treatment, the company's financial statements may not fully reflect the company's obligations with respect to the SPE or its arrangements. Transactions with SPEs commonly are structured so that the company that establishes or sponsors the SPE and engages in transactions with it is not required to consolidate the SPE into its financial statements.

Enron provides a great example of the improper use of off-balance sheet transactions for fraudulent purposes. The company's former CFO and another high-ranking Enron official were convicted of engaging in a complex scheme to create an appearance that certain entities that they funded and controlled were independent of the company. This allowed Enron to incorrectly move its interest in these companies off its balance sheet. The U.S. Securities and Exchange Commission (SEC) alleged that these entities were designed to improve the company's financial results and to misappropriate millions of dollars representing undisclosed fees and other illegal profits.

In response to the Enron off-balance sheet transactions, the AICPA issued an interpretation — FIN46 — regarding entities that need to be consolidated for financial statement purposes. FIN46, which was later amended to FIN46R, is now referred to as the Consolidation Topic under the FASB Codification.

Notes no one can comprehend

Companies can also commit financial statement fraud by misrepresenting their financial condition through misstatements and omissions of facts and circumstances in their public filings, such as the management and discussion analysis, nonfinancial sections of annual reports, or footnotes to the financial statements. In this situation, management does not provide sufficient information to the users of financial statements. As a result, the users cannot make informed decisions about the financial condition of the company.

Companies must disclose related party transactions in accordance with securities laws and accounting rules. Moreover, transactions with board members, certain officers, relatives, or beneficial owners holding 5 percent or more of a company's voting securities that exceed $60,000 must be disclosed in the management section of the annual report. Failure to disclose related party transactions hides material information from shareholders and may be an indicator of fraudulent financial reporting.

In 2002, the SEC alleged that Adelphia engaged in numerous undisclosed related party transactions with board members, executive officers, and entities it controlled. One of these transactions involved the construction of a golf course on land owned or controlled by senior management. The SEC alleged that Adelphia failed to disclose the existence of these transactions or misrepresented their terms in its financial statements. Over $300 million of company funds were diverted to senior management without adequate disclosure to investors.

The SEC alleged that three top executives — the CEO, CFO, and Chief Legal Officer — failed to disclose to shareholders the multimillion dollar loans from the company that they used for personal business ventures and investments, and to purchase yachts, fine art, estate jewelry, luxury apartments, and vacation estates. These senior officials also allegedly failed to disclose benefits such as a rent-free $31 million Fifth Avenue apartment in New York City, the personal use of corporate jets, and charitable contributions made in their names.

Uncovering Financial Statement Fraud

Financial analysis techniques can help accountants and investigators discover and examine unexpected relationships in financial information. These analytical procedures are based on the premise that relatively stable relationships exist among financial accounts. If the relationships among those accounts become unstable, especially in a public company, the financial statements should offer full disclosure of the facts that explain what happened.

Unexpected deviations in relationships most likely indicate errors, but they may indicate illegal acts or fraud. Therefore, deviations in expected relationships warrant further investigation to determine the exact cause. As a fraud investigator, you can use several methods of analysis to examine the parts of financial statements that are most likely to be tainted by fraud. We explore those analytical methods in this section. To learn more about any of these methods, check out *A Guide to Forensic Accounting Investigation* by Thomas Golden, Steven Skalak, and Mona Clayton (Wiley).

Comparative techniques

As a forensic accountant, you could use the following techniques to identify the relationships among any financial data that present red flags:

✔ **Comparison of current period information with similar information from prior periods:** Prior period amounts are used as the basis for analyzing current period information. This time series analysis can show unusual changes that may be indicative of fraud.

✔ **Comparison of accounting information with budgets or forecasts:** Pressures on management to meet budget estimates may result in financial fraud. This comparison should include adjustments for expected unusual transactions and events.

✔ **Study of relationships of financial information with the appropriate nonfinancial information:** Nonfinancial measures are normally generated from an outside source. For example, *retail stores sales* is a common measure of the performance of retail companies, where sales are expected to vary with the number of square feet of shelf space.

✔ **Comparison of information with similar information from the industry in which the organization operates:** Studying a company's financial metrics and comparing them to other industry participants for unusual trends may indicate discrepancies. These discrepancies need further analysis to investigate financial fraud.

✔ **Comparison of information with similar information from other organizational units:** This technique involves comparing the financial performance of various subunits. For instance, a company with several stores may compare one store with another store.

Ratio analysis

Ratio analysis is a comparative technique that you can use to study data on a *time series basis* (meaning year over year or over a period of time) so that different trends can be identified. You should perform these analyses at the company level and at the business-unit levels (meaning within each department or unit of the company). Earlier in this chapter, we explain the various categories of ratios you can use to assess the financial health of companies. In this section, we study some of these ratios from a forensic perspective to help you understand how financial fraud can be detected from this analysis. Ratios related to inventory and revenues/receivables are covered in upcoming chapters.

✔ **Current ratio:** This ratio measures the ability of the company to pay its current obligations from its current assets, such as cash, inventories, and receivables. The current ratio decreases when cash is embezzled or when liabilities go unrecorded in the financial statements. The formula for calculating this ratio is as follows:

Current ratio = <u>Current assets</u>

Current liabilities

✔ **Debt to equity ratio:** This ratio measures the degree of debt a company has in relation to its *equity* (ownership resources). In other words, it shows the use of borrowed funds (debt) as compared with resources from the owners. This ratio can be manipulated by decreasing the accounts payable so that debt covenants can be met. Or, accounts payable can be reduced by recording unauthorized expenses, which will result in higher income. The debt to equity ratio can be expressed as follows:

$$\text{Debt to equity ratio} = \frac{\text{Total liabilities}}{\text{Total equity}}$$

✔ **Profit margin ratio:** This ratio measures the margins earned by a company from selling its products or services. It helps you understand the company's pricing structure, cost structure, and profit levels. You should look at profit margin trends because this ratio is expected to be consistent over time. Management can play around either with manipulating revenues or costs in order to maximize this ratio. Thus:

$$\text{Profit margin ratio} = \frac{\text{Net income}}{\text{Net sales}} \text{ or } \frac{\text{Net sales less costs}}{\text{Net sales}}$$

✔ **Asset turnover ratio:** This one measures the effectiveness of the usage of assets in terms of generating sales. This ratio can be manipulated by booking fictitious sales, thereby increasing the numerator in the asset turnover ratio, which is expressed as follows:

$$\text{Asset turnover ratio} = \frac{\text{Net sales}}{\text{Average assets}}$$

CASE FILE

The Satyam financial statement debacle

Vijay coauthored an article that appeared in *Business Week* about the financial statement scandal that occurred at Satyam Computer Services. This scandal rocked India's outsourcing industry in 2008. The extent of the accounting fraud was $1 billion. We analyzed the financial statements of Satyam and its two major competitors: Infosys and Wipro. The analyses revealed no indications of financial statement manipulation.

The vital clue was a relatively obscure item in Satyam's financial statements: investments in bank deposits. As of March 31, 2008, Satyam reported in its consolidated balance sheet approximately $825 million of its $1.1 billion cash and bank balances as investments in bank deposits. The disclosures made by the company about these deposits in its financial statements did not include the names of the banks where the deposits were invested — customary in India under generally accepted accounting principles (GAAP) — nor did they explain the reasons as to why a significant portion of the company's assets were invested there. In retrospect, this was the gaping hole in the financial statements that was ignored for many years.

Beneish model

The *Beneish model* is a mathematical model that is used to predict the likelihood of a company cooking its books. To use this model, you calculate indexes based on changes in account balances between the current year and the prior year. Professor Messod Beneish developed the model after finding that on average, companies that manipulate their financial statements have significantly larger increases in days' sales in receivables, greater deterioration of gross margins and asset quality, higher sales growth, and larger accruals than companies that don't manipulate their financial statements.

Here are the indexes of the Beneish model:

- ✔ **Days sales in receivables index:** The ratio of days sales in receivables in the current year to the corresponding measure in the prior year. This variable gauges whether receivables and revenues are in or out of balance in two consecutive years. A large increase in days' sales in receivables could be the result of a change in credit policy to spur sales. However, disproportionate increases in receivables relative to sales may also suggest revenue inflation.

- ✔ **Gross margin index:** The ratio of the gross margin in the prior year to the gross margin in the current year. When this index is greater than 1, it indicates that gross margins have deteriorated, which increases the probability of earnings manipulation.

- ✔ **Asset quality index:** The ratio of noncurrent assets other than property plant and equipment (PPE) to total assets. It measures the proportion of total assets for which future benefits are potentially less certain. This ratio compares asset quality in the current year to asset quality in the previous year. An increase in this index indicates an increased propensity to capitalize expenses and thus defer costs (red flags for the forensic accountant).

- ✔ **Sales growth index:** The ratio of sales in the current year to sales in the prior year. Growth does not imply manipulation, but growth firms are viewed as more likely to commit financial statement fraud because their financial position and capital needs put pressure on managers to achieve earnings targets.

- ✔ **Total accruals to total assets:** *Total accruals* are calculated as the change in working capital accounts other than cash less depreciation. This ratio is used to gauge the extent to which cash underlies reported earnings. Higher positive accruals are associated with a higher likelihood of earnings manipulation.

By calculating these ratios, you create a score that you can compare with the scores of other companies. The following table shows the average scores for each index for *nonmanipulators* (companies that don't mess around with their financial statements) and *manipulators* (companies that do). If your calculations show that a company's scores are close to those of a *manipulator,* you have reason to keep investigating.

Index Type	Nonmanipulators	Manipulators
Days sales in receivables index	1.031	1.465
Gross margin index	1.014	1.193
Asset quality index	1.039	1.254
Sales growth index	1.134	1.607
Total accruals to total assets	0.018	0.031

Data mining

Whereas all the analytical methods introduced so far in this chapter involve analyzing aggregated financial statements, *data mining* uses queries or searches within financial accounts to identify anomalies. Identifying anomalies involves searching for large and unusual items for further review. For instance, a query can be performed on payment amounts to identify double payments. Other examples of data mining techniques include:

- Identifying gaps in document numbers like invoices, checks, or purchase orders

- Identifying duplicate vendors or duplicate payments to vendors or employees

- Finding fictitious customers, vendors, or employees

- Noting payments of commissions to agents that are unusually high or above-market

Chapter 6

Investigating Inventory Fraud

In This Chapter

▶ Getting an inventory refresher

▶ Knowing why and how companies fudge inventory numbers

▶ Keeping your eyes peeled for inventory fraud

*I*nventory is at the center of many a financial statement fraud. In this chapter, we review what inventory is and why and how it is at the center of so many frauds. We also discuss how sharp accountants can uncover inventory frauds in the course of an audit or forensic examination.

Reviewing Inventory Basics

Before we get specific about how inventory fraud may be committed, we need to quickly review what inventory is and how it's accounted for.

Defining our terms

Generally, *inventory* is merchandise that is being held for sale to customers. You find inventory in both merchandising and manufacturing businesses. Inventory can come in three forms:

✔ Raw materials

✔ Works in process

✔ Finished goods

A merchandising operation usually has only finished goods inventory. Sometimes a merchandising operation may do some slight modification to a product before selling it, but generally it just repackages and sells what it has purchased. Think of a company like Macy's. It buys sweaters, socks, and towels from various sources. It hangs those items on hangers or refolds them to fit on tables, and it sells them to consumers — that's it.

Manufacturing operations, on the other hand, buy raw materials or partially fabricated materials, process them, and then sell finished goods; therefore, they likely have all three types of inventory on hand at any given time. Think about a company such as GM. It buys many types of raw materials, as well as whole components of cars. It may buy sheet metal to bend into fenders and buy whole transmissions. It puts all these raw materials and components onto its assembly line, flips a switch, revs up some auto workers, and voilà!, a car comes off the end of the line.

Valuing inventory

Now that you recall what inventory is, think back to what your accounting courses have taught you about how it's valued on a company's balance sheet and its effect on the related income statement. Inventory is valued at the lower of its cost or market value.

Determining cost

To determine cost, we need to determine which of our widgets (the fictitious product manufactured by all accounting students) is left in inventory at the end of the year. There are four methods of determining which widgets we have on hand: One method is an actual valuation, and three are models or approximations. Understand that a business may use one method for management purposes (the day-to-day running of the business) and another method for financial statement purposes. Which method(s) a business chooses has to do with tax considerations, financial statement considerations, and industry standards. The methods are:

- **Specific Identification Method:** In this method, a business actually identifies each item that is in inventory and how much the business spent to purchase and prepare that item for sale. This method is generally used when a business has few items in inventory, and each item has a high cost. The only time we've seen this method used was by a client who was an art dealer. He never had more than 20 items in inventory, and each came with a hefty price tag.

- **Last-In-First-Out (LIFO):** This method assumes that the last items purchased are the first sold and, therefore, the remaining items in inventory are the first items purchased. In most cases, this method defies reality because the older items will spoil or become outdated. For example, if the Ford Motor Company were to use LIFO, it would be assuming that the cars in its inventory were Model As — not a realistic assumption.

  Note: Though LIFO is recognized under U.S. Generally Accepted Accounting Principles (GAAP), it has little acceptance internationally. The process of converging GAAP and International Financial Reporting Standards (IFRS) is underway. As a result, LIFO may no longer be applicable for GAAP. If this were to happen, the U.S. tax code would have to be changed as well. Under the current IRS Code, a taxpayer cannot use LIFO for tax purposes unless it also uses LIFO for financial statement purposes.

✔ **First-In-First-Out (FIFO):** This method assumes that the earliest items purchased are the first ones sold, and the last items purchased are the ones remaining in inventory. This method often reflects reality. Suppose you go to the supermarket for milk. The milk display is actually the front of a large refrigerator. A supermarket employee, wearing multiple sweatshirts, is inside the refrigerator. She slides the containers of milk onto the shelf. You come along and buy the first container that was slid in because it's in front. After a few customers have taken milk, the shivering worker slides in more milk, and so it goes all day long.

✔ **Dollar Cost Average:** This method does not assume anything about the flow of the inventory. Rather, it is a mathematical model that averages the cost of a company's inventory based on its opening inventory and the purchases it makes during the year.

Figuring out market value

Determining inventory's market value is a three-step process. First, you compute each of the following three values for a company's inventory:

✔ **Net realizable value (NRV):** The anticipated selling price of the product less any selling costs required to complete the product and bring it to market.

✔ **NRV less normal profit margin:** NRV includes a profit margin embedded in it that reflects the minimum rate of return that the inventory would generate alternatively. This minimum rate of return, called the *normal profit margin,* is deducted from NRV to arrive at market value.

✔ **Replacement cost:** The cost that a company would have to pay today for replacing the inventory.

After computing these three values, you line them up and take the middle value to determine the market value.

When you determine both the cost and market value of a company's inventory, you choose the lower of the two to put in its financial statement.

We can't offer a lengthy discussion of the accounting entries here, but if you're itching for more info, be sure to check out your intermediate accounting textbook. Or pick up a copy of *Intermediate Accounting, 13th Edition* by Donald E. Kieso, Jerry J. Weygandt, and Terry D. Warfield, published by Wiley Higher Education.

LIFO, FIFO, GIGO?

GIGO is sometimes jokingly referred to as an inventory method. It is not. GIGO stands for Garbage-In-Garbage-Out. It's a term often used by our friends over in Information Technology (IT) to refer to faulty output that results from faulty input.

When is inventory an asset?

Just because a company has goods on its premises doesn't mean it should add those goods into its inventory. Conversely, not all of a company's inventory may be on its premises. You need to have a handle on this topic because it plays into fraud issues in a big way.

Remember way back in Accounting 101, your professor taught you about FOBs? The initials stand for "Free on Board" or "Freight on Board." The *FOB point* is the point where the ownership of goods-in-transit changes hands, and it's a source of angst for accountants trying to figure out what inventory belongs to a client at the closing date of its financial statements.

Here's a quick refresher: If a client is on the receiving end of goods with an FOB point of the shipper's warehouse, the goods should be added into that client's inventory, even when they are still on a ship in the middle of the ocean. Conversely, if the goods are being shipped by your client with an FOB point of the receiver, the goods belong in your client's inventory even if the ship is still in the middle of the ocean. If the ship has been boarded by pirates, that's a whole other ball of wax!

A client may also have the issue of *consignment goods.* These inventory items are shipped to a customer, but not purchased by the customer until he sells them to *his* customers. This was a very common method of doing business for the music industry when music only came on CDs. A music publisher would ship CDs to a retailer on consignment. The retailer did not own the CDs; they belonged to the publisher. When you or I went into the store to purchase a CD, the retailer simultaneously purchased that CD from the publisher when the sale was rung up. The problem for financial statements is that the retailers sometimes do not give timely reports to the publisher about sales and remaining inventory. They wait as long as they can because doing so allows them to hold off paying the publisher for purchases. The publisher may not get the reports until after it has to prepare financial statements. The publisher may deal with this problem by using estimated inventory amounts (and sales figures) to prepare its financials. We often see the use of estimates in preparing financial statements. However, sometimes over-exuberant estimating borders on fraud.

You need to understand how your client does business and the nuances of its industry in order to know how its inventory is handled.

The Motives and Means of Misrepresenting Inventory

Before you can sniff out inventory fraud, you need to get inside the mind of a company that would commit it. In this section, we explain what motivates businesses to fudge their inventory numbers, as well as how they may accomplish those fudges.

Pumping up the volume: Creating phony inventory

Companies have powerful motivations for inflating inventory valuations. Two of the biggies are improving their financial statements and satisfying their bank covenants.

Back to Accounting 101 again. Remember the "Cost of Goods Sold" section in the income statement? Beginning inventory + purchases − ending inventory = cost of goods sold. Do the math: The higher the ending inventory, the lower the cost of goods sold. A lower cost of goods sold leads to higher gross profit and higher net income.

In addition, inflated inventory shows up in the current assets section of the balance sheet. Having more current assets does all kinds of wonderful things to a company's *liquidity ratios,* which measure the ability of a company to meet is debts or obligations in the short run. This ability is measured in terms of current assets (cash and cash equivalents, marketable securities, accounts receivable, and inventory) that a company has to pay off its short-term debts.

When a company borrows money from a bank, the bank often puts covenants (conditions) into the loan agreement. Among the covenants there is a lien on inventory and requirements that the inventory and/or liquidity ratios be maintained at certain levels. By inflating inventory values, the company can keep its lenders happy.

But *how* does a company go about inflating its inventory? Keep reading for the most common schemes.

Stocking the shelves with empty boxes

The empty box scheme is one we've seen over and over again. Here's the basic rundown.

To run this scheme, a company must have an inventory that comes in boxes . . . let's say electronics. We know of schemes where the client has shown the auditor empty boxes of TVs, stereos, and so on. If the auditor asks to see a TV, the client claims it can't open the box because then it can't sell the TV as new and will lose money. What auditor wants his client to lose money?

Here's a great story from professor Sy Jones of New York University. A company in the electronics business knew its auditor was going to be a stickler about the possibility of empty boxes during the inventory audit. The CEO and CFO spent all night before the audit filling TV boxes with rocks. During the count, the auditor asked that a box be opened. The client demurred but said that the auditor could feel the box and know that the box wasn't empty.

Inflating inventory counts

Another trick that companies often try is simply to inflate the inventory count. In the earlier section "When is inventory an asset?" we discuss consignment goods. It's easy to overestimate consignment goods because they aren't on the company's premises. In the case of CD sales, the music publisher wouldn't have physical custody of all the consigned CDs; instead, those items would be stocked on retailers' shelves.

Companies can over-count inventory in many other ways; here's just one more example. There was a case in the 1960s involving a company called Allied Crude Vegetable Oil in New Jersey. Upon learning that the company could obtain loans using its inventory of salad oil as collateral, owner Anthony DeAngelis devised a scheme wherein he had the tanks containing the salad oil filled mostly with water and only a few feet of salad oil on top of each tank. Mr. DeAngelis used warehouse receipts that confirmed the existence of the fictitious inventory to fool the company's lenders into loaning the company more than $175 million. Mr. DeAngelis then used the borrowed funds to speculate on the soybean futures markets. The scheme unraveled when the soybean futures markets crashed and DeAngelis was unable to come up with the collateral to cover his large bets.

Counting obsolete inventory

Another means by which a company could artificially inflate the value of its inventory is by delaying or ignoring the required write-down of inventory that has become obsolete. Such inventory is referred to as *dead* or *excess* inventory.

Inventory that sits in a warehouse waiting to be sold is subject to decay or obsolescence. The product may not be usable anymore in the company's business because it may be at the end of its life cycle or may have passed its expiration date. To account for this situation, accounting rules require a company's management to establish a reserve for inventory obsolescence. In the event that slow-moving inventory becomes obsolete before the company can sell it, management must write down the value of that inventory, sometimes even to zero value.

Be aware of your clients' motives to fool you during an inventory count, and don't be lulled into a sense of security just because a client seems to have its act together. Always keep your radar working to pick up any possible signs of inventory fraud.

Turning down the volume: Letting inventory walk away

Okay, so the previous section makes clear that companies have some strong motives for inflating inventory numbers. But why on earth would a company intentionally underestimate its inventory?

One of the causes of missing inventory is *shrinkage*. Shrinkage may result from inventory becoming spoiled or broken, but too often it's caused by inventory just walking out a company's door. In this situation, the crux of the issue is that the inventory isn't walking out by itself. Someone is benefiting from the stolen inventory. If that someone is an employee (or a group of employees), the company may try to hide the shrinkage from its accountant because it doesn't want anyone to know that the problem exists. If that someone is a manager, that person has very personal motivation to hide the shrinkage from the accountant and the financial statements.

The key to avoiding shrinkage from theft is for the company to establish strong internal controls. In a retail situation, for example, a store may install magnetic detectors on its doors that set off alarms if magnets embedded on items aren't removed or demagnetized. Or a store may hire security guards (whether in uniform or undercover).

Someone who is truly motivated to take a company's inventory can get pretty creative. Consider this story, told to Frimette by one of her students: This girl's cousin had worked for a clothing store and was not treated well. To get back at her bosses, she stole the machine that removed the magnetic tags from clothing. After she and her job were separated, she went shopping along with her tag-removal machine. She'd borrow a baby from a friend or relative, put the machine in the bottom of the stroller, and cover it with blankets and diapers. She'd take a pair of jeans into the fitting room. If they fit, she'd remove the tag and put on the jeans. She'd put her old jeans on the hanger to give back to the lady at the entrance to the fitting room, and she'd walk out wearing the new jeans.

We could write volumes about missing inventory, and we cover the topic in much more depth in Part VI. For the moment, the bottom line is that you can't assume companies only inflate inventory numbers. You have to be aware of the possibility of missing inventory as well.

Crazy Eddie

Crazy Eddie Antar ran a chain of electronics stores in the New York City area for many years. In the mid-1980s, he took the chain public, which meant he had to keep Wall Street happy. If he had spent as much energy running his business as he did scheming, he could have been very successful. Among his other schemes, he played tricks on his auditors during the inventory count.

The inventory in Crazy Eddie's warehouse consisted of boxes of merchandise on pallets arranged in a square and piled high. The auditors came to the inventory count wearing their suits, which of course they didn't want to get dirty. To help keep their suits clean, Eddie sent a young female employee up on a ladder, to the top of the boxes, to count how many rows of boxes there were. Picture the young female employee in a short skirt, high on a ladder, while young male auditors in their pristine suits watched from below. Eddie's female employee would call down to the auditors how many rows deep of boxes she saw. The auditors would then multiply by the number of rows high and get the count of items. However, the square was hollow. Therefore, the count was very inflated.

Another trick that Eddie played on his auditors was the big inventory move. When auditors finished counting inventory in one store, Eddie would treat them to a big long lunch. While the auditors were being fed, Eddie's employees moved the merchandise to the second store. Hence the inventory was counted twice, and total inventory value was very inflated.

Inventory manipulation was only one of many complicated frauds committed by Crazy Eddie Antar. If you want to learn more about this and other fraud cases, check out www.whitecollarfraud.com. This Web site is run by Sam Antar, Eddie's cousin and former Crazy Eddie CFO.

Preventing and Unearthing Inventory Fraud

Frauds involving inventory are very popular, so you should always take special care when auditing a client's inventory. In this section, we walk you through steps you should take when observing inventory counts and explain what to look for on a client's financial statements that may signal inventory fraud.

Observing inventory counts

When it comes to inventory, one of the most basic tests an accountant can do is to observe a client's inventory count. Periodically, a company's management should do an actual physical count of the inventory to determine how many items are on hand and the condition of those items. If the company has strong internal controls in place, it is acceptable to count inventory in the middle of the accounting period and then roll the inventory value forward to the end of the year or use its perpetual inventory records to determine its end-of-the-year inventory value. If a company's controls are weak, the inventory count should be done as close to the *closing date* — the end of the accounting period — as possible.

In addition to observing the inventory count, you should also perform cut-off tests. *Cut-off tests* are close examinations of shipping documents (for shipments in and out of the business) for a certain number of days around the closing date. The point of these tests is to determine if all inventory transactions were recorded in the proper period, either in the accounting period under audit or in the period after.

If your client has inventory that is not on hand, such as consignment items or inventory stored in a public warehouse, that inventory may be accounted for via third-party confirmations. You don't need to visit every consignment site or warehouse. Instead, you should request that the company send letters to its consignees and warehousemen asking for written confirmation of the amount and type of inventory they are holding. Occasionally, you should visit a third-party location to perform a stock count — just to make sure those third parties are being honest.

Limiting fraud with audit techniques

The level of a client's inventory values should grow or contract with the level of its sales. For example, say a client does $1 million of business one year and has an ending inventory of $100,000. In the next year, it does $2 million of business and claims that its inventory grew to $500,000. It's possible that such a significant change in inventory could happen; maybe the company has made huge purchases in anticipation of even more business. But in this situation, you should consider the significant change in the company's financial ratios a red flag that requires more investigation.

Here are some other red flags to be aware of related to inventories:

- ✔ Journal entries recording the purchase or sale of inventory that are unsupported by invoices and other documentation.

- ✔ Journal entries made after the close of the accounting period that reverse inventory purchases in the following period.

- ✔ Unusual or suspicious shipping or receiving reports.

- ✔ Unusual or suspicious purchase or sales orders.

- ✔ Excessive movement of inventory between company plants.

- ✔ Ratios that are not in line with expectations, such as inventory turnover, days in inventory, net sales, and profit margins. The expectations come from prior years' performance or industry norms.

Another thing to look at is the comparison of actual inventory counts to accounting records. Any business knows what its approximate rate of *shrinkage* (inventory loss) should be. If the difference between the actual counts and the quantities recorded in the books exceeds that approximation, you could be seeing a sign of trouble.

CASE FILE

Cooking the books at a university bookstore

This is a true story of inventory fraud. We can't tell you when and where, or we'd be violating confidentiality.

At the end of a fiscal year, the internal audit department at a large university observed the inventory count at the university bookstore. The actual count was about $300,000 less than the accounting total, a much larger than expected amount. The internal auditors recommended an investigation, but the university administration didn't want to go through the trouble. At the end of the following year the actual inventory was $1.2 million below the accounting amount! At that point, there was a total of $1.5 million dollars of books missing, which could not be ignored.

The internal auditors were given the go-ahead to do a full-fledged investigation. They did a thorough examination of underlying documents. One thing they found was that many checks to book vendors did not have purchase orders or invoices to back them up. The investigation process included interviews with the accounts payable clerks who cut the checks. The clerks told the investigators that from time to time the

purchasing agent would run up to their office in a panic. He would say that an order had been screwed up at the publishing house and for some reason the UPS driver or postal driver had a COD package and was demanding immediate payment. "Don't worry," he would say, "I'll bring the paperwork up later." Needless to say, the paperwork never came.

An examination of the checks used to pay these CODs revealed that the endorsements did not quite match the payees. For example, a check for John Wiley & Sons was endorsed by the Wiley Company.

At that point, the FBI got into the act. Because the university received federal funds, the FBI had jurisdiction. It got warrants to obtain information from the banks where the checks were cashed. Apparently the purchasing agent had several accounts in the names of proprietorships that he owned, and those accounts had names very similar to several major publishers. The last we heard, the purchasing agent was taking an extended (four-year) vacation at Club Fed and was required to make restitution.

Chapter 7

Examining Revenue Recognition Problems

*B*usinesses exist to make money, and making money starts with selling. *Revenue* is the total amount of money earned by a company by selling goods, providing services, and/or allowing the use of its assets in a given period of time. In other words, revenue refers to the productive use of a company's assets or capital. Revenue is also called *sales* and *turnover*.

Unfortunately, sometimes businesses want you to believe that they are making more money than they really are. According to the U.S. Securities and Exchange Commission (SEC), revenue recognition fraud schemes were the most prevalent among the various financial statement fraud schemes committed between 2000 and 2008. A March 1999 report sponsored by the Committee of Sponsoring Organizations (COSO) of the Treadway Commission, *Fraudulent Financial Reporting 1987–1997: An Analysis of U.S. Public Companies*, noted that more than half of frauds involved overstating revenue.

In this chapter, we review what revenue is, how it is recognized, and various types of revenue-related schemes that are perpetrated. We also discuss how forensic accountants and auditors can uncover and prevent such frauds.

Reviewing How to Account for Revenue

Some people confuse the terms *gross revenues* and *net revenues*. Gross revenues equal the quantity of goods or services sold multiplied by the sales price; they are the invoice values of goods sold or services rendered. When a company sells products, it makes allowances for discounts, products that may be returned, products lost during transit, and so on. The difference between the gross revenues and these allowances is net revenues (or *net sales*).

Is revenue the same as profits? No. In accounting parlance, revenue is referred to as the "top line" because it is the topmost item in a company's income statement. Profits, or net income, are commonly referred to as the "bottom line"; they equal the difference between total revenues and total expenses. What happens when expenses exceed revenues? The difference is called *losses* or *net loss*.

Let's quickly go through some of the principles or rules that apply when revenues are accounted for or recognized in the financial statements. Remember the *cash basis* of accounting — the method that recognizes revenue when cash is collected? Great — but that's not our focus here. We're interested in the *accrual basis* of accounting, which means the revenue is accounted for in the financial statements when goods are sold or services are rendered. According to the International Financial Reporting Standards (IFRS), revenue is recognized when substantially all the risks and rewards of ownership transfer from the seller to the buyer. The SEC requires the following four criteria to be met in order for revenue to be recognized:

- **Persuasive evidence that an agreement exists:** Written sales agreements that are signed by the customers represent the best form of evidence that supports the existence of a contract.

- **Delivery has occurred or services have been rendered:** This occurs when the customer takes title, and the risks and rewards of ownership have transferred to the buyer.

- **The seller's price is fixed or determinable:** Some sales contracts may contain customer cancellation or termination clauses. The sales prices in arrangements that are cancelable by the customer are neither fixed nor determinable until the cancellation privileges lapse.

- **Collectability is reasonably assured:** This means that the customers have the ability to pay, and that the company is reasonably guaranteed to collect its receivables.

Accounts receivable is recorded in a company's books and records at *net realizable value*: the amount of receivables that will be converted into cash. Net realizable value is calculated as the difference between the balance of accounts receivable and an estimated allowance for doubtful accounts.

Identifying Common Motives for Altering Revenue Statements

Now that you recall what revenue is and how it's supposed to be accounted for, let's focus on the juicy stuff: the motives for committing revenue-related fraud. In this section, we cover four of the most common: the desire to lower a company's tax burden, exceed analyst expectations, pocket big bonuses, and keep lenders happy.

Trying to evade taxes

Tax evasion refers to concealing taxes owed to the government by illegal means. Businesses engaging in tax evasion conceal or misrepresent the true state of their financial affairs. Tax evasion is a serious crime per the Internal Revenue Service (IRS), which estimated that it lost $350 billion in tax collections because of this type of fraud in 2007. Recently, the U.S. Department of Justice brought a case against UBS, the largest Swiss bank, to reveal the names of 52,000 U.S. taxpayers alleged to have evaded paying taxes and used the bank to hide $15 billion in assets.

Tax evasion can take many forms; the two most common forms are income tax and sales tax evasion. To accomplish either one, companies understate their sales, thereby concealing the real amount of revenue earned. Cash sales, for example, may not be accounted for in a company's books. This type of fraud has two effects: both income taxes and sales taxes go unreported.

People convicted of tax evasion are often sentenced to jail terms and stiff penalties and fines.

Knowing that every penny counts

One of the main motivations to distort financial results is to meet analyst expectations. If a company misses its earnings estimates, called the *consensus estimates,* by even as little as a penny, the company gets punished by the market as reflected by a tumble in its stock price. By contrast, a company that beats consensus estimates is likely to see the price of its stock jump. Thus, market pressures may compel a company to resort to questionable, often fraudulent, practices.

Making extra bucks

Companies motivate employees by offering incentives for their performance. Both employees and managers have a lot riding on meeting sales or earnings targets. Salesmen are paid commissions based upon achieving sales goals. Top management members get paid bonuses upon attainment of certain performance metrics. Sometimes, these bonuses can run into millions of dollars and take the form of cash payments or stock awards. There is tremendous motivation to fudge the numbers.

Adhering to debt covenants

Many companies borrow money from creditors for various needs, including meeting their day-to-day operational needs and investing. These debts generally come with conditions that require the company to operate within certain limits. These conditions, called *debt covenants,* are crucial for a company to follow. If it does not follow them, the lender can recall the debt owed, putting the company in financial jeopardy. Therefore, companies may be tempted to resort to fraudulent means in order to meet debt covenants.

Getting to Know Types of Revenue Fraud

There are three forms of improper revenue recognition:

- ✔ Companies prematurely recognize revenue through legal means. That is, they recognize revenues in earlier periods than they actually occurred.

- ✔ Companies record fictitious revenue either from false sales or to false customers.

- ✔ Companies play with the amounts of revenue recognized by inflating values. For instance, a contractor is building a bridge that will take four years to complete. In each period, under the percentage-of-completion method, the contractor is required to recognize the portion of the revenue that corresponds with the completion of the construction. It can do so if it can reliably estimate progress on the contract. This situation presents opportunities to overstate the percentage of completion, increase the costs incurred, or underestimate the costs of completion. For example, say that at the end of year one, 20 percent of the bridge is complete. The contractor may account for 25 percent of the revenues.

In this section, we study some of the common fraud schemes that tap into these forms of improper revenue recognition, and we show you how to keep your eyes peeled for them.

Fictitious sales

This fraud is a bit like a magician pulling a rabbit out of a hat. A company can create either fictitious customers or fictitious sales orders. Remember this adage: To cover a lie, you need to tell more lies. In this case, the company fabricates documentation to cover up the fake sales. Then, it creates a fictitious customer account that, as time passes, shows up as past due.

This past-due customer account would draw attention from an auditor. To conceal it, the company may write off the customer account as being uncollectible. Bad debts are a common occurrence in businesses. As long as the company's total bad debts do not fluctuate drastically from period to period, the fake customer in our example whose balance has been written off may never come to light.

Another way to conceal the fictitious sale is to charge the transaction to an account commonly called "Sales Returns and Allowances," with the explanation that the customer returned the product.

As an auditor or a forensic accountant, you should be aware of the following red flags for fictitious sales:

✔ Large amounts of discounts, credits, sales returns, and allowances

✔ Receivables balances that rise faster than sales

✔ Large increases in sales and receivables at the end of the period

✔ Commissions paid on sales generated rather than on collection of the customer balance

✔ Excessive write-offs of customer balances after the period end

✔ Long extensions of aging receivables

 Take the case of Cendant back in the late 1990s. Its executives were tried for manufacturing more than $500 million in fake revenues over a three-year period in order to meet analyst estimates. In 2007, Walter Forbes, the former chairman of Cendant, was sentenced to 12½ years and ordered to pay restitution of more than $3 billion.

Lapping

Lapping is the concealment of a transaction where the fraudster steals the cash received from a customer and then diverts the cash received from another customer to the first customer's account. This is a "Robbing Peter to pay Paul" scheme that's best explained with an example.

Say the fraudster steals the payment intended for customer Adam's account. When a payment is received from customer John, the fraudster credits that money to Adam's account. When customer Charlie pays, John's account is credited. To keep this fraud going, the trickster resorts to further diversions and misapplications of collections over and over again. This fraud usually comes to light when the employee loses track of the payments or is unable to obtain additional payments.

Most lapping occurs because of inadequate control over incoming payments. Lapping can usually be detected by comparing the dates of the customers' payments with the dates the customers' accounts are posted. The best way to prevent it is to have proper segregation of duties so that the employee handling the checks received from customers has no access to the recording of the accounts receivable records.

Beware of employees who do not take vacations, and rotate the duties of employees. Most lapping schemes come to light when employees are out of the office for extended periods of time, and other employees look at the customer ledgers.

Redating

The longer a customer receivable balance remains outstanding, the less the chance that it can be collected. In this scheme, the fraudster revises the receivable to reflect a more current date so that it does not get charged to the company's bad debt reserve account. What's the point to this scheme? The fraudster doesn't want an auditor scrutinizing this particular receivable. The balance is then charged against other accounts, such as sales discounts and allowances.

Look out for journal entries that record sales transactions outside the normal invoicing process or for entries that do not have adequate documentation.

Side agreements

An auditor's antenna should go up when she becomes aware of side agreements. Such agreements made outside the normal course of business represent red flags. These agreements, which are usually done at the same as the main agreement, alter existing agreements. As one commentator noted, "What the main agreement giveth, the side agreement taketh away."

Management may use side agreements to inflate sales because side agreements are tough to detect, especially when they're oral agreements rather than written.

Fraud schemes associated with side agreements may include allowing customers to cancel orders at any time, extending payment terms, or providing customers with unconditional rights of return. Why is this problematic? Such terms may affect the recognition of revenue, including the time period in which it needs to be recognized.

In the mid-1990s, Informix was the third largest database maker (behind Oracle and IBM). The SEC charged its executives of inflating its financial performance over a three-year period by puffing its revenue by $295 million and earnings by $244 million. Informix restated its earnings for the period 1994 to 1997. Informix no longer exists today; it succumbed to its fraud and was sold in a fire sale to IBM in 2001.

The heart of the fraud at Informix was the use of side letters to inappropriately record revenues. Informix sold licensed software to companies, which in turn resold the licenses to third parties. Informix recognized revenues from the sales of licenses upon receipt of a signed and dated license agreement. But, through side letters, Informix violated its revenue recognition policies. It used many schemes through side letters, including extending payment dates beyond the traditional 12 months, purchasing hardware from customers that offset the license fees paid by them, and refunding customers' licensing fees by diverting the company's future revenues.

Channel stuffing

Perhaps you've heard of selling tomorrow's products today? That is channel stuffing, which is accomplished by offering incentives to customers like deep discounts and extended payments terms to induce them to buy products that they may not currently need. Though this practice may be legitimate, companies must adequately disclose these transactions to avoid creating misleading financial statements. By pushing sales from future periods into the current period, the company risks that future sales will decrease if all other factors remain constant.

The auditor has to be watchful for deep discounts being granted at period ends. Additionally, you may notice a marked increase in shipping costs, which is a possible sign of channel stuffing.

Does the name "Chainsaw Al" ring a bell? Al Dunlap, nicknamed "Chainsaw Al," was known for turning around companies from the brink of failure. When he took over the reins at Sunbeam in the 1990s, he cut Sunbeam's costs by closing plants and slashing payroll. But those measures were not enough to maintain Sunbeam's rising share price.

In 1997, the company got caught pulling $62 million in sales from future periods into the present. Sunbeam offered deep discounts, favorable payment terms, and extended rights of return to distributors so that they could purchase products before the end of the year. For instance, according to the

SEC complaint, electric blankets that had been packaged for a certain retailer were sent to a distributor who agreed, in return for a guaranteed profit, to hold the blankets until the retailer was ready to accept them.

Mr. Dunlap agreed to a $500,000 fine and accepted to be banned from ever serving as an officer or director of a public company.

Bill and hold

One of the conditions for recognizing revenue is that delivery has occurred or services have been rendered. (See the earlier section "Reviewing How to Account for Revenue"). *Bill and hold* is a fraudulent scheme designed to circumvent the delivery requirement. The seller raises a legitimate sales order and invoices the customer, but it ships the goods in the future. The seller holds the good either in its premises or off-site in a third-party warehouse until the buyer is ready to accept the goods. However, the seller recognizes the revenue now.

A note of caution here: Bill and hold transactions may be proper if certain criteria are met. For example, if a customer has legitimate reasons to request delay of shipment (such as the lack of available temporary storage space), revenue recognition is permissible. The key to a proper bill and hold arrangement is that the buyer — not the seller — requests it.

Look out for the following landmines when you're trying to recognize fraudulent bill and hold transactions:

- Unusual sales transactions occurring shortly before the end of the accounting period
- An abnormal number of shipments made to third-party warehouses rather than to a customer's regular address
- Invoices that are missing shipping information
- High shipping costs incurred at the end of the accounting period

Also be on the lookout for marked increases in off-site rental expenses at period end. Something fishy may be going on!

Multiple deliverables

Certain revenue transactions may contain multiple deliverables. A seller not only sells the product but also has other obligations, such as installing and activating the product after delivery, conducting product testing, or training employees to use the product. The smell test for recognizing revenues in these circumstances is to scrutinize whether the undelivered portion is essential to the functionality of the delivered item.

To test whether a company is reporting revenue correctly when multiple deliverables are involved, contact some of its major customers. Confirm that all services have been performed with respect to the products that they purchased.

Round tripping

Companies conduct round tripping by recording transactions that have no economic benefit. They have resources that they can sell, and they find buyers who sell the resources back to the company. (The resources make a round trip, as opposed to a one-way trip to the buyer.) The net effect on the profit and loss statements for both the buyer and seller is zero. Each of the parties assumes the roles of seller and buyer at the same point in time.

This collusion results in both companies recording revenues and expenses of the same amount. Though the companies earn no net profit from the transactions, they benefit from recording higher top-line sales. These transactions are usually complex in structure, and the challenge presented to auditors and forensic accountants is to decipher the intent of the parties.

How can you possibly identify round tripping? In addition to looking for complex business transaction structures, you should examine documentation to see whether funds were exchanged between the parties and whether there was an independent purchase of goods or services. The absence of these conditions may be indicative of round tripping. Also, look out for customers who are involved in the same line of business as your client, and scrutinize transactions with these parties. Plus, look for parties that appear on both the vendor and customer lists.

Improperly keeping the books open

A company may record sales at the end of a period by improperly keeping the books open for a few days longer. The company invoices the customer during this extended period, but ships products after the end of the period. Standard cut-off testing (which we explain later in the chapter) often brings these schemes to light. You should also make direct inquiries of accounting personnel, billing clerks, and warehouse personnel to determine whether the books were held open past the end of the period. In addition, using forensic technology (see Chapter 15) would help in detecting such schemes.

Executives at the software giant Computer Associates were accused of keeping the books open for an extra five days after the end of the reporting period so that revenue could be counted a quarter earlier than it ought to have been. Though this backdating may sound innocuous, it results in recognizing tomorrow's revenues today.

The scheme began around 1998 and continued through September 2000. Computer Associates is alleged to have prematurely reported $3.3 billion in revenue from 363 software contracts. During the four quarters of fiscal 2000, revenues were improperly inflated by 25 percent, 53 percent, 46 percent, and 22 percent, respectively. The SEC said the goal was to meet or beat per-share earnings estimates of Wall Street analysts, a key to keeping a company's stock price rising.

Other revenue frauds

Here are a handful of other schemes to know about:

- **Defalcation:** This scheme involves embezzling cash received from customers. When a check is received from a customer, the fraudster alters the check to make it payable to himself or endorses the check to his benefit.

- **Skimming or larceny:** *Skimming* occurs when cash is stolen before it is recorded in the company's books. *Larceny* refers to taking cash receipts after they have been recorded in the accounting systems.

- **Inflating the value of receivables:** This fraud involves underestimating the allowance for doubtful accounts or delaying the write-off of receivables deemed uncollectible.

- **Partial shipments:** Some companies recognize the full amount of revenue on an order even though the shipments are incomplete.

- **Multiple element revenue arrangements:** This type of revenue arrangement occurs when sales of products are combined with sales of services. You typically see such arrangements in the computer software industry, where the sales of computer software may be accompanied by services related to installation and integration of the software and the sale of a software maintenance agreement. Each of these elements may require different revenue recognition treatments, thereby increasing the possibility of fraud.

Uncovering Revenue Recognition Problems

To determine whether your client is trying to pull a fast one when it comes to revenue recognition, you can employ a handful of standard auditing and forensic accounting techniques that we review in this section. If these actions raise any red flags, you know to keep digging for more information.

Accounts deceivable! The ZZZZ Best case

In 1987, ZZZZ Best Company perpetrated a massive financial statement fraud that fooled its auditors and its investors, who lost a reported $100 million. The company was a carpet cleaning business started by Barry Minkow at the age of 13. Within five years, the company went public.

The fraud involved recording fictitious revenues and accounts receivable. The company fabricated revenues by claiming to clean and restore buildings damaged by catastrophes. Thus, it claimed to earn its revenues through insurance restoration jobs. On one occasion, its management found a large building under construction and placed signs around the building stating that it was the contractor for the restoration. In reality, this building had not been damaged. The auditors were fooled into believing that this site was a multimillion dollar restoration site.

On another occasion, when the auditors visited another restoration site, ZZZZ Best leased some floors of a new building. For the floors that weren't completed, it spent approximately $1 million on subcontractors to restore the floors.

Minkow was sentenced to 25 years in federal prison for perpetrating this fraud (and was paroled after serving 8 years).

Testing the cut-off dates

Performing cut-off procedures or observing the client perform these procedures can be an effective method for deterring revenue fraud. Accounts receivable testing is usually conducted in conjunction with inventory cut-off procedures. Such procedures include:

- ✔ Examining purchase orders, invoices, and shipping documents
- ✔ Testing payments from customers
- ✔ Examining ending inventory
- ✔ Comparing quantities shipped with quantities billed
- ✔ Checking credit and debit memoranda for sales returns and claims from customers
- ✔ Determining whether there are unusually high volumes of returned goods after the end of the accounting period
- ✔ Analyzing contract cancellations after year-end

Looking at related-party transactions

Related-party transactions include those that occur between a parent company and its subsidiary; between affiliate companies; and between a business and its principal owners, managers, or members of their immediate families. These transactions present the highest risks for financial statement fraud, including revenue fraud. The chances of colluding increase when the parties involved are related.

Even finding related parties may pose challenges. You can accomplish this task by asking management whether any relationships exist between the management of both companies and, in some cases, performing searches of public records or conducting background investigations.

An important consideration when reviewing related-party transactions is to see whether the transactions were conducted at *arm's length*. That is, the transactions occurred between the parties as if the parties were independent or unrelated and on an equal footing.

Common warning signs of revenue frauds with related parties include:

- Round tripping sales arrangements
- Goods sold or purchased at prices less than cost
- Loans to and from related parties with unusually favorable terms
- Write-offs of customer balances
- Monies transferred between parties without transfers of goods and services
- Unusual transactions at period end
- The detection of a hitherto undisclosed related party
- Difficulty in determining who owns or controls an off-balance sheet entity
- Overly complex business structures that make it difficult to ascertain the underlying business purpose
- Significant bank accounts or operations in tax-haven jurisdictions

What can the auditor do in these circumstances? Examine such transactions with a sense of heightened awareness or skepticism. Here's how:

- Review relationships and the nature of business transacted with major suppliers and customers.
- Analyze advances and cash disbursements to determine if the company is funding a related third party.
- Test contracts and transactions with such parties to see whether they meet the criteria for recognizing revenue.

✔ Inquire about the presence of side agreements and undisclosed third parties from the legal counsel and predecessor auditors to the company.

✔ Send confirmation letters to customers asking them to confirm dates, quantities, and amounts. Follow up on unreturned confirmations or confirmations with discrepancies.

✔ Perform substantive procedures such as identifying and analyzing subsequent collections from customers after period end.

 Read the publication by the American Institute of Certified Public Accountants titled "Accounting and Auditing for Related Parties and Related Party Transactions — A Toolkit for Accountants and Auditors." To find it online, go to http://ftp.aicpa.org/public/download/news/relpty_toolkit.pdf.

Investigating and analyzing accounts receivable

The numbers won't lie! Put on your Sherlock Holmes hat and search for clues in the company's accounts receivable:

✔ Revenues or accounts receivable that appear to be too high as compared to previous periods or to competitors in the same industry

✔ Sales discounts, allowances, allowances for doubtful debts, and bad debt expenses that appear to be too low

✔ Increases in sales return percentages on total sales

✔ Accounts receivable balances that are rising too fast as compared to the rise in sales

✔ Cash collected from revenues that is low compared to sales

✔ Unusual journal entries prepared at the end of a reporting period that affect revenues

✔ Nonstandard journal entries posted by top management

✔ A sudden increase in new and unknown customers

✔ Revenue adjustments made at the last minute before closing the books (or immediately thereafter)

✔ A lack of supporting documentation or photocopies of documents

✔ Transactions that are not authorized

✔ Management overrides of internal controls related to the revenue cycle

✔ Weaknesses in cutoff procedures

✔ The receivables have been outstanding for a long period of time, generally over 90 days

CASE FILE

Cleaning up with Regina

Regina Company, Inc. was a 100-year-old company reputed as a reliable manufacturer of vacuum cleaners. In the 1980s, its management changed. Don Sheelan acquired a controlling interest in the company by taking on a large amount of personal debt. He needed Regina to be profitable so that he could repay his debts. Regina, under Sheelan's direction, introduced new products that had plastic parts that apparently melted when the product was used for a period of time, rendering the vacuum cleaner useless.

Consequently, the sales returns were getting out of control. Sheelan rented a warehouse off-site to store the returns and removed the underlying documentation — bills of lading, warehouse count sheets, and inventory return forms. The sales returns were not reflected on the financial statements. This fraud could not be perpetrated indefinitely. Before long, word of the defective design began to spread among consumers, and sales began to drop. Eventually, the company collapsed on the weight of its fraud, and investors and creditors lost about $40 million.

Certain ratio analysis techniques are also good ways to check for discrepancies. Significant and unusual changes in these ratios would warrant further analyses:

- **Sales growth index:** This ratio shows the increase in current year sales to prior year sales. High-growth companies are motivated to commit fraud when the growth trend reverses. Investors expect that growth to continue, and those expectations pressure managers to produce.

- **Gross margin ratio:** This ratio measures how well each dollar of a company's revenue is utilized to cover the costs of goods sold. Cost of goods sold includes the direct costs, material, and labor of producing goods sold by a company. A decrease in this ratio may signal negative prospects for the company. The management may be motivated to show better numbers by increasing these ratios.

- **Days sales outstanding:** This ratio measures the average number of days taken from the sale of a product to the collection of its receivable. Sales and receivables typically follow a consistent trend. If the ratio detects a disproportionate rise in receivables relative to sales, the change may be due to revenue inflation.

TIP

Another tool to use to detect revenue recognition issues is to create a trend analysis, such as a line graph with the monthly sales, gross profit, and net income. This could show whether there are significant fluctuations during the year, and possible adjustments at period-end (quarter- and year-end).

Chapter 8

Studying Securities Fraud

The securities markets are places where a lot of money changes hands very quickly. The New York Stock Exchange, one of the world's largest exchanges, reported that in 2009 it managed 1,331,995 transactions for 16,126,680,649 shares at a value of $11,488,719,043. That's an awfully big amount of money and trades. We've all heard of people getting rich in the markets. Some of the stories are real and some not. A lot of people believe the stories they hear and think they, too, can become rich by "playing" the markets.

Because of the large amounts of money being moved around and so many people wanting to become rich easily, the securities markets have become fertile grounds for fraudsters. The fraudsters come from all ends of the industry: listed companies, analysts, brokers, investors . . .

In this chapter, we tell you about some of the most common security frauds and discuss methods of uncovering them. We also explain how you can talk to your clients about not becoming victims.

Falsifying Information in Financial Statements

We devote Chapter 5 to a detailed discussion of financial statement fraud. Here, we just touch on the basics and explain how falsifying financial statements constitutes securities fraud.

The financial statements are reports issued by company management that present a snapshot of the company's financial position at a certain date (the balance sheet) and a summary of the company's activities for a certain period of time (the income statement, statement of owners' equity, and statement of cash flows). Additional disclosures (footnotes) are presented with the statements. If the statements have been audited (which is required if the company has publicly traded securities), reviewed, or compiled by a CPA, an accountant's report accompanies the statements and disclosures. Together, these documents should give a comprehensive view of the company's financial issues.

When management issues a set of financial statements, it makes the following assertions:

- ✔ All transactions have been recorded and at the proper amount.

- ✔ All transactions have actually occurred.

- ✔ All transactions have been authorized.

- ✔ All transactions have been recorded in the proper period.

- ✔ All assets, liabilities, and equity items exist.

- ✔ Management has rights to use all assets and has disclosed any impingement to those rights. All obligations have been recorded and/or disclosed.

- ✔ All assets, liabilities, and equity items have been recorded.

- ✔ All assets, liabilities, and equity items are presented at their correct valuation.

- ✔ The financial statements are complete.

- ✔ The financial statements are properly presented and are understandable.

Any intentional, material misstatement that makes these assertions untrue may be considered financial statement fraud.

Why do managers falsify financial statements? A lot of research has been done on this question, and two answers rise to the top:

- ✔ **The company needs to secure financing.** Financing, whether equity or debt, is based on the financial statements. If things are shaky for the company, that fact shows up in the financial statements. A poor showing in the financial statements makes financing difficult to get or more expensive. Therefore, management has incentive to paint a picture that is rosier than may really be the case.

- ✔ **Management's compensation package is related to the company's performance.** Many companies incentivize management by relating their compensation package to financial results. Financial results may be measured many ways, including changes in net income, changes in stock price or *market capitalization* (market price times the total number of outstanding shares), and changes in earnings per share. If a manager wants to increase his pay, all he has to do is play with the numbers and manipulate the results.

Wall Street generally likes to see that a company's earnings grow in a nice smooth line over time. Wall Street gets very cranky if a company's earnings deviate from what analysts have estimated they'll be. To smooth earnings and meet analysts' expectations (and, therefore, boost stock prices), management may manipulate the earnings shown on the financial statements. Doing so constitutes securities fraud because it means that investors are basing their stock purchase decisions on false information.

One way to manipulate earnings is to play with the *accrual entries,* which are often estimates of certain expenses (such as warranty and guarantee liabilities and bad debt expenses). Management should be making good faith estimates for these expenses, but who's to know if the estimates are being rigged so as to achieve a particular earnings goal?

Accounting researchers have actually figured out ways to measure what they call "abnormal accruals." The explanation is long and detailed, but you can refer to a graduate-level financial statement analysis text if you're just itching to find out more!

Lying to Auditors

An auditor is a professional who examines underlying data in order to give an opinion on someone else's assertions. An auditor must be independent and objective and perform his audit in a systematic way. In the United States, in order to perform a financial statement audit, an auditor must be a Certified Public Accountant licensed by one of 54 jurisdictions. Auditors are guided by Generally Accepted Auditing Standards (GAAS).

In the United States, the Sarbanes-Oxley Act of 2002 makes it illegal to lie to a financial statement auditor. (The same restriction applies in the United Kingdom under the Companies Bill of 2003.)

How can a company lie to an auditor in order to manipulate its financial statements? It takes creativity and/or collusion to do so successfully. In one of the most famous audit failure cases, ZZZZ Best founder Barry Minkow piled lies on top of lies in an effort to keep his auditors from learning the truth about the business. The truth was that about 85 percent of reported revenues never existed. How did he pull this off? According to Minkow, he and his senior managers mastered the use of the copy machine. They cut and pasted from magazines, telephone books, and newspapers to create fake contracts and invoices that looked real. (Their fraud predates Google and the explosion of the Internet.) Then they moved the little money they had in circles, from one account to another, to make it look like they were getting payments for these invoices. When the auditors started asking too many questions about areas management knew to be troublesome, they slyly guided the auditors to other areas of the audit.

For more about how Barry Minkow pulled off what was at the time the largest corporate fraud, check out *Cooking the Books: What Every Accountant Should Know About Fraud.* This is a DVD from the Association of Certified Fraud Examiners (ACFE), with an interview of Barry Minkow with commentary by Professor Steve Albrecht, an authority on corporate fraud. You can find it in the Bookstore section of www.acfe.com.

Crazy Eddie Antar, who ran a chain of electronics stores in New York City for years, took lying to the auditors to a whole new dimension. When the auditors went out to lunch, Eddie's underlings would actually change numbers on the auditors' work papers. Learn an important lesson here and never leave your work papers unsecured! (To read more about Crazy Eddie, see the sidebar about him in Chapter 6.)

Cheating Investors

False financial statements are just one way that fraudsters stick their fingers into the pockets of investors. Wall Street pros and Wall Street wannabes have also found ways of stealing from investors, which we cover in this section.

Operating a boiler room

Boiler rooms are one of the most common forms of perpetrating stock frauds. These schemes are called *boiler rooms* because at one time they operated out of basements in large, dingy rooms with rows and rows of old desks.

The settings may be nicer these days, but the idea is the same: You have a room full of people sitting at desks with phones and lists of people to call. They call number after number on their lists all day long. If a caller gets a live person on the other end, she engages that person in conversation and cunningly convinces him to buy whatever security (or insurance product) she's selling. To close the sale, she may shade the truth, tell outright lies, and/or use high-pressure sales techniques. Sadly, many of the victims are elderly. (See Chapter 10 for a discussion of the many types of fraud perpetrated against the elderly.)

Manipulating penny stocks

If you have the choice of buying a stock that costs $109 per share or a stock that costs $.109 per share (that's 10.9 cents), which would you choose? Because you're an accountant (or soon to be one), you should know that the price per share is not such an important number on its own. You have to consider the value of the stock and its future potential and then compare that information to the current price.

Unfortunately, not all investors are as sophisticated as you are. Many are not sophisticated at all. It's easy for a sleazy broker to convince them that the 10 cent stock is a bigger bargain. Any stock that sells for less that $1 is called a *penny stock,* but similar scams proliferate with any low-priced stock.

One of the most common schemes with low-priced stocks is the *pump-n-dump.* (The SEC refers to this fraud as a *hype-and-dump manipulation.*) In the pump-n-dump scheme, the fraudsters hold some of the target stock in their own accounts. Then they start selling the stock to the unsuspecting public. Simultaneously, they may start selling and buying stock among themselves. One of the measurements watched by Wall Street is the *volume* or number of shares traded. If the volume is up for a particular stock, Wall Street watchers may assume that there is something exciting going on with the stock. A very sophisticated pump-n-dumper may hire a public relations firm to create even more excitement about the stock.

All the buzz and excitement will probably cause the stock price to start rising. When the price of the stock gets to where the fraudsters want it to be, they sell their shares at a tidy profit. They shut down their boiler rooms and public relations machine and walk away with their money. After the hype and the trading stop, the price of the stock plummets back down to pennies, and the victims are left holding stock with a huge loss.

To perpetrate this fraud, the criminals may use a legitimate stock that is *thinly traded* (meaning it doesn't trade often) or that just happens to have a low per-share price. Sometimes they create phony companies and go through the process of getting them listed, just to have a stock to play with. They typically use boiler rooms as a method of pushing sales of the targeted stock. With the advent of the Internet, they now have new methods of perpetrating their frauds. We've received hundreds of spam e-mails that appear to be from friends telling us about this great stock that's about to have its price go way up. The e-mails encourage us to buy now before the stock goes up — to get in on the deal while the stock is still a value. We delete this clutter from our inboxes immediately and encourage our clients to do the same.

These schemes are illegal. The exchanges and the SEC closely watch stocks that seem to have large sudden increases and decreases in price. When they find a stock like this, they send their forensic investigators to look at the trading patterns and see who has been buying and selling.

Conducting insider trading

One of the core philosophies about the stock market is that all investors have equal access to knowledge about the companies. If a particular investor has information about the company from someone who works inside the company — information that is not available to the general public — and trades on that knowledge, that situation is called *insider trading*. Sometimes the investors are actually employees of the company. Other times, the information may not come from a company employee; inside information could be leaked by lawyers, brokers, and even messenger service employees and printers working for the company.

Insider trading is highly illegal. The SEC and the exchanges look for large purchases or sales of stocks just before important announcements. These transactions are scrutinized to determine if they were made by people working for the company or people who know people who work for the company.

The accusations against Martha Stewart

Martha Stewart was well known and very wealthy. She was also a friend of Samuel D. Waksal, founder of the bioresearch company ImClone. ImClone developed an anticancer drug called Erbitux and applied to the FDA for approval to sell Erbitux. Stewart was an ImClone shareholder.

On December 27, 2001, Waksal, members of his family, and Stewart sold their shares in ImClone. The next day, the FDA announced that it did not approve Erbitux. The stock price dropped precipitously.

The government alleged that Waksal had information that the FDA would not approve Erbitux and that he notified his family and friends ahead of the official announcement. Waksal, Stewart, and Stewart's stockbroker, Peter Bacanovic, were indicted on various charges related to the incident. Waksal pled guilty and received a sentence of not less than seven years and three months. Stewart and her broker went to trial.

Stewart was very vocal about proclaiming her innocence. The day after her indictment, she took out a full page ad in *USA Today* proclaiming her innocence and started a Web site to promote her innocence. During the trial, the judge threw out the charges of securities fraud related to the alleged insider trading. There was simply not enough evidence. Stewart, however, was convicted of conspiracy, obstruction of justice, and two counts of lying to federal agents. Stewart and her broker were both sentenced to five months in prison, five months of home confinement, two years probation, and fines. Stewart paid fines of $195,000 — three times the amount she profited from the alleged insider trading.

Remember: Lying to a government agent is a crime. Keeping quiet is a constitutional right. We train our clients that when they are confronted by a government agent, they should politely say "I'd rather not answer your questions without the advice of an attorney" and then go get an attorney. The agents may be a bit annoyed because this delays their investigation, but they can't arrest you for staying quiet.

The flash crash

On May 6, 2010, we experienced what came to be known as the *flash crash*. The Dow Jones Industrial Average, the most popular measure of the value of stocks traded on the New York Stock Exchange, dropped almost 1,000 points in less than a half hour. As far as we can tell, no one knows exactly what happened. It's believed that a broker or trader in Chicago, at about 2:42 p.m., made a typo in a trading order for Procter & Gamble stock. More shares were traded than intended. When the computerized trading systems saw the large sell, they too started selling, and then it kept going like a snowball downhill.

At one point, Accenture dropped over 90 percent and became a penny stock.

This incident was considered a very serious issue by authorities — so serious that at 3:15 p.m., Secretary of the Treasury Timothy Geithner was in the Oval Office briefing the president. Geithner then spent most of his evening on conference calls with world central bankers about this "crisis." By the close of the day, the market had largely recovered and was down only about 345 points.

Front running

Front running occurs when a broker or brokerage house takes advantage of knowledge of stock orders that are about to be placed at the stock markets. The broker or brokerage house places its own order first. For example, say that you call in an order to buy 500,000 shares of IBM. A large trade like this may push the stock price up. Knowing your order is in the pipeline, the broker places his own order for IBM stock before your order goes to the floor of the exchange.

This practice is both illegal and unethical. If the broker's order drives the price of the stock up even a smidgen, the client then overpays for the stock.

Related to front running are two other practices that are not illegal but are very questionable ethically:

✔ **Tailgating:** A broker sees a client making a trade and puts his own trade in immediately after. The broker is betting that the client may have some superior knowledge of the stock or ability to pick stocks. Let's take the previous example. The broker sees your trade for 500,000 shares of IBM and figures you're on to something. He places your order in the system and then immediately places his own order.

✔ **Flash trading** (sometimes called *high-frequency trading*): This is a computerized version of tailgating. We live in a world where computers have access to data before humans can see or analyze the data. In flash trading, computers are programmed to watch for big trades or patterns of trade. When they see these phenomena, the computers execute their own trades trying to make some money off the knowledge about these other trades. It has been estimated that flash trading accounts for 50 to 75 percent of all trading on the markets.

Day trading

Another popular phenomenon is day trading. Day trading by itself is not illegal or unethical, but some of its promoters may be fraudsters.

Day trading is a trading system whereby traders use computer systems to closely watch the movement of stock prices. If they see a certain stock is trending upward on a particular day, they may buy the stock and take the upward ride. As soon as they see the stock start to go down, or by the end of the day, they sell the stock. They trade in large volumes, hoping they may make only a few pennies on each share traded. Because the stock is sold the same day, the trader never has to actually pay for the stock.

You may have been invited to a seminar about a system guaranteed to make large amounts of money in the stock market with only a small investment. At the seminar, you find out that if you take the full training, which comes with a hefty price tag, you will learn all the details of how to become rich using the system. After completing the training, you might be offered a position with the firm so you can use its system. You're not really getting a job. You get a desk with a computer and access to the proprietary software, which watches the markets for evidence of intraday stock price movements that meet the criteria for initiating this type of trade. When you actually execute a trade, it goes through the firm's systems, and you get charged a brokerage fee. Of course, the brokerage fees are very high.

We've seen people who actually make money doing this, and we've seen people lose a lot of money doing this. The only ones consistently getting rich are the promoters.

Abusing the short-selling process

A *short sale* is when someone sells a stock she doesn't own. The seller does so in the hope that the price of the stock will drop and she can then buy it back at a cheaper price and "cover the short." In many cases, the seller is actually borrowing the stock from someone who owns it. If you or I traded shorts, we would be borrowing the stock from our brokers. Our brokers just might own the stock in their inventory or be holding it for other clients. If, during the period that the short position is open, there is a dividend paid by the company, the seller is responsible for paying any dividends to the lender of the stock.

Selling short can be very risky. What if the price of the stock starts going up? Usually at some point the brokerage house asks the seller to "cover the short" by buying the stock or putting up some security that the broker can sell to buy back the stock, if it needs to, at the higher price. If you don't watch the short positions carefully, the stock price can rise dramatically, and the seller's loss may be limitless.

Naked short selling is considered abusive and very problematic. In a naked short sale, the seller doesn't actually borrow the stock. Because he's not borrowing the stock, he can sell as much as he wants. Selling limitless numbers of these phantom shares puts pressure on the markets and causes the price of the stock to drop.

Because Overstock.com shareholders became a victim of naked shorting, Overstock's CEO Patrick Byrne has become a leader in promoting regulation of this practice. As a result, in recent years the SEC has enacted various regulations to curb short selling. You can learn more about Patrick Byrne's crusade at www.overstock.com/naked-short-selling.html.

Offering the wrong investment advice

There are more stories about bad investment advice than we can recount. Here are some of the reasons why your client may get bad advice from a broker:

- ✔ The broker is selling whatever security the firm is pushing without regard to a particular investor's needs.
- ✔ The broker doesn't understand what he's selling.
- ✔ The broker is diverting funds from a client's account without the client's knowledge.
- ✔ The broker has little or no regard for the client's true needs.

Unfortunately, we've seen many instances of these situations. How can these types of problems happen? Just about anyone can become a stockbroker. Go to any job fair, and you'll see the brokerage houses soliciting every warm body that walks by to become a securities salesperson. Understanding the securities markets, as well as understanding the financial needs of investors, is very complex. These brokerage houses will take any willing person, give them a crash course, have them take the licensing exams, and then sit them down to make sales calls. We've been amazed by how many securities sales-people we've seen who are nice, honest, hardworking people who have no clue what they're doing.

There are two major components to properly advising clients: understanding the client and understanding the securities. Clients are not all from the same mold. Every client has a different level of wealth, a different income stream, a different *risk tolerance* (willingness and ability to take financial risk), and a different family situation. A high-yield investment that is also high risk may be appropriate for a 25 year old who has another 40 years of potential earnings to make up any losses. A 60 year old who is planning to retire in a few years should be looking at more conservative investments. Yet, the broker who doesn't understand these issues is likely to put both these clients into the risky stock because that's what his brokerage house is pushing this week or because he's heard on the grapevine that this is a "hot stock."

When first taking on a new client, all brokerage houses have the client fill out a questionnaire that is used to assess the client's financial situation and risk tolerance. In every case we've seen, the questionnaires are then promptly buried in the client's file and never referred to again.

Rapid-fire stock orders

This practice, also known as *quote stuffing,* has recently come to the attention of the SEC for its potential to manipulate markets and market prices. This is the practice of issuing large stock orders quickly and then canceling the orders just as quickly. This practice may have been, at least in part, the cause of the "flash crash" of May 6, 2010. (See "The flash crash" related sidebar in this chapter.)

In a recent *New York Times* article, Mary Shapiro, chairwoman of the SEC, was quoted as saying that her investigators are trying to determine if this practice "violates existing rules against fraudulent or other improper behaviors."

Churning stocks

Brokers make commissions each time they help clients buy and sell stocks. *Churning* is the practice of urging clients to buy and sell too often in order to raise the commissions. Sometimes churning is done without the clients' knowledge. The broker will enter buy and sell orders because the client isn't watching or the broker had obtained a general consent but is trading for his own gain and not the clients' best interests.

Preventing Your Clients from Becoming Victims

We use several tools to keep our clients from becoming victims of stock frauds. First is financial education. We try to talk to clients about how to spot problems. A salesperson who talks about all high-yield securities, doesn't have answers to questions, or says he's never had a client lose money is probably someone to stay away from. We tell our clients to choose salespeople who come by recommendation rather than from cold calls or other types of solicitation.

We also find that tax season is the perfect time to review our clients' portfolios. When we're tax planning at the end of the year or looking at their statements to do a tax return, we look at the investments, not just the information required for taxes. If things don't look right, we quiz the client about what we're seeing. If we're not comfortable with the answers, we have the client come back in as soon as possible for a more detailed analysis of her investments. As part of our analysis, we look at suitability of investments, potential churning, and excessive trading costs.

We also recommend that our clients use a *fee-based* investment advisor: someone who gets an hourly fee rather than making a commission for selling securities. This type of advisor will give the client an overall investment plan (recommending what types of securities the client should be invested in) rather than sell specific securities and earn commission. This type of advisor has less incentive to steer the client to inappropriate investments and is less likely to be in a position to commit a fraud because he doesn't actually handle the clients' accounts.

Investors can measure their potential for getting involved with risky investments or scams at the Web site of the Financial Industry Regulatory Authority, www.finra.org.

A study in securities fraud: Bernie Madoff

Bernard Madoff was born and raised in Queens, New York. In 1960, he graduated college and started his investment firm: Bernard L. Madoff Investment Securities. He started out trading *penny stocks* (stocks that sell for less than a dollar) and *pink sheet stocks* (stocks that trade infrequently). He also developed computerized systems that were incorporated into the NASDAQ. The firm grew because of the innovative use of technology and because Bernie's father-in-law, an accountant, referred his family and friends.

Over time, Bernie developed a sterling reputation in the investment community. He, his brother Peter, and his sons Mark and Andrew were prominent members of the investment community. They sat on boards, including for the Securities Industry and Financial Markets Association (SIFMA), NASDAQ, and the Securities Industry Association. They were philanthropists who contributed large amounts to a variety of community organizations.

Except for Bernie himself, no one knows for sure exactly when his investment operation turned into a fraud. Bernie has said this happened in the early 1990s. Some investigators say it began in the 1980s or that his firm may never have been legitimate at all.

The most often heard version of the story is that Bernie had been genuinely earning high rates of return for his clients for quite a while. At some point, the market turned against him, and the rates of return significantly decreased. Bernie didn't want his clients to see that he had lost his luster, so he continued giving them the high returns. To pay for the high returns, he used new funds coming into the firm. He intended to stop the scheme and pay everyone off as soon as the market strengthened and he was legitimately earning high returns again. But he increasingly needed more new funds in order to pay off old investors. He was never able to catch up.

When the recession of 2007–2008 hit, Bernie became desperate. Clients were pulling out money to survive the recession, and little new money was coming in. At some point, he was not able to keep up with the demands for cash withdrawals and confessed to his sons what he had done. On December 10, 2008, his sons notified authorities of what their father had done, and the next day Bernie was arrested. Bernie pleaded guilty in March 2009 to swindling approximately $65 billion. On June 29, 2009, Bernie was sentenced to 150 years in prison.

Ironically, a fraud investigator had notified the SEC as early as 1999 that something was amiss at Madoff Securities. Harry Markopolos, a financial analyst and fraud investigator, was retained by some institutional investors who were considering investing with Madoff. Markopolos tried to duplicate the rates of return that Madoff claimed to be giving his clients, but could not perform this feat. He realized, through his mathematical computations and simulations, that Bernie's returns were impossible. Markopolos notified the SEC several times about his findings. The SEC failed to act. Markopolos also told his story to a *Wall Street Journal* reporter, as well as to New York State Attorney General Elliot Spitzer. They, too, failed to act. You can learn more about Markopolos in his book *No One Would Listen: A True Financial Thriller* (Wiley).

Part III
It's All in the Family: Fraud against Individuals

The 5th Wave   By Rich Tennant

"Sorry, Cedric the King cut my budget for additional fools. He said the project already had enough fools on it."

In this part . . .

Not every fraud case involves a business. Many times, forensic accountants are asked to help individuals who are trying to shield themselves against fraudsters — or to recuperate losses after a fraud has been committed.

In this part, we start with perhaps the most personal type of fraud investigation: one in which someone hires the forensic accountant to search for a spouse's assets (which are sometimes ingeniously hidden!) in the midst of divorce. We continue with a discussion of how forensic accountants can help elderly people (and their families) protect themselves from fraud against their estates and trusts. And we conclude this part with a chapter about the common (and sometimes shockingly easy) ways that fraudsters try to separate homeowners from their most precious asset.

Chapter 9

Divorce with a Side of Fraud

. . . .

In This Chapter

▶ Knowing where and how to look for assets

▶ Assigning value to a business

▶ Figuring out where income may be hiding

▶ Trying to avoid the IRS

. . . .

Divorce proceedings are unlike any other type of legal proceeding. Emotions can run very high. People who once loved each other deeply now hate each other with the same magnitude. When they go at each other, anyone in their path may also get hit with mud, including lawyers, accountants, and social workers.

In this chapter we talk about how forensic accountants play a role in divorce proceedings. We'd like to be able to tell you how to stay out of firing range, but we haven't figured that one out yet.

Searching for Hidden Assets

Often in divorce cases the spouses try to hide assets in order to avoid paying maintenance (alimony) or child support to the other spouse. Sometimes spouses go to great lengths to hide assets. Other times they just forget to list items on the required disclosure forms. Either way, attorneys often hire forensic accountants to help them get a full accounting. In this section, we introduce some of the more common schemes (and occasionally honest mistakes) that you may encounter when working on a divorce case.

If a client asks your advice on transferring assets, be careful when advising her. Some asset transfers may have costs associated with them or trigger tax issues. If the person who is holding the asset has debts, her creditors may have liens against the asset being transferred. Also, the courts may consider any transfer made when litigation is foreseen or pending as a fraudulent conveyance.

Locating assets given to family, friends, or holding companies

Usually a divorce is not contemplated long in advance, which means the people involved have little time to do deep hiding of assets. (However, sometimes people hide assets deeply for a variety of other reasons.) If you know where to look, you can often uncover hidden assets with just a bit of research.

Transfers to 529 or other cash accounts

One way to hide assets is to put them in the name of another entity: another person, a trust, or a holding corporation. Someone could take this action with the intention of truly hiding the money from the other spouse, or he could do so with the honest belief that by giving the money to a third party such as his children, he's taking a good (and allowable) step to ensure that they're covered financially no matter how the divorce proceedings play out.

For example, Dad realizes divorce is imminent, and he happens to have a lot of cash. He moves the cash to 529 accounts (college savings accounts) for the kids. When he fills out the financial disclosure for the divorce paperwork, he leaves off the cash that was transferred because he honestly believes this is now money that belongs to the kids. But the judge would probably consider this a sham transfer and consider the cash part of the *marital estate* (assets belonging to the couple as a married couple).

How would a forensic accountant find out about this type of asset transfer? One way is get bank statements going back as far as possible. Most judges will let you get at least five years of statements. Do an analysis of all cash transfers. The transfers to the 529 accounts should pop right up. Another way is to get the couple's tax returns. Depending on the type of 529 account, information about the accounts may appear on the state tax returns.

The 529 account is an example of a common asset hiding scheme. Cash is often moved to all kinds of accounts belonging to relatives and friends. You use the same techniques of analyzing cash transfers on bank statements to uncover any such schemes.

Real estate transfers

Sometimes people will be so bold as to change the title on real estate, putting the realty in the name of a family member or friend. Clearly, the motive here is to greatly reduce the person's net worth on paper.

Almost all jurisdictions have real estate ownership listings available online. Just a few minutes online will reveal any transfers of real property. One Web site to check out is www.zillow.com. This site's purpose is to analyze prices at which real estate transfers. If you can find the name of someone involved in your divorce case and the asset transferred for an amount that seems to be below market value, you may have discovered a sham transaction.

A nest of holding companies

Another way to hide assets is to put them in holding companies that are inside holding companies that are inside holding companies. (No, that's not a typo — bear with us here.) Envision a set of Russian nesting dolls: The assets are tucked inside the innermost doll and have several layers of ownership surrounding them. Hiding assets like this takes quite a lot of time and effort, which means it occurs when someone is planning divorce for a while (or is hiding assets for reasons other than the divorce).

Ownership of corporations is a matter of public record. It may take time and patience, but any investigator can dig up the information on corporate ownership. Investigators can also find clues to these corporations in other places, such as payments to lawyers to set up corporations and income on tax returns.

Every once in a while you land a case where the assets are actually physically hidden. In one case, the wife was so angry with her soon-to-be ex-husband that she literally started tearing the house apart. Inside a dropped ceiling she found documents that she didn't understand, so she brought them to her lawyer who turned them over to a forensic accountant. The documents detailed a large amount of assets that had not previously been disclosed. The judge was so mad that instead of a 50/50 split of marital assets, he gave the wife 75 percent of all the identified assets.

Artful deception

Sheila was in a bitter divorce battle. She told her soon-to-be ex-husband's attorneys that the artwork in her apartment was not hers, but was owned by a friend. The ex's lawyer sent in a forensic accountant with special expertise in the art world. The accountant was able to trace the provenance of the artworks to a London dealer. The dealer provided copies of sales receipts that showed the art was really sold to Sheila and that she purchased the art using foreign currency. Not only did Sheila look like a fool in front of the judge when this information was revealed, but the lawyer then wanted to know why Sheila was doing transactions in foreign currencies. Were any other foreign currency transactions hidden away?

Sheila was forced to add artwork into the assets to be distributed. She wasn't happy about that!

Banking on foreign accounts

Sometimes people stash their money in offshore accounts, which are harder to find and sometimes hard for the lawyer to *attach* (meaning to put a lien on the assets and have them transferred per court orders). However, it's not impossible.

You search for these accounts as you would any other. Look for transfers that don't have reasonable explanations. Also, look for overseas travel. To do this, analyze credit card statements and look for the purchases of airfare and hotels. Any travel that can't be explained by normal business travel or vacations — or any travel to locations known for being "cash stash" havens (such as the Cayman Islands or the Isle of Man) — is suspect. If you discover evidence of such travel, notify the attorney you're working for.

Also keep in mind that the U.S. government now requires that U.S. citizens annually report all foreign bank accounts in which they have an interest or have signatory authority when the value of the account is $10,000 or more at any time during the year. The penalties for not filing a Foreign Bank and Financial Accounts (FBAR) disclosure are formidable. Ask the attorney you're working for to subpoena copies of the individual's FBAR reports. If they were properly filed, they should give you clues to the presence and whereabouts of foreign accounts.

If you have sufficient proof to create suspicion that overseas bank accounts exist, the attorney you work for may go to the judge and request *Letters Rogatory*: documents sent from courts in one country to the judiciary of a foreign country asking for judicial assistance. The attorney will then retain an attorney in the other country who will present the Letters Rogatory to that country's court and request that the court issue a subpoena to be served on the bank where you suspect cash is hidden.

Studying tax returns and other financial documents

When dealing in divorce issues, you need to understand how to read tax returns and other financial documents. The astute reader can find a lot of information that can be used in a divorce.

Tax documents

A lot of assets show up on a tax return. A couple's joint returns may show *passive loss carry-forwards* or *capital loss carry-forwards* (tax benefits that may be used on future tax returns), or large tax refunds. These may be considered assets of the marital estate and should be reported to the lawyers and the court.

We can't emphasize enough the importance of carefully reviewing tax returns. Every forensic accountant we know uses the tax returns as a tool for uncovering income and assets. If one of the parties owns a business, you need to be looking at the tax returns and financial statements of the business, too. If you haven't looked at a tax return since your tax course in college, it's time to hone your tax skills.

One of our colleagues told us about examining the tax returns of her client's husband. The husband claimed that he had suffered a big drop in income. (We note in the upcoming section "Identifying Hidden Income" that some people try to claim poverty to avoid paying alimony or child support.) As proof, he showed his tax return, which really did have a relatively small taxable income. By reading the return carefully, our colleague realized that he had a huge charitable deduction for a contribution to a charitable trust. Because he still controlled the trust, it became part of the marital estate, which meant the wife was entitled to her share of it.

When studying someone's tax documents, don't just look at the federal tax return. If there's a large deduction for state taxes on a federal return, it may also be a hidden asset. Check out the state return. We've seen taxpayers make overly large prepayments of state taxes in the hope that no one would look and realize that a large refund of state taxes was imminent.

Don't use the copy of the tax return that's been given to you by the other side. It doesn't take much to make up a phony tax return. Instead have the other side sign an IRS form 4506, "Request for Copy of Tax Return." When properly filled out, this form will direct the IRS to send a copy of the filed return directly to you. Form 4506-T will get you a transcript of the taxpayer's account. The transcript will also show any corrections made by the IRS, amended returns filed by the taxpayer, and all payments.

Loan applications

Bank loan applications are another great source of information because they require the applicant to list all assets. Financial statements such as these (both personal documents and those from a closely held business) can be obtained by serving subpoenas on banks where loans were applied for.

Something to keep in mind: People often inflate their assets on a loan application. If assets claimed on the bank loan application are not really owned by the applicant, the application may be considered false. Filing a false bank loan application is considered banking fraud. As we explain in the upcoming section, "How is this information used?", discovering a fraudulent application can come in handy during a divorce as well.

We recently heard of a case where the husband said he had very few assets because everything was owned by his family. But the loan application for his new apartment showed $60 million worth of stock in the family business. Well, who owned the stock: the husband or the "family"? Did he commit fraud on the loan application or perjury on the financial statement to the divorce court? (Either way, the wife's attorney had something to use against him!)

Requesting a Business Valuation

One of the largest assets someone may own is a business. When one spouse is the owner of a business, that business may be part of the marital estate. And the business owner may be tempted to hide some of the value of that asset in order to avoid giving the spouse his or her fair share.

To ensure the equitable distribution of assets, you have to place a value on the business. To accomplish this step, we recommend calling in a business valuation (BV) expert because BV is a complex process. During the course of a BV engagement, the valuer needs to determine the exact income and expenses of the business. In the process of doing so, he will also be doing forensics: making sure that all income is recorded and all expenses are true business expenses.

What types of business expenses might raise a red flag for the valuer? Consider this scenario: Our friend Bob was called in to help a small business prepare for a sales tax audit. As part of his preparation, he reviewed all the expenses on the books of the business. He came across some checks marked as "matron expense." Not understanding what this was, Bob went to the controller. The controller made him close the door before he began his explanation. Apparently the business owner was having an affair. The "matron expense" checks were made out to the mistress.

To save time, money, and arguments during a divorce proceeding, often only one business valuation is presented to the courts. Either the attorneys decide on one neutral BV expert or the judge appoints one. BV is an art and a science. If each side hired its own expert, not only would it would pay twice the amount for the service but also the net valuation would likely be very different from each expert.

However, even if the judge appoints an expert, that fact doesn't preclude either side from hiring its own expert to review the valuation report.

For more information on business valuation, check out *Business Valuation For Dummies* by Lisa Holton and Jim Bates (Wiley).

Identifying Hidden Income

In divorce proceedings, one (or both) of the spouses may ask the other for maintenance and/or child support. The usual response is that the other spouse doesn't have enough income to pay the maintenance and child support being requested. Is that response honest? Sometimes, and sometimes not. The spouse being asked for money may be hiding sources of income to avoid the payments. In this section, we introduce ways to recognize that someone may have phantom income that needs to come to light.

Whenever you're researching someone's financial documents, work with an attorney who will get you proper subpoenas so that you're always on the right side of the law.

Starting with basic research

To seek out hidden income, you start by employing standard research techniques. You trace financial documents (such as bank statements and tax returns) to look for any abnormalities. For example, you want to note any unusual transactions that suggest money is being funneled to other family members, friends, or foreign banks. Then you conduct interviews with the person whose income you're investigating and anyone close to that person who may have key information.

You also need to look at credit card statements. Analyzing them will alert you to spending habits that are not in line with the income that the spouse has declared. And you can do a lifestyle test: If the spouse is driving a Corvette and vacationing on the Riviera, but tells the divorce court he's so poor he can barely afford to eat, put up a red flag. Sometimes the other spouse is very keen to an ex's lifestyle changes, so you may want to interview that person to start getting clues.

Often, hidden income is an issue when a spouse owns a business. As we note in the earlier section on business valuations, someone who owns a business may be motivated to hide the true value of that asset during a divorce proceeding so the spouse doesn't get a fair share. But a business owner can also try to fudge the numbers when it comes to how much money he's pocketing as income.

Take the case of Jay, a non-CPA accountant with a small practice. He told his soon-to-be-ex-wife's lawyer that he didn't have enough income to pay her maintenance. The lawyer sent out a business valuation (BV) expert to look at the business. The BV expert engaged Jay in a casual conversation about the practice of accounting. Jay told the expert that most of his clients were small businesses that paid monthly fees. The BV expert began analyzing Jay's receipts. She laid out his receipts on a grid showing how much each client was paying each month. She noticed that some clients didn't pay every month. When she reported this finding, the judge ordered Jay to explain the missing payments. At that point he revealed his secret: a second account to which some of his income was being deposited.

CASE FILE

Missing teeth

Merry, a dentist, was in a bitter custody and child support battle with her ex. She told the courts that she was hardly making any money from her dental practice. The court sent in a neutral business valuation (BV) expert to look at her business. She really had very little in the way of deposits to the business checking account. Her day sheets and patient charts, however, revealed a somewhat busier practice. The BV expert had the courts subpoena records from some insurance companies in her area. The insurance companies supplied information revealing a rather large income. When the BV expert examined the backs of the canceled checks from the companies, he noticed that the checks were deposited in foreign banks. Apparently, Merry had been sending her checks to family members who lived abroad, and they were depositing the checks in her overseas accounts. The judge was not happy!

To look for income that is being hidden in a business, you need to understand the nature of the industry your target is in. For instance, if you were examining a doctor you wouldn't just look at deposits in the bank. You might also look at that person's *day sheet*: the list of all the patients who come in on a particular day. If the number of people walking through the door is higher than the number of people who seem to be paying for the doctor's services, you have reason to suspect that some of the income is being diverted from the main accounts. (For a doctor's office, you might also ask to see statements from insurance companies or patient charts.)

TIP

If a judge finds out that a tax fraud or other crime has been committed, she is required to notify authorities. If a litigant hides something from a judge, the judge has the right to hold that person in contempt and put her in jail. Often when these issues arise, the lawyers settle them among themselves. They avoid letting these issues get to the judge and escalate into a criminal matter or jail time.

Taking a look at the new girlfriend (or boyfriend)

Very often a new girlfriend or boyfriend is the trigger for divorce proceedings. Sometimes it pays to take a look at the new pal's lifestyle. If the new girlfriend or boyfriend is driving a Ferrari that can't be explained by that person's own income, you should see a red flag pop up. The errant spouse may be deferring income to this person but trying to explain away the reduction in income as gambling losses or just hard times.

Looking at business contracts

Contracts — especially employment contracts — are another good source of information about income. One of the spouses may legitimately state that her salary is X dollars. The problem is that X is not the whole story. Reading the employment contract may lead you to bonus money and stock plans, which are not part of the weekly paycheck. There may also be generous expense allowances that the spouse is using as a private piggy bank.

Jerry and Harold were having lunch one day. Jerry, Harold's boss, had just been through a very bitter divorce. Jerry hated all wives and wives' lawyers. Harold started to tell Jerry how he was now in the process of divorcing and how his wife's lawyer was taking him for a ride. Jerry told Harold that he had a wonderful idea. He would cut Harold's pay in half. Then Harold could tell the lawyer that he had a precipitous drop in income and could prove it with his new pay stubs. To make up the difference, Jerry would give Harold a company credit card, which Harold could use for his personal expenses. The wife's lawyer started to wonder how Harold was living the same lifestyle with a 50 percent drop in income. The forensic accountant, working for the wife's lawyer, got subpoenas to examine the books of Harold's employer. It didn't take long to figure out the scheme.

Keeping the IRS at Bay

As much as the parties in a divorce may hate each other and don't want to see the other get any money, they hate the IRS more. They would rather see a hated ex-spouse get money than see the IRS get any. When you find a potential bank fraud, let the lawyer you are working for know. The lawyer will use this information as leverage. He knows the other side doesn't want to deal with a potential IRS audit, so he'll use your information as leverage to force a favorable settlement.

Palimony and divorce in one

Rita found out that her husband Tom had been cheating, and started divorce proceedings. Tom claimed that he had hardly any income and couldn't give Rita maintenance. The forensic accountant retained by Rita's attorney began to wonder how Tom had been supporting his girlfriend and their baby. The girlfriend also began a suit for palimony and child support.

The forensic accountant had the lawyer subpoena employment records from the company Tom worked for. He found that Tom indeed put all the income reported on his W-2 into his joint account with Rita. However, he hadn't told Rita that he was also earning commissions! He used the commission money to support the girlfriend and baby.

More bugs than ants at a picnic

There are all sorts of ways to get information about a spouse's income and assets. Sometimes the parties to a divorce go to extremes.

We had a tax client, Roy, who was a licensed private investigator. His specialty was electronics. He was known, in the community of investigators, as the go-to guy when you suspected bugs (listening devices) and wanted them detected and removed.

New York City has been the epicenter of many famous divorce cases: the Trumps, the Perelmans, and the Wildensteins, to name a few. Each of these cases was very long and bitter. They hogged the tabloid headlines and gossip columns for months. In one case the separated couple lived in separate apartments in the same building. Roy was called in by one spouse who suspected that the other was bugging the apartment. A few weeks later he got

a call from the second spouse, who also suspected the apartment was being bugged.

Roy worked alternately for each spouse, debugging the apartments. Many times, as he was entering or leaving the building, he would see friends who he knew from the very tight-knit community of investigators. When Roy saw his comrades in the building, they were almost always disguised in the uniforms of repairmen or delivery services. They had been in the building because they were hired by one spouse to bug the apartment of the other. They each knew what the other was doing, but no one let the cat out of the bag. Why should they? They all made quite a bit of money bugging and debugging until the divorce was over and settled.

Each party was trying to listen in on the business dealings of the other in order to uncover potential missing assets or undeclared income.

After practicing forensic accounting for a while, you will develop antennae that are very sensitive to fraud. If you can't find any solid evidence of fraud in a particular case, but your antennae rise up high, let the attorney you're working for know. That person may be able to use your hunch to bluff the other attorney. It doesn't always work, but sometimes this trick brings amazing results.

If a judge finds out about bank fraud, tax fraud, or any other legal activity, she is required, by law, to give that information to the proper authorities. The lawyers, therefore, know that having damning information of the other party can be used to leverage a settlement without the judge learning of the improprieties.

Recognizing injured and innocent spouse issues

Reporting a known tax fraud to the IRS can be a sticky thing to do. If joint tax returns were filed, both parties signing the return have obligations to the IRS.

If the other party was the instigator to a false return, that person is the one primarily responsible. The other spouse can declare to the IRS that he was an innocent or injured spouse and therefore does not have obligations to the IRS. Here's what these terms mean:

- ✔ **Injured spouse:** The IRS uses this term if someone can prove that his or her spouse has run up debts or other financial obligations in the injured spouse's name. If someone gets designated an injured spouse, the IRS will withhold the couple's joint refund so it can be applied to those debts or other financial obligations.

- ✔ **Innocent spouse:** If a couple files a joint return but one of the spouses' reports false information on the return, the other spouse can try to convince the IRS that he or she had no knowledge of the falsehoods. If the IRS agrees, that person is designated an *innocent spouse* and does not face legal action.

CASE FILE

Behind locked doors

Jim and Sue were involved in a divorce. Jim owned a small retail business that he ran out of a kiosk at a local mall. Most of his sales were for cash. Our friend Carol was asked by Sue's attorney to see what she could uncover. At their initial meeting, Carol engaged Sue in some casual conversation. During the conversation Sue let out that Jim had a locked room in the basement. He would go in there for hours at a time. No one else was allowed in, and he didn't even want anyone knowing about the room. Carol casually mentioned that she'd love to see what Jim was hiding in there.

Carol's casual comment got Sue thinking. The next time Jim went to work, Sue searched the entire house until she found a key she didn't recognize at the bottom of Jim's sock drawer. She quickly ran downstairs to try the key, and it opened the lock to Jim's lair. In the room Sue found all sorts of ledgers and stacks of papers that were meaningless to her. She quickly loaded it all into the car and took it down to a nearby

copy center. A few hundred dollars (and a large stack of copies) later, Sue hurried home. She put all the ledgers and papers back in the room, locked the door, and returned the key. She then drove all the copies over to Carol's office.

Carol took one look at the stack and knew they had hit pay dirt. A few days later she had a meeting with Jim to ask him about his income. Jim, as expected, pleaded poverty. Carol told Jim that she didn't think his declaration of low earnings was correct. She thought the number should be *much* higher. Jim insisted that Carol was wrong until she dug into her briefcase and pulled out a photocopy of a general ledger. Jim instantly recognized the ledger that was his second set of books.

Carol told us that the case was quickly and quietly settled within a few weeks of her meeting with Jim. Besides committing tax fraud, Jim had been committing a fraud against the mall operators. In most malls the rent is based, at least in part, on sales.

Although the IRS does hear innocent/injured spouse pleadings and does often rule favorably, the whole process can be a small nightmare while it's going on. No lawyer wants to get their clients into the position of having to defend themselves before the IRS.

Identifying common tax considerations

We can't get into a long discussion of taxes here (please try to control your disappointment!). However, we need to let you know that when you are a professional accountant you may be asked about taxes in divorce, too.

There are many tax considerations in how funds are dealt with in a divorce. Here, we note just a few of the major issues:

- ✔ Assets that are divided at the time of divorce generally do not trigger a taxable event. However, questions may arise as to taxable basis if and when the assets are later sold. Advise your client to get as much of this information as possible at the time of the divorce.

- ✔ A spouse who moves out of the marital home may not be eligible for certain tax advantages if and when the house is sold at a profit.

- ✔ Maintenance payments (alimony) are a deduction to the payer and income to the receiver. The payer, in order to get the deduction, is required to list the receiver's name and Social Security number on his tax return.

- ✔ Child support payments are not taxable. The custodial parent is entitled to the exemption for the child(ren) unless there is an agreement to the contrary. The noncustodial parent must get the custodial parent to sign form 8332, *Release to Claim or Exemption for Divorced or Separated Parents,* each year and attach it to her tax return. For more information, see IRS Publication 4449 at www.irs.gov.

Unless you're knowledgeable in this area, you should refer these questions to a tax expert.

Chapter 10

Protecting Estates, Trusts, and the Elderly

. . . .

In This Chapter

▶ Realizing why the elderly are targeted by fraudsters

▶ Identifying common frauds that hurt the elderly

. . . .

*T*he sad truth is that the elderly are prime targets for fraudsters. As much as their loved ones try to protect them, the frailties and economic realities of old age combine to make them targets. In this chapter, we talk about why the elderly are susceptible to fraud and introduce you to some of the most common scams that are run against the elderly.

As an accountant, you can play a vital role in helping to prevent frauds that prey on your elderly clients. One of the most important ways to help is simply to spend some time talking to your elderly clients when they call or visit you to discuss taxes or financial planning. They may be more willing to talk to you than their family members about their concerns — and to listen to your warnings about potential frauds. That's because they may fear that if they admit to falling for a fraud, for example, a family member will deem them incompetent and try to put them in a nursing home.

What if you're approached by an elderly client's family member who wants to discuss that client's business or state of mind? Keep in mind that talking to a family member about a client may be a violation of confidentiality. Certified public accountants (CPAs) are bound to confidentiality by the AICPA Code of Ethics, the IRS Rules of Practice, and the Code of Conduct of your state CPA board. However, if a client is truly no longer mentally competent, he may be a danger to himself or others. Before calling a family member to discuss such a situation, call the ethics committee at your state society or consult your malpractice insurance carrier. Most malpractice carriers have lawyers you can talk to.

Becoming Prime Targets for Fraud

No surprise here: Most elderly people don't function as well — either physically and mentally — as they did when they were younger. Yet the elderly often try to live as if everything were the same as when they were in their prime. Sometimes they don't realize that they're having problems.

Frimette's mother-in-law had such poor hearing when got older that she had to keep her TV on very loud and sometimes didn't hear the phone. When she didn't answer the phone, we would run over to see if she was okay. Yet she refused to believe that she had a hearing problem. We installed a special phone that lit up when there was an incoming call, and she disconnected it. This type of response is very common. She believed that if she acquiesced to her disability, she would be reliant on her family for help and would lose her independence. She avoided letting us take care of her needs (economic, health, and day-to-day living) even though letting us help her would have given us peace of mind and probably made her safer. We've seen this same story played out hundreds of times with clients, relatives, and friends.

Decline in mental function is a big problem. Some statistics indicate that as much as 30 percent of people over 80 have some form of dementia. Dementia diseases cause the patients to be forgetful, lose their language skills, lose track of their surroundings and reality, and become incapable of rational decision making. We've seen some people with dementia make the strangest decisions. They may go to the bank and remove cash for no apparent reason, dress totally inappropriately for the weather, and buy things that they absolutely don't need. They sometimes think that they are in a different time and place.

Many elderly people who were in the middle class during their working days also have a great fear of outliving their money; they fear that they will run out of savings before they die. Many of them also want to maintain whatever savings they have, and even grow their nest egg, so they can leave something for their children.

When you combine these health, mental, and economic issues, you get a dangerous brew. The result is that the elderly become prime targets for fraud.

Spotting Some Common Scams

In this section, we discuss some of the more common fraud schemes that target the elderly. We also note the protective measures you can take to help a client or loved one avoid such a scam.

Preying on hearing loss over the telephone

Imagine that you're at a rock concert and your phone rings. How clearly will you be able to hear? What if you're at home, but the caller is at the rock concert? Or one of you is just in a spot where phone reception is bad? For an elderly person with even a little bit of hearing loss, every phone conversation may be as difficult to hear as the ones we've just described.

Now imagine that an elderly person with poor hearing gets a call from a shyster who is trying to sell inappropriate investments, subscriptions, or other items. If the elderly person is afraid to show that she doesn't fully hear (or understand) what the caller is talking about, she may agree to all kinds of things that are potentially harmful.

One common scam involves the needy grandchild overseas. Sadly enough, many grandparents don't hear from their grandchildren often enough to be able to recognize the grandchild's voice on the phone — or to know what's going on in that grandchild's life. Imagine that an elderly grandparent is sitting at home with the TV on loud and gets a phone call. The caller says that he is Dan, the grandson who hasn't called in a long time. "Dan" says that he is in a foreign country, has been robbed, and has no money. He's ashamed to call Mom and Dad, and he wants to know if Grandma would be so kind as to wire a few thousand dollars right away. And, by the way, please don't tell Mom and Dad. What a beautifully constructed scam. It plays on Grandma's difficulty in hearing, her vanity about her hearing loss, her desire to be a good and loving grandmother, and her hope that she'll be loved forever for doing this favor and not telling anyone.

Variations of this scam exist as well. Perhaps a salesman calls who has some new and great health apparatus that will cure the hearing loss, blindness, wrinkles, and anything else that may be bothering the elderly person (who, as a potential victim of fraud, is referred to as the *mark*). The salesman claims that this offer is only for this person, and, therefore, he or she shouldn't tell anyone about it.

Reading the meter to gain home access

Meter readers, cable guys, and repair people also make for great scammers. Mind you, we're not talking about *real* meter readers, cable guys, and repair people — they're fine folks who work hard just like the rest of us. We're talking about scammers who buy uniforms and print their own ID cards. Do you know what the ID card for a worker from your utility company looks like? Most people don't know, which makes it easy for a scammer to use the ruse of needing to read a meter or check a wire to gain entry to an elderly person's home. When they're inside the home, they find "repairs" that need to be made — and, of course, they recommend their cousin to do the repairs. They may also find "violations" that can be cured with a small cash payment.

Sometimes such scammers work in pairs. While one talks to the resident and distracts that person's attention, the other cleans out cash and jewelry. We've even heard stories of scammers using physical violence against the elderly after gaining access to the home.

Pressuring someone to buy life insurance

Life insurance is a complex, multifaceted insurance product. It was originally designed to provide financial security for the family of a deceased person, but these days it's being sold as an investment and to defray estate tax costs.

Some life insurance salespeople use outright lies and prey on the fragile emotions of the elderly to sell insurance. They will give the elderly person all kinds of reasons to buy an unnecessary policy, and they'll become complete nuisances until they get a signed application. Here are some of the tales these fraudsters spin, along with the truth behind the tales:

- ✔ **Life insurance is a great way to invest to leave an inheritance to the grandchildren.** Life insurance is insurance — not an investment.

- ✔ **The insurance will pay for inheritance taxes so your children won't have to pay.** Estate taxes come out of the estate, not out of the pockets of the heirs. Some salesmen use this story even when the situation is such that there won't be an inheritance tax.

- ✔ **The insurance will pay for funeral expenses.** Yes, it will. However, there are better ways to cover those expenses. Many funeral homes offer prepaid, preplanned funerals. Also, many people are members of religious or fraternal societies that will cover a lot of the funeral costs.

- ✔ **Life insurance costs only pennies a day.** Yes, it can cost just pennies a day, but if you want a substantial insurance policy, those pennies add up. Very cheap policies are often advertised on TV and in magazines. For the low premium stated in the ad you get a policy with a very small benefit — usually $10,000. To buy additional units of $10,000 of insurance, the costs can go very high. These policies are usually expensive compared to more conventional policies sold by the more reputable insurance companies.

An ounce of prevention is worth a pound of cure, so you should be advising *all* of your clients to have a comprehensive estate plan, regardless of their age. You should also review any major transactions with them at least once a year when they come in for their income taxes. You should also have a list of reliable insurance people to refer your clients to.

Promoting high-yield investment schemes

The elderly are particularly vulnerable when it comes to fraudulent high-yield investments. Many elderly people worry that they will outlive their money — that they'll use up their nest eggs before they die. And, of course, everyone with children and grandchildren wants to leave something behind for the kids. Because most elderly people don't work and aren't earning money, the only way they can grow their money is by investing it. The more money they make on their investments, the faster they grow their nest eggs. Sounds logical!

A slick fraudster can quickly make a *mark* (a potential victim) forget one of the principles of investing: The rate of return is correlated with risk. In other words, the higher the rate of return, the riskier the investment is. With risk comes greater potential to lose the funds being invested. A person who has little likelihood of replacing lost funds and really needs those funds should not be investing in high-risk securities.

When your clients come in for their tax returns, do a little math in your head. If the interest and dividends that you have to put on their income tax return represent a rate of return that seems high, raise the red flags and start asking questions. Even if your client has already invested in something that smells like a scheme, you may be able to get him or her out of that investment before the money disappears.

Cashing in a life insurance policy

Did you know that you don't have to die to collect on a life insurance policy? Collecting on a life insurance policy before your death is called getting a *viatical settlement* or *life settlement.* These settlements became popular during the late 1980s and early 1990s when AIDS patients were dying because no long-term treatments were available to them. They knew they were going to die, and if they needed cash during their lifetime, they turned to their life insurance policies for help.

Here's how such a settlement works: The person whose life is insured is either elderly or gets a diagnosis that will lead to death within a few months. That person needs money for living expenses (or for one last hurrah). She doesn't have any ready cash, but she has a life insurance policy. The owner of the policy (who may or may not be the insured) sells the policy for a lump of cash. Now the insured person can get some money to use during what is left of her life.

When these settlements started, a lot of fraud was going on. Can you figure out what a life insurance policy is worth when the insured is still alive? Most insured people can't figure it out, and people cashing in their insurance policies were getting very little money compared to the worth of the policy.

Sometimes the policies were then sold to strangers, and sometimes they were sold back to the insurance companies.

The insurance regulators are very concerned about these settlements. Some of the purchasers of these policies have no *insurable interest* in the life of the insured. An insurable interest means that you have a reason to care whether the insured person lives or dies besides being able to collect the benefit. Also, computing the value of the settlement is a very complex affair. The regulators have written rules for these transactions to try to avoid letting people get fleeced. If you have a client who is considering one of these transactions, we strongly recommend that you seek out the advice of a professional who is very experienced in this area, which may mean an accountant, economist, actuary, or business valuation expert.

Bernie Madoff enticed investors, a number of them elderly, into his supposed high-yield investments. You should always have a list of reputable investment advisors to recommend to your clients. If you see any red flags, such as overly high yields, excessive trading, and so on, send your client to someone you trust for a review. If your recommended investment advisor also sees too many red flags, it may be time to recommend a forensic investigation.

Getting Grandma to change her will

One purpose of a will is to give direction to the survivors of a *decedent* (the person who died) on how the decedent wished to have his worldly goods divided. Other purposes include giving directions on the funeral and naming guardians and trustees for minor children. (*Guardians* are people who will take care of the kids, and *trustees* are people who will take care of the money for the kids.)

A person can change his will as often as he likes. We've heard stories of people changing their wills almost weekly! If you show up to Sunday dinner and spill wine on Grandma's favorite tablecloth, she may go to her lawyer Monday morning and change the will, leaving you out and giving Cousin Itt a bigger portion.

If Grandma changes her will because she freely changes her mind, fraud doesn't come into play. But if she changes her mind under duress or when she is suffering from dementia, that's another story.

Using coercion

Sometimes a relative who really needs money coerces Grandma into changing her will in his favor. He may come to Grandma with a great story of woe. He may tell Grandma about how much money he owes to the loan shark who has promised to break the grandchildren's knees if he doesn't pay. If only

Grandma will change her will so the loan shark can be paid after Grandma passes, everything will be fine. This person may play on Grandma's sense of guilt by pointing out all the times over the years that Grandma favored Cousin Itt. Now it's time for Grandma to prove her love and change her will, cutting out Cousin Itt altogether.

The use of coercion to influence a will is certainly immoral and may even be illegal. If you suspect that a client is being unduly influenced or coerced, you may want to notify family members or the authorities.

Taking advantage of dementia

Dementia diseases (including Alzheimer's) cause an elderly person to lose his mental abilities. Someone suffering from dementia starts to lose his memory, get confused, and become unable to perform tasks that used to seem simple. Simply put, he's not in his right mind. Therefore, he may not have the mental capacity to sign legal documents such as wills, powers of attorney, or health-care proxies.

Some fraudsters approach people with dementia and get them to sign updated wills that leave the bulk of the estate to the fraudster. The fraudster may be a stranger, a family member, or a caretaker.

CASE FILE

He doesn't know what he's signing

A client called this morning to tell us that she got a call from the assisted-living home where her father resides. He's in his 80s and has an advanced case of dementia. The administrator who called decided that her father should have a *healthcare proxy* (someone who can make healthcare decisions on his behalf), so the administrator is going to get him to sign the required paperwork. This news is very, very troubling. The administrator probably means well, but someone with advanced dementia does not have the legal capacity to sign documents. What if the administrator also got him to sign a power of attorney form and then cleaned out his bank accounts?

As accountants and auditors, this story bothers us for another reason. The client told us that her father had given her power of attorney and healthcare proxy years ago, when he still had the legal capacity to do so. She gave the assisted-living home copies of these documents when he was first admitted. Why can't the nursing home find the documents in his file? What is the status of their internal controls?

We're guessing, based on the larger story in this case, that the home just finds it easier to take care of the residents without having to bother to call family members. Also, if they are in charge, they get to choose the caretakers and vendors for medical supplies. It's entirely possible that the assisted-living home is getting kickbacks from its vendors — something that, unfortunately, is not uncommon for assisted-living and nursing facilities. If the home can make patient decisions that bring more business the vendors' way, the home stands to profit.

CASE FILE

The strange tale of Brooke Astor

Brooke Astor was a prominent New York socialite and philanthropist. Her third husband, Vincent Astor, died in 1959, leaving Mrs. Astor a very wealthy woman. She reportedly said that money is like manure — it should be spread around. From the time of her husband's death until the onset of her dementia, she gave away close to $200 million to a variety of charities. In her will, she bequeathed the bulk of her estate to her favorite charities.

Sometime in the 1990s Mrs. Astor started exhibiting the signs of dementia. Her estranged son, Anthony Marshall, came to her aid. Or maybe not. In 2006 her grandson, Phillip Marshall, found her to be living in her New York City apartment in squalid conditions. He accused his father of neglecting Mrs. Astor's care. He notified authorities, who stepped in. As a result, her longtime friend, Annette de la Renta, wife of the famous fashion designer Oscar de la Renta, was appointed her caretaker. Also, a criminal investigation was started. Mrs. Astor died on August 13, 2007 at the age of 105.

Anthony Marshall and his lawyer, Francis Morrissey Jr., were indicted in November 2007 on various charges including conspiracy, grand larceny, and forgery. It was alleged that Anthony had his mother sign *codicils* (additions) to her will, naming him as primary beneficiary. The two men were also charged with looting Mrs. Astor's funds to the tune of almost $200 million and forging a deed to one of Mrs. Astor's homes. Many witnesses came forward to say that Mrs. Astor's dementia was fairly advanced, and that she did not know what was going on when the codicils were signed. They also said that Mrs. Astor would never have left the bulk of her estate to her son because she thought his wife was a fortune seeker and did not like her.

Mr. Marshall and his lawyer were both convicted. Mr. Marshall was convicted on 14 of 16 counts, including grand larceny. He was sentenced to one to three years.

Presenting a forged will or hiding the will

In a sidebar in this chapter, we tell "The strange tale of Brooke Astor," a wealthy New York socialite whose son stole her money by having her sign changes to her will when she was suffering from advanced dementia. Unfortunately, Mrs. Astor's story is not unique. As we note in the previous section, sometimes fraudsters are able to get wills changed by coercing an elderly person or by taking advantage of the loss of mental faculties.

But what if the fraudster can't get the elderly person to make changes to the will? That's when two other types of fraud emerge:

- **The fraudster forges a will.** In this situation, the person committing fraud simply writes a new will and forges the necessary signatures. (To uncover this fraud, a handwriting expert may be helpful. Most people aren't *that* good at forging signatures.)

✔ **The fraudster hides the real will.** If a person finds out that her elderly relative recently changed his will to exclude her, she has great motivation to get rid of the most recent version of the will. This situation becomes complicated when the elderly person changes his mind and makes additions or revisions to the will frequently. The last version of the will prior to the person's death is the one that's considered valid. But if prior versions of the will are still floating around, a former beneficiary may be tempted to eliminate those versions that are least beneficial to her.

CASE FILE

When it may be beneficial to hide a will

We were involved in one case where the decedent's will was hidden from the courts. Here's the story.

Essie was a divorced mother of three. She was a music teacher and had a modest amount of assets. In her 40s she was diagnosed with a virulent form of cancer. She fought a brave fight and passed away about five years after her diagnosis. To save some money, Essie researched online to learn how to prepare and execute a will. She typed the will herself and went to a local pharmacy where she found a notary and some witnesses (total strangers) to watch her sign the will.

At the time of her death, two of her children were over the age of 18 and living on their own. Her youngest son was 15 and living with his father. After her funeral her daughter, Millie, went through her Mom's desk and found the will. She brought us the will and a list of Essie's assets. Essie's principal asset was her condo, worth about $180,000. With all her other assets the estate was worth about $240,000, way below the requirement to file a federal estate tax return.

When we looked at the will we were astounded. The will was on two sheets of crumbling paper held together with tape. The signatures of Essie and the witnesses were illegible. There were notes we could barely read, which were written in the margins. Essie had left everything to her three children, but it was not an even division. She made specific bequests, meaning that specific things went to each child. Furthermore, she did not name a trustee for her

youngest son. We advised Millie to consult an attorney who specialized in estates.

The attorney advised Millie to hide the will. They would go to the courts and say that Essie died *intestate* — without a will. The judge would then divide everything into three equal parts. The lawyer said that the will may not have been executed properly and that the estate would languish in the courts while the judge figured out what to do. Presenting Essie as intestate would be a lot easier and save thousands in legal fees. All three children agreed.

The judge, as predicted, divided the estate into three parts. He also named Millie as administratrix for the estate. Because Essie hadn't named a trustee, the judge appointed one of his cronies as trustee for the youngest son. After legal fees, court costs, and some other expenses, the son was to inherit about $75,000. Before any funds were transferred, Millie got a letter from the judge's appointed trustee explaining that his minimum fee for being a trustee was $50,000. Millie was incensed. She started writing letters to the judge and refused to turn over any money to the trustee. By the time the judge ruled that the fee should be reduced, the youngest son was close to his 18th birthday. Millie just held out a few more months, and her brother inherited the entire amount without any fees.

In this case, hiding the will worked out because all the children agreed and they had a smart lawyer. Moral of the story: It doesn't pay to be cheap when preparing a will.

CASE FILE

Getting adopted after death

Wouldn't it be wonderful if you could find someone rich who recently died, get yourself named his/her adopted child after death, and inherit the fortune? Here is a true story of how this almost happened.

Joseph DiPace, a chemical engineer who worked on the atomic bomb, died on November 19, 2002, in Florida. He and his wife did not have any children. His wife, Jeanette, had died several years before, leaving about $800,000 in a trust.

After Joseph was widowed, his niece-by-marriage Shirley DiPace, who lived not far away, became a close companion of Joseph. She saw him about twice a week. She took him to doctors' appointments and shopping, had him to her home for holidays, went out to dinner, and so on. Before his death many of the nieces and nephews had not seen Joseph for upwards of 20 years. By all accounts, Joseph and Shirley were close.

At one point Joseph began proceedings to formally adopt Shirley. He did this so that she would inherit Jeanette's trust as well as his own trust, worth about $700,000. He left his other nieces and nephews $5,000 to $10,000 apiece. At the adoption hearing Joseph's doctor, and others, testified that Joseph was of sound mind when he made this decision. On November 18, 2002, Joseph signed the adoption papers, one day before he died; however, the adoption order was not signed by the judge until November 21, 2002.

Joseph's other nieces and nephews were incensed that Shirley, a "stranger," would inherit the bulk of the estate. After all, they were Joseph's flesh and blood. They sued to have Shirley's adoption overturned. They argued that Shirley had used coercion and undue influence over Joseph to get him to change his trust.

Shirley lost the case. Unfortunately for her, an adoption after death is not valid.

TIP

The person writing the will — or making additions and changes to it — must be careful to destroy all copies of the previous will. Some people also videotape their wills (which makes for a grand presentation after death). Before doing so, check with an attorney to see if this is a valid form for a will.

Stealing Uncle Joe's house

Stealing a house form an elderly person is easier than you think. Remember, the elderly are often easily persuaded and do not always have sharp senses of sight and hearing. Some fraudsters (whether strangers or family members) just get the elderly person to sign over the deed to the house. That signature is often all that's needed to assume ownership!

Other times, a fraudster may ask Uncle Joe to co-sign a loan, which is actually a mortgage on the house. When both signatures go on the paperwork, both people are suddenly co-owners.

Chapter 11

Recognizing Real Estate Fraud

*W*hen most people talk about real estate, the three words they focus on are "location, location, location." In this chapter, we encourage you to focus on "prevention, prevention, prevention" — of real estate fraud, that is.

For our purposes, *real estate* encompasses all transactions related to buildings, land, rental units, and loans for these types of properties. Many creative frauds are perpetrated in this area of business against individuals, businesses, and banks. Fraudsters can fairly easily victimize individuals who are unsophisticated and don't seek help or advice from accountants or lawyers. You can't change that reality, but you can encourage your clients to consult you before making any major real estate decisions — and to develop a healthy dose of skepticism whenever someone is pitching a deal that's just a bit too good to be true.

In this chapter, we show you how some of the most common real estate frauds are perpetrated, how to uncover them, and how to prevent them.

Helping Homeowners Fight Fraud

Many real estate frauds are perpetrated against homeowners who are elderly, are not financially astute, or are having serious money problems. The best defense against these frauds is to train your clients to always contact you before any major financial decision. Sometimes just a few minutes on the phone, or a quick e-mail, can save your clients from losing their life savings and their home.

In this section, we outline some of the common frauds perpetrated against individual homeowners, and then we explain how accountants can help homeowners protect themselves.

Stealing a home with a false deed

A *deed* is a document that is evidence of ownership of real property. When the ownership of property transfers, the seller signs the deed and gives it to the buyer. Because the buyer doesn't need to sign the deed, the buyer has no actual evidence of ownership other than having access to that document. If the deed were filed in the buyer's sock drawer, anyone who opened that sock drawer could claim ownership to the property.

To reduce fraud — as well as to aid in the collection of property taxes — deeds are *filed* (recorded) with a government office. Usually they're filed at the government office in the county in which the particular real property is located.

Getting a home for a song — or a signature

To transfer a deed, in many jurisdictions, all that is necessary is a signature on the deed. That means if you can get your hands on a deed, you can pretend to be the seller and sign the property over to someone other than the real owner.

Given this fact, you'd think that getting your hands on a deed must require jumping through a complicated series of hoops. To prove that you — and only you — are the real property owner, you must need to produce at least a half-dozen photo IDs, a few government-issued numbers, and a letter from your mother, right?

Wrong. To get a deed on a particular property, you simply go down to the government office that records the deeds in your area and ask for a copy of it. Copies of deeds are usually available for just a few dollars. You must sign your name, but the registrar of deeds does not always check the signature or ask for any proof that the signature on the deed is valid. After all, what would the registrar check the signature against? The real home buyer wasn't required to sign the deed in the first place, so the registrar doesn't have a signature to compare yours with.

So to steal a home (or another building), a fraudster can forge the signature of the legitimate owner on a created deed document and file it at the registrar's office. Easy as pie!

Feeling some protection from title insurance

Getting queasy? Take a deep breath: Homeowners do have some protection against this type of fraud. *Title insurance* is an insurance policy that indemnifies the owner of real estate for problems with the title prior to the date the policy was issued. So let's say you buy a property from a seller, and you get title insurance. Some years later you find out that the seller really didn't own the property he sold to you. You can ask your title insurance company to refund you the purchase price of the house.

A title company usually researches the ownership of the property before issuing the policy. The company often demands that the conveyor of the deed present appropriate identification at the time the deed is transferred. If you borrow money from a bank to buy the property, usually the bank requires title insurance. A title insurance company also checks to see if any *liens* (legal claims) have been placed on the property, such as unpaid real estate taxes, prior mortgages, or other types of tax liens.

Stealing a home through mortgage fraud

A *mortgage* is a loan that is secured by real property; if the loan is not paid, the lender can take the property to pay off the loan. Many types of mortgage fraud exist. Sometimes the borrowers commit the fraud, and sometimes the lenders do. In this section, we take a look at a few types of schemes.

Usurious mortgages

Usury means charging very high interest rates, so *usurious* mortgages are those that come with outrageous interest rates attached.

Why would anyone agree to pay such high rates? Sometimes a borrower doesn't qualify to get a loan from a reputable lender; the lender does a credit check, identifies problems, and turns down the loan application. If the borrower is desperate, he may turn to a less-than-reputable lender. That lender takes on the risk of a less-than-qualified borrower but charges a very high interest rate in exchange. Sometimes the lender manages to structure the transaction so it can charge rates in excess of the legal limits.

We've seen usurious loans in two common situations:

- ✔ A homebuyer doesn't have enough money for a substantial down payment. Lenders consider the loan-to-value (LTV) ratio when they structure the terms of the mortgage. A low down payment means a low LTV, which means higher risk to the lender so it charges a higher rate. The borrower has a higher interest rate and a very large principal balance. The lender may also add other requirements like mortgage life insurance. Add it all up, and the borrower has a huge monthly payment that's hard to meet.

- ✔ Homeowners get into credit trouble. They'd like to borrow money against the equity in their home as their own personal bailout. Because they're in trouble, they have a poor credit rating. That means higher risk to the lender, who compensates by charging a high rate of interest. The result: A large monthly payment that is hard for the borrower to deal with.

Desperate borrowers are already in a financial pickle, so they often struggle to make the payments on a high-cost mortgage. A shark lender is well aware of this fact, and it just sits back and waits. As soon as the borrower defaults on the loan, the lender forecloses and takes title to the property. If the loan is small relative to the value of the property, the lender profits big time.

Anyone borrowing against real property should have a lawyer review all the documents related to the mortgage. The borrower should ask the lawyer to explain all the terms of the transaction and all the possible pitfalls in understandable language.

Mortgages that are really sales

There are two versions of the mortgage that's a sale:

- A desperate property owner can't qualify for a mortgage. A less-than-scrupulous lender offers the owner a great deal: "Sign the building over to me. I will get the mortgage, and you will pay me rent so that I can pay the mortgage. When your credit improves or the mortgage is paid off, I will give you back the building." Unfortunately, the owner does not get the property back and actually has sold the building for a pittance.

- The building owner signs what he believes to be mortgage documents but in reality signs sale documents. Before he knows what has happened, he no longer owns the property.

In each case, the unscrupulous lender takes advantage of a desperate borrower. This problem can easily be avoided if the borrower consults an attorney to read and explain the documents before signing anything.

Think this type of fraud would be pretty impossible to pull off? It's not. Here's just one example: In April 2005, Troy Keith of Springdale, Ohio, received a 46-count indictment in a mortgage scam for approaching homeowners and offering to take over their mortgages while they paid him rent. He was supposed to pay their mortgages, but didn't. If any of those 46 homeowners had really checked into Keith's credentials, they likely wouldn't have been victimized. Urge your clients to deal only with reputable mortgage brokers. Most states license mortgage brokers, so your state banking department is a great place to start. If you're lucky enough to work with astute clients who ask your advice, make sure you have a list of reputable financial professionals to refer them to.

To get a sense of how prevalent mortgage frauds of all types really are, visit www.mortgagefraud.org, which highlights new articles about schemes that put homeowners at risk.

When a home has no mortgage: The risks of not owing money

So if taking out a mortgage puts you at risk for fraud, you'd think owning your home clear and free would be keep you out of harm's way. Unfortunately, life just isn't that simple. Here's how you can be a victim of mortgage fraud even if you don't have a mortgage.

When someone takes out a mortgage or another type of real estate loan, the lender (such as a bank) has a *lien* (a legal claim) placed against the property. If the property changes hands, the lien holder is notified. Any change in ownership is probably a violation of the loan agreement, which prompts the full amount of the loan to come due.

If there is no mortgage on a property, a fraudster can easily file a mortgage. Here are two types of fraud perpetrated against homeowners who don't have mortgages:

- ✔ A fraudster presents herself to a lender as the owner of the property and takes out a mortgage.
- ✔ A fraudster places a lien on the property and waits patiently until the owner tries to sell the property.

Protecting your clients' homes

As an accountant, you can do several things to help protect clients from the types of frauds we've introduced so far in this chapter. If you have clients who fall victim to such schemes, the best way you can help them is by uncovering the fraud sooner rather then later.

Helping clients make key decisions

As we note many times in this chapter, you want to encourage your individual clients to call you before they make important real estate decisions. In particular, they should call you before they buy or sell a house or take out a second mortgage. (In fact, they should call you before making all sorts of life decisions, such as changing jobs, getting married, or having a baby. But most people aren't accustomed to using their accountants as resources in these situations, so you have some client training to do!)

If you encourage your clients to lean on you during these key real estate transactions, you can help them make appropriate decisions that will affect their financial well-being and mitigate their tax obligations. The key is that they must call you *before* signing on the bottom line.

As a financial professional, you can help your clients spot bad or fraudulent real estate deals. And to make sure you're providing the best service possible, you should develop a network of honest, hardworking bankers and lawyers to recommend to your clients if they need advice that's beyond your scope of your expertise.

Yes, we know, many people dislike lawyers. But the truth is that a good lawyer is like an insurance policy. Sometimes it may seem like you're paying that person for nothing, but if you're in a pickle he can really bail you out.

Consider this lesson on the worth of lawyers from Frimette's own experience: I was refinancing a home mortgage and arrived at the bank for the closing a bit early. The bank's paralegals encouraged me to start signing papers, but I insisted on waiting for my lawyer to come. When the lawyer arrived, he went through an almost foot-high stack of documents and discarded three-quarters of them with a gruff "My clients are not signing that." He also found that the remaining documents contained many erroneous computations of funds due the bank. I took out my portable adding machine, plugged it into the wall, and started to recalculate. The paralegals had never seen such a thing. They called others from the office to come and see the borrower who was recalculating the mortgage numbers! Together, my lawyer and I found numerous errors and saved several hundred dollars by being watchful and distrustful of the bank.

Encouraging property liens and lien searches

You should counsel your clients to take two specific actions that can help them protect their real estate assets: take out a lien on their own property, and do regular lien searches on that property.

Taking a lien on your own property

Everyone should have a lien on their own property, even if they don't owe any money on it. In the earlier section, "When a home has no mortgage: The risks of not owing money," we outline two types of fraud that can steal a home right out from a homeowner who doesn't even have a mortgage.

The prime victims for these types of fraud are elderly people who have worked for years to make mortgage payments and have finally paid off their houses. Their heirs, or the homeowners' trust, should file a large lien on the property to prevent fraud. However, this strategy has potential dangers and should not be done without consulting an attorney.

Kira heard about how fraudsters steal the homes of seniors who have paid off their mortgages. She was concerned because her Mom had paid off the mortgage. Kira had one brother, and she and her brother were Mom's only heirs. We recommended that she and her brother file a $1 million lien on Mom's house. That way, anyone trying to place a phony lien in order to steal Mom's house would first have to pay off the $1 million lien. Of course, we recommended that they talk to the family attorney about making the arrangements.

Doing a lien search

One way to protect an interest in real property is to do frequent lien searches. All real property ownership deeds and mortgages are filed with a government office — usually your county clerk. Many of these government offices now have these records online. To do a lien search, you just go to the Web site of that office and search for your property. You can find the owner's information and all the liens on the property.

Each real estate registrar organizes its records differently. Some organize the records by identifying numbers, and others organize the records according to block and lot numbers. Most have ways of looking up these numbers by searching the address. Some also allow searches by last name.

If you find a lien on a client's property that you don't think belongs, *act quickly.* The sooner you discover a phony lien after it has been placed, the easier it is to clean up. Sometimes unrecognizable liens may just be errors on the part of a government agency (such as the real estate tax board) or improperly filed mechanics' liens.

If you believe a lien is fraudulent, help your client to contact the authorities right away. For example, you may want to contact:

- ✔ The registrar of records in that area
- ✔ The district attorney or state's attorney
- ✔ The FBI — if you see any indication that the fraud came from someone out of state
- ✔ The U.S. Postal Inspector — if you suspect that the fraudster used the U.S. mail to perpetrate the fraud (for example, by mailing documents to the registrar)

Remind your client to keep a record of all contacts with authorities. If the fraudster should contact your client and ask for a payoff, tell the client to call the local police immediately.

Manny recently contacted us about a problem his mother was having. She tried to refinance her house. The potential lender did a lien search and found a lien dating back to 1985. Mom thought the lien was filed by a roofer who did repairs, but she couldn't quite remember. The lien was in a corporate name, and the corporation couldn't be found. We referred Manny to a real estate lawyer. If Manny's mother had been doing regular lien searches on her house, she could have spotted the lien while the corporation was still in business, and the problem surely would have been easier to fix.

Even small frauds matter

Here's an example of a common type of fraud that even legitimate banks perpetrate on their mortgage borrowers. It may seem small, but you should advise your clients to look out for it nonetheless.

When a homeowner refinances a mortgage, typically the bank does not pay off the old mortgage for three days. The delay is legitimate because consumers have a right to undo any contract for three days. However, the bank starts charging interest on the new mortgage from day one. Three days of interest isn't usually a lot of money for the homeowner, but over hundreds of borrowers the amount does add up for the bank. If the bank's lawyer refuses to waive the three days' interest at the time of closing, a letter to the appropriate state banking authority usually triggers a refund.

Focusing on Repair Schemes

Repair schemes are pervasive. Most often the elderly and unsophisticated homeowners are the victims, but businesses certainly aren't immune. In this section, we outline the most common schemes and explain what an accountant can do to help a client who's been victimized.

Shielding homeowners from unnecessary and improperly done repairs

You're just about to sit down to dinner when someone rings your doorbell. You don't recognize the man standing on your front porch, but he identifies himself as a roofer. Here's his pitch: "I happened to be driving by and noticed that some of your shingles are missing."

In this type of scheme, roving fraudsters pretend to be repairmen and convince homeowners that they need certain repairs. A repairman gets a deposit and has the homeowner sign forms and contracts. Included in the pile of forms is usually a form for a mechanic's lien — something we explain in detail in the next section. The repairs may or may not be done; usually, they're started and not completed. The homeowners are left with undone work, the deposit is gone, and they may have to deal with a lien on the house.

But even if the person you hire is a legitimate repairman, you may be taken for a ride. For example, say you call a repairman because you know you have a problem that needs fixed, such as a leaking toilet. While he's working on that problem, the repairman "discovers" another, more serious (and expensive) problem, such as a slow leak under your floorboards. Depending on how closely you pay attention, that repairman may be able to convince you that the problem exists — and that he's fixed it — when in fact he just wasted a few hours doing not much of anything. If you aren't very handy around the home (which is likely why you called the repairman in the first place), you may not feel comfortable questioning what you're being told. Chances are you'll pay the bill and let the repairman walk out the door with stolen money.

Improperly done repairs are usually done by unlicensed or just incompetent repairmen. These people have learned how to talk the talk, but that's as far as their expertise goes. When they leave your home (with your payment firmly in hand), they leave behind just as much of a mess as you had before. And if you try to call the next day or the next week to ask them to return and do the repair correctly, you may find that you can't reach them anymore.

Here's how homeowners and business alike can avoid being the victims of these types of schemes:

- ✔ Always, always get a second opinion. Even if a problem needs to be fixed urgently, take a bit of extra time and ask more than one repairman to look at it and give you a quote for the work required.

- ✔ Avoid dealing with repairmen you don't know. If you're new to the area or have a problem you haven't encountered before, find a reputable repairmen by recommendation.

- ✔ Check for licenses and complaints with the local licensing bureau or the Better Business Bureau.

In addition to offering your clients the preceding advice, how can you help when it comes to phony repair schemes? If your client is a business, you can unearth phony repairs by doing financial statement analysis. Is there a reason for repair expenses being higher this year than last? Is there a reason why repair expense is a higher percentage of sales than usual? Getting answers to these questions can help uncover frauds. If your client is a home-owner, preventing and uncovering fraud comes down to having trained clients. Get them used to asking the right questions and consulting with you regarding any large transactions.

Mechanic's lien: Knowing what it is and how to avoid it

Contractors and repairmen often file a mechanic's lien when they work on large jobs. A *mechanic's lien* is a lien on the home or business property for the cost of the repairs or remodeling. That way, the contractors and repair-men have some guarantee that the person or company hiring them will pay for their services. Sometimes the lien is in place from the onset of the job, long before payment is even due.

Here's the problem: Down the road, the property owner tries to sell the prop-erty, and a title search reveals a mechanic's lien from a repair company that may be long gone. You can't even find them to pay them. This hampers your ability to sell the property. Sometimes these liens are placed for legitimate work, and when the job is complete the contractor just forgets to remove the lien. But as we explain in the previous section, phony repairmen sometimes place mechanic's liens on homes as well.

If the contractor is legitimate, getting a mechanic's lien removed is not a prob-lem. Just ask the contractor for a *release of lien* form, get it filed with the real estate registrar, and the lien is removed. But if the contractor is not legitimate or has gone out of business, finding that person to get the lien removed can be a big hassle. You may have to help your client and her attorney prove that the lien was phony or paid off so that the attorney can get a court order to remove the lien.

In certain situations, the IRS or another taxing authority such as a county or state department of revenue will file a lien on real estate for unpaid taxes. But sometimes the lien doesn't get removed when the taxes are finally paid. If you or a client are in that situation, simply ask that taxing authority for a *release of lien* and take it to the county clerk to clear the records.

Here's how you should advise your clients to prevent a mechanic's lien issue:

- ✔ A contractor or repairman must get the property owner's signature for the lien documents to take effect, so never sign anything without a lawyer's review. Ask the lawyer to make sure the contract includes a clause that prohibits the filing of a lien. A legitimate contractor may agree not to have a lien placed or to have the paperwork held *in escrow.* This means that the lien will be filed only if the homeowner does not pay at the end of the job.

- ✔ As we note in the earlier section "Doing a lien search," check for liens frequently. If a mechanic's lien has been filed against your property, take care of it sooner rather than later.

Keeping Commercial Leases Honest

As a forensic accountant, you may work on either side of a commercial real estate deal. If you're working with a business client that is signing a lease for new office space, you need to advise your client to pay close attention to how usable square footage is calculated. If you're working with a landlord that's renting space to a retailer, you need to help your client ensure that a lease based on the percentage of retail sales is being honored. We explain both situations in this section.

The square footage scheme

Many commercial leases are stated in terms of a dollar amount per square foot of space. The $64,000 question is this: What parts of the premises are or are not included in the square footage? If a support pillar exists in the middle of the floor, is that counted or not? If the property includes an internal staircase, how is that counted? Leases are often vague about these types of issues. The remedy is to tell your client to demand a lease that is specific about how the square footage is calculated.

If your client wants to verify the amount of space it will actually occupy, you can help it find a lease auditor. *Lease auditors* are engineering types with all kinds of fancy measuring instruments that verify the usable and nonusable square feet of space. You might also recommend bringing a lawyer into the conversation.

The landlord as retail partner

In retail leasing, the landlord often asks for a percentage of sales. For example, a landlord may charge a base rent (to make sure it receives a set amount of money it month) and then charge a percentage of sales on top of that base amount.

The unfortunate side effect of this type of lease agreement is that the store owner has the incentive to hide sales. Landlords know this. Therefore, the terms of the lease often include a provision allowing the landlord to audit the books of the tenant.

But what if the tenant manages to keep some sales off its books as well? Another way to uncover reduced sales reporting is to use mystery shoppers to observe sales. Let's say that the tenant is a coffee shop. You estimate that on average a customer has a $5 tab. (Sometimes customers order just coffee, which is only $1.50. Sometimes they get coffee and a bagel, which is $4.50. At lunchtime, customers who order coffee and a sandwich pay about $7.) If you simply stand as an observer across the street to count people walking into the store, you can get a sense of the sales activity.

Another way a forensic accountant can uncover an underpayment of rent is to audit coffee cup purchases. Hang out in front of the store on the day that cups are delivered. Slip the delivery guy a tip, and inquire about how many cups are delivered each week. Do a little math to come up with how many cups of coffee are sold. Then multiply by the average sale, and voilà! You now have the total sales amount. Sales tax auditors have been known to use this technique when auditing restaurants and pizza parlors.

We once had a client who ran a very popular local catering hall. The hall was particularly popular with brides whose fathers had cash businesses, so the hall was often paid in cash. Unfortunately, it chose to hide some of this cash and not report its true sales to the tax man. The sales tax bureau suspected what was going on and sat investigators in cars across from the catering hall for an entire month. All the investigators did was count people entering the catering hall for each party. They already knew the average per-head charge for a wedding. They used this calculation to send the catering hall a substantial bill for unpaid sales taxes.

Boosting Banks' Fraud Defenses

So far in this chapter, we've focused on many frauds that harm individuals and some that can affect businesses. Here, we turn our attention to frauds perpetrated against banks. We show how those frauds take place and how you can advise bank clients to protect themselves.

Spotting phony mortgage applications

If you're a homebuyer desperate to buy a house, but you don't earn enough to qualify for a mortgage, what do you do? If you're like many people (and we hope you aren't!), you lie about your income on the mortgage application.

This fraud is so pervasive that banks have become wise to it. Banks often demand that the mortgage application package include an IRS form 4506. The form gives the IRS permission to share information with the bank about the applicant's income as reported on income tax returns. Taking this step should help banks verify applicants' true income — if only the banks would follow through. Many banks just leave the form 4506 in the file and never request the information from the IRS. The result? If a homebuyer really can't afford the mortgage or runs into unexpected financial problems, she eventually defaults, and the bank is left holding a bad mortgage.

Why doesn't every bank file form 4506 for every mortgage application? One reason is that it sometimes takes the IRS weeks or even months to send copies of the tax returns. That kind of delay can seriously disrupt a potential homebuyer's timetable.

If you are advising staff members at a bank or another mortgage lender, tell them to have mortgage applicants call the IRS and request that an income transcript be faxed to the bank. The IRS usually faxes these transcripts within 24 to 48 hours.

We once represented a family-owned business during an IRS tax audit. (We did not prepare the original tax returns.) The sons of the owners worked in the business. During an expansion, the business purchased an adjacent piece of property in the name of one of the sons for $1 million. A small down payment was placed on the property, which translated into a large mortgage. The son, a family man with three children of his own, had been reporting about $20,000 of income from the business. The IRS agent was wondering how he qualified for a mortgage of close to $900,000 with only $20,000 of income. The IRS agent said that either the son was underreporting his income (which is a felony violation of tax law) or had lied on the mortgage application (a felony violation of banking law). Either way, he was in big trouble! Falsifying information on mortgage applications is serious business.

Being wary of phony appraisals

Another common fraud perpetrated against banks is phony appraisals. This fraud usually involves the mortgage broker, the property buyer, and the real estate appraiser.

Here's how it works: The buyer identifies a target property. The property may be purchased specifically for perpetrating this fraud or it may already be owned by the buyer and just refinanced for the fraud. The buyer goes to a complicit mortgage broker, who prepares a loan application package for the bank. The package includes an appraisal of the property value. (Keep in mind that banks will lend only up to a certain percentage of a property's value.) The appraiser, who participates in the fraud, appraises the property for an amount well above its actual value. The bank then issues a loan based on the phony appraisal. The buyer/owner pays off the broker and appraiser for their services and walks away with the cash. He never pays the bank on the mortgage. The bank is left owning a building that is worth less than the loan it issued.

You can advise your banking clients to avoid this scam by taking several steps:

- ✔ The bank should check out the reputation of the brokers and appraisers that bring mortgage deals to the bank.

- ✔ The bank should perform its own appraisals. Full appraisals can be expensive, but a less costly option is the *drive-by* appraisal: Instead of a full detailed analysis of the property, the appraiser just takes a quick look at the outside of the building and gives an estimated appraisal. If too many drive-bys are coming back with values much lower than the full appraisals, the bank should suspect that the original appraiser may be up to something nefarious.

- ✔ Banks should look back on past mortgages that have gone bad and see if the same broker or appraiser is associated with too many of the mortgage defaults. Doing so shines a spotlight on the fraudsters. Usually this step is done by federal investigators, but only after many frauds have been perpetrated.

As we were writing this chapter, the Kings County District Attorney in New York announced an 82-count indictment against seven people charged with buying and selling the same house four times over four years, stealing one woman's identity, and securing four mortgages worth $2 million. The defendants allegedly misled banks in making loans, recruited *straw buyers* (people who allowed their credit to be used to secure mortgages), and created fake employment and financial records. Two of the defendants are mortgage brokers who were charged with putting together the fraudulent deals — proof positive that banks must be diligent about performing background searches not only on prospective buyers but also on mortgage brokers.

We heard of an accountant with a client who regularly bought and sold real estate. The client was approached by buyers regarding the purchase of a few homes. At the closing, the client noticed that the selling price and mortgage were way overvalued for the true value of the home; however, the client was still walking away with a fair price and adequate cash from the sale. The client was a little suspicious of the buyers, but his cash from the sale was reasonable. A few months later, the authorities showed up at the client's house to ask him some questions about the home sales. Come to find out the buyer was working with an appraiser to inflate the values of the homes. They were taking the excess cash and defaulting on the loans. They thought he was in on the scam.

Part IV
Meeting Your Methods of Investigation

The 5th Wave   By Rich Tennant

"This is classic voodoo economics, Grace, right down to the chicken blood it's written in."

In this part . . .

This field of accounting is named "forensic" because the information you uncover is used in a legal setting of some kind. Many forensic accounting engagements involve litigation, and in this part we walk you through what that means. We also provide detailed suggestions for how to counsel small and large businesses on being proactive in the fight against fraud. Because so many types of fraud are perpetrated by employees, we devote an entire chapter to making certain that the company does what it can to ensure employee satisfaction — thus eliminating one major motivation for committing fraud.

We start by explaining the types of reports that forensic accountants are often asked to create based on their investigations. We continue with a detailed discussion of the role a forensic accountant plays in helping attorneys prepare for business litigation. The next chapter is devoted to explaining what it means for a forensic accountant to serve as an expert witness and how to prepare for that responsibility. We then look at government litigation, which involves its own set of players and standards of proof.

Chapter 12

Walking through the Investigation Process

*A*ny fraud investigation starts with an accusation. When you're talking about fraud perpetrated against individuals (which we discuss in Part III), the accusation may come from a soon-to-be former spouse, the child of an elderly person who has been victimized, or any other individual who believes that he or someone he cares about has been defrauded.

With occupational fraud (the type we discuss in Part II), the accusation often comes from within the company — from employees willing to blow the whistle when they think they smell something rotten — or from people closely related to the company, such as customers or vendors. The accusation can also arise as a result of routine company procedures such as internal audits of company processes, external audits of the company's books and records, or specific inquiries undertaken to investigate red flags. No matter where the accusation comes from, the company must look into it — at least enough to determine whether a full investigation is warranted.

In this chapter, we offer a big-picture view of what forensic accountants do after an allegation has come to light. We focus on occupational fraud for two reasons: It's often a forensic accountant's bread and butter, and the process for conducting an occupational fraud investigation is fairly standardized. (We say *fairly* because these investigations are not straightforward by any means; they usually have many moving parts requiring myriad resources.) That's not the case for investigations into fraud against individuals; the investigative steps you take during a nasty divorce may differ greatly from those you take when a fake repairman bilks an elderly person out of thousands of dollars.

Forensic accountants often assist attorneys in conducting corporate investigations. Here, we discuss how companies decide whether to pursue full-blown investigations, what the team of investigators looks like, how the team creates a workplan for the investigation, and what types of tools they most often use to gather information.

Figuring Out Whether to Fully Investigate

When an accusation of occupational fraud or other corporate misconduct is made, the company whose managers, directors, or other employees have been accused may ask its counsel whether to investigate or not. The circumstances giving rise to the allegations are a key factor: Has the company learned of the allegations via legal proceedings, such as the execution of a search warrant or receipt of a grand jury subpoena? If so, more often than not, the company may have no choice but to conduct an internal investigation to assess whether the allegations are true.

If the company is aware of allegations of misconduct, but no lawsuit has been filed and/or the government has not started an investigation, the investigation question is more difficult to answer. Here are some considerations:

- ✔ Should the company investigate the allegations, which, if true, would lead to legal liability?
- ✔ Do the allegations have the ring of truth given what the company managers know about the individuals accused of wrongdoing?
- ✔ Should the company throw good money after bad if the allegations turn out to be false?
- ✔ Is it better to ignore the problem and hope that the allegations never become public?

Although there is no rule mandating an investigation, here are the key tools the company must use to make the decision:

- ✔ The law
- ✔ Good business judgment
- ✔ Common sense

The company management (*not* including anyone named in the accusation!) should ask its legal counsel to spell out the law related to the accusation. The next step is to walk through potential consequences to the business of choosing one path versus another. For example, here are some possible disadvantages of conducting an internal investigation:

✔ An investigation may yield damaging information that may be subject to legal discovery. In other words, if the company discovers that the accusations are true, it may be required to share its findings with the opposing party in litigation.

✔ The costs of conducting the investigation may turn out to enormous in terms of legal and forensic accounting fees, lost management and employee time, and damaged reputation.

✔ The company must be prepared to deal with the consequences if the inquiry leads to the discovery of widespread corporate misconduct.

During its deliberations, the company must also decide whether to disclose to the government the allegations and any findings from its internal investigation.

In spite of all these potential disadvantages, common sense dictates that it's almost always in the company's best interests to conduct an investigation. That's because the company can't know with any certainty whether allegations are true until an investigation is done. If the investigation reveals that the accusations are patently false, the company is in a stronger position to defend its managers, directors, or employees should the issues become public. If the investigation shows that the accusations are potentially true, the company can immediately begin taking steps to shore up its defenses against the negative publicity and damage to its reputation.

Assembling an Investigative Team

After a decision to conduct an investigation has been made, the company has to marshal its resources, consider what preliminary actions to take against the alleged wrongdoers, and secure any evidence before it can be destroyed. Then it has to determine the nature and scope of the investigation. The company should line up its investigative team immediately to help with these preliminary tasks and jump into the investigation as soon as they're completed.

Depending on the significance of the allegations and the scope of the investigation, the company should consider assembling a multidisciplinary team consisting of experienced lawyers and forensic accountants. Of course, in-house personnel need to participate as well. Here's how each of the players may contribute:

✔ **Legal counsel:** Conducting a successful investigation involves navigating through an array of legal and regulatory intricacies, pitfalls, and landmines. The investigative team consists of both the company's external and internal counsel. Experienced lawyers are well equipped to manage the various issues affecting the investigation, including issues of law and liability.

If an investigation spans multinational jurisdictions, the company needs to hire lawyers who have expertise in dealing with both U.S. and international regulators and law enforcement agencies.

✔ **Forensic accountants:** A good forensic accountant can offer advice on matters such as staffing the investigative team, defining the scope of the investigation, devising an investigative plan, conducting the investigation, reporting on the findings, and counseling on the business consequences.

A corporate investigation should be conducted by a forensic accounting team that is separate from the company. Because financial accounting investigations are their livelihood, forensic accountants are capable of deploying more resources at a faster pace than the company can. For instance, when interviewing a potential witness, an experienced investigator who has conducted numerous interviews is better suited than an employee who works for the company, such as an internal auditor.

Forensic accountants also have the requisite skills to retrieve and analyze relevant data stored electronically, including e-mails. They can even retrieve electronic information that may have been deleted. For a better understanding of the use of technology in investigations, be sure to read Chapter 15.

✔ **In-house personnel:** Often, employees in the company's human resources or security departments have roles to play in a fraud investigation. Forensic accountants may also consult the internal audit department because internal auditors have an in-depth knowledge of the company's operations, such as the organizational structure, transaction processes, and internal controls. (Past internal audits may also be a great source of information for the forensic accountant.) Internal auditors can also assist in collecting and corroborating documentation, sampling, interviewing, testing and analyzing data, and following up on matters discovered during the investigation.

Planning the Investigation

The company's goal should be to conduct a thorough investigation that will withstand future regulatory inquiries or litigation. To achieve that goal, the team should investigate all allegations of misconduct and ensure that the relevant leads are examined. Team members must interview witnesses and review relevant documents. At the same time, the investigators must be cognizant of not engaging in any wild goose chases or investigating baseless or frivolous allegations. In this section, we help you determine how to keep your focus during an investigation, and we discuss why the location of the alleged fraud matters.

You should conduct your investigation as if it will go to trial. Make sure that the entire investigation is by the book so nothing can be questioned. Make sure your research is pristine: neat, understandable, and without extraneous material.

Finding your focus

How do you figure out what to focus on and what to ignore? Before starting any investigative procedures, a forensic accountant should understand the following:

- ✔ **The exact nature of the allegations or concerns:** This helps you determine the individuals to interview and documents to secure and review.

- ✔ **The time frame when the misconduct is alleged to have occurred:** You need to establish a starting point for the investigation. As the investigation progresses, the team can decide how far back in time to go.

- ✔ **Who within the organization is alleged to be involved in the misconduct?** Is the problem confined to lower-level employees, or does management appear to be involved? Has the company taken steps to deal with these individuals? Based on what you know, do you think such individuals do or don't have incentive to cooperate with the investigation?

- ✔ **Has the company already performed a preliminary investigation into the matter?** Have reports documenting any conclusions or facts been issued? If so, review the reports to determine whether the matter was investigated satisfactorily or whether additional work may be required.

- ✔ **Has the company already self-reported or disclosed the problem to regulatory authorities?** If so, your investigation should mirror the plan that was disclosed to the authorities. You need to know whether there are any deadlines that the company must meet in investigating the matter.

- ✔ **Does the company have a documented history of similar misconduct?** How and where did the previous problems occur, who was involved, and how were they resolved?

- ✔ **The location of the alleged misconduct:** If the accusation relates to misconduct in a foreign location, you have several issues to consider to ensure a successful investigation. Keep reading to find out what we mean.

Going global

If the accusation relates to misconduct that occurred in a foreign location, you need to make sure your team can overcome any language and cultural barriers, and you need to understand the laws of the foreign jurisdiction governing the investigation. You also need to research any risks inherent in the location, such as terrorism, political instability, and health-related issues.

If you're going to conduct a foreign investigation, you should discuss country-specific issues with in-country legal resources before you begin. Doing so will help you understand what you can and cannot do in each country or region of the world. Specifically, here's what you need to find out:

✔ **Legal and employee rights:** Because laws, regulations, and employee rights are different from country to country, it's easy to get into trouble by not knowing what is and is not permissible when conducting an investigation. Do the upfront research in order to protect yourself and the company from legal risk.

✔ **Data privacy:** In certain parts of the world, such as in Europe, maintaining data privacy is critical. For instance, in Germany, you cannot access an employee's computer or review his e-mail. Obviously, you need to understand any such restrictions.

✔ **Business culture issues:** In the United States, the Foreign Corrupt Practices Act (FCPA) prohibits the payment of bribes to foreign government officials by an American company to obtain or retain business. But bribes are an accepted practice in some parts of the world. You need to understand such cultural differences before your investigation begins.

Take the time to learn about the customs of any locality where you'll be conducting interviews. And be certain to hire skilled interpreters if you don't have a member on your team who has the necessary language skills; you never want to risk misinterpretation by overinflating your estimation of your own language skills.

Developing workplans

After the investigative team has determined the scope and nature of its task, it develops a workplan that provides a roadmap for the investigation. The workplan addresses the procedures related to the specific allegations at hand. For instance, if the allegation concerns the embezzlement of cash, the workplan should focus on the company's procedures that are designed to discover this precise problem.

If the investigation is conducted in multiple locations by different teams, the workplan is shared with all the teams. The plan should be sufficiently detailed to enable the team to achieve its objectives while being flexible enough to allow team members to pursue other issues that may arise during the course of the investigation.

A workplan includes the following:

✔ Background information about the company's accounting processes and how it prepares its financial statements (information that is crucial for all team members to know)

✔ Information that needs to be gathered and preserved

✔ Documents and financial accounts to review

✔ Individuals to interview

✔ Analytical procedures to perform to narrow down the existence of the fraud

✔ Internal controls to test

Gathering and Reviewing Evidence

With a workplan in hand, the process of gathering evidence commences. A company's financial statements, books, records, and supporting financial documents are almost always going to be crucial. The investigative team must be extremely careful to preserve and store this evidence; in Chapter 15, we explain the role that technology plays in accomplishing this task.

The documents you're dealing with are sometimes physical but often electronic. Whatever form they take, you must maintain appropriate controls over any documents that you request and receive.

But documents alone usually don't cinch an investigation. In most cases, interviews provide crucial evidence as well. In this section, we also show you how to become a stellar interviewer so you can glean the right types of information.

Dealing with documents

Most likely, you'll be dealing with a wealth of electronic evidence during an occupational fraud investigation. We're talking about e-mails, computer files (including deleted and encrypted files), instant messages, electronic voicemails . . . the list goes on. The sheer volume of such evidence can be overwhelming, and it demands the strictest level of information management. Before you start tapping into your client's electronic files, you need to know exactly how you're supposed to organize, manage, and analyze the data you discover. Chapter 15 is a great introduction to working with electronic evidence; be sure to spend some quality time with it.

Here are other types of documents you want to be sure to review at the start of an investigation:

✔ The company's organizational charts

✔ Personnel listings (so you can select individuals for interviews)

✔ Audit work papers and other internal reports that may provide background information about the company's financial practices

✔ Copies of the company's trial balance and financial statements

In some cases, you may need to cross borders or even continents to gather all the documents you need. For example, the company may have operations in Africa, but its accounting operations are done in India and its data is in Europe. Part of your task is to figure out how to efficiently and effectively get the relevant information in your hands.

After you've identified the documents you need and have them in hand, your task is to review them and build a case. You must take the document review step seriously. Documents often contain a lot of potentially relevant information, some of which may not be obvious at first glance. For example, a document that doesn't seem to contain any relevant information may refer to another document that *does* contain crucial information. Or a document may contain information that seems benign unless you're giving it an eagle-eye review. For instance, an invoice submitted from a vendor that contains a P.O. Box return address should raise the question of whether the invoice is fictitious.

Bottom line: After you've jumped the necessary hoops to get the documents in your hands (or on your computer screen), take the time necessary to review them carefully. And trust that as your experience grows, you'll be able to home in on the relevant information more and more quickly.

Conducting interviews

Document review is a necessary step in any fraud investigation, but often it reveals only part of the story. Documents can be destroyed, altered, or structured to present information that suits the needs and purposes of the fraudster.

But if done correctly, a structured interview may reveal information that the forensic accounting team can use to build a more complete picture of the events preceding and following the misconduct. With that information in hand, the team can assess the credibility of the fraud allegations and circle back to obtain any relevant documentation to support them.

Just as you need to take your time to review documents thoroughly, you need to take the time to prepare yourself for interviews. Otherwise, you could derail the investigation. When you first begin a forensic accounting career, you probably want to leave the interviewing to a member of your team with more interview experience. Effective interviewing requires certain skills that come with experience. To learn how to frame and ask questions to illicit certain responses, as well as how to read body language during a response, try to spend some time with an experienced interviewer before tackling this task on your own.

You should consider the order in which you conduct your interviews. Each interview is a stepping stone to the next and helps build your knowledge of the facts. The interview of the prime suspect should be done toward the end.

Looking for information or an admission of guilt

Investigators can use many different types of interviewing techniques, and each is done with a different end purpose in mind. One thing to remember is that an interview is not an interrogation: You rarely want to be confrontational.

There are two main categories of interviews that dictate the form of the questions asked and the manner in which the interview is conducted:

✔ **The information-seeking interview:** This type is done for the purpose of obtaining additional information regarding the facts and circumstances of the case.

✔ **The admission-seeking interview:** This type of interview is trickier and requires more skill on the part of the interviewer. It's usually done when the interviewer knows the subject is guilty and is seeking to extract an admission of guilt from him. An interviewer can try to obtain an admission in several ways:

- *Direct or logical approach:* The investigator tells the interviewee what he knows and then explains to the interviewee the futility of not confessing.

- *Nondirect approach:* The interviewer allows the person being interviewed to talk openly and possibly confess. The interviewer tries to appeal to the subject's sense of morals and values.

- *Rationalization approach:* The interviewer attempts to justify the subject's behavior by providing an excuse: "You had to steal the money from the vault because you were not getting paid enough for your services."

As an interviewer, you have to determine when the chosen method isn't working and know how to switch between methods during the interview if you aren't getting the responses you seek.

Asking a variety of questions

Here are the different types of questions you can use during an interview:

✔ **Closed-ended:** You're looking for a "yes" or "no" answer, or you give the interviewee a limited number of answers to choose from. This is called a *forced choice.* The downside of this format is that the correct choice may be missing, which would means that you wouldn't uncover the evidence you're looking for.

✔ **Open-ended:** You provide very little guidance about what type of answer you're looking for. The interviewee is allowed to talk about his or her feelings in response.

✔ **Connecting:** These questions try to connect or tie details together to determine where the fraud took place.

✔ **Positive-reaction:** These types of questions are similar to closed-ended questions, but they're set up to get the person being interviewed to say "yes." They're designed to put the person being interviewed into a cooperative mood.

✔ **Clarifying:** You ask this type of question to build on a response to another question.

✔ **Secondary:** With this type of question, you repeat something the interviewee said in hopes of getting further clarification.

Here are two types of questions to avoid:

✔ **Compound:** These questions touch upon more than one issue, but allow for only one answer. (For example, "How satisfied are you with you pay and your work conditions?") The questions can be confusing, as can the answers.

✔ **Confrontational:** Obviously, you don't want to turn the interviewee off. Being confrontational may have its place during an admission-seeking interview if the subject isn't responding to other approaches, but generally you want to stay away from this approach.

You should be careful to take note not only of the responses given but also of the other verbal and nonverbal cues offered by the subject. Verbal cues include tone of voice and inflections, which could alert you to uncertainty or discomfort. Nonverbal cues include crossing the arms over the chest or crossing legs, which may convey that the interviewee is feeling closed off and is possibly hiding something.

Ensuring interview success

Here are other things to do to be an effective interviewer:

✔ Before conducting an investigative interview, prepare yourself on all the important documents and issues.

✔ Research thoroughly the background of each interviewee. Online research can be very helpful.

✔ Have a list of prepared questions to ask, but don't feel like you have to follow it precisely.

✔ Make small talk in the early part of the interview to put the interviewee at ease.

✔ Don't conduct interviews in public, such as in a noisy restaurant.

✔ When you expect the interviewee to be cooperative, schedule the session in advance. When you expect someone to be uncooperative or adversarial, conduct a surprise interview.

✔ Listen! Let the subjects talk when they want to talk.

✔ Observe and read body language.

✔ Don't put a time limit on an interview. For example, don't schedule an interview an hour before a lunch meeting; the interview may take three hours.

✔ Don't lose your temper and/or allow the interviewee to get under your skin.

✔ Don't use ploys, tricks, or lies as an interview strategy. If you're caught doing so, you'll lose credibility, making the interviewee less likely to cooperate.

✔ Consider having a witness to the interview, especially if you're going to broach issues that may be key points in court. Or, after you prepare your interview report, consider having the interviewee confirm its accuracy.

✔ Use a neutral, nondefensive, and nonaggressive approach during the interview.

✔ Seek permission from the interviewee to call him later if needed, and be sure you obtain his contact information.

✔ Obtain legal advice regarding whether or not to record any interview.

✔ Take notes during the interview, and dictate and clean them up within a day or two.

Other items to consider prior to conducting the interview include:

✔ **Timing of the interview:** Whereas you should try to accommodate the schedule of the subject, you have to be careful not to let too much time pass before conducting the interview or else you run the risk of information becoming stale or the subject forgetting relevant facts.

✔ **Location of the interview:** The ideal location for conducting an interview is a place that has few or no distractions. This way, you can focus on the subject and also control the interview.

✔ **Positioning of the interviewer and interviewee:** Studies suggest that the best place for an interviewer to sit is facing the interviewee, in between the subject and the door. This positioning makes it uncomfortable for the interviewee to walk out if he wants to.

✔ **Legal issues:** Give consideration to legal issues raised in any interview process, such as attorney-client privileges, advice to employees, and the company's obligations to employees. In addition, conducting an aggressive interview can open the company and the investigation team to legal liabilities.

✔ **Participants:** Ideally, two or more people should conduct the interview so that one can ask the questions while the other takes notes. An interview should be treated as a conversation with a purpose. Stopping to take notes of responses will disrupt the flow of the conversation. If possible, outside counsel should also be present during the interview in case legal issues arise.

Remedying the Outcome

This phase occurs either during the investigation or when it is complete. One of the important objectives of the investigation is to find remedies so that the chances of similar events occurring are minimized, if not eliminated. The forensic accountant plays the following roles during this phase:

✔ Providing litigation support to counsel in litigation proceedings

✔ Representing the company before regulatory and law enforcement agencies

✔ Quantifying damages that the company may be liable for as a result of the incident

✔ Helping the company work through the business implications of the investigation, such as possible loss of contracts if the company makes its vendor contracts stricter (to strengthen its controls and reduce the risk of future fraud)

✔ Assisting in financial recovery from the subject and other parties

✔ Conducting fraud risk assessments and compliance audits of the company to prevent the occurrence of similar misconduct

✔ Advising on strengthening necessary internal controls

✔ Monitoring business activities in the future

In Part VI, we offer details about how to advise small and large business clients on fraud prevention efforts, including assessing risk and strengthening internal controls.

Chapter 13

Tracing the Flow of Money

*W*ithin a business, cash can be manipulated in two ways: It can either be misappropriated or "created" in a company's financial statements. The first type of fraud occurs when employees or managers steal cash from a company. Small businesses are more susceptible to *defalcation* (misappropriation) of cash because they have fewer internal controls in place to detect the fraud. In large businesses, management can override the controls to perpetrate fraud.

The second type of fraud is rare and extremely difficult to carry out. The assumption here is that the cash and bank balances reported in the company's financial statements are fake. To carry this out, someone has to artificially inflate the revenues first.

This type of financial statement fraud occurred in one of the largest corporate frauds in history involving Parmalat, a multinational Italian dairy and food company. Parmalat's management fabricated invoices to inflate revenues and then "created" cash to make the inflated revenues seem genuine. Management also forged a bank confirmation showing a balance of $4.9 billion. This type of fraud is difficult to pull off without getting caught because cash is cash, and it's virtually impossible to "create" cash without raising some obvious red flags.

As a result of this fraud, Parmalat was forced to declare bankruptcy at the end of 2003. It was estimated that a billion Euros were missing. That's a lot of cheese!!

When investigating occupational fraud (and other types as well), following the money trail is essential. In this chapter, we discuss the methods you use to trace the money so you not only detect fraud, but also build a case to bring the perpetrators to justice.

Identifying Potential Red Flags

There are many red flags for missing money, and many of them dovetail with the general signs and symptoms of fraud. We focus here on occupational fraud (the subject of Part II of this book) and review some of the signs of missing cash that can be found on a company's financial statements.

Analyzing financial statement basics

As we discuss in Chapter 5, financial statements are a picture of a company's financial condition and a record of business for a certain period of time. One quick way to determine if cash is a problem (for example, it's disappearing) is to compare the company's revenues, accounts receivable, and cash flows.

In a properly functioning business, accounts receivable should grow with sales, and revenues and cash flows should be closely correlated. If sales are staying the same, and accounts receivable are up, you have to ask why. It's possible that there are collection problems or that someone is stealing cash. If sales are up, accounts receivable down, and cash flows steady, you might ask, "Where's the money?" In short: If business is up, the company should have more money. If the financial statements don't show more money, ask why. Maybe the business is extending more credit to its customers (which may or may not be a problem), or someone is walking off with the money. This basic analysis is sometimes called the *smell test:* Do the financial statements smell right?

Detecting earnings management

Earnings management is the practice of manipulating a company's income statement to achieve a desired net income. We like to call it *bottom line accounting.* A publicly traded firm may practice earnings management to please Wall Street. A closely (privately) held firm may do so to keep its lenders happy or to reduce its tax burdens. Let's talk about some ways that earnings management is done and how to spot it.

Normally, cash flows should be correlated with net income. However, when net income is being manipulated, cash flows and net income may not be correlated. A simple way to spot this problem is to graph cash flows and net income and see if the lines rise and fall together, more or less. If you're graphing these on a weekly or monthly basis, make sure to take seasonal business into account. For example, if your target's primary customer is a larger retailer, you may see heavy sales in October, November, and early December. However, you may not see the cash flows until January, February, or March.

Manipulating gross profits

The *gross profit method* of determining inventory may be used as part of this type of scheme. When a business doesn't know what the value of its inventory is, in certain circumstances it's permitted to estimate *gross profits* (net revenues less cost of goods sold) using its historical average gross profit percentage. If the business has a number for gross profit, it can then back into the cost of goods sold. If it has an ending cost of goods sold number, you can back into an estimated ending inventory number.

We saw one case of a garment manufacturer who was barely making ends meet. She relied on bank loans to keep her company afloat. To keep the bank happy, her accountant did *bottom line accounting*. He knew what he wanted the net income to be. He started with his net income and then backed into a gross profit. From there he backed into an inventory number. After just a few years, the financial reports from this small clothing manufacturer were showing that it had several hundred thousand dollars of inventory. In reality, the company had very little inventory and had no cash because it really didn't have the net income that was reported.

Estimating abnormal accruals

Abnormal accruals are another way of managing the bottom line. *Accruals* are a way of estimating expenses versus prepaid expenses, as well as estimating unearned revenues. In your basic accounting courses, your professors taught you how to collect and analyze relevant information and make good faith estimates. When management is practicing *bottom line accounting*, the estimates are skewed to what the company needs the numbers to be rather then prepared in good faith.

We saw an instance of a contractor with long-term contracts. For such contracts, generally accepted accounting principles (GAAP) require using the percentage of completion method to determine the revenue for a particular period. (If 50 percent of the contract is completed in a given financial period, 50 percent of the revenue should be booked during that period.) To determine revenue, we divide the actual costs by the estimated total costs and multiply that amount by the revenue amount in the contract. But this contractor played with the estimates. He figured out what he needed his bottom line to be and then he told his staff engineers to play with the estimated total costs. If estimated total costs went down, the current period revenue went up because there was a higher percentage of the contract completed. If estimated total costs went up, the revenue went down.

We've also seen schemes where companies purposely overestimate taxes to increase accruals and lower their bottom line. We've actually seen *cash basis companies* (those that use the cash basis of accounting to prepare financial statements and tax returns) overpay estimated taxes to their state so as to lower their federal tax burden. In the following year, they just apply to the state for a refund.

Accounting researchers have many ways to determine if a company's accruals are abnormal. If you want to find out more, ask your accounting professor or hit the library!

Looking Closely at Bank and Other Records

Bank records are a primary source of information about where money is flowing to and from. Depending on the nature of the forensic accounting engagement, you may not have easy access to bank records. But if litigation is involved, the attorney you're working with may be able to subpoena bank records.

Examining bank records and other related documents is particularly useful in occupational fraud, but it's also useful in many other types of fraud cases. The techniques we describe in this section can be used if you're looking for tax fraud, hidden assets in a matrimonial case, underreporting of income for contractual reasons, business valuation, and more.

In this section, we explain the value of regular bank reconciliations, as well as how 1099 forms and credit card statements play into forensic investigations.

Reconciling bank statements routinely

The timely performance of bank reconciliations is the number one control for cash frauds. Every business *must* establish systems to ensure that bank reconciliations don't fall through the cracks. There are two great reasons to do reconciliations in a timely manner:

✔ If a fraud is found while someone is performing the bank reconciliation, and the bank may be partially responsible, there are time limits for filing claims.

✔ In the case of an ongoing fraud, the sooner it's found, the sooner it can be stopped.

Moral of the story: Make sure your accounting clients get those bank recs done pronto!

Here are some forensic techniques to use to uncover signs of fraud while performing the bank reconciliation:

✔ **Check the endorsements.** Is each endorsement the same name as the payee? Is it the same name as in the purchase and/or disbursement journals? Was the check cashed or deposited? We've seen frauds where checks were deposited to accounts with names very similar to legitimate vendors. Most businesses deposit checks into their bank account and endorse the check with a rubber stamp. Double endorsements or cashed checks (besides payroll checks) are unusual and warrant further investigation.

Banks now send back photos of checks rather than the originals. Therefore, it's become harder to see if a check has erasures or Wite-Out. If you suspect that a check may have been altered, and the picture of the check with the bank statement is not clear enough for a determination, ask the bank if it can provide better pictures.

✔ **Look for checks made payable to "Cash."** Checks made payable to "Cash" are a problem. Although a business may sometimes cash a check to fund the petty cash fund, it's unusual for checks to be made payable for Cash. If you see this during the course of an investigation, ask questions about why checks are being written this way. If the company managers say the checks are covering expenses, ask for supporting documents.

Recently, a part owner of a scrap metal business was arrested and convicted for various fraud and tax evasion charges. The way we heard the story, he had been cashing checks to get cash to pay for scrap metal. This process is normal in that industry. However, as the story goes, he did not have any supporting documents to prove he paid for metal. Even a diary with a record of sellers and amounts may have kept him out of jail.

✔ **Look for handwritten checks.** These days, most businesses generate their checks from a computerized accounting system. It is unusual, in some entities, to see handwritten checks. Therefore, any handwritten check is cause for more investigation.

✔ **Check for (real) supporting documents.** Any item paid for by a business should have support documentation. Any payment without support is cause for concern. When examining documentation, make sure it's real! In the world of computerized accounting, verifying documentation has become more and more difficult because anyone with access to accounting software can create a bill.

✔ **Be suspicious of checks with lots and lots of zeros.** We were once called into a small plumbing business by one partner who was suspicious of his other partners. During our examination of the checkbook and bank statements, we found lots of checks with lots of zeros made out to the other two partners. When we asked about the purpose of the checks, we couldn't get an answer that made us feel comfortable about their legitimacy. During the course of our investigation we found other indications of fraud. We advised our client to retain an attorney to sue his partners. (We've since heard that there was an out-of-court settlement because the partners feared criminal prosecution for some of the frauds.)

✔ **Don't overlook commonplace expenses.** When performing a forensic examination, you may want to look more closely at seemingly innocent expenses. We rarely see auditors looking at the postage expense. If checks are made out to, and endorsed by, the U. S. Post Office, that would seem to be sufficient. But consider this story:

The management at a nonprofit agency got wind that one of its employees was running a mailing house business on the side. He was addressing, stuffing, and mailing envelopes for large mailings for businesses and other nonprofits. When they heard this, something clicked, and they realized that their postage expense had been running a bit high. They asked their auditors to do a forensic examination. The auditors found that a number of the checks to the post office were made out to the postmaster of the town where this employee lived, and not where the nonprofit agency was located.

In addition to postage, take a look at the types of expenses that someone might incur at home. If the electric bills seem too high for this business, or if there are more than 12 checks issued per electric meter, look more closely at the checks made out to the electric company. Is someone's personal electric bill also being paid from the business?

✔ **Find out who really owns the fixed assets.** If business funds are being used to purchase fixed assets, check to see that the assets are really in the business. For example, is the car that was just purchased being used by a salesperson or by the manager's wife?

We once had a client who installed boilers in large buildings and was under audit by the IRS. The IRS agent found checks made out to a local lighting store. She insisted that the owner of the business was buying chandeliers for his home. We told her that this was not so because (a) what would he do with so many chandeliers?; (b) commercial boilers run off of fuel, but the thermostat and ignition are managed by electric components; and (c) this lighting store had a division in the back that sold the electrical components that this contractor needed. She refused to believe us. We offered to take her to the store and show her the area in the back where these components were purchased. She still refused to go see. Finally, we had to make a call to her supervisor to get the issue straightened out. (Take-home lesson: You must understand the industry you are examining.)

Studying 1099 forms

U. S. tax law and regulations require that a company issue an IRS Form 1099 whenever it pays $600 or more to a noncorporation entity, for items other than inventory, and to all attorneys. As we write this book, the law is expanding to require 1099 forms for *any* entity receiving more than $600 in a year other than banks. The IRS is requiring this step in order to reduce tax fraud. It will help forensic accountants in other examinations, too!

An artful deception

During the course of a sales tax audit at an art dealership, a New York State auditor found what appeared to be suspicious shipments to the headquarters of Tyco, Inc. in Exeter, New Hampshire. The shipping charges seemed awfully small for a painting sold for about $12 million. The auditor paid a visit to the Tyco offices in Exeter. He could not find the painting anyplace in the premises. The State of New York was then able to execute a search warrant for the New York City home of Dennis Koslowski, the former CEO of Tyco, Inc. That was where they found the painting hanging. This was also the start of the unraveling of Koslowski. He ended up paying $21.2 million to New York for sales tax he had avoided paying on 13 different paintings, as well as other taxes he had evaded. And the painting investigation led to further investigation. Mr. Koslowski was found to have paid for a lot of personal expenses with Tyco monies. He ended up having to pay Tyco $97 million in restitution and about $70 million in fines. And, of course, he went to jail.

When examining a company's 1099 forms, ask management about any names that appear suspicious. We all understand payments made to trade vendors and the electric company, but what about payments to individual names? What are these people doing for the business? (Was this person really a consultant for the company, or was she someone's entertainment?)

1099s with employees' names are a cause for concern. If an employee is on payroll, he shouldn't also be getting 1099s. If board members are getting 1099s for their board membership, check that the 1099 amounts are equal to the designated fees for board members.

Any 1099s or checks issued to companies without adequate explanation deserve further investigation. Something we've done occasionally is a *corporate search.* If you know which state a corporation or LLC is organized in, you can search the corporation's office online at the state's Web site. Check the name of the person designated to accept service (such as receive legal documents and summonses). If the name shown for that corporation is a familiar one (such as the name of one of your target's board members or employees, or the spouse of a board member or employee), you need to investigate further.

A company with good internal controls should have an antinepotism policy that limits the employment of staff or board members' family members.

Cruising through credit card statements

Credit card statements are another wonderful source of information. Credit card statements often list the phone number of the vendors, so it's very easy to verify what type of business they are and what the transaction may have been.

We once did a forensic audit of a clothing manufacturer on behalf of its lender. When we looked at credit card statements, we found a lot of checks to restaurants, department stores, and retail stores, so we started to ask questions. The restaurants were explained as business entertainment. We then wanted to know why a clothing manufacturer, in the heart of midtown Manhattan, would entertain a buyer at a Fuddrucker's in New Jersey, which just happened to be in the town where the salesman lived. We got a lot of *ahems* when we asked our questions. We then asked about the department and retail store purchases. The salesman told us he was buying samples. This may have been legitimate because clothing manufacturers often buy designer clothes and then copy the design. However, we failed to see how a manufacturer of adult women's clothing would need to buy a sample at Children's Place. The bank was not happy with our findings!

Another thing to look for on credit card statements is airplane tickets. Frequent travel to locations that are known tax havens (such as the Cayman Islands and Isle of Mann) should be further investigated.

Gathering Witness Testimony

In Chapter 12, we offer lots of specific advice for becoming a great interviewer. Witness interviews, coupled with your document review, can help you trace the trail of money and spending, whether you're investigating fraud in a business or the hidden assets of a party in a divorce. If you can find the right people, you may learn a lot.

The angry girlfriend or boyfriend (or ex-husband or ex-wife)

Since "hell hath no fury like a woman scorned," you can bet that a scorned lover is a great source of information, whether in a divorce case or an occupational fraud investigation. For the person who's been scorned, tattling on the fraudster is an easy way to get payback.

If you can find a target's ex-spouse or ex-lover, ask that person about your target's spending habits. Find out where your target likes to dine and shop.

An ex may also know where there's a hidden safe with cash or assets hidden overseas.

Neighbors

Most of us have at least one neighbor who has nothing to do but sit at the window all day and watch what goes on in the neighborhood. This person is often lonely and has nothing else to do. He or she may also be the person on the block who accepts some package deliveries on behalf of other neighbors because this individual is the only one consistently at home.

When someone asks the right neighbor about the goings-on at a particular home on the block, that person may spew forth with a wealth of information. She can tell you about the regular visits by a tomato-red Ferrari, the boxes that come from Bloomingdale's, the flower deliveries, and so on. This information, together with information gathered from examining documents, helps paint a very big (and sometimes colorful) picture of the target of your investigation.

Disgruntled employees

A disgruntled employee can be the most dangerous person to a business fraudster. Such an employee may be privy to certain transactions. If he is angered or feels disrespected on the job, he can turn on his employer and do a lot of damage by revealing frauds. If you can find a disgruntled employee or ex-employee, that person can be even more valuable than an ex-girlfriend.

We were asked by an attorney to review the transactions of a new client: an electrician in an upstate New York county. He had a large operation with several trucks on the road 24/7. At one time, he gave all his electricians a raise. The bookkeeper asked if she would be getting a raise, too. The boss told her that she wasn't entitled to a raise because she was a woman, and only the men were entitled to raises. This wasn't a very smart move! The bookkeeper dropped a dime to the IRS. The next thing the electrician knew, the U.S. Attorney was knocking on his door to investigate. The only smart thing he did was box up all the financial records and bring them to his attorney. The attorney then delivered 30+ boxes of documents to our office. The attorney asked us to perform an analysis and tell him just how bad things were.

During our analysis of the business checkbooks, we found regular checks written to "Cash." The owner was writing weekly checks to himself, for cash, supposedly to reimburse out-of-pocket expenses. He was also giving his electricians smaller cash checks. There weren't any supporting documents for these expenses. We also found many, many checks payable to credit card companies, Macy's, and other department stores. In English, the check stubs were marked that these were payments for business supplies. (To Macy's?) However, there were notations in another language that indicated these checks were actually for his wife's shopping sprees. Because one of us just happened to be fluent in this language, we were able to give the attorney a detailed report on how bad it was. Had we not known the language, we would have found a translator. If the U.S. Attorney had gotten his hands on the books before us, it would have been very bad for the client because the IRS and the U.S. Attorney have access to translators for any language you can think of.

When we gave the attorney our news, he said that he would try to plea out the case (make a plea bargain deal) before the U.S. Attorney had a chance to examine the records.

Conducting a Lifestyle Analysis

Another title for this section would be "How to Afford a Mink Coat on a Poverty Level Salary." According to the Association of Certified Fraud Examiners (ACFE) *Report to the Nation 2010,* fraudsters often display warning signs that they are engaging in illicit activity. In 43 percent of cases, the perpetrators are living beyond their means. In 36 percent of fraud cases, they're experiencing financial difficulties.

An important investigative tool is the lifestyle test. Is the target of your investigation living a Bergdorf's lifestyle on a Walmart salary? If the IRS suspects this is the case, its agents may do a "garbology" investigation. After you put your garbage at the curb for pickup, your garbage becomes the property of the town. The IRS can then go through your garbage without the need for a search warrant. Its agents will look for shopping bags, price tags, and merchandise wrappings. If your garbage and your reported income don't jibe, you're in trouble.

An investigator may also just surreptitiously take photos of a target. Why are you seen in a fur coat leaving an expensive restaurant when you have reported income that qualifies you for Medicaid?

CASE FILE

Bringing down Al Capone

Alphonso Caponi (Al Capone) was born in Brooklyn, New York, to Italian immigrant parents. He dropped out of school in the sixth grade to join a gang. In 1920 he moved to Chicago, where he became involved in organized crime including prostitution, *bootlegging* (the illegal sale of alcohol during prohibition), and gambling. When then-mob boss Johnny Torrio

retired in 1925, Capone became the boss of organized crime in Chicago.

In addition to Capone's usual crimes, police also believed that Capone was the mastermind behind the Valentine's Day Massacre. On February 14, 1929, four men (two dressed as policemen) entered a garage that was used as a liquor warehouse by the Bugs Moran Gang. The four men came with machine guns and let loose 150 bullets, killing six of the seven men working there. Despite all the serious crimes alleged to have been committed by Capone, police at the time weren't able to get him for more than illegal gun possession.

However, IRS Intelligence Unit watchdog Elmer Irey was closely watching Capone. Capone was reputed to have been making $100 million yearly from his various criminal operations. He lived a lavish lifestyle, yet he did not report any income or pay income taxes. Capone was smart, sly, and slippery. None of the assets reputed to be his were in his name. All his purchases were done through agents. Irey was not deterred and kept his men on Capone's tail. The major exception to Capone's asset-less life was his purchase of a 14-room estate on Palm Island in Biscayne Bay in 1928. Capone's wife, Mae, also went on a huge shopping spree at that time. Irey knew that Capone couldn't afford the mansion and a shopping spree unless he had a huge source of income.

While Irey was watching Capone's spending, the FBI's Chicago office put Elliot Ness on the Capone case. A free Al Capone was a thorn in the side of FBI Director J. Edgar Hoover. He charged his men with the importance of getting Capone behind bars. In 1930, Irey sent an agent into deep cover in the Capone organization. Agent Frank Wilson got very lucky when he overheard two of Capone's men talking about how stupid the IRS was because they had Capone's books and didn't do anything with them. Apparently, in a raid on a Capone business site several years earlier, the Feds had removed mountains of documentation, including bookkeeping records. The bookkeeping records were in code and in a handwriting not recognized by the IRS. Wilson casually asked about what happened to the bookkeepers. They apparently had left Capone's Chicago operation

for other places. Wilson's information led Irey to the bookkeepers, who agreed to help Irey decipher the ledgers.

After Irey was able to decipher the ledgers, he had Capone! During the early part of 1931, U.S. Attorney George E.Q. Johnson had grand juries hand up indictments against Capone and some of his men for failure to report and pay income tax and for violation of prohibition. Capone faced 34 years in jail. Because some of the crimes were past the statute of limitations, Johnson was worried that the indictments and possible subsequent convictions would not withstand Supreme Court scrutiny. He agreed to a plea bargain where Capone would serve only two years. Capone boasted proudly about the light sentence, and the press was angry about it. Judge James Wilkerson was also incensed and announced that he was free to hand down any sentence he chose. Capone revoked his plea deal and pleaded not guilty.

While waiting for the trial to start, Capone got busy bribing potential jurors. When he arrived in court on the morning of October 6, 1931, he was extremely confidant and cocky. Then Judge Wilkerson surprised everyone. He announced that another judge had a trial starting that day and that he and the other judge would switch jury panels. No one on the new jury had ever been approached by Capone's men with bribe money. During the less-than-two-week trial, the U.S. Attorney showed the jury Capone's flamboyant lifestyle, and Capone couldn't explain how he supported it. Capone was convicted and sentenced to 11 years in prison. He served in various federal penitentiaries, including Alcatraz.

Capone was released in 1939 because he was extremely ill with an advanced case of syphilis. He died in his Florida estate as a powerless recluse in 1947.

Chapter 14

Going to the Source: Obtaining Records

In This Chapter

▶ Playing private investigator: locating relationships and assets

▶ Detecting public and business records online

▶ Learning background investigation search tips

▶ Steering clear of trouble when conducting background searches

*I*magine picking up one end of a long rope. You know that at the other end of that rope, which you cannot yet see, is the misappropriated money you are tasked with trying to find. As you follow the rope, the end may become frayed and splay off into different directions. A good forensic accountant collects all the frayed pieces and diligently follows the rope to its other end.

Tracing the flow of money, for instance, inevitably yields the names of *payees*: individuals or businesses that have received money or some other form of compensation. These parties will be the subjects of your investigation. Understanding who these payees are and how they relate to each other, as well as to other individuals and entities, assists you in uncovering the fraud scheme.

Conducting background investigations, with an initial focus on public records, is a key component to any forensic accounting investigation. It is a useful way to discreetly obtain information without tipping off subjects that they're on your radar. The information obtained from background investigations helps you narrow your list of potential suspects. It may also help you identify recoverable assets.

For example, some simple preliminary background research could uncover that an individual has several tax liens filed against him, recently filed for personal bankruptcy, or had several judgments filed against him by healthcare providers. These financial difficulties could certainly put that individual on your list of subjects to be investigated because they may explain the motive behind a fraud. Having information in hand about a subject's background is also enormously helpful when it comes time further down the road in your investigation to interview the subjects or other relevant parties.

Identifying Relationships and Assets: Background Investigations

In a forensic accounting investigation, you come across some natural or obvious targets: individuals who had access to or control over funds, and businesses or individuals that received significant sums of money. You should investigate the backgrounds of the most logical subjects first and then expand the scope of your investigation to include less obvious subjects, if necessary. Background investigations play a key part in finding assets lost due to fraudulent acts, such as assets that have been misappropriated.

To help identify your targets, you should keep in mind the *fraud triangle*: motive, opportunity, and rationalization (see Chapter 1). An example of *motive* could be that an employee has encountered some type of financial hardship (a spouse who lost a job, a college education to pay for, or gambling debts, for example). The *opportunity* part could be that the business that employs this individual has weak internal controls and a system that allows for one person to direct payments without being detected. The *rationalization* angle could be that the fraudster believes he is entitled to the money he is stealing because he is underpaid, or he believes that he will eventually repay the money.

Figuring out relationships

When conducting an investigation, identifying relationships among individuals — and among individuals and entities — is often critical. Conducting background investigations and obtaining public records that corroborate the relationships is a necessary part of most forensic accounting investigations and may contribute to unraveling the fraud.

Assume that you are called in to investigate a potential fraud at Ace Computer Co., which has been losing $1 million annually for the past three years. The following are examples of the types of significant relationships that could be identified in background investigations:

- The vice president of Ace Computer Co.'s accounts payable department lives on the same street as the owner of Computer Shell, Inc., who just received a large payment from Ace. The vice president is also listed in the corporate registration records as a director of Computer Shell, Inc.

- Computer Shell, Inc.'s owner has a bio on the company Web site that states he graduated from Penn State University in 1982, which coincidentally is the same year as the employee at Ace Computer who manages the corporate bank accounts.

- The contact person for Computer Shell, Susie Smith, is the maiden name of the wife of an employee in Ace Computer's accounts payable department.

✓ Ace Facilitator LLC was formed in New York only a month before it began receiving payments from Ace Computer, and Ace Facilitator appears to have only one client: Ace Computer Company.

Focusing on assets

Locating assets held in the names of individuals and entities can quickly help narrow the list of possible fraud suspects by shining a spotlight on those who are living beyond their apparent financial means. For example, an employee earning a $60,000 salary who purchases a new Mercedes and a $2 million home in the Hamptons should raise a red flag to the investigator. In the area of asset recovery, background investigations can point the forensic accountant in the direction of misappropriated funds and hidden assets that may ultimately be recovered.

Investigating the asset profile of payees is a logical component of any background investigation. If $3 million was paid to Ace Facilitator LLC, obviously you want to gather more information about Ace Facilitator. Who owns the business? When was it formed? What does the business do? You may determine that Ace Facilitator does not have an actual business location, only a post office box. You may also discern that a former business partner of an employee at Ace Computer is listed as an officer on the incorporation records of Ace Facilitator. Or you may discover that Ace Facilitator has recently acquired multiple parcels of property in its name.

In investigating a Ponzi scheme, Eureka Forensic Accountants uncovered an outgoing wire of several million dollars from one of the corporate bank accounts to a law firm. An auditor might check the flow of funds and trace it to the underlying records, but a forensic accountant will ask many questions about the payment. In this instance, background investigations of the owner and his family members revealed a luxury apartment owned in the name of one of the owner's sons. A review of deed and mortgage documents showed that the property was purchased right around the time the money was wired to the law firm. These documents also proved that the name of the law firm that handled the property transaction was the same as the payee firm, and that the purchase price of the apartment was the same as the amount wired to the law firm.

Locating Corporate and Business Records Online

Public records are documents recorded by city, county, state, or federal agencies that are available to the general public for free or for an administrative fee. In this section, we explain what records are available and the databases you use to access them.

Knowing the types of records available

Some of the categories of public record information include:

- ✔ Secretary of State and other business registration records
- ✔ Real property ownership records (deeds and mortgages)
- ✔ Motor vehicle registrations
- ✔ Aircraft and watercraft ownership records
- ✔ Criminal records (state and federal)
- ✔ Civil litigation filings (state and federal)
- ✔ Bankruptcy filings
- ✔ Tax liens (state and federal)
- ✔ Regulatory filings (such as SEC filings)
- ✔ News media

You can also look at *judgments* — court orders stating that a person (the *plaintiff*) who sued someone else (the *defendant*) is in the right. A judgment issues the method to right the wrong (such as fines), the actions required from the defendant in order to correct the violation, or the amount of money the defendant needs to pay the plaintiff.

In addition, you can look at *Uniform Commercial Code (UCC) filings.* The UCC was created in an attempt to harmonize laws governing sales and other commercial transactions in all 50 states. The UCC Section is the central filing office for certain financing statements and other documents.

And you must be aware of *watch lists,* which are available from multiple sources. One source to consider is a list created by the Office of Foreign Assets Control (OFAC) of the U.S. Department of the Treasury, which administers and enforces economic and trade sanctions based on U.S. foreign policy and national security goals. The Specially Designated Nationals (SDN) list is an OFAC publication that reflects individuals and organizations with whom U.S. citizens and permanent residents are prohibited from doing business.

Other watch lists name *politically exposed persons* (PEPs). This term refers to people who have been entrusted with prominent public functions, such as politicians and government officials, and individuals closely related to those people. By virtue of their positions and the influence they hold, PEPs present a higher risk for potential involvement in bribery and corruption. Companies have to continuously identify PEPs for purposes of protecting against money laundering, foreign bribery, terrorism, and illicit financing. DowJones and World Compliance are two organizations that provide online databases containing information about PEPs.

An in-house investigative unit or outside investigative firm will also have access to information that is not fully "public" but that is provided to licensed investigators as part of a package of database offerings. This information would include someone's address history, residential and mobile telephone numbers, motor vehicle information, and credit reports — all of which provide useful information in background investigations. Due to various data privacy and consumer protection laws, including the Driver's Privacy Protection Act (DPPA) and the Gramm-Leach-Bliley Act (GLBA), licensed investigative groups sign contracts with database providers that require them to indicate a "legal permissible purpose" under the Fair Credit Reporting Act (FCRA) when accessing certain types of information.

Feeling the love for databases

If you are a forensic accountant and your calculator is your best friend, online databases should be your second best friend. That's because most public records are now aggregated and compiled by various database providers into searchable databases to which you can subscribe. These database aggregators are useful tools that allow you to efficiently and easily conduct nationwide or even global searches for any public record of your subjects. (They save you the time and expense of having to visit courthouses to search their records, checking every state government Web site for the information they contain, and so on.)

Most of the subscription databases charge fees to allow access. If the firm you are working for does not maintain an in-house investigative unit with subscriptions to these services, you may need to contract with an outside reputable third-party firm that routinely performs background research on individuals and entities.

Realizing what a database can do for you

Two of the most attractive aspects of these online databases are their efficiency and their breadth of coverage. For example, they provide the ability to find in a matter of seconds a business anywhere in the United States that names your subject as an officer, director, registered agent, or owner. Using such a database avoids the cumbersome task of having to search each individual state's Secretary of State Web site.

The online databases also tend to offer greater functionality than government-maintained Web sites. For example, an individual state's Web site listing corporate records may allow you only to search for business names in that state. But what if you don't know the business name and have only the names of individuals? The business databases in some online databases allow you to search by an individual's name, by a business name, and by an address. Similarly, when searching for assets, instead of having to guess the jurisdictions in which a subject may have purchased property, some databases allow you to search the entire United States for property in that person's name. And if you become aware of suspicious locations during your investigation, the databases allow you to easily search by address to identify the owners of those locations.

Several of the online databases have the ability to use *Boolean search logic,* which increases the likelihood that you are capturing all the information possible on a particular subject. Boolean search logic allows you to search name variations. For example, if your subject is formally named Elizabeth Smith, and you are looking for business records naming her as an officer or director, your search could be constructed like this:

(Elizabeth or Liz! or Beth or Bets!) w/3 Smith

The "!" at the end of the words would make sure you captured "Liz" and "Lizzy" and "Betsy" or "Betsey." The "w/3" stands for "within three words of" and allows for one or more middle names.

Because "Smith" is such a common last name, you may still receive hundreds of results, but you can then further narrow your search by focusing on areas where you know she has lived or worked:

((Elizabeth or Liz! or Beth or Bets!) w/3 Smith) and (New York or Boston or Miami)

Having access to these online databases allows you to cast a wide net for useful information, which typically yields key pieces of the puzzle and provides a higher degree of confidence that you have covered all the bases. The results often give you solid investigative leads in identifying significant relationships and assets so you can zero in on potential suspects in the fraud and safely eliminate others.

Avoid the Google trap! Budding forensic accountants not reading this chapter may believe that all you have to do when conducting a background investigation is type a name into Google and voilà — anything there is to know about a person or business will be revealed. Not true. Whereas trolling the Internet is necessary in any investigation, the results are random and haphazard. Online databases offer you the ability to perform organized and comprehensive searches in key areas, such as businesses, assets, litigation, criminal records, and media.

Working with subscription databases

Although many of the databases we list in this section have a great deal of overlap in coverage, some provide information that others don't, and each offers a particular way of accessing the information. Therefore, you may find it advantageous to use one database over another during a particular investigation. To conduct thorough background investigations of subjects with a high degree of confidence, ideally you want to have access to multiple database aggregators because they complement each other.

For example, the media-searching portion of Lexis may offer access to certain publications not covered by Factiva, and vice versa. If you are searching for any businesses affiliated with your subject, Lexis and Westlaw offer the most comprehensive coverage for Secretary of State records and other business registration filings. But after you have identified those businesses, you would likely then proceed to conducting a search in Dun & Bradstreet to obtain more detailed information on each entity.

Here are some of the most frequently used databases:

- **Mergent:** Mergent Online is a database that provides information on company financials, description, history, subsidiaries, officers, and directors. Its search capabilities are combined with access to risk ratings, credit information, and recommendations under one platform. The online content includes:

  - **U.S. Company Data:** Consists of a fully searchable database with financial details of 25,000 active and inactive companies

  - **International Company Data:** Provides access to companies representing over 95 percent of non-U.S. market capitalization

  - **Global Annual Reports:** Contains over 300,000 annual reports from globally listed companies

  - **Corporate Family Tree:** Contains information on direct and indirect subsidiaries and percentage of ownership in these subsidiaries

  - **Executive Profile:** Features over 200,000 executive profiles from all U.S. publicly traded companies, including biographies, compensation, and performance

- **Lexis** and **Westlaw:** These two databases are competitors, but we discuss them together here because they have a lot in common. Both databases provide access to several categories of public record information. For example, they both have people-finder databases that allow you to identify or locate individuals across the United States. They also provide access to the other categories of public information including business registration records, state and federal litigation, tax liens, judgments, UCC filings, assets, government watch lists, voter registration records, and news media.

  Both Lexis and Westlaw evolved from legal databases that were used by attorneys performing legal research. Therefore, they both include extensive information on case law and reported decisions. They also offer other categories of information such as a Social Security death master index, which allows you to confirm whether someone with a certain Social Security number is alive or dead.

✔ **Accurint** and **LocatePlus:** Again, these two databases are competitors. (Accurint is owned by Lexis.) But they're both referred to as *identifier* databases because they are often an investigator's first stop to try to identify or locate individuals or businesses. You can enter a name and a state; and each database will give you the names, Social Security numbers, and addresses of all the individuals with that name in that state. Or you can enter a street address to see what individuals or entities are associated with a particular address. Or you can enter a Social Security number to determine the name of the person to whom it is issued.

One unique aspect of these databases is that by running a full report on an individual you typically receive a full address history, the names of relatives and neighbors, and the names of other individuals who have addresses in common with your subject. Both databases also let you search concealed weapons permits, professional license information, aircraft registration, driving records, and some court filings, real property ownership information, and Secretary of State records.

✔ **Dun & Bradstreet (D&B):** D&B offers information on businesses globally, including location, date of formation, sales figures, credit information, banking relationships, corporate hierarchy, and the names of key management personnel. The caveat is that not all businesses are covered, and the information is largely self-reported by each business. For example, a business could report that its latest year's sales were $2 million, but this number could be factually incorrect because D&B does not independently verify the information.

One aspect of D&B that is particularly useful in forensic accounting and background investigations is the ability to search by an address or a telephone number to see what business(es) are associated with those identifiers. The History portion of the D&B reports also provides background information on the officers or directors of the business, which may yield previously unknown affiliations with your subject. The D&B report also typically indicates the Standard Industry Classification (SIC) code for a business, so you can learn what line of business the entity purports to be in.

✔ **Factiva:** This database, owned by the news corporation DowJones, offers the ability to search literally thousands of newspapers, journals, and trade publications for any mention of your subject. It also allows for searching in foreign language publications. As the world becomes smaller, and corporate investigations become more global in nature, having access to media from around the world is vital to obtaining relevant background information.

✓ **PACER:** PACER is an acronym for Public Access to Court Electronic Records. It provides online nationwide access to court documents filed at the federal level, including civil, criminal, and bankruptcy filings. You can search by a case number or a party name. If you find your subject named as a plaintiff or defendant, you can obtain a copy of the docket, which will tell you the status of the matter and list the filings. Most docket reports in PACER offer you the ability to hyperlink to specific filings including the complaint, various motions, and final dispositions.

Searching SEC records

EDGAR (the Electronic Data Gathering, Analysis, and Retrieval system) is a free database (no subscription required!) that contains more than 500,000 company records that are publicly filed with the U.S. Securities and Exchange Commission (SEC). It allows you to search for basic company information, such as company name, address, and fiscal year end, as well as more in-depth information. For example, a company's registration statement includes descriptions of its properties, securities for sale, management information, and financial statements. Company disclosure filings can also include comments and response letters from government agencies.

The EDGAR database provides access to all the SEC filings relating to publicly traded companies. Information that may be useful in a background investigation may be found in a company's annual (10-K) or quarterly (10-Q) financials, including the names of officers or directors, parent companies, or subsidiaries. Other SEC filings that could provide information useful to your background investigations include *13-Ds,* which would indicate a subject's beneficial ownership of 5 percent or more in a publicly traded company; and *8-Ks,* which are notifications of a company's "material events" (such as acquiring or selling a subsidiary).

Take the following steps to use this database:

✓ Go to the EDGAR Web site at www.sec.gov.

✓ Read the EDGAR Guide for Investors and the FAQs on how to use the database.

✓ Try EDGAR's Next-Generation Full-Text search engine for company filings from the past four years. Enter a company name for a simple search, or do a more focused search by clicking the Advanced Search option.

✓ Try an advanced full-text search. With this option, you can search for broader company info by selecting a Standard Industrial Classification. You can also search for specifics via Central Index Key (CIK) numbers, which are assigned to companies and individuals by the SEC.

Background Investigation Search Tips

Now that you know about the various sources of public information, we want to offer you some search tips. This section is your introductory guide to conducting online searches.

Follow a logical searching order

It often makes sense to first locate the people who are subjects in your investigation. Knowing where a subject currently resides and where he lived in the past helps focus your searches in other areas and ensures you are not missing relevant information because you failed to search in all the right locations. For example, learning that a New York-based subject resided in Los Angeles seven years ago could lead you to a prior criminal record filed in California, along with litigation alleging fraud, which may indicate a pattern of prior fraudulent activity involving your subject.

If you discover that your subject has lived in Los Angeles, conduct searches for any business records filed in that area that might name your subject as an officer, director, registered agent, or owner. A search for litigation, tax liens, judgments, and regulatory filings should then be conducted in the name of the individual, as well as for any businesses with which he is connected. You should then conduct searches on all these same names in asset files for any real property, vehicles, boats, and planes. Lastly, make sure to conduct searches in news articles, journals, and trade publications for any mention of the individual and/or the business entities.

Verify the information you already have

Typically in forensic accounting investigations it is possible to review the personnel files of internal employees who are the subjects of your investigation. Reading the subject's initial employment application (which may include a credit report), his résumé, and performance reviews is a great starting point and could yield useful clues that may factor into your investigation as it progresses. A healthy dose of skepticism is sometimes warranted:

- ✔ Did he really get the MBA from Harvard that is listed on his résumé? Call the registrar's office of Harvard University to verify the degree. (Because degree verification is currently commonplace, many colleges and universities now require that inquiries go through a service called the National Student Clearinghouse: www.studentclearinghouse.org.)

- ✔ Why did he work for so many firms over such a short period of time? Call former employers and verify dates of employment.

✔ If he says he was the owner of a prior business, was that business ever sued? Conduct online searches in state- and federal-level court records to identify any prior litigation. The opposing parties in litigation may provide valuable insight about the subject you are investigating.

✔ If a subject's employment agreement allows for the employer to obtain credit reports, consider going through the proper channels to obtain a recent credit report. This often provides clues regarding a subject's personal financial stability.

If at first you don't succeed . . .

You should expect that the prime suspect in a fraud investigation is not going to wire money directly from the company he works for into a bank account in his name. You will not always be able to waltz right in and find all the evidence displayed out in front of you. Where's the fun in that, anyway? On occasion, you need to go through the back door. You may find that you have only random, disparate pieces of information — also known as clues!

If you are not finding results using a person's name or business name, use other pieces of information you already do have and work backward, or reverse your searches. Search by business or residential addresses, by telephone numbers, or by Social Security numbers to see what names are connected to those bits of information. A telephone number might link to more than one business entity, or a Social Security number may have been issued to a deceased person. If you are searching by a company name and cannot find a match, searching by the address may reveal that the name was spelled wrong in the database: for example, Turkan, Inc., instead of Turkam, Inc.

Perseverance is the investigator's greatest tool. Do not give up easily; be diligent about your searches.

Peel back the layers

Many fraudsters who misappropriate money assume they will never get caught, or they have every intention of ultimately returning the money. Therefore, some do not go to great lengths to cover their tracks. But more clever fraudsters attempt to conceal their transactions by creating layers of companies to hide assets, or they put assets in the names of others. When conducting an investigation, you need to think like a bad guy when hunting for clues. For example, when searching for assets, do not forget to search under the names of business entities connected to the subject, or under the subject's spouse's name, children's names, or maiden name.

If what you uncover begs another question, keep going! Remember, your goal is to follow the rope to its other end. For example, if you dig into the background of a suspect company only to discover that it is owned by yet another company and no individuals' names are mentioned, take the next step to research who is behind the second company. It may be one of your individual subjects or someone with whom he or she has a business or familial relationship. The extra step taken is critical in forensic investigations and often yields the best results.

An investigator looking for hidden assets in a recent global fraud investigation identified a company that listed L. Nominees in Gibraltar as the corporate secretary. No other names of people or entities were listed. Further investigation revealed L. Nominees was wholly owned by L. Asset Management, which was in turn wholly owned by L. Holding Company. And L. Holding Company was owned by Runaway Trust in the British Virgin Islands (BVI). Obtaining information from the BVI about the owners of an entity is difficult without a subpoena, but just knowing that an entity has so many suspicious off-shore layers is a clue in itself.

Keep in mind that a conspicuous lack of information is considered useful information and perhaps indicative of fraudulent activity. For example, an entity receiving a significant amount in payments would be expected to have a physical address, actual operations, a Web site, a Dun & Bradstreet report, and a registration filed with the Secretary of State's office. A lack of this type of information may suggest the business is just a fraudulent shell that exists in name only.

Avoiding Investigative Pitfalls

Unfortunately, background investigations are not all simple or foolproof. Investigations require thought, curiosity, and some creative thinking. There are a few inherent pitfalls in conducting public records research that could greatly alter your results if you are not aware of them. Here, we offer a few words of caution to guide you in your investigative efforts.

Double- and triple-sourcing your information

You shouldn't rely on a single source for information about your subject. Here's why:

✔ **Online databases have limited coverage:** When conducting searches on online databases, keep in mind that not every record in every public record category may be available online in a particular source. In certain instances, some records may not be available online at all. For example, civil litigation filings for some counties in some states are not available in database aggregators. Real property ownership coverage is not available online for every county in every state, and only select states offer criminal records online.

✔ **Human error comes into play:** Even though several of the online databases purport to have the same coverage, invariably one database will have a record that another may not. Also, keep in mind that some of the information contained in these databases was entered in by people, and thus occasionally you run across inaccuracies in the records. An address could be one digit off, or the spelling of a subject's name one letter off. To be thorough in your investigation, conduct the same searches in multiple databases to ensure you are not inadvertently missing relevant pieces of the puzzle.

✔ **Jurisdictional coverage varies:** Coverage of public records also varies by country, and learning what is available in the country you are searching in is necessary before you begin investigating your subjects there. For example, Austria does not make its court records public, although the parties in the litigation often "leak" information about these matters to the media. Criminal records are infrequently available in non-U.S. jurisdictions. Corporate registry records are available in many countries, but you can typically only search by an entity name, making it difficult to uncover other entities with which your subject may be affiliated. The same holds true for property records: You can search by an address but not always by an owner's name. And in many of these countries, although the information may in fact be "public," it may not be available online in a database. Hiring record retrievers to manually search through records in relevant jurisdictions often is necessary outside the United States.

Going to the source

When you find information you think will be relevant to your investigation, you always want to trace it back to its source to verify its accuracy. In the previous section of this chapter, we explain how great online database aggregators are. Well, here comes the qualifier: Online databases are a great starting point for researching the backgrounds of individuals and companies, but they aren't the ending point. They are like springboards that help you advance to the next phase of your investigation. Don't rely on them as evidence. Whenever possible, you should obtain the actual source document.

For example, an online record from a database may tell you that your subject is the defendant in three civil court cases filed within the last few years. You would be remiss if you did not then take the next step and obtain copies of the complaint, the docket, and the final disposition. These documents may provide leads to other assets or describe a previous scheme or pattern of fraudulent behavior. The documents may also reveal the names and details about other parties in litigation who you might want to consider contacting as your investigation progresses.

As another example, an online nationwide search of Secretary of State records may identify your subject as an officer in a company based in Connecticut. Next, you should go to the Connecticut Secretary of State Web site to search by the company name to verify the date of formation, status, and any other information provided. Then, obtain a copy of the actual corporate documents from the Secretary of State's office. These documents may provide additional information including the stated purpose of the company's organization, other officer names, and additional addresses. Importantly, these underlying documents may also contain signatures that could be useful for comparison purposes with other internal documents uncovered in your investigation.

There are networks of record retrievers in the United States and globally whose sole business is obtaining copies of source documents including business registration records, litigation, property records, and other filings. However, before going that route you should feel free to pick up the phone and "smile and dial." In many instances, you can identify the source agency on the Internet and call the agency yourself to request copies of underlying documents.

If it's practical, you should also consider going to see first-hand the locations that are relevant to your investigation. (Trench coat and fedora are optional.) If you and the subjects you are investigating are located in the same city, a site visit could be illuminating. A visit to an office location of a business that has received substantial payments may reveal that it is in fact a residence, not an office building, and that the "suite number" is actually just an apartment number. Or, if the location is in a legitimate office building, the receptionist of the building may tell you that the business has no physical space but just receives mail there, or that the business abruptly packed up and moved recently (perhaps to avoid detection!).

A visit to a subject's apartment building may reveal an opulent residence well beyond his financial means or, conversely, a dilapidated apartment in the projects. The doorman or a neighbor in the building may be willing to tell you a bit about the subject, or you may discover names of other individuals or entities on the list of tenants that may have some relevance in your investigation. You can write down and later research the license plates of vehicles found in a driveway at a residence or office location because the owners of these vehicles may also be relevant. You should compare the information you have gleaned from site visits with what you already know "on paper" about the subject.

Using Internet searches (with caution)

Earlier in the chapter, we explain that you can't just put a subject's name into Google and think your investigation is complete. However, you should not forego searching the Internet. Although databases are a good starting point and offer the ease and efficiency of organized searching, you should also conduct general Internet searches. Findings on the Internet are always a good complement to your targeted public record searches and help ensure a thorough and comprehensive background investigation. Without them, you may miss a key piece of your investigative puzzle.

General Internet searching can yield useful pieces of information that would not otherwise be obtained from public record database searches. Social networking sites such as Linked-In, ZoomInfo, and Facebook can provide clues as to where a subject is currently employed, where he lives, who his "friends" are, or other affiliations. Searches on Bing or GoogleMaps will allow you to view what a particular property looks like and can be useful in "seeing" the location of a business or a home without having to actually go there.

The *whois* Web site (www.whois.net) allows domain name searching on Web sites to identify the underlying site owners. If your subject has been clever enough to keep his name from appearing in Secretary of State records or in the Dun & Bradstreet database or on a company Web site, uncovering that he was the person who established the domain name for the Web site of a suspicious entity could be particularly useful. Another Web site, www.internetarchive.org, allows you to search for previous versions of Web sites or Web sites that no longer exist.

Staying legal

Some investigators get so caught up in the thrill of the chase that they will stop at nothing to find out the information they need. Because you will likely be working at the request of a client, and your work will certainly be recorded and possibly become part of future litigation, staying within the boundaries of the law is imperative. After all, your goal is to continue being a forensic accountant — not to end up in prison with the fraudsters you are chasing!

The forensic investigator should always conduct his investigation with the thought that the case will go to trial. To reiterate, follow the law in all circumstances!

It is critical to be aware of the laws in the jurisdiction in which you are conducting your investigation. When in doubt, ask the general counsel of your employer for advice or the law firm that hired you to perform the investigation. Some tips to keep in mind:

✔ Do not misrepresent yourself by claiming to be someone you are not.

✔ Do not go "dumpster diving" through the garbage bins in the backyard of a subject's house.

✔ Do not trespass on private property or break other laws to obtain information.

✔ Do not threaten or intimidate a subject of your investigation or hold that person against his will.

✔ Do not illegally record conversations. Several states require two-party consent, and it is illegal in *all* states to record a conversation to which you are not a party.

Taking the Next Steps

After you have discreetly completed your search for background information on your subjects, you may need to open up the investigation to the next phase and go beyond public record or other document review. This step would entail interviewing opposing parties in litigation, former employers, colleagues, neighbors, and ultimately the subjects themselves. Knowing key facts about a subject's background will allow you to conduct thorough and useful interviews — and to better determine if someone is being truthful.

Chapter 15

Tapping into Electronic Evidence

. . . .

In This Chapter

▷ Comprehending the scope of electronically stored information (ESI)

▷ Making sure ESI is properly preserved

▷ Collecting and processing data

▷ Performing complex data analysis

. . . .

*T*echnology is everywhere in a company's life, from electronic accounting systems and financial records to e-mail or instant messages both within and outside the organization Companies create a *lot* of data, including customer information, supplier data, product blueprints, and accounting files. The data grows by leaps and bounds every year. With this growth comes the challenge of collecting, processing, and preserving the data should an investigation require analyzing or reviewing that data.

Electronically stored information (ESI) is an extremely valuable source of evidence in financial fraud investigations. Corporate financial systems are sophisticated electronic systems that document and monitor everything from payroll and expense reimbursements to large accounts receivable and inventory write-downs. Financial fraudsters often make use of sophisticated technology in their schemes.

As a forensic accountant, knowing where the relevant electronic evidence resides can help you develop an appropriate and efficient review plan. Whether you're looking for a fraudulent journal entry within a complex general ledger system or an e-mail communication discussing kickbacks, you need to take the whole universe of available electronic information into account as you develop the scope of an investigation.

You also need to know how to prevent a company from "losing" information relevant to your investigation. And to make certain that the electronic evidence you discover can be used by your client (in court or any other setting), you have to properly collect and process that evidence.

Advanced forensic technology tools come into play with the topics we discuss in this chapter, and we just scratch the surface here. The take-home point is that you need to spend time learning how to locate, collect, and analyze financial records, e-mails, and any other electronic communications. Doing so can allow you to uncover the story of *who* knew *what* and *when* during a fraud investigation. If you decide that this subject matter is your cup of tea, you may decide to become one of the computer gurus or electronic data processing (EDP) auditors who specialize in the type of data retrieval we discuss here. If not, at least you'll be able to hold your own when working with such an expert.

Defining Electronically Stored Information (ESI)

According to the *Federal Rules of Civil Procedure* (a set of rules that govern civil lawsuits in U.S. district courts), electronically stored information (ESI) is information that is created, manipulated, stored, and utilized in digital form through the use of computer hardware and software. There are two types of ESI found in an organization: structured and unstructured ESI.

Structured ESI

Structured ESI refers to information that you can find within the electronic systems that are usually used to maintain a company's financial transaction data or other systems. Examples include general ledger systems such as Oracle Financials and SAP, human resources systems such as PeopleSoft, and proprietary databases such as inventory tracking systems.

Typically, structured ESI is a highly accessible source of evidence for a fraud investigation. Depending on the size and complexity of an organization, the majority of this information likely resides in a single location that is centrally managed by a company's information technology (IT) department.

Whereas this information is relatively easy to locate, it may be extremely difficult to review and analyze. Here's why:

- ✔ A company has a *lot* of data related to its financial transactions.
- ✔ The database may be very complex.

These days, the systems that track a company's financial transactions are sophisticated, and they tend to grow exponentially as the organization grows or utilizes additional modules or features. As a result, you can spend a lot of time trying to conduct a broad analysis of a company's transactions — an analysis that isn't focused on a particular issue, timeframe, or organizational segment. This fact can be particularly problematic during the early stages of an investigation when you're still trying to define the key issues you need to focus on.

Structured data is rich with information and provides an enormous amount of evidence to aid in the fact-finding stage of the investigation. Although most of the available information can be accessed through a *user interface* (the system by which you interact with the data through the use of hardware and software components), you shouldn't ignore other behind-the-scenes data elements that can be helpful as well. For example, you want to pay attention to statistics that provide the timing of each record entry and the user who entered the information.

Unstructured ESI

The phrase *unstructured ESI* refers to data that does not have an assigned format, such as audio, video, and text documents. Examples include electronic files such as Microsoft Office documents (including memos, letters, and spreadsheets), text typed into the body of e-mails, instant messages, and electronic voicemails.

Unstructured ESI is often spread throughout an organization, which makes it difficult to locate and quantify its volume. For example, whereas a typical e-mail environment has a centrally managed server, additional e-mails very likely exist elsewhere in the company's electronic infrastructure. Old e-mails may be archived in locations off the main server to preserve hard drive space and increase speed and efficiency. Employees may store other electronic files in multiple locations as well.

Because unstructured ESI is amorphous, you have to develop a systematic approach so you can preserve, collect, index, and review the files. If you discover great information during your investigation but don't document it properly, your efforts may be in vain.

Unstructured ESI can be a tremendous asset during a fraud investigation. That's because in addition to containing relevant facts, these files can also be examined for metadata. *Metadata* is information that is not readily visible to users, such as information as to when a document was last edited, printed, and saved.

Preserving ESI with Legal Holds

Here's what usually happens at the start of a fraud investigation: A certain issue (or series of issues) comes to light that is the catalyst for the investigation. The legal team determines whether the issue has the potential to develop into legal action, often based on the preliminary findings of the investigators. (Other events, such as whistleblower letters or regulatory inquiries, can also provide the legal basis for this action.) If the answer is yes, the attorneys issue a *legal hold notice* to the employees or custodians who maintain any ESI that is potentially relevant to the potential litigation. When the notice is sent, the employees or custodians are being asked to conduct what's referred to as a *preservation hold.*

The legal hold notice should clearly identify the types of documents and transactional systems (both paper and electronic) that are potentially relevant, and it should provide instructions to the recipients not to delete or modify these documents. Because the organization being investigated may not want to disclose many details to some or all of the ESI custodians, this document must be worded carefully.

One of the most difficult tasks here is to define the scope of the preservation hold. You have to figure out who the relevant ESI custodians are, as well as the types of documents and systems to cover. When identifying the custodians, don't just limit the list to those key custodians who are directly associated with the issues being investigated. Include support staff and other custodians who have access to the documents or interact with the key custodians on a regular basis.

When thinking about which documents and systems to cover, keep in mind that you want the hold to be broad enough to capture *all* documents that are potentially relevant to the investigation. As the investigation progresses, the hold should be updated to refine the scope. E-mail systems, financial systems, files, voicemail, and backup tapes are examples of some of the areas you should consider when developing the scope of ESI.

After the hold notice is issued, you need to have legal resources available to the ESI custodians to answer any questions that arise. Often, custodians have questions about the types of documents included in the notice or technical procedures that prevent the accidental modification or deletion of the pertinent documents.

If you expect a legal hold to last for an extended period of time, you should issue regular reminders to the recipients. Doing so reaffirms the requirements that are outlined in the hold.

Working with backup tape systems and other archives

Backup tapes and other archive systems require special attention. Large organizations often use backup tapes to store electronic data located on network servers in the event of a disaster. These tapes, known as *disaster recovery tapes,* are often created on a rotation schedule so that older tapes are overwritten periodically. For example, a company may rotate and overwrite its tapes on a weekly basis.

Disaster recovery tapes can be backed up using one of two methods:

✔ **Full backup:** Includes all the selected data present on the device targeted for backup.

✔ **Incremental backup:** Captures only those files that have changed since the last backup was performed.

You need to understand which type of backup is contained within a tape when you're selecting which disaster recovery backups to restore.

In addition to disaster recovery tapes, organizations maintain *archive backups,* which represent snapshots in time. For example, an organization may store archive backup tapes for a period of seven years. Archive backups are usually full backups of particular application servers. Organizations may create archive backups on a regular schedule (weekly, monthly, quarterly, annually) or based on a particular event. For example, many companies created archive backups prior to the turn of this century based on Y2K concerns.

Due to the massive volume of tape media required to store archive backups, many organizations house them at offsite facilities, such as with a company called Iron Mountain (www.ironmountain.com), for long-term storage. During a preservation hold, you should consider notifying the people responsible for the storage and maintenance of the archive tapes to prevent the deletion of historical backups.

Preparing for ESI collection

Custodians who are subject to the legal hold notice should *not* attempt to segregate or copy any pertinent documents on their own. The act of doing so has the potential to permanently alter the documents (and seriously mess up your investigative efforts). Modifying or deleting potentially relevant files, called the *spoliation of evidence,* can have disastrous effects on a legal case. In some cases it can lead to *summary judgment:* a court judgment without a full trial. Bottom line: A trained electronic discovery professional must perform this work so that the investigation is not exposed to questions surrounding the authenticity of the documents being examined.

Rather than gathering or segregating documents subject to a hold, here's what the document custodians *can* do to help your investigation: prepare an index of the documents covered by the hold, including their locations. That way, when you start your search for relevant information, you have a roadmap to guide your way. If this request is not made through the legal hold notice, you can make it verbally during an interview with a custodian.

Collecting Preserved ESI

You may think that collecting the preserved ESI within an organization would be similar to using a cut-and-paste feature to copy files to an external hard drive. Unfortunately, the work is more complicated than that. It's a good idea to perform this work with a degree of professional skepticism and to document your efforts so that the authenticity of the collected ESI will not be questioned and scrutinized.

In this section, we walk you through the best practices for collecting various types of ESI.

Getting more details with physical collections

Hard drive imaging is a process that essentially takes a snapshot of all of the electronic information contained within a computer's hard drive at a particular point in time. It's a useful tool, especially because if a computer crashes you have all the information you need to reconstruct the hard drive. And if you're conducting a forensic investigation, hard drive imaging gives you access to previously deleted documents and prior versions of documents that can help you find what you need.

Investigations often require the creation of hard drive images. This step is commonly referred to as a *physical collection* because the image maintains an exact replica of the data stored on the original device. Imaging computers is beneficial because it allows you to review and evaluate deleted files and file fragments.

Consider a scenario where a member of a company's accounting team is creating, printing, and subsequently deleting fraudulent vendor invoices. These invoices are submitted for payment and approved by the fraudster who created them. A check is then cut to the entity listed on the manufactured invoice and mailed to a post office box rented by the fraudster. In this scenario, the key source of evidence resides on his computer as a deleted file. Thus, physically collecting the custodian's computer provides a significant benefit to the investigation.

Given the detailed steps associated with performing a forensic image, physical collections are usually performed by electronic discovery professionals who are trained to use the specialized imaging tools. Should the authenticity of the ESI ever be called into question, these professionals can testify to the process and validate that the image was created correctly and completely.

Common software applications that are used by forensic technology professionals include Guidance Software's EnCase, Forensic Tool Kit, and Linux DD.

Working with logical collections

Hard drive imaging requires specialized tools and experienced electronic discovery professionals to perform — and not every case requires it. If you're collecting electronic data and you *don't* perform hard drive imaging, you're working on what's commonly referred to as a *logical forensic collection.* During a logical forensic collection, you target the collection of files or folders within a file system. For example, you can perform a logical collection of a custodian's My Documents folder, which is likely to be found at C:\Documents and Settings\[*username*]\My Documents\.

This type of collection will not capture some of the more notable aspects of a hard drive image, such as deleted files or file fragments. However, when a logical collection is performed using the right tools, the collection will preserve the metadata associated with the files being collected. For example, common file system metadata fields include the files' creation date, the last modified date, and the last accessed date.

Commonly used tools for logical collections include these programs:

- ✔ **NTBackup:** This is a Windows-based program that allows you to browse computer folders, and select folders and files to back up. The resulting backup is a single self-contained file that contains the selected files and folders and maintains their original metadata. This program comes standard with most of the currently available versions of Microsoft Windows.

- ✔ **XXCopy:** Similar to NTBackup, this program allows the user to preserve the metadata associated with the selected files; however, the resulting copy cannot be stored into a single backup file. This program is available for download on the Internet.

- ✔ **RoboCopy:** This program, which shares similar features to NTBackup and XXCopy, is also available for download online.

After the collection is completed, you need to document your effort in a standardized way so you can describe the effort in detail at a later date. Here are some common attributes of the collection that you want to note:

- ✔ The investigator's name (that's you!).
- ✔ The date and time of the collection.
- ✔ The date and time reported by the computer.

- A description of the files being collected.
- The name of the custodian who uses the computer.
- The directory location of the files within the computer.
- The physical location of the computer.
- A *hash value* (or unique identifier) provided by the forensic tool used for the collection. This value allows you to authenticate the collected ESI to the original image at a later date.

You may also want to take photographs of the computer equipment when the data is collected. Doing so provides a visual record of the computer that you are examining for ESI.

Branching out to network collections

Data collection is not limited to the personal computers. Servers can store a significant amount of ESI across a corporate *network*, a collection of computers and devices among which resources and information can be shared. A significant amount of ESI, such as e-mails, voicemails, and databases, is stored on the company's network infrastructure. This data is often centrally located but accessed by many custodians, so you need to develop a map of the organization's security settings to identify which network-based ESI corresponds to the subject custodians. Using security information about the network *file shares* (files that reside on the network that are shared by many users or groups of users), you can identify the network locations that a custodian cannot see, those she can see but not edit, and those she can edit in order to create new ESI. These distinctions help you define the scope of the ESI you need to collect.

When collecting network-based file shares, you often need to utilize logical collection methods rather than hard drive imaging. Here's why:

- Imaging the server could potentially take a significant amount of time based on the overall size of the server.
- A server image may capture large amounts of data not relevant to the investigation.

At the conclusion of the ESI collection, it's a good practice to prepare a backup of the collected data onto a new set of storage media. Doing so is your insurance policy in case the storage media that contains the collected ESI mechanically fails. In addition, the backup can be used as a working copy while the original collection copy can be stored for safekeeping. The working copy is the copy you use for data processing, review, and analysis (subjects we tackle later in the chapter).

Avoiding common mistakes when collecting e-mails

The process of collecting e-mail is different than the document collection methods we discuss in the previous sections. E-mail systems are like post offices: They organize messages by the respective user mailbox on the system. Therefore, if you want to collect e-mail from one or more mailboxes (those associated with the custodians who fall within the scope of your collection effort), you usually do so without collecting e-mail data from the entire network server. The e-mail platform, such as Microsoft Exchange, Lotus Notes, or Groupwise, dictates the particular method of capture you need to use, but in most instances the collection effort results in separate e-mail container files associated with each collected mailbox. An e-mail container file is a standalone file that contains multiple e-mail messages, such as a *PST* file for Microsoft Exchange platforms.

When you're collecting e-mails, you need to know that investigators sometimes fail to get complete collections. Here are examples of ways to avoid common mistakes:

✔ **Working around data storage limits:** In some e-mail platforms, the extracted mailbox containers are limited to 2 gigabytes (GB) of data. This limitation, which is more prevalent in older e-mail platforms, may curtail the e-mail extracted from the server. To avoid this from occurring, review the available documentation related to the e-mail environment and take alternate steps to collect the data should the server have this limitation. For example, divide the server e-mail into date ranges (so the messages within the date range do not exceed the 2GB limit), and create multiple e-mail containers for each date range. Be sure to thoroughly document any and all steps you take that fall outside of the typical collection protocol.

✔ **Knowing how many mailboxes a custodian can access:** In some cases, custodians send and receive e-mails from multiple mailboxes on the server. For instance, administrative assistants may have access to one or more executive mailboxes within the e-mail environment. You need to fully understand the custodians' access rights and make sure that all relevant mailboxes are collected.

✔ **Looking for e-mail archives as well:** Don't assume that the server contains all the e-mail for a given mailbox. E-mail can be easily archived to multiple locations throughout the organization's technology infrastructure. If you rely solely on the e-mail server, you may have large gaps in the e-mail collection resulting from the archival habits of the custodians. Therefore, you need to review the contents of the computer as well as other network file share locations for e-mail archives.

Processing Data to Simplify Your Review

After you're done collecting ESI, your next step is to inventory the contents of the collection and identify the files for review. This process is commonly referred to as *native file processing*. Native file processing allows you to cull the collected files, index the culled file set, and apply keywords in order to facilitate an efficient review and is performed with the help of an electronic discovery software application. Many of the most commonly used electronic discovery applications (such as Law, Concordance, Summation, Attenex, or Ringtail) allow for native file processing.

Why the term "native file"? When a file is saved using a certain program, the file is often saved in a proprietary format or *native file* format that only that program can recognize.

In this section, we show you how native file processing applications remove system files (which you can't and don't need to review), eliminate duplicate files, and allow you to search for keywords in the data you've collected. We also introduce advanced language analytics, which can speed up your search for relevant information even more.

Removing non-reviewable system files

Upon completing the inventory of the data, you must identify and eliminate any non-reviewable system files that reside on a collected computer image. What does *non-reviewable* mean? A software application or operating system requires certain files to be saved to a computer in order for particular applications to run. Files that end in the following extensions are common examples of non-reviewable files: *.exe*, *.com*, *.dll*, and *.sys*. These files are commonly referred to as *system files* and could represent a sizable population of files stored on the custodian's computer.

The National Institute of Standards and Technology (NIST) publishes a list of system files that are embedded within common software applications. Many of the commonly used native file processing applications rely on the published NIST listing to identify and cull files from a document collection. Removing the system files aids the remainder of your native file processing effort by decreasing the volume of data that you have to index and search.

Tossing out duplicate files and e-mails

After you've removed the system files from the inventoried file collection, you start a process called *de-duplication,* which is a fancy word for "removing duplicates." You identify copies of files or e-mails that reside in multiple areas of the collected data, and you remove all but one of these copies from the documents selected for review. You can do this process either across all custodians or within a collection of files associated with a single custodian. De-duplication significantly reduces the number of files slated for review, which saves you a significant amount of time.

In addition to standard de-duplication, many native file processing systems adopt an advanced de-duplication method for e-mails called *thread de-duplication.* An *e-mail thread* refers to a series of replies back and forth pertaining to a certain message. Thread de-duplication identifies e-mail threads that contain all of the content from prior e-mails sent to and from the same parties on the same topic and eliminates the earlier, incomplete messages. For instance, if custodian A and custodian B are discussing a new product over a series of e-mails back and forth, thread de-duplication would identify that the most recent message in the chain contained all the prior messages within its body and eliminate those prior messages from being reviewed separately. This de-duplication method can significantly reduce the volume of e-mails you have to review.

Searching for keywords

After your collection has been culled for system files and duplicates, it can be indexed. *Indexing* is an automated process that extracts the text associated with the file collection and allows you to search that text. After the data is indexed, you can search for keywords that appear anywhere in the collected documents, which is a huge time-saver. Common indexing engines include DTSearch and X1.

Using advanced language analytics

Advanced native file processing systems go beyond keywords; they use advanced language analytics that speed up your data review. These tools analyze the documents for language content to identify nouns and other contextual roots to the discussion. They then organize the documents so that collections of documents or e-mails discussing the same people, places, and things are presented and reviewed together. These advanced analytics have been shown to increase investigators' review efficiency by five to ten times when compared with a standard keyword search review. Some examples of advanced electronic discovery tools include Ringtail, Attenex, and Stratify.

Reviewing Documents, E-mails, and Other Data

Electronic document review tends to consume the most amount of time in an investigation. How much time does this review take? It depends on how many documents you need to review and how many investigative teammates are helping you. Suffice to say that you'll be devoting a good amount of time to this step. The good news is that some technical and process-oriented solutions can decrease the effort you need to make during document review and simultaneously increase the accuracy and completeness of your review.

To determine how to tackle your document review, you need to carefully consider the specific objectives and deadlines associated with the investigation. Often, fraud investigations require an extremely fast-paced review. This is particularly true for investigations that are brought on by regulatory agencies that impose stringent reporting deadlines on the organization being investigated.

When time is extremely tight, you definitely want to use advanced language analytics to identify and review key documents. (We introduce this process in the previous section.) This technology employs a process called *document seeding,* which means that a document with known characteristics is injected into a collection of documents being reviewed. Because advanced language analytics can organize documents based on key concepts, you can perform a search to locate the injected document and instantly see a collection of documents that discuss the same people, places, and things. Doing so quickly takes you to the most relevant documents.

Another review method is to focus on the documents associated with those custodians who are centrally involved in the investigation. You review these documents completely and identify specific words or phrases that appear. You then use these words or phrases to perform a targeted review on the remaining custodian documents. At the same time, you sample a random set of documents that are not responsive to given keywords. In the event that you identify relevant documents within the sample, you introduce additional keywords to the review to expand the number of documents you review. You repeat this process until the number of false negatives within the random sample is rendered insignificant. (A *false negative* is a negative search result that occurs when the concept you're looking for actually exists in the documents.)

Performing Complex Data Analysis

Analyzing structured data in an investigation is a cumbersome task. With the variety of structured data systems on the market (including Oracle Financials, SAP, PeopleSoft, JD Edwards, Hyperion, and Quick Books), the most common way to speed up your review of a transactional financial system is to extract the schema components of the database that are potentially relevant to the investigation and convert the data into a common format. A database *schema* is the logical definition of the structural elements of the database (such as tables, views, indexes, and field definitions). After you've converted the data into a single format, you can test it for common indications of fraud. For instance, one indication of fraud may be that vendor payments exceed a certain dollar threshold.

Data mining applications are available that read the data in an organization's financial system and perform tests that allow you to identify potentially fraudulent activity. These tools generally allow you to review flagged transactions so you can figure out which ones really indicate fraud and which are false positives.

Identifying ESI on the Web

The Internet contains a mountain of information that may be useful to you during your investigation. External communication media, such as Webmail and instant messaging, are often managed outside the walls of the organization. Many other communication systems exist on the Internet as well. For example, the custodians whose documents you're investigating may write blogs, post tweets, or use Facebook postings. Any of these communications may include relevant information to your investigation. Here's a bit more information about some key online resources:

✔ **Webmail:** Web-based e-mail services (such as AOL, Gmail, Hotmail, and Yahoo!) allow people to access e-mails through an online browser rather than a company server. People who use a Webmail program can communicate without corporate oversight. Fraudsters often use Webmail because it's beyond the purview of the company's e-mail infrastructure. This technology could be used to send e-mails that contain organizational trade secrets or intellectual property.

Collecting Webmail for investigative review is a difficult task and often requires a subpoena. In addition, online e-mail services often have auto-delete mechanisms that limit the investigator's ability to retrieve deleted messages over time. If you determine that Webmail is within the scope of your investigation, you need to address the issue of deleted messages.

Keep in mind that some businesses do not allow access to Webmail from work computers in order to prevent employees from sending out data that can't be monitored. (It also keeps employees from being busy with personal e-mail during work hours.) Be sure to ask the company about its policies before your search begins.

✔ **Blogs:** Blogging is a relatively new phenomenon and consists generally of an author's thoughts on a range of topics. Blogs can be updated regularly, which makes them akin to an online diary. If a custodian of documents relevant to your investigation writes a blog, be sure to check it out.

✔ **Twitter** and **Facebook:** We discuss these two together because they represent two common media for making public or semiprivate announcements. With Twitter, the author crafts messages that are delivered to the author's followers. Followers can comment on the messages, and a record of these communications can remain available for public review. With Facebook, users often link accounts with other users and communicate in a semiprivate forum.

You can use these online sources of evidence to aid in custodial interviews, build a more detailed story of the fraud, and identify other potential custodians or parties involved. They are a valuable asset to an investigation.

Capturing Web-based ESI can be accomplished by implementing a *Web crawler* that saves a copy of the publicly accessible Web site to your own computer. After the Web site is saved, you should prepare proper documentation to capture the Web address, the date and time of the capture, and the name of the investigator who performed the capture (that's you!).

Chapter 16

Who Wants to Know?
Reporting on Your Findings

*R*eporting the results of an investigation is a critical step — as important as conducting the investigation itself. You may be asked to communicate your investigation procedures and findings either in writing or orally, depending on the purpose and scope of the investigation or litigation, your target audience, and the client requirements. Most often, a report that's going to be used as evidence must be written. If you're asked to provide an expert opinion on matters that are in dispute, you'll do so in writing as well. But when you provide periodic updates to clients or law enforcement authorities on the status of an investigation, your report will likely be done orally.

In this chapter we cover some of the most commonly used reports that you will prepare as a forensic accountant. We explain how to tailor a report to your target audience, how to communicate clearly, and how to structure various types of reports.

Determining Your Audience

When you prepare investigative reports documenting the findings of a fraud investigation, you must know your reader(s). This advice applies to anything you write, of course; it's a universal guideline of effective writing. Here are the people most likely to read an investigation report:

- ✔ **Client:** If you've been hired by a company — or by certain company insiders, such as the management or the board of directors — that's your client. Your *engagement letter* (the contract you sign when you agree to conduct the investigation) should spell out exactly who your client is and what type of report the client expects.

- ✔ **Attorneys:** Your audience will include attorneys who work for a company or attorneys investigating that company. Sometimes, attorneys hiring you will include your findings in their own reports. Other times, you may be asked to prepare reports under your or your firm's name so the reports can be covered by attorney-client privilege (which means the communications between you and the attorneys are protected from pre-trial discovery).

Always be aware that the defense attorneys will probably gain access to your reports during the discovery phase of civil litigation. They will scrutinize the report for errors, omissions, and misstatements. Therefore, it behooves you to make sure the report is accurate in all respects.

- ✔ **Court:** Judges and juries may receive your reports as well. You are generally required to submit your reports to court prior to testifying. Juries get access to your reports at the end of the trial.

- ✔ **Law enforcement agencies:** In criminal cases, prosecutors and other law enforcement personnel will review your reports. They look primarily at evidence and witness statements that will best sustain a criminal prosecution.

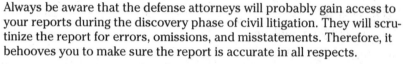

Organizing Your Work Papers

At the outset of an investigation or litigation, you should discuss with the client and its counsel how you are going to document your findings. As the investigation progresses, the scope of the engagement may change, and you may be required to provide other forms of reports. It's important to properly organize all your working papers, exhibits, and supporting documents so that you can respond quickly to changing reporting requirements.

Writing effective reports requires a high level of attention to detail. Take ample care in planning, organizing, documenting the information obtained, and ensuring compliance with applicable professional standards. There are no second chances for defective analysis, faulty reports, and inefficiencies — the damage to the case and your reputation will be done.

Work papers document any work you perform during the investigation or litigation. Whether they're electronic files or hard copies, they contain information that supports the facts, analyses, and findings in the report. You *must* organize them properly because work papers can be subpoenaed at a later date and may be subject to discovery. You should prepare the work papers with the assumption that a regulatory authority will review them at some point.

If the engagement involves working under the direction of an attorney, and you want to try to keep your work papers privileged (so they aren't subject to discovery), always mark your papers this way: *Privileged & Confidential, Attorney-Work-Product, Draft — For discussion purposes only.*

Each work paper should stand on its own. Work papers should be easy to read and understand by an independent reviewer. The information in work papers should be cross-referenced to the source documents as well as to your report. Any documents provided by the client or prepared by the client should be marked as such.

During the course of your investigation, you must determine what documents constitute work papers and what documents don't. Handwritten notes, miscellaneous electronic files, and other documents not relevant to the subject matter of the investigation may or may not be required depending on the nature of the information. You should be cautious about taking notes because even they may be read by others.

Documenting Interviews

Conducting interviews is an integral part of an investigation. Even after you pore through every document available to you, you probably won't have the whole picture of what transpired. Interviewing witnesses often provides the missing part of the puzzle. When you gather information with interviews, you need to bring two critical qualities to the table:

- ✔ **Adequate preparation:** You must adequately prepare prior to any interview. Proper preparation requires knowing what you're looking for (which means understanding your client's expectations) and having a pretty good idea of what information each witness may be able to provide.

- ✔ **Active listening:** Obviously, you must have good listening skills so you can absorb all the information that emerges in an interview and respond to it with further questions. Active listening involves participating with the interviewee, not just throwing questions at him.

As with work papers, you must be very organized when conducting and documenting interviews. After each one, you write an *interview memorandum* that contains the following information:

- ✔ Your name
- ✔ The witness' name and contact information
- ✔ Any evidence provided by the witness, such as documents
- ✔ A statement that the interview was voluntary and the witness was informed of the nature of the inquiry

- The date of the interview
- How the interview was conducted (for example, in person or by phone)
- The date the memorandum was prepared
- Whether the interview was electronically recorded
- The facts learned during the interview

You file each interview memorandum along with your work papers and cross-reference it to any source documents and to your final written report.

Creating a Masterpiece

No matter what types of reports you're required to provide, you need to keep a handful of tips in mind. These fundamentals will allow your writing — and your reputation as a fraud investigator — to shine:

- **Be objective:** Any report you create should be based on facts. You should maintain your objectivity to exclude any bias. For example, do not provide speculative interpretations of the underlying facts.

- **Plan:** Plan your investigation and the report well in advance. Respond to any changes in the scope of your work or events that affect it, and address issues immediately when they pop up. A thorough investigation results in good, efficient reports. The information should flow logically. The evidence, procedures, and analysis should be prepared in a way so as to support the conclusions reached in the report.

- **Keep it simple:** All reports, whether written or oral, should contain simple language and concepts. A skilled forensic accountant can communicate complex transactions in a manner that can be understood by all. In the event the report includes complicated concepts, trade jargon, or industry terms, you should provide explanations for each of these concepts and terms. A good practice is to use tables and graphs to explain your findings.

- **Pay attention to details:** The information you provide should be factual and correct. Any facts or numbers that are incorrectly represented affect not only the credibility of the report but also the credibility of the investigation as a whole. Check your language and the tone of the report to ensure consistency, and avoid grammatical errors and spelling mistakes.

- **Be both thorough and concise:** The report should not leave out any substantial facts material to the investigation or litigation, and it should not waste the reader's time with irrelevant information.

✔ **Avoid using certain words:** Avoid words that may exaggerate facts such as *greatest, maximum, highest, always, never, topmost, unparalleled,* and *absolute.* Avoid using phrases that may have legal implications and may not be understood, such as *not to exceed* or *time is of the essence.* Avoid judgmental comments or words such as *unacceptable* or *inappropriate* (unless you are writing an advocacy report, which we explain later in the chapter).

✔ **Be careful about opinions:** Unless the engagement requires you to provide an opinion, do not render one. Stay focused on the facts.

✔ **Address internal control issues separately:** Discuss the findings of your investigation separately from internal control issues. Although your client may be interested in knowing about such control weaknesses, address these separately from the core findings of your report. (Need a refresher on what internal controls are and why they matter? Check out Chapter 20.)

When writing your report, keep in mind that you are not assessing guilt. You are expressing your opinion on the underlying facts.

Getting Familiar with Investigation Reports

A fraud examination should answer the questions of *who, what, where, why, when, how,* and *how much.* You write investigation reports after you conduct fraud examinations (such as investigating the embezzlement of cash, employee fraud, or financial misstatements). Investigative reports do not provide opinions; they provide information on the procedures you performed, the facts learned, and your findings from the investigation.

You may be asked to provide affidavits regarding the facts you discovered, your opinions, or other matters involving your investigation. *Affidavits* are voluntary declarations of facts or oaths made by an individual. They're usually considered stronger statements than regular reports because affidavits are communicated in written form and attested to in the presence of a notary public or an officer authorized to administer such an oath.

Investigation reports should adhere to the following five standards (as reported in the *Fraud Examiners Manual* from the Association of Certified Fraud Examiners, 2003):

✔ **Accuracy:** The report must be accurate and devoid of mistakes in dates, amounts, or spelling. Carelessness leaves the entire report open to question and criticism.

✔ **Clarity:** You need to use clear language that isn't subject to different interpretations.

✔ **Impartiality:** You should avoid bias or foregone conclusions. Avoid expressing opinions; let the facts speak for themselves.

✔ **Relevance:** In every investigation, the forensic accountant uncovers facts not relevant to the case. Your job is to exclude such information from the report.

✔ **Timeliness:** You should prepare reports during the course of the investigation and not long after its conclusion. If you don't prepare a report on a timely basis, you run the risk of omitting or distorting important data.

An investigative report includes the following information, in this order:

✔ The date the report was issued

✔ The name and contact information of the recipient(s)

✔ A reference to the engagement letter, including scope of the engagement

✔ A disclaimer of responsibility for the adequacy of procedures

✔ A description of the procedures performed

✔ A statement of the facts and findings (but no opinions or legal conclusions)

✔ A restriction on the distribution of the report

✔ Your signature

Figure 16-1 shows an example of what an investigative report looks like.

Crafting Expert Reports

An expert report is used to convey the opinion of an expert in a dispute environment (meaning litigation or arbitration). Expert reports lay out the facts surrounding the dispute, the forensic accountant's opinion, and the basis of the opinion.

Writing an expert report is no small endeavor. Depending on the case, you (or people working under your supervision) may need to sort through mountains of evidence, including e-mails, company memos, presentations, policy manuals, transcripts of witness testimony provided at depositions, and auditor work papers. You may also need to research information outside the company, such as how other companies in the same industry accounted for and disclosed similar transactions.

John Span
Director
Spick and Span Company
555 Big Blvd
New York, NY 10001

August 19, 2010

Top Notch Investigators LLP was retained by Spick and Span Company (Spick-Span) for evaluating the franchise fees receivable from Super Clean Inc. (SC) during the period January 1, 2008 to December 31, 2008. Spick-Span franchises commercial cleaning products to 135 franchisees including SC. Our work was performed pursuant to our engagement letter dated March 1, 2010.

The sufficiency of the procedures is solely the responsibility of Spick-Span. Consequently, we make no representation regarding the sufficiency of the procedures described below either for the purpose for which this report has been requested or for any other purpose.

1. We read Spick-Span's franchise agreement with SC dated September 1, 2007. The agreement calls for franchise payments of 10% on sales made by SC to its customers. Our interpretations of the agreement were based on discussions with Spick-Span representatives.

2. We interviewed SC employees listed in Exhibit A about SC's franchisee calculations.

3. We traced the sales amounts listed on the franchisee fee statements to the transaction-level sales detail reports and to SC's general ledger.

4. We selected 125 sales items out of a total population of 7,056 sales items listed on the detailed sales reports using a stratified statistical sampling method. We divided the population of SC's customers into three strata: supermarkets with sales in excess of $1 million; medium stores with sales between $200,000 and $1 million; small stores with sales of less than $100,000.

5. We traced the selected items to source documents such as invoices and shipping records.

During our testing of the amounts reported on the franchisee statements, we compared the sales amounts listed on the sales reports to the sales amounts listed on the franchisee statements. For sales in the Brooklyn Heights section of New York, we noted that the sales amounts listed on the sales reports did not agree to the amounts listed on the franchisee fee statements. SC's employees were unable to explain these differences, which totaled $980,000. Consequently, we have calculated additional fees of $98,000 due to Spick-Span, as presented on Exhibit B.

This report is intended solely for the information and use of Spick-Span and is not intended to be and should not be used by anyone other than Spick-Span.

Yours truly,

Robert S. Holmes

Robert S. Holmes

Figure 16-1:
Sample
investigative
report.

The report must delineate your opinions and the basis for those opinions. Keep in mind that if you don't express a certain opinion in the report, you probably cannot address that issue at trial. So if you want to express an opinion in the courtroom, you must first express it in the expert report.

The more reasonable and supportable the assumptions you make in your report, the more defensible the report will be, and the more difficulty the opposing lawyer will have in attacking your position. Given these circumstances, you need to know a lot about the facts of the case and weigh carefully everything included in the report.

An effective expert report is drafted using active voice, states opinions clearly, and uses correct language. Define complex and technical terms, and avoid absolute words such as *always* and *never*, and unnecessary qualifiers such as *extremely* or *highly*.

Following the Federal Rules of Evidence

In federal court, expert reports and testimony must comply with Article 7 of the Federal Rules of Evidence. The following list highlights the more salient provisions of the pertinent rules:

- ✔ **Rule 702**: Expert testimony may assist a jury or judge in areas requiring specialized knowledge as long as it's based on sufficient facts or data, it's the product of reliable principles and methods, and the witness has applied the principles and methods reliably to the facts of the case.

- ✔ **Rule 703**: The expert may base her opinion on certain facts or data that she knows prior to the hearing if that information is the type that's ordinarily relied upon by experts in her field and if it doesn't need to be submitted as evidence in order to be admitted.

- ✔ **Rule 705**: An expert may offer her opinion in testimony without first testifying to the underlying facts unless the court decides otherwise.

Federal Rules of Civil Procedures: Rule 26(a)(2)(B) requires that all the following be included in an expert report:

- ✔ A complete statement of all opinions

- ✔ Information considered by the expert in forming her opinions

- ✔ An explanation of the basis and reason for the opinions

- ✔ Any attachments to be used as a summary of or support for the opinions

- ✔ Qualifications of the witness, including a list of publications authored by the witness in the preceding ten years

- ✔ A listing of any other cases in the preceding four years in which the witness testified as an expert at trial or by deposition

✔ Compensation to be paid to the expert

✔ Signature of the witness

Facing a Daubert motion

If a lawyer believes that an expert's testimony should be inadmissible, he files a Daubert motion, which leads to a Daubert hearing before the judge (who is the gatekeeper on such issues). At the hearing, the lawyer argues that the opinions formulated by the expert were developed through techniques not recognized by peers or that the expert does not have the requisite qualification to opine on a particular topic. If the argument is successful, the expert's opinions will not be admitted at trial.

A successful Daubert hearing against a forensic accountant can have a devastating effect on her career because she will be asked in all future depositions whether any of her expert opinions have been excluded. An affirmative answer causes negative connotations to be attached to her credibility, and lawyers will be extremely reluctant to use someone who has in the past been successfully challenged under Daubert. Therefore, you need to guard against this situation by not being in the position of acting as an expert in matters for which you are not qualified. You also never want to offer opinions on matters for which you don't have sufficient evidence.

Following the report template

An expert report features the following information, in this order:

✔ **A caption:** This is the heading of your report and usually contains your name, the name of your employer, and the date the report was issued.

✔ **Background:** This section broadly describes the nature of the engagement and what you have been hired to do.

✔ **Qualifications:** Your qualifications and experience are briefly described in the report with the notation that your résumé (or curriculum vitae) is attached as an exhibit.

✔ **Compensation:** You must include your fees and those of the professionals assisting you per the engagement letter you signed with the client. Fees are generally paid on an hourly basis.

✔ **Information Considered:** You should describe all the relevant information you have considered in arriving at your opinion. The information itself is included in an exhibit or appendix to the report.

✔ **Engagement:** Here, you describe what you have done — the analysis and procedures conducted.

✔ **Opinions Reached:** This is the main part of your report — you express your opinion and the bases for expressing it. When you issue your report in response to an opposing expert's report, you should discuss the reasons why you disagree with the other expert's findings.

✔ **Reservation of Rights:** Because the report is issued at a particular point in time, your opinion may no longer be valid with passage of time as new information becomes available. Therefore, you should reserve the right to change your opinion as new facts come to light.

✔ **Signature and Date:** The signature almost always comes from the individual expert rather than that person's employer.

Figure 16-2 features a sample expert report so you can see these elements in action:

Preparing Oral Reports with Care

Oral reports require slightly less time and effort than written reports, but the preparation for an oral report should be as comprehensive as that for a written report. Oral reports are not only less expensive from a client's perspective, but they also are interactive in nature. Oral communications and presentations of findings give a forensic accountant the opportunity to provide updates of the investigation or clarifications about the findings. They also allow the recipient to seek clarifications on a one-to-one basis.

Periodical status update reports are often provided orally to clients. For instance, you may be asked to provide updates of the investigation to a company's board of directors or to the regulators, such as the Securities and Exchange Commission (SEC). In our experience, you should prepare talking point memos for providing such updates. When preparing these memos, you should try to anticipate any questions that may be asked of you when providing the updates.

You may also be called to give a *deposition* in your role as an expert witness. During a deposition, the opposing counsel has an opportunity to question your analysis, procedures performed, and findings. You may also need to testify in court relating to information provided in your expert report. (See Chapter 18 for the lowdown on what to do in the courtroom.) Especially in these situations, you should take just as much care to prepare your oral communications as you do your written communications.

SUPREME COURT OF THE STATE OF NEW YORK | Index No. 987654321

JOHN BLAKE,
Plaintiff,
vs.
ORANGE COMPANY,
Defendant.

**EXPERT REPORT OF SAM ACE
ECONOMIC ADVISORS, LLP**

AUGUST 10, 2010

I understand that John Blake (Plaintiff), an executive employed by Orange Company (Defendant), was terminated by Defendant on December 31, 2009 following a 30-year career as an executive with the Company. I have been advised by counsel for the Plaintiff that Defendant has been found liable for breach of contract in the wrongful termination of Mr. Blake. I have also been advised that the amount of damages for breach of contract is to be determined at trial.

I am a Managing Director at Economic Advisors LLP (EA). EA specializes in economic advisory and valuation services. My professional responsibilities include providing economics, statistics and financial modeling services.

I received my Ph.D. in economics from the University of Pennsylvania in 1996, and a B.S. in Accounting from New York University. I am currently an adjunct professor at Pace University, where I teach graduate and undergraduate courses in economics and statistics.

During my tenure with EA, I have been involved in calculating economic damages in the context of litigation relating to a wide range of areas, including intellectual property, patent infringement and wrongful termination. My curriculum vita is attached as Exhibit 1.

EA is compensated at the rate of $675 per hour for my services in this matter. The billing rates of other persons involved in the preparation of this report range between $225 and $650 per hour. My fees are not dependent upon the outcome of this case.

Information considered in the preparation of this report is listed in Exhibit 2. I have been asked to perform economic analyses of the amount of damages suffered by Plaintiff as a result of wrongful termination by the Defendant. The amount of damages suffered by Plaintiff as a result of the wrongful termination is calculated at $1,099,000. The basis for this opinion is discussed in section II of this report.

My work is ongoing, and my opinions are subject to revision based on new information or data (including new reports or testimony by Defendants' experts), which subsequently may be provided to, or obtained by me.

Sam Ace
August 10, 2010

Figure 16-2:
A sample
expert
report.

Crafting Advocacy Reports

Certified public accountants and economists may serve as arbitrators in resolving certain disputes. (We discuss this situation more in the next section.) Forensic accountants are sometimes asked by their clients for assistance in presenting the client's position during arbitration. For instance, you may be asked to assist either the buyer or the seller in an arbitration proceeding regarding a purchase price adjustment dispute. In such situations, you act as a consultant or ghost writer for the client, supporting and advocating the client's point of view. You review the information, analyze the data, and assist your client in drafting his position.

Unlike expert reports, advocacy reports do not contain your independent opinions; they contain only your client's opinions. They are also not issued on your firm's letterhead; instead, the client's letterhead is used.

The normal audience for this type of report is an arbitrator or a mediator. The parties present their own positions in these proceedings (with the assistance of attorneys) rather than having prosecution and defense attorneys speak for them. For this reason, advocacy reports are issued in the names of the respective parties.

There is no model or standard format for writing advocacy reports — the format differs from client to client and from situation to situation. Sometimes, the client or its attorney may write the report and ask for your assistance in drafting sections related to finance, accounting, or economics. At other times you may be asked to write the entire report yourself. In both situations, you must constantly get feedback from the client as to the tone and substance. You may be told to tone up or tone down the language based on how much the client believes he has been wronged by the other party.

Rendering Decisions in Arbitrations

In addition to writing advocacy reports, forensic accountants may be asked to render decisions during Alternate Dispute Resolutions (ADR) proceedings such as arbitrations. In these circumstances, you play the role of both judge and jury. Decisions rendered in these forums are usually final and binding on the parties.

If you're asked to serve in this capacity, your contract should prescribe in detail the procedures to be followed in arbitration. Arbitration proceedings consist of the following elements:

✔ **Preliminary hearing:** During the hearing, the arbitrator discusses the rules of the arbitration and the expected procedures — defining the issues in dispute, setting up a schedule with a timetable for various deadlines to be met, scheduling the submission of written statements to the arbitrator, and establishing a time frame for the preparation and delivery of the decision.

✔ **Discovery:** The extent of discovery is limited when compared to litigation. Discovery may include exchanging information and interviewing witnesses. In rare cases, witnesses are deposed in an arbitration proceeding.

✔ **Written statements:** Each party prepares a written statement of its position for submission to the arbitrator. (As we explain in the previous section, forensic accountants can help prepare such advocacy reports when representing one of the parties.) These submissions can occur either simultaneously or separately. Usually, there is more than one round of submissions.

✔ **Interrogatories:** The arbitrator directs questions to the parties through written interrogatories. The arbitrator may ask questions about providing additional information or clarifying issues raised in the parties' written statements.

✔ **Hearings:** If the arbitrator believes that he has received all the information necessary to render his decision, the parties do not have a hearing. When hearings occur, they resemble court trials that consist of testimony, presentation of evidence, and cross-examination of witnesses.

✔ **Decision:** The arbitrator renders his decision in writing after reviewing all the evidence. He states his decision, the amount of the award, and the reasons for the decision. The format of this document will change depending on the specifics of the dispute, but will include the following elements:

  • A direct reference to the contract that brought the arbitrator into the case

  • The accounting or other professional standards that apply to the case and led the arbitrator to his decision

  • The arbitrator will usually sign the decision as an individual on the letterhead of the firm for which he works.

Figure 16-3 shows a sample of a decision written by a forensic accountant.

Roger Lee
555 Big Blvd
New York, NY 10001

Dear Buyer and Seller:

As provided by Section 4 of the Purchase Agreement dated as of January 15, 2009 (the "Agreement"), between Good Health Hospital (the "Seller") and Quality Health Services (the "Buyer") (collectively, the "Parties"), the Parties have engaged Best Forensics to serve as the "Arbitrator" by letter dated May 31, 2010. This letter summarizes our findings in connection with our arbitration of the issue related to classification of the 2008 Medicaid liability in the Closing Balance Sheet, set forth by the Parties.

We have concluded that the liability related to the 2008 Medicaid account amounting to $754,000 should be treated as a current liability in the Closing Balance Sheet. GAAP recognizes that the current liability classification include obligations that, by their terms, are due on demand. The preponderance of the evidence submitted to us indicates that under GAAP, the 2008 Medicaid obligation was due on demand and as such should have been classified as a current liability as of the Closing Date.

Very truly yours,

R. Lee

Roger Lee
Partner, Best Forensics

Figure 16-3:
An example
of an
arbitrator's
decision.

Chapter 17

Preparing for Trial: Business Litigation

*I*t's no surprise that the United States is the most litigious country in the world. As businesses take risks to get rewards, they're exposed to litigation of all types. When a business faces litigation, it needs not only experienced legal counsel but also the support of a forensic accountant. We explain why in this chapter — and we show you what exactly a forensic accountant does to support the business.

When a business is accused of fraud, either the whole company or specific people who work there must defend themselves in a criminal case, a civil case, or both. Being notified of a criminal or civil complaint is downright frightening to company executives because they know the potential ramifications:

✔ Significant out-of-pocket and opportunity costs associated with litigation

✔ Potentially significant costs of damages paid to settle the case or as a result of the court's findings

✔ Reputational damage to the company name

✔ Negative effects on the company's stock price

✔ The personal impact on individuals named in the complaint

Being served a complaint can have a paralyzing effect on even the most intrepid of executives. To overcome the paralysis, they need skilled and experienced professionals — including forensic accountants — to help them take appropriate and timely action.

Where Do Fraud Lawsuits Come From?

Businesses receive fraud complaints because someone is complaining. Who is that someone? It could be an individual employee in the company who figures out that a senior manager is lining her pockets. It could be a government agency that gets word a company is engaging in fraud to make its financial reports glow when the revenue and profit numbers really aren't all that healthy. It could be a shareholder angry over a dip in the price of the company's stock. In this section, we introduce the most common fraud watchdogs.

U.S. Securities and Exchange Commission (SEC)

If you ask someone on the street who is responsible for chasing business fraudsters, the answer may likely be "the SEC." (Or the answer may be steely silence; not everyone on the street likes being asked questions by complete strangers.) The SEC is very visible and undoubtedly the granddaddy of the fraud watchdogs. It has broad powers of enforcement with respect to publicly traded securities.

The SEC was established by the Securities and Exchange Act of 1934 and is an independent federal agency headquartered in Washington, D.C. Its stated mission "is to protect investors, maintain fair, orderly and efficient markets and facilitate capital formation." It enforces compliance with federal securities laws by all market participants and actively monitors the securities markets to detect, deter, and prevent fraud.

If the SEC perceives any wrongdoing, it can respond by taking several courses of action, including administrative law hearings, sanctions, and *civil litigation*. The word *civil* means that these cases are private disputes, and damages are sought to rectify some wrong allegedly inflicted by one party (the defendant) on the other party (the plaintiff).

Public Company Accounting Oversight Board (PCAOB)

The PCAOB was created by the Sarbanes-Oxley Act (SOX) in 2002 primarily in response to the Enron and WorldCom scandals. It is a private-sector, nonprofit corporation that oversees the auditors of public companies. As of April 2009, there were approximately 2,000 registered accounting firms. The PCAOB consists of five members, each of whom is appointed by the SEC.

U.S. Department of Justice (DOJ)

Whereas the SEC can enforce federal securities laws with civil litigation, the DOJ has jurisdiction over the *criminal* enforcement of those laws. What's the difference? Criminal cases don't involve two private parties. Instead, local, state, or federal governmental authorities charge individuals or businesses with a violation of law in criminal cases.

Each state, as well as Washington, D.C. and certain U.S. territories, has at least one U.S. Attorney who works to criminally enforce federal laws within that state or district. On fraud matters, the DOJ may work cooperatively with the SEC or independently.

State attorneys general

Each state has either an elected or appointed attorney general. The powers of this office vary from state to state, but virtually every state has *blue sky laws* that can be used to protect against securities violations. These laws were passed in most states before the enactment of the federal securities laws, and they enable states to take action against bogus stock sales. (For example, New York's Martin Act was passed in 1921.) State attorneys general also have the power to enforce other types of fraud, such as insurance fraud.

Whistleblowers/plaintiffs

Individuals also play a role in the fight against fraud. Many companies now have fraud hotlines that allow employees to call anonymously and blow the whistle on perceived wrongdoing. The complaints are monitored by an independent ombudsman and investigated as he deems appropriate. If a whistle-blower raises an issue regarding the misapplication of accounting standards, the ombudsman often involves a forensic accountant in the investigations.

One of the more commonly known whistleblower allegations is a *qui tam* action under the False Claims Act. This provision allows individuals who aren't affiliated with the government to file fraud claims against federal contractors. Initially, the DOJ investigates the whistleblower's claims and then decides to pursue or not pursue the action on behalf of the government. If the DOJ determines that the claim doesn't justify the assignment of government resources to proceed, the person making the claim can continue to pursue the claim without the government's participation. If that person is successful, the claim can be very lucrative for the whistleblower because a sizeable percentage of the award or settlement amount is paid to him.

Sometimes groups of individuals take action together in the face of potential fraud. For example, securities class action lawsuits may be filed if a group of investors suspects a company is issuing fraudulent financial information. (In a *class action lawsuit,* a large group of people bring a collective action before the court.) Typically, these cases are motivated by a dramatic drop in the market price of the stock. Upon investigation, investors may discover that they were purchasing the stock based on intentionally misleading information from the company. Or, they may find that the company failed to follow generally accepted accounting principles or SEC disclosures.

It's important to keep in mind that the definition of fraud varies among jurisdictions. In some courts, fraud requires an intentional act, whereas in others it requires only a *willful blindness,* meaning that someone issuing financial reports should have known the information was false but chose to turn a blind eye.

Something else to remember: Not every business fraud case has merit, and — obviously — fraud litigation is always filed after the supposed wrongdoing has occurred, which can make it difficult to prove exactly what was happening at the time. So the system of prosecuting fraudsters isn't perfect. But because the cost and consequences of being named in litigation — especially in a securities class action lawsuit — are so dire, the fear of litigation very likely deters some instances of fraud.

Other watchdogs

Many other regulators are also on the lookout for fraud. For example, the Internal Revenue Service, the Federal Deposit Insurance Corporation, the Controller of the Currency, the Financial Industry Regulatory Authority, the Postal Inspector, and the stock exchanges are all on the case. And virtually any law enforcement organization can investigate fraud if the wrongdoing occurs within its jurisdiction. For example, local law enforcement may investigate and prosecute a check-writing scheme or employee theft from a company.

With so many people watching, it seems astounding that perpetrators are bold enough to think that they can get away with fraud. Nonetheless, people continue to develop increasingly creative methods to obtain funds through financial theft, proving that greed cannot be legislated out of the human genome. Luckily for you, that means there will always be a demand for the services of forensic accountants.

Looking at the Litigation Process

In this section, we study the lifecycle of fraud litigation. A forensic accountant who understands the five components of the litigation process can be more effective in her role as a litigation consultant or an expert witness. (We discuss those roles later in the chapter.)

At any time prior to the case being adjudicated in court, the parties to civil litigation can *settle.* This simply means that the parties agree to terms outside of court, which eliminates the need to try the case. Settlements can occur during any phase, including in the midst of the case being tried or even after a trial but during the appeal. The majority of civil cases settle.

The term *settle* doesn't apply to criminal cases, but a defendant in a criminal case may avoid being tried through plea bargaining. Typically a plea bargain involves the defendant pleading to a lesser charge or a reduced sentence.

Pleadings

A legal *pleading* is a formal written statement filed with a court in a civil matter. There are three types of pleadings:

- ✔ **Complaint:** This is the first pleading submitted by the plaintiff. It sets forth the allegations of fact that prompted the legal action, and it includes something called a *prayer for relief,* which is a statement of the remedies that the plaintiff seeks from the court. The complaint usually contains information about the defendants, the court where the case is filed, and the law and legal theories that support the plaintiff's position.

- ✔ **Demurrer:** This pleading is filed by the defendant to challenge the complaint filed by the plaintiff on grounds that it hasn't met the legal standards of a proper complaint. A demurrer pleading essentially states that the defendant has no legal liability even if the facts alleged by the plaintiff hold true. The reasons for filing a demurrer are threefold: to force the plaintiff to clarify the complaint, to buy time in preparing a response, and to eliminate claims that don't have merit.

- ✔ **Answer:** This pleading is the defendant's response to the complaint. In it, the defendant admits to any allegations with which it agrees and denies other allegations. A defendant may also include a *cross complaint* in the answer, meaning that the defendant makes claims on the plaintiff (who becomes a *cross-defendant*).

Discovery

Discovery refers to the pre-trial phase in a lawsuit during which the parties request documents and other evidence from other parties. They can also compel the production of evidence by requesting the court to issue a subpoena. Here's what discovery usually includes:

- ✔ *Interrogatories,* which are written questions asked by a party of the other party, who must answer the questions in writing under oath.

✔ Requests for the production of documents, which may come in the form of court-issued subpoenas. These requests or subpoenas seek internal documents, e-mails, policy manuals, and other tangible evidence relevant to the case for which attorney-client privilege cannot be claimed.

✔ Requests for *admissions* that seek the opposing party's verification of information as fact.

✔ *Depositions,* which are oral testimonies provided by witnesses under oath by an attorney. Depositions allow lawyers to ask questions of potential witnesses in the case, and the witnesses' answers constitute sworn testimony. Depositions are taken before a court reporter so that an exact transcript of the questions and answers is created. These days, it's fairly common for depositions to also be videotaped.

The forensic accountant performs most of her work during the discovery phase. She collects the underlying facts, analyzes them, and reaches conclusions. When serving as an expert witness, she may give a deposition or help the attorney in taking a deposition. We go into more detail about these tasks later in the chapter.

Trial

Ah, yes — the stuff that TV shows are made of! Whereas most civil cases are settled out of court, and many criminal cases are resolved with plea bargains, some do end up in a courtroom. If a case goes to trial, it can be either a *jury trial* or a *bench trial*:

✔ In a jury trial, the judge determines the admissibility of evidence and instructs the jury on the applicable law. The jury determines the facts based on the credibility of the witnesses and the weight of the evidence.

✔ In a bench trial, the parties to the case waive a request for a jury trial and agree to have the judge fill the role of the jury as finder of fact.

Jury trials have the following five phases:

✔ **Jury selection:** The judge and attorneys question the jurors until 12 jurors are selected by all sides. Jurors who may have difficulty rendering a fair and impartial verdict are excused.

✔ **Opening statements:** These brief statements made by the attorneys to the jury lay out each side's case and what they hope to prove. The plaintiff's attorney in a civil case or a prosecutor in a criminal case gives the first statement. The defense attorney follows. In a civil case, the plaintiff bears the burden of proof at trial and must meet the standard of a preponderance of the evidence. (See the later section "Knowing the Standards of Proof.")

✔ **Presentation of evidence:** Witnesses are called to testify in this order:

- The plaintiff's witnesses testify first.

- Witnesses for the defense come next.

- Rebuttal witnesses are called at the end.

The attorney who calls each witness conducts a direct examination of that witness. Then the attorneys for the opposing party cross-examine the witness. This step can be followed by a *redirect* examination (where the first attorney asks more questions) and a *recross* examination (where the opposing party attorney steps up again).

✔ **Closing arguments:** This is the final opportunity for the attorneys to address the jury. The plaintiff's attorney makes a closing argument first, followed by the defense attorney. Each attorney summarizes the evidence and tries to persuade the jury why her client should prevail.

✔ **Jury deliberations:** The judge instructs the jury on the law(s) it must apply in the case. After the jury finishes deliberating, it reaches a verdict. The verdict is read by a jury foreperson elected by his fellow jurors.

In a bench trial, the jury selection phase doesn't apply, and deliberation is done by the judge alone or by a panel of judges.

Outcome

The most common type of litigation outcome is a *verdict*: the formal decision or finding rendered by the judge or jury in a jury trial. The jury may render either a general or a special verdict:

✔ In a *general verdict,* the jury finds for either the plaintiff or the defendant on all issues.

✔ In a *special verdict,* the jury decides on the facts of the case and leaves it to the judge to decide on the application of the law.

Appeal

An *appeal* is a process for requesting that a superior court reverse the decision of a lower court on the basis that the lower court committed an error in rendering its decision. A ruling by a judge or jury can be appealed if legal errors were made by the court in ruling on motions, admitting evidence, or instructing the jury.

The appeals court will examine the original ruling of the lower court and decide if the lower court committed any legal error or made a mistake in its reasoning.

Forensic accountants rarely provide any services during this phase because the appeals court analyzes the case based on the law rather than the facts.

Knowing the Standards of Proof

The phrase *standard of proof* refers to the magnitude of evidence that the prosecutor (in a criminal case) or the plaintiff's attorney (in a civil case) must present at trial in order to win. Depending on the type of fraud case, the trial lawyer needs to meet one of these standards:

- **Beyond a reasonable doubt:** In a criminal case, the prosecutor must prove his case so that the jurors have no reasonable doubt that the defendant committed whatever crime he is charged with. Criminal cases have the highest standard of proof.

- **Preponderance of the evidence:** In most civil cases, this standard of proof applies. It means that a plaintiff's attorney must show that it is *more likely than not* that his client's contention is true. This is the lowest level of proof; the plaintiff or the defendant (in certain instances) has to prove that there is greater than a 50 percent chance that his contention is true.

A third standard of proof you may be familiar with is "clear and convincing evidence." It doesn't apply to fraud cases; instead, this standard is used in cases in which a state seeks to terminate parental rights.

Getting the Forensic Accountant Involved in Litigation

Litigation involving financial issues or fraud can be complex, to say the least. Professionals with specific knowledge of accounting, economic, or financial information are critical to a company's hopes of seeing an appropriate outcome of the case. Forensic accountants may act as litigation consultants, expert witnesses, or both. We explain both roles in this section. In special circumstances, a judge may appoint a forensic accountant as a *trier of fact*, a role we also explain here.

Forensic accountants may be involved in either civil or criminal cases. They may also be involved in alternative dispute resolutions that are held out of court to resolve grievances either as an advocate to one of the parties or as a neutral arbitrator (a trier of fact).

Alternative dispute resolution

A court case is usually time consuming and costly. Therefore, parties engaged in disputes sometimes opt for alternative dispute resolution (ADR) mechanisms. Two forms of ADRs are arbitration and mediation:

In *arbitration*, the parties submit the dispute to one or more unofficial persons (meaning people who aren't judges or juries) who resolve the dispute privately. The results rendered by an arbitrator are generally binding on all parties.

Mediation usually occurs in marital dissolution cases. A mediator plays the role of reconciling the parties' dispute. A mediator helps the parties understand the strengths and weaknesses of both parties' positions and may suggest compromises to resolve the dispute. Unlike arbitration, this process is nonbinding.

Serving as a litigation consultant

Trial lawyers litigate suits of all types, from patent infringement to medical malpractice to accounting fraud. Try as they might, lawyers can't possibly be adequately trained in every discipline that may be at issue in legal disputes. In some cases, lawyers hire forensic accountants to help them sort through and understand the arcane accounting issues in their cases.

Sometimes, trial lawyers hire a single forensic accountant to act both as litigation consultant and expert witness (a role we explain next). But on occasion, lawyers hire litigation consultants separately from expert witnesses. If you're hired by a trial lawyer, you want to clarify up front — preferably in writing — what role you're expected to play.

Why wouldn't the trial lawyer just hire you to do both jobs? Because of *discoverability issues.* Here's what we mean: Any work performed by a consultant who is hired directly by the lawyer to assist with the case is protected as an attorney work product. On the other hand, any work performed by the expert is *discoverable*: It can be introduced into the case if requested by the other party. Sometimes, lawyers need to have open discussions on the technical issues with knowledgeable people without fear that the other side will have access to those conversations or memos. To allow these open discussions to happen, lawyers hire litigation consultants separate from experts to perform protected work.

Just to keep life interesting, you can be hired as a consultant and later asked by the trial lawyer to become an expert witness on the issues reviewed. If this situation occurs, existing rules states that all work performed both previous to and after being named the expert is discoverable. So both you and the trial lawyer(s) should make certain that nothing was said or prepared during your consultation that would be detrimental to your expert testimony. (If the terms of your previous engagement were set forth in a written engagement letter, that letter should be amended to reflect your additional role as a testifying expert.)

As of this writing, a movement is afoot to try to protect some of the work of the expert and eliminate the need for a separate litigation consultant, thus reducing the cost of litigation. Changes to the Federal Rules of Civil Procedure (FRCP) that pertain to expert testimony have been recommended to alleviate some of the inefficiencies and burdens associated with hiring experts. The proposed rule changes would provide work product protection for drafts of any expert reports and any communications between an expert and the attorney, except in the following three areas:

- ✔ Those that relate to compensation of the expert

- ✔ Any information provided by the attorney to the expert that was considered in the formulation of the expert's opinions

- ✔ Assumptions provided by the lawyer and upon which the expert relied in forming his or her opinions

We expect that these rule changes will be approved by the U.S. Congress and go into effect shortly after this book's publication, so by the time you read these words, they may be in place. If the changes take place, the separate role of litigation consultant will essentially disappear.

Taking the stand as an expert witness

Expert witnesses are hired to assist the judge or jury with understanding topics that are beyond common knowledge. A witness may be called to testify about certain expert opinions he has formulated based on complex factual issues within the case.

Disclosing expert witnesses

At some designated point in time before the trial begins, both parties must disclose to each other and to the court whether they intend to produce experts and who will act as the expert witnesses. Keep in mind that simply because an expert is disclosed by one party doesn't suggest that the expert's opinions are expected to be totally favorable to that party. The expectation is that the expert will be fair and objective to all sides.

The trial lawyers have to follow the rules of the court where the case is filed when disclosing expert witnesses. If an expert is disclosed past the required deadline, the expert may not be allowed to testify. Also, any opinions or other potential testimony of an expert that are not adequately disclosed to the other side and to the court can result in such opinions being impermissible at trial.

Following federal court rules

The rules governing expert disclosures can vary from venue to venue, so we can't very well summarize them here. Your state CPA society or bar association may have courses that cover the rules for expert witnesses in your state.

But there are specific rules for federal court embodied in the Federal Rules of Civil Procedure (FRCP). The FRCP covers many topics, but the rule that is pertinent to expert witnesses is Rule 26. The expert's opinions must be set forth in a written report signed by the witness, and the report must contain the following:

✔ A complete statement of all opinions the witness will express and the basis and reasons for them

✔ The data or other information considered by the witness in forming them

✔ Any exhibits that will be used to summarize or support them

✔ The witness's qualifications, including a list of all publications authored in the previous ten years

✔ A list of all other cases in which, during the previous four years, the witness testified at trial or deposition

✔ A statement of the compensation to be paid for the study and testimony in the case

The court may order experts to prepare additional documents, affidavits, and other supplemental reports. On occasion, experts may be asked to prepare a rebuttal report in response to the opinions expressed by the opposing expert.

Being deposed and heading to trial

Typically, after an expert witness is disclosed, he or she may be *deposed*: asked to provide oral testimony to the opposing counsel under oath. This step is taken so the opposing attorney can gain further knowledge with respect to that expert's opinions and possible testimony.

If the case proceeds to trial, experts who have been disclosed as witnesses may be called to testify. The party who engaged the witness first asks questions during the direct examination. The opposing attorney can then ask questions on cross-examination, leading to possible further questions by the attorney who originally called the witness. The expert and the lawyer who hires her usually spend considerable time in pretrial consultations in an effort to prepare the expert for trial testimony. In particular, they want to anticipate and prepare for the battery of questions that will come on cross-examination.

Being appointed a trier of fact

In cases that have complex accounting, economic, or financial issues, the court may appoint a forensic accountant to decide certain factual matters in a dispute. In this situation, the accountant is referred to as a *special master*. The expert is appointed to assist the judge in deciding these issues.

In contract disputes, the parties can stipulate that the issues should be resolved in an arbitration setting wherein an accounting or financial expert is the adjudicator or arbitrator. In instances where the judge appoints the special master, the expert's compensation is decided by the court. When the expert acts as an arbitrator in a private matter (such as a contract dispute), she is paid by the parties to the dispute.

Providing a Variety of Services

When an attorney hires a forensic accountant as a litigation consultant or expert witness, he relies on that person to provide assistance in a host of different ways. Especially in large cases, forensic accountants provide a plethora of services, which may include assisting with discovery, managing documents, developing case strategies, gathering intelligence, and calculating damages — subjects we touch on in this section.

Assisting with discovery

During the litigation process, discovery occurs between the time the original pleadings are made and the trial. In discovery, each party tries to ascertain the other side's facts and theories. Experts perform most of their work during this phase. The documents produced in discovery can be voluminous. Forensic accountants can assist attorneys in framing document requests and analyzing the data both during depositions and in cross-examinations of the other side's experts.

Managing documents and data

In Chapter 15, we discuss the uses of technology in retrieving and storing data. Technology experts help attorneys collect, organize, and analyze large data sets. They use computer systems for this purpose. These data sets include documents obtained from the client that are generally scanned to a document management system in the form of images.

Developing case strategy

Forensic accountants participate in the development of case strategy in terms of advising on the business issues in the case. When working as a litigation consultant, a forensic accountant can discuss the different analyses that she can perform on the accounting, economic, and financial data, and the theories that can be used based on the underlying facts and circumstances. The important thing to keep in mind is to be objective and independent.

Gathering intelligence

Forensic accountants can help attorneys in gathering intelligence to support their client's case. This task is usually done in the discovery phase. For instance, forensic accountants can investigate where former employees and other persons of interest are situated, conduct background searches, and identify the presence of assets and funds. We discuss the process of gathering intelligence in Chapter 14.

Calculating damages

In commercial litigation, forensic accountants often calculate damages as expert witnesses. The central concept here is that the defendant's harmful act reduced the plaintiff's earnings or streams of economic value. These streams may be the profits earned by a business or the sale of a business or its property. The harmful act could be a breach of contract or the occurrence of an event (such as an oil spill).

After a defendant's liability has been established (which is a legal question), the forensic accountant conducts a damages study. We explain how that happens next.

Quantifying lost profits

There are two components of lost profits:

- *Historical lost profits* reflect the actual performance experienced by the damaged party from the time of the event through the trial date.

- *Future lost profits* (also called *but-for-value*) refers to the calculation of financial performance that the damaged party would have experienced had it not been for the harmful action or event.

A financial statement that is prepared based on what would have been is called a *pro-forma* financial statement. CPAs must follow specific requirements for the presentation of a pro-forma statement. You can find these requirements in an auditing textbook such as *Auditing and Assurance Services: Understanding the Integrated Audit,* 1st edition, by Karen L. Hooks (John Wiley & Sons).

But-for studies are conducted both pre-trial and post-trial. The pre-trial damages calculation shows the financial performance that the damaged party would have achieved during the period from the event date through the trial date if not for the harmful event. The post-trial *but-for* scenario refers to the financial performance that would have been achieved subsequent to the trial date, either for a fixed period of time into the future or into perpetuity, but for the harmful action or event.

The forensic accountant performs the following steps in quantifying lost profits:

- ✔ **Reconstructing financial records:** The forensic accountant assesses the availability of financial records to calculate actual performance. An important component of this task is determining whether the financial records are reliable.

- ✔ **Analyzing mitigation issues:** This step involves determining what the injured party *could have done* to minimize the damages stemming from the harmful action or event and what it actually did. If the injured party didn't do anything to minimize the damages, it may be necessary to decrease the calculated losses. That's because the injured party must assume responsibility for some of the losses that were within its control.

- ✔ **Calculating costs:** This task involves determining the *normal* level of expenses incurred by the injured party historically. (The forensic accountant should make sure that extraordinary and personal expenses are not included in this calculation.) In a *but-for* performance calculation, the forensic accountant calculates the projected costs that the injured party would have incurred in the future. The projected costs should be reasonable from the perspective of how close they reflect reality, which is truly a challenging proposition.

- ✔ **Determining market impact:** The forensic accountant studies a company's market impact by first looking at the market or size of the industry that the injured party operates in. She then determines the extent that the injured party has penetrated the market, and the extent to which it could have done so if not for the harmful action or event.

- ✔ **Projecting lost sales and operating cash flows:** The forensic accountant estimates the level and the quality of sales and cash flows that the injured party could have generated if not for the harmful event. Toward this end, she estimates a growth rate that is reasonable. Issues to keep in mind include whether the party has the infrastructure or sufficient working capital or cash flow to have achieved the projected sales.

Calculating prejudgment interest

Prejudgment interest is the interest that an injured party could have earned on the revenue it would have been making if not for the harmful action or event. The time period for calculating this interest spans from the date of the event until the date of judgment by the court.

State law may dictate how the forensic accountant must calculate prejudgment interest when calculating damages to an injured party. The law may call for excluding the interest altogether, limiting interest to a statutory rate, or excluding compounding interest. There is no hard and fixed rule about using simple or compound interest. Similarly, disagreements may arise between the parties regarding whether the interest should be calculated before or after taxes — or, for that matter, whether the interest rate represents the lending rate of the injured party or the borrowing rate of the defendant. Obviously, this is pretty technical territory, but that's where forensic accountants thrive!

Projecting future earnings

When calculating damages, the parties in a litigation may disagree regarding the injured party's projections of future earnings. Maybe the injured party doesn't have a long track record of profits (it's a recent start-up, for example). Or the two sides may disagree about whether to project inflation when considering future earnings. When losses are projected into perpetuity, issues such as inflation can mean a lot. Or, they may mean nothing: Forensic accountants may not consider future inflation in their projections at all. If they choose to ignore inflation, they are projecting future losses in *constant dollars*.

Discounting future losses

The forensic accountant calculates the amount of damages needed to replace future lost profits. To do so, he performs a present-value calculation of the losses by discounting those losses to the current period. A *discount factor* calculates the amount of dollars needed at the time of the trial to compensate for the loss of a dollar in the future. Usually, the discount factor uses a compounded interest rate called the *discount rate*.

Taking Care of Business

If you're going to hire yourself out as a litigation consultant or expert witness, you need to know a few things about the business of doing those jobs. We cover the essentials in this section.

Getting paid

For a forensic accountant providing litigation services, the most common fee arrangement is billing based on hours worked: You charge a standard hourly rate plus out-of-pocket expenses. Sometimes, forensic accountants work on a fixed-fee basis.

You want to avoid a *contingent fee arrangement*, which means that you get paid if you help the party hiring you prevail in court. The American Bar Association considers it an ethical violation for its members to put up an expert witness and compensate him on a contingent basis. That's because if the expert's compensation is tied to the outcome of the case, his independence and objectivity are impaired.

Consider taking a retainer from the client that you can adjust against your final invoice. Doing so reduces the chances that you won't be paid fully for your services.

Understanding the work product privilege

Most of us know about the attorney-client privilege thanks to TV shows and movies set in the courtroom. In short, certain communications between the attorney and the client are protected and, thus, kept confidential.

The *work product privilege* is broader in scope than the attorney-client privilege. It means that any materials prepared in anticipation of litigation are protected from discovery by the opposing counsel. As a result, your preliminary opinions, observations, draft schedules, reports, and impressions prior to the issuance of your final expert report will not be discoverable. The opposing party can negate this privilege only by proving that it cannot otherwise obtain the information without undue hardship.

When you work on litigation, label or stamp all the documents you prepare prior to issuing your expert report. Use the following wording: Privileged and Confidential, Subject to the Attorney-Client and Work Product Privileges.

Protecting your work papers

As an expert witness or a litigation consultant, you generate work papers supporting the work you perform. If you're hired as an expert witness, the opposing counsel can gain access to the materials you have prepared in supporting your opinion, including notes and calculations. But if you're hired as a litigation consultant, the attorney representing your client can assert the work product privilege, which means your work papers may not be discoverable.

Chapter 18

Organizing Evidence and Serving as an Expert Witness

*E*xpert testimony is used in a lot of litigation these days. When you're hired to serve as an expert witness, you must understand your primary target audience: the jury. Jurors take their work seriously, but are placed in the difficult position of needing to evaluate complex technical matters that they may know nothing about. They generally cannot ask questions during the trial and are not permitted to take notes, do any research on their own, or discuss matters with each other until they deliberate the final outcome of the case.

The most important function of your expert testimony is to *persuade* the jury. Jurors are more likely to be persuaded when they trust you. To be persuasive, you have to establish and maintain credibility, and credibility requires honesty. In the words of Edward R. Murrow, "To be persuasive we must be believable. To be believable we must be credible. To be credible we must be truthful."

To demonstrate your credibility, you have to prepare diligently for your testimony. Preparation is critical because when you are unprepared, the chances of making errors increase and you appear nervous. Preparation enables you to be confident and self-assured during testimony. It makes you more persuasive.

In this chapter, you discover various techniques and skills you can use to effectively communicate with the judge and the jury. With this information in hand, you'll be in a position to excel in your testimony.

Are You an Expert Witness or a Fact Witness?

Fact witnesses are involved in trials as a result of having direct knowledge about the issues relevant to the case. This type of witness testifies about what he has seen, heard, or experienced. For example, a controller of an organization may be called to testify in a financial fraud case about the process of preparing the financial statements. Sometimes fact witnesses volunteer to testify. In other instances, they're required to testify because they've been served with a *subpoena:* a formal, written court order compelling their witness testimony or the production of evidence under a penalty for failure. In either case, fact witnesses must limit their testimony to facts of the case.

An *expert witness* testifies by virtue of his knowledge, skill, experience, training, or education in a particular area. His expertise and specialized knowledge is meaningful to one of the litigation parties as it attempts to prove its side of the case. An expert testifies voluntarily by agreement with one of the parties or the court.

A key distinction between fact witnesses and expert witnesses is that an expert witness usually provides an opinion. Also, unlike a fact witness, an expert is entitled to compensation for participation in the case.

There are two types of expert witnesses: non-testifying and testifying experts. Here's how their roles differ:

- **Non-testifying expert:** Someone would hire a non-testifying expert to evaluate her case. In this circumstance, the expert advice or opinion is protected from discovery by the opposing party or its counsel. (*Discovery* is the phase before the trial in which each party requests documents and other evidence from other parties. The requesting party has the right to compel the production of evidence by using a subpoena or requests for the production of documents and depositions.)
- **Testifying expert:** A testifying expert takes part in the trial itself. His identity and the documents used to prepare his testimony are discoverable to the other side in litigation.

Knowing What Is Expected from an Expert

When you're an expert witness, bringing great qualifications and experience to the table is like winning half the battle. The other half involves avoiding common mistakes, choosing the right methodology to form an opinion, and taking steps from the start to ensure your success.

Steering clear of failure

To be an effective expert witness, it helps to study why some financial experts fail in this role. Here are some common reasons for failure:

- ✔ The expert is not knowledgeable about the important facts of the case.

- ✔ There are inconsistencies between an expert's direct testimony and cross-examination. For instance, the expert seems clear and concise during direct testimony, but evasive and hesitant during cross-examination. These inconsistencies create the wrong impression in jurors' minds, and they start to question the expert's credibility.

- ✔ The expert uses unnecessary jargon and terms of art. A *term of art* is a word or phrase that has special meaning in a particular context. (One example is *punitive damages,* which means that monetary compensation is awarded to an injured party that exceeds the losses suffered as a result of the injuries sustained; it is intended to punish the wrongdoer.) Using unfamiliar words and phrases creates a distance between you and the jury. When using a technical term, take the time to explain it succinctly and clearly. And don't ever use acronyms — you'll confuse the jury.

- ✔ The expert has not practiced his testimony in a meaningful manner. Practice allows an expert, even an experienced one, to be exposed to what he would encounter in a live trial setting. Sometimes cross-examination is really stressful. Having a meaningful practice can help you get used to responding under pressure.

Choosing your methodology carefully

If the methodology you use to form an opinion is unsound, you'll very likely face a *Daubert challenge:* a hearing with the judge requested by opposing counsel to challenge the validity of your testimony (see Chapter 16). If the judge agrees that your methodology is shaky, your testimony will not be admissible. Even if your testimony survives a Daubert challenge, opposing counsel can still challenge your methodology during cross-examination.

How do you select the right methodology? Keep in mind that the methodology must meet these criteria:

- ✔ **It can and has been tested.** Testing is often considered the most important factor in a Daubert challenge because it verifies your methodology and conclusions and bolsters your opinion.

- ✔ **It's been subject to peer review and publication.** Peer-reviewed articles in prestigious journals support the theory you are using by showing that it has been previously scrutinized by other experts who are best able to detect flaws in the methodology.

- ✔ **It has a known or potential error rate that indicates you've used a precise methodology.** There is no requirement that expert testimony is admissible only if the expert is able to state her opinions with a quantifiable degree of certainty. Experts are required to merely mention the error rate.

- ✔ **It's accepted in the relevant professional community.** Your opinion should be accepted in your professional field of expertise. For example, if you are opining on a valuation matter, the valuation approaches that are accepted in the valuation community are the income, market, and asset approaches.

- ✔ **It existed before the litigation.** You don't want to create a methodology solely for the litigation at hand.

- ✔ **It adequately accounts for alternative explanations.** Your methodology should also test for alternative explanations. The question to be raised here is: Does the data support reasonable alternatives that may also explain the *facts* of the case?

Aiming for success

Here are some do's and don'ts to keep in mind as you prepare to be an expert witness:

- ✔ **Ask for sufficient time to prepare.** When you sign your *retention contract* (the agreement with the party that's hiring you), make sure your engagement letter states that you'll be given adequate time to review the evidence, conduct research, and formulate your opinion.

- ✔ **Conduct a thorough investigation.** Do your research, and examine the evidence. Obtain and review all relevant documents with care. Give the jury the impression that you have done your homework.

- ✔ **Be careful about note taking.** Your notes related to your testimony are generally discoverable. Don't create any notes that are inflammatory, show bias, or could be misconstrued and used against you. Moreover, don't destroy or discard your notes. Doing so can be very damaging to your role as an expert.

- ✔ **Do not share draft reports with retaining counsel.** This material is fodder for opposing counsel, who will try to show that the retaining counsel directed subsequent changes to your report.

- ✔ **Be transparent about changes to your report.** If you *do* show a draft report to retaining counsel, and if he or she requests legitimate changes to your report, issue an addendum to the original report. Don't try to hide the fact that changes have been made.

- ✔ **Do not testify outside your area of expertise.** If you have any doubts about whether you're qualified to testify on the subject in question, don't do it.

✔ **Prepare extensively.** We repeat this advice several times in this chapter. That's because preparation goes a long way not only in building your self-confidence but also in persuading the jury that what you say is true.

Presenting Your Credentials: Preparing Your CV

As an expert witness, you'll be asked to provide copies of your most recent *curriculum vitae* (CV) to the attorneys for both sides and to the court prior to trial or the deposition hearing. A CV is similar to a résumé but provides more details. An expert's CV outlines her qualifications to testify as an expert witness and highlights her knowledge, skill, experience, training, and education in a particular field of expertise.

Preparing a CV is an important part of your role as an expert — don't underestimate its importance! Set aside the necessary time to proofread and review it. Have another set of eyes take a look at it. Here are some other suggestions to help you make it bulletproof:

✔ **Ensure the accuracy of every item on your CV.** Has anything changed since you wrote your CV? If so, update that information.

✔ **Make sure timelines are accurate.** Also, explain any gaps that exist. For example, if you took a year off after college to backpack around Europe, don't fudge your CV to try to cover up that gap; acknowledge what you were doing during that year.

✔ **Be consistent.** Your CV is going to change over time, but don't make changes that create inconsistencies among the various versions. Add your new experiences, and remove those that seem less relevant as time passes, but don't change facts.

✔ **Give everyone the same version.** If you're serving as an expert witness for multiple clients, give them all the same CV.

✔ **Be honest about professional societies and certifications.** If you paid a fee to obtain credentials from an organization but haven't otherwise participated, remove that organization from your CV.

✔ **Include any writing you've done.** Make sure that the titles are complete and accurate, the dates of publication are correct, and co-authors are listed.

✔ **List previous cases you have worked on.** List all cases you have worked on as an expert at trial or by deposition within the last four years. Don't list the outcome of the cases because cases are generally won or lost based on the strength of the underlying facts.

✔ **Remove unnecessary information.** Don't include your political affiliations, Social Security number, or activities unrelated to your professional qualifications.

> ✔ **Avoid padding.** Examples include unearned degrees and designations and continuing education courses. Also, if you've authored articles, don't list them more than once.
>
> ✔ **Refrain from puffery.** You don't need to claim to be the "world's leading expert" or even "nationally known." If you're nationally known, the parties involved will already know that!

Preparing Your Files

After reviewing the evidence at hand, and before going to trial, you create a report that contains an opinion about the issue at hand (such as economic damages). The report usually contains, as an appendix, references to documents that formed the bases for your opinion. That way, this information can be easily accessed at trial.

In reality, you're likely to review many documents that you don't specifically reference in your report. If that's the case, you should also create an index listing all the information and data that has been provided to you.

In larger engagements, where the data to be reviewed is enormous, you generally have a team of qualified professionals assisting you in reviewing the data. In this case, you would use an electronic repository for storing the information. These repositories usually come with index formats. Ask the other team members reviewing the data to diligently complete the index and cross-reference it to your report.

You also need to maintain other documents created during your engagement, including billing records, field notes, correspondence with counsel, and any existing draft reports. Any of these items may become the subject of subsequent discovery by the other party.

Is every document you create leading up to the trial subject to discovery? Probably. The Federal Rules of Civil Procedure say that *privileged* information is not discoverable, and examples of privileged information include attorney-client, spousal, and doctor-patient communications. However, in most jurisdictions there is no attorney-client privilege between the attorney and the expert because the expert is not represented by the attorney. Therefore, any communication between the expert and retaining counsel is not protected by this privilege. Most federal courts will not protect any "data or other information considered" by the expert in forming his opinion. Also, no work product privilege exists to protect anything provided by retaining counsel to the expert.

Giving Live Testimony

Prior to testifying, you need to think about what you must do to make your testimony resonate with the jury. Accounting and economic testimony is generally complex and rarely piques the interests of jurors. In other words, you run the risk of boring the jury to tears! Your challenge is to get at least one juror to actually listen to you.

In this section, we show you how to present yourself during your testimony so the jury will actually listen, as well as how to hold up under cross cross-examination. We also spell out what you should and shouldn't say and how to become aware of what your body language is saying.

Getting the jury to listen

Your testimony generally will not occur in the early stages of a case's lifespan. Keeping the jurors' attention — especially after they've heard lots of other testimony — can be tough. To persuade the jury that what you're saying is correct, you have to make sure the jury remembers your testimony when they start deliberating.

Should you wear fluorescent colors? Present your testimony in the form of a song? You can't be anything but professional when you're in the role of expert witness, so being flashy definitely won't help (and will likely ruin your reputation in the field). Instead, you need to put yourself in the shoes of a juror and understand what jurors expect from financial experts.

 First and foremost, jurors expect experts to be prepared and organized. They have little patience for a presentation that is disorderly and haphazard. Jurors also expect experts to explain in simple and clear terms why their testimony matters and why the jury should listen and try to comprehend. To accomplish these objectives, you must be at ease on the witness stand. Be your normal self, and don't be deceptive. Jurors will forgive your flaws if they believe you to be credible.

Here are some other tips to keep in mind when providing live testimony:

- ✔ Respect the jury, and convey this point to them.
- ✔ Try to come across to the jury as an excellent teacher and communicator.
- ✔ Make sure that the jurors can hear you.
- ✔ Maintain eye contact with the jury without appearing to stare at them.
- ✔ Appear confident in yourself and in your opinions.

✔ Do not appear to convey that you are an advocate of the party who hired you.

✔ Provide analogies to drive home points to the jury.

✔ Use effective visual aids to assist in your testimony.

✔ Cite specific references, including published and peer-reviewed research.

✔ Don't talk down to the jurors, but keep your explanations simple. Imagine that you're explaining the material to an eighth grader.

✔ Don't come across as a number-cruncher; you want your message to go beyond numbers. Tell a story that the jurors understand and care about.

✔ Make sure your opinion seems reasonable.

✔ Tell the truth.

✔ Know the facts of the case and your analysis like the back of your hand.

✔ Answer only questions that you understand; ask counsel to explain ambiguous questions.

✔ See and fully read the documents presented to you.

✔ Consider alternative opinions and have reasons for rejecting them.

✔ Stay in your sandbox. In other words, don't stray from your area of expertise. This is important because if your testimony is found to be incompetent or inadmissible, it will damage your reputation as a professional and an expert.

✔ Do not use terms that you cannot define. Doing so would imply that you are testifying beyond your area of expertise

Surviving cross-examination

Cross-examination is all about control. Attorneys maintain control by asking leading questions that limit your ability to explain and questions that the attorney knows how you'll answer.

Attorneys typically map out a strategy for cross-examining expert witnesses. Put simply, attorneys will try their best to undermine your credibility and destroy the merit of your testimony. Understanding how attorneys prepare to cross-examine you allows you to prepare effectively for their questions. Here's what you need to do:

✔ Before the trial, determine the limited number of points the attorney will try to make during cross-examination. The party hiring you can help with this step by pointing out which parts of your testimony the opposing counsel will likely focus on.

✔ Anticipate that the attorney will try to get you to say something to support the other party's case. Be prepared for those attempts to get you to admit that an opposing opinion may be true or to concede that your testimony is weak in a certain area. Again, your own preparation is key so you can stand firm in your opinions.

✔ Realize that the attorney wants to show that you are weak or deficient in some way. She may try to point out your potential biases or any inconsistencies between your report and prior statements you've made.

Knowing what to say, what not to say, and when to shut up

The witness box is the stage on which you perform. To be a good expert witness, you must know that there are things you should and shouldn't say in a courtroom. Cases are won or lost because of testimony. When you're giving yours, be aware of these general guidelines:

✔ If you do not understand the question, say so. Do not guess the meaning; have the counsel rephrase the question.

✔ Never exaggerate your qualifications.

✔ Do not volunteer information. Answer only the question asked.

✔ Do not offer opinions outside your area of expertise.

✔ Don't lose your temper.

✔ Pause and think before answering.

✔ Avoid jokes, sarcasm, and inappropriate remarks.

✔ Use your qualifications as an opportunity to teach and bond with the jury.

✔ Mention any local roots or affiliations you may have.

✔ Explain how you obtained your training and certifications in your field of expertise.

✔ Discuss your work history.

✔ Let the jury know whether you have any military history.

✔ If you have obtained your degree from a prominent university or worked for easily recognizable and reputable organizations, mention them.

✔ Get to the point and give your conclusions early on in your testimony.

In many cases, the opposing party may hire an expert witness of their own. Here's how to handle that situation:

✔ Don't try to trash the opposing expert; you may appear biased and appear to be an advocate for the party that hired you.

✔ Show respect to the other expert.

✔ Succinctly discuss your disagreements with the other expert. Point to reasons why you disagree, such as:

- The expert's opinion is outside his area of expertise.

- The methodology that has been used is unreliable.

- The expert has made incorrect factual assumptions.

- The expert has used standards and regulations that are not generally accepted in the field.

- The investigation performed is incomplete at best.

Above all, make sure you do the following:

✔ Speak clearly and distinctly. Do not mumble.

✔ Testify only within your area of expertise.

✔ Respect the collective wisdom and intelligence of the jury.

✔ Use words the jury will understand.

✔ Address and acknowledge your own weaknesses.

✔ Demonstrate an absolute command of the facts.

✔ Never overstate your opinion.

Mastering your body language

Your nonverbal actions are extremely important in communicating your credibility and believability. You need to work on eliminating any distracting behavior. Straightening your tie, twirling your hair, adjusting your glasses, or shifting around in your chair will come across as a sign of nervousness or defensiveness; the jury may think you have something to hide. You need to be calm to be credible.

Does that mean you need to sit in your chair as stiff as a board? Absolutely not! Effective nonverbal communication includes leaning forward, listening attentively, and using minimal hand gestures. Maintain eye contact with the attorney when the question is being asked. Your goal is to appear confident, relaxed, and comfortable. If you slouch, you will come across as being nonchalant, unconcerned, and bored with the court proceeding. You do not want to convey this message with your body language.

Preparing for an examination before trial (EBT)

Another form of live testimony takes place before the trial and requires just as much preparation. When you testify during a *deposition,* you are examined under oath and outside of the courtroom. The opposing counsel usually takes your deposition to learn about your background and the bases for your opinion. The deposition often affords the only opportunity prior to trial for counsel to question you. If you're required to submit an expert report, the deposition will be conducted after your report is done.

In case you're wondering, courts usually require the party seeking discovery to pay the expert a reasonable fee for the time spent on responding to discovery. So don't worry; no one expects you to volunteer!

A stenographer is present to scribe the deposition proceedings. Some depositions are also videotaped. As an expert witness, you should do your best to excel during your deposition. Depositions are a critical part of the outcome of the case for two reasons: First, most cases settle before going to trial. Second, your deposition can be used against you if the case goes to trial.

Here are some things you want to avoid during your deposition:

- ✔ Appearing to be uncomfortable, nervous, or anxious
- ✔ Fidgeting
- ✔ Searching for answers
- ✔ Showing arrogance, anger, or combativeness
- ✔ Eating, drinking, or chewing on gum, pens, or pencils
- ✔ Attending to cell phones or pagers

In federal cases and in many state courts, you have the right to read, sign, and correct your deposition. You generally have 30 days upon completing your deposition to review the transcript or the recording of the proceeding. This step enables you to change any part of the transcript that you believe to be incorrect. You will sign a statement reciting such changes and the reasons for making them.

Dressing for court or a deposition

You should wear conservative clothing while testifying in court or getting deposed. A dark business suit with a white or light blue shirt is appropriate for men. For women, a suit or a long-sleeved dress is preferred. Avoid excessive jewelry or accessories. Makeup and hair should be simple and neat.

Creating Visual Testimony

So far in this chapter, we've focused mainly on how to present your words and your physical appearance to a jury in the most effective way. But visual aids can be very helpful as well. Many people retain information presented visually better than information communicated verbally. If you want the jury to really remember your key points (and trust us, you do!), consider adding visual communications to your testimony.

Here are some simple rules to follow when it comes to visual communications:

- ✔ **Create a story with your testimony.** Use a combination of different visual aids to showcase your testimony including charts, graphs, and copies of important documents.

- ✔ **Select an optimum number of visuals; don't overdo it.** Too many charts and visuals will dilute the impact of the important ones.

- ✔ **Follow the five-second rule.** Design your visuals in such a way that a juror can digest the main points in five seconds.

- ✔ **Make the visuals colorful.** For example, for charts viewed from a distance, use light type on a dark background. For accounting information such as a balance sheet, select one or two salient pieces of information and make them stand out from the rest.

- ✔ **Emphasize what matters most.** When you are visually presenting an important piece of evidence, highlight or enlarge the important portions of the document that you want jurors to focus on.

Chapter 19

Peeking Inside Federal Government Fraud Cases

. . . .

In This Chapter

▶ Knowing the basics of federal law and crime categories

▶ Meeting some federal agencies involved in financial crime cases

▶ Learning the steps involved in a federal case

▶ Reacting when a government agent knocks on your client's door

. . . .

The reality of life is that not everyone who commits a financial crime is caught. Many people do get caught, however, and if the agency doing the catching is an arm of the federal government, the penalties they face can be very steep.

In this chapter, we look at how financial crimes, including occupational fraud, are investigated and prosecuted by the U.S. government. Federal prosecutors possess tremendous power — the mere prospect of an investigation sends chills down a person's spine. For a company, a federal investigation or indictment can wreak havoc on its business, including damaging its reputation.

One of the toughest decisions that federal law enforcement agencies face is *who* to investigate. Law enforcement agencies face many challenges, such as resource constraints in terms of personnel, equipment, time, and money. Federal investigators juggle many assignments; they cannot spend their whole careers working on only a few cases. Consider this example: Tracing all the transactions in just one Ponzi scheme alone could take years. There comes a point in time when the investigator stops an investigation, summarizes the evidence, refers it for prosecution, and moves on to the next case.

In other chapters, we show you how forensic accountants conduct investigations on behalf of companies and individuals. In this chapter, we discuss the roles played by various government agencies in investigating civil and criminal financial frauds. Just as they do in other cases, forensic accountants who work for federal agencies apply accounting methods and financial techniques to assist in solving crimes.

An important point to understand is that the primary goal of the federal law enforcement officer (and, by extension, forensic accountants working for federal agencies) is to identify and document specific events involving the movement of money during the course of a crime. When money is exchanged, it involves two or more people or entities, and someone is inevitably giving direction to move the money. This action generates witnesses. Documentary evidence plus witness testimony help in prosecuting financial crimes.

Understanding Some Basics of Federal Law

To gain a basic understanding of how federal fraud cases work, you first need to know that there are many categories of law. To start, here are two key groupings:

- **Civil law:** The body of law that deals with conflicts and differences between individuals or entities. Remedies are usually in the form of money damages or court-ordered actions, such as doing (or refraining from doing) specific things.

- **Criminal law:** The branch of the law that deals with offenses of a *public* nature — wrongdoing committed against federal and state statutes. If you violate a criminal law, you face penalties, fines, and/or incarceration.

Within the "criminal law" category, crimes are further divided into two types:

- **Felony:** A serious crime punishable by incarceration for a period exceeding one year, a fine, and loss of certain civil rights.

- **Misdemeanor:** A less serious crime than a felony, which usually results in a fine and/or incarceration for less than one year.

Proving the elements of a crime

The elements of a crime are those component parts that must be proven in order to convict someone. The elements of federal crimes are embodied in the *United States Code*, a publication of the text of statutes enacted by Congress. This code is updated every six years with cumulative supplements being issued during intervening years. The United States Code is usually found in the reference section of any library. You can also access it online at http://uscode.house.gov.

All federal laws (*statutes*) are grouped according to subject matter within the United States Code. (They are *codified.*) The United States Code has 50 titles, or broad categories, of statutes. Titles may be further subdivided into parts, subchapters, or chapters. Let's say that you are reading a story about a financial crime. You research the press release issued by the United States Attorney's Office, and it states that the defendant was convicted of violating 26 U.S.C. §7201. "U.S.C." stands for United States Code, "26" is the title number within which the statute is found, "§" is the symbol for section, and "7201" is the actual section of the statute.

In 2008 and 2009, the most common federal investigations resulting in sentences related to drug trafficking and fraud. Money laundering and tax evasion cases were significantly lower, but don't let the numbers fool you: Money laundering and tax evasion cases are among the most complex financial investigations and are very time-consuming to investigate.

Realizing how federal financial crimes differ from others

Federal financial crimes have certain characteristics that are not seen in other federal or state crimes:

- ✔ **They often have better** *jury appeal* **than other criminal cases.** In other words, the people being prosecuted may be business professionals such as bankers, lawyers, investment brokers, and accountants — professionals whom many jurors can relate to seeing in their everyday lives. In another type of case, such as a state murder trial, the jurors may believe that they have little in common with the defendant.

- ✔ **These cases tend to have better informants than cases tried at the state level.** For example, a federal case may be built around the testimony of a *whistleblower:* an inside person with access to detailed information about an alleged crime.

- ✔ **Severe sentences are meted out in federal financial cases.** Financial crimes create economic losses and are crimes of greed. (Other types of crimes, such as murder, assault, or rape, are crimes of passion.) At the federal level, these cases can carry some pretty stiff penalties.

From an investigation perspective, the federal approach is similar to that used at the state level: Evidence is obtained by issuing search warrants, and assets are forfeited or seized. As with any financial investigation, a federal investigation may uncover assets that would not normally be discovered, resulting in their forfeiture.

Fighting Fraud in the Government Sector: The Enforcers

Many government agencies deal with financial crimes, both on a civil and criminal level. City agencies, municipalities, state agencies, and federal agencies all have some form of jurisdiction over financial crime cases. There are even agencies at the global level that may have jurisdiction.

In each state, district attorneys, state's attorneys, attorneys general, and county and city prosecutors all share responsibility for prosecuting financial crime violations. Much of the work at the state level focuses on identity theft, but some prosecutorial offices have jurisdiction to investigate more complex financial fraud, such as money laundering.

But the juiciest cases involving financial crimes occur at the federal level, where the Federal Bureau of Investigation (FBI) has historically been the main agency dealing with financial crime. Ready for a surprise? The FBI doesn't have jurisdiction over every financial crime. The Criminal Investigation Division of the Internal Revenue Service, the Securities and Exchange Commission, the Drug Enforcement Agency, the United States Postal Service, the Department of Housing and Urban Development, and the U.S. Secret Service are a few of the other agencies charged with the power to investigate financial crimes as well.

And none of these agencies, including the FBI, actually prosecutes the crimes it investigates. Instead, when these agencies' investigations are complete, they provide information to the U.S. Attorney who has jurisdiction over the particular case. The U.S. Attorney actually handles the prosecution.

In this section, we start by introducing you to the U.S. Department of Justice, which is the agency overseeing all the U.S. Attorneys who prosecute federal cases. We then describe the efforts of just four of the federal agencies that are kept busy investigating occupational fraud and other financial crimes: the IRS, the Security and Exchange Commission (SEC), the FBI, and the recently created Office of the Special Inspector General for the Troubled Asset Relief Program (TARP).

The U.S. Department of Justice

The U.S. Attorneys serve as the nation's principal litigators under the direction of the Attorney General. There are 93 U.S. Attorneys stationed throughout the United States, Puerto Rico, the Virgin Islands, Guam, and the Northern Mariana Islands. U.S. Attorneys are appointed by, and serve at the discretion of, the President of the United States, with the advice and consent of the United States Senate. Each U.S. Attorney is the chief federal law enforcement officer within his particular jurisdiction.

Each U.S. Attorney assigns cases to Assistant U.S. Attorneys (AUSAs), who serve as prosecutors for those cases. An AUSA can be likened to a quarterback on a football team. This person is managed by a coach (the U.S. Attorney) but calls the plays on the field with the input of all the other players (such as Special Agents of the investigating agencies).

The federal prosecutor has a great deal of power but also a great deal of responsibility. (We're reminded of a scene in *Spiderman* here.) He has the responsibility of representing the United States in court and making critical decisions affecting individuals and the public. He is also responsible for each case from inception through trial and appeal to the United States Court of Appeals. Experienced AUSAs handle complex and sophisticated investigations and prosecutions that have national and international significance. Some of these legal actions result in media attention and intense public scrutiny.

Other law enforcement agencies refer investigations to the local U.S Attorney's Office. For example, the IRS and the FBI do not prosecute investigations. Some financial crime cases may be assigned to specialized units of the Department of Justice, such as the Anti-Trust Division or the Tax Division.

The Internal Revenue Service

The Criminal Investigation (CI) Division of the Internal Revenue Service stands apart from other investigative agencies. To qualify as a Special Agent for the agency, you need a minimum of 15 accounting credits. Although the FBI, the U.S. Department of Housing and Urban Development (HUD), and the Secret Service also hire Special Agents with accounting backgrounds, none of them requires the accounting credits that the IRS does. Most of the Special Agents hired by IRS Criminal Investigation have accounting degrees and prior accounting experience.

The CI division serves the American public by investigating potential criminal violations of the Internal Revenue Code and related financial crimes with the goal of fostering confidence in the tax system and compliance with the law. A criminal action is brought against a taxpayer who *willfully* attempts to hide income from the federal government. Willful behavior is also an integral part of proving other criminal activity, including fraud, money laundering, or Bank Secrecy Act violations.

The agency is composed of approximately 4,100 employees worldwide, about 2,700 of whom are Special Agents whose investigative jurisdiction includes tax, money laundering, and Bank Secrecy Act laws. How many cases do these agents handle? In 2009, the CI division initiated 4,121 investigations and recommended prosecution 2,570 times. More than 2,100 people were convicted that year based on the work of the CI division.

Whereas other federal agencies also have investigative jurisdiction for money laundering and Bank Secrecy Act violations, the IRS is the only federal agency that can investigate criminal violations of the Internal Revenue Code.

Securities and Exchange Commission

The SEC is a law enforcement agency that protects investors and is charged with maintaining fair, orderly, and efficient capital markets. The Division of Enforcement within the SEC prosecutes violations of securities laws. It recommends the commencement of investigations and civil actions in federal court or before an administrative law judge; it also prosecutes these cases on behalf of the Commission.

The Division of Enforcement is organized into the following five specialized units:

- **Asset Management:** This unit focuses on investigations involving investment advisors, investment companies, hedge funds, and private equity funds.

- **Market Abuse:** This unit focuses on investigations involving large-scale market abuses and complex manipulation schemes by institutional traders, market professionals, and others.

- **Structured and New Products:** This unit focuses on complex derivatives and financial products, including credit default swaps, collateralized debt obligations, and securitized products.

- **Foreign Corrupt Practices Act:** This unit's focus is on violations of the Foreign Corrupt Practice Act, which prohibits U.S. companies from bribing foreign officials for obtaining or retaining business.

- **Municipal Securities and Public Pensions:** This unit focuses on misconduct in the large municipal securities market and in connection with public pension funds. That misconduct may include offering and disclosure fraud, tax fraud, public corruption violations, and public pension accounting and disclosure violations.

The Division of Enforcement employs forensic accountants. Led by the Chief Accountant for the Division of Enforcement, these employees provide technical accounting expertise during financial fraud investigations.

An SEC enforcement action is composed of three sequential events or proceedings:

- **Trigger event:** A trigger event is a disclosure of potential violations that comes from the company itself. Common trigger events include whistleblower charges, voluntary company disclosures, financial restatements, auditor changes, unusual trading in the firm's shares, delayed SEC filings, and management departures.

✔ **Investigation event:** After the trigger event, the SEC gathers information about the allegations through an informal inquiry, which could lead to a formal investigation. Prior to filing civil litigation charges, the SEC sends the target individual or company a Wells Notice indicating its intent to file charges. The SEC provides the target a last chance to respond with reasons that civil charges should not be filed. Some enforcement actions are resolved immediately upon the SEC's initial release of information about the case.

✔ **Regulatory event:** If the SEC decides to proceed with the case, it continues with administrative or civil litigation proceedings. If criminal behavior is suspected, the case is referred to the U.S. Department of Justice so it can be prosecuted by a U.S. Attorney.

In civil suits, the SEC seeks *injunctions:* orders that prohibit future violations. In other words, a person who violates an injunction is subject to fines or imprisonment for contempt. The SEC also seeks civil money penalties and the *disgorgement* of illegal profits (meaning the profits have to be forfeited).

The SEC also brings a variety of administrative proceedings, which are heard by administrative law judges and the SEC itself. A proceeding for a *cease and desist* order may be instituted against any person who violates the federal securities laws. In such cases, the respondent may be ordered to forfeit any ill-gotten funds. With respect to regulated entities (such as brokers, dealers, and investment advisers) and their employees, administrative proceedings may be instituted to revoke or suspend their registration or to impose bars or suspensions from employment. The SEC can also order regulated entities to pay civil penalties, as well as to forfeit illegal profits.

Federal Bureau of Investigation

By far, the FBI has more jurisdiction than any other federal agency with respect to financial crime. It investigates matters relating to general fraud, theft, or embezzlement occurring within or against the national and international financial community. These crimes are characterized by deceit, concealment, or violation of trust. Such acts are committed by individuals and organizations to obtain personal or business advantage.

The focus of the FBI's financial crime investigations are corporate fraud, healthcare fraud, mortgage fraud, identity theft, insurance fraud, mass marketing fraud, and money laundering. The Financial Crimes Section of the FBI deals with these areas. The majority of corporate fraud cases pursued by the FBI involve accounting schemes designed to deceive investors, auditors, and analysts about the financial condition of a corporation. They involve the following:

✔ False accounting entries

✔ Bogus trades designed to inflate profit or hide losses

✔ False transactions designed to evade regulatory oversight

✔ Insider trading

✔ Kickbacks

✔ Backdating of executive stock options

✔ Misuse of corporate property for personal gain

✔ Obstruction of justice designed to conceal any of the previously noted types of criminal conduct, particularly when the obstruction impedes the inquiries of the SEC and other regulatory and law enforcement agencies

In the following sections, we discuss some of the FBI's primary program areas.

Securities fraud

The SEC does not have the power to investigate corporate criminal fraud; therefore, the SEC often joins other law enforcement agencies, such as the FBI, IRS, and Postal Inspectors, through the grand jury investigative process with a local U.S. Attorney's office. These partnerships capitalize on each agency's expertise and jurisdiction.

Combating securities and commodities fraud is a priority for the FBI. The losses arising from these frauds total $40 billion annually. They are associated with decreased market value of businesses, reduced or nonexistent return on investments, and legal and investigative costs. The victims of securities and commodities frauds include individual investors, financial institutions, public and private companies, government entities, and retirement funds.

In 2006, the FBI investigated 1,653 cases of securities and commodities fraud and had 157 agents dedicated to the problem.

Healthcare fraud

The FBI's mission in the area of healthcare fraud is to provide guidance and assistance to support investigations targeting individuals and organizations who have defrauded the public and private healthcare systems. The FBI, along with its federal, state, and local law enforcement partners, the Centers for Medicare and Medicaid Services (CMS), and other government and privately-sponsored program participants, work closely together to address vulnerabilities, fraud, and abuse.

Some common types of healthcare frauds include the following:

✔ **Medical equipment fraud:** Equipment manufacturers offer free products to individuals. They then charge insurers for products that were not needed or may not have been delivered.

✔ **Rolling lab schemes:** Unnecessary and sometimes fake tests are given to individuals at different locations such as health clubs or shopping malls and billed to insurance companies.

✔ **Services not performed:** Providers bill insurers for services never rendered by changing bills or submitting fake ones.

Mortgage fraud

The FBI investigates mortgage fraud in two distinct areas:

✔ **Fraud for profit:** Sometimes referred to as *industry insider fraud,* the motive here is to falsely inflate the value of the property, or issue loans based on fictitious properties. Eighty percent of all reported fraud losses involve collaboration or collusion by industry insiders. Each mortgage fraud scheme contains some type of material misstatement, misrepresentation, or omission relating to the property or potential mortgage relied on by an underwriter or lender to fund, purchase, or insure a loan.

✔ **Fraud for housing:** This area involves minor misrepresentations by the mortgage applicant solely for the purpose of purchasing a property for a primary residence. Applicants may make misrepresentations by embellishing their income or concealing debt. This scheme usually involves a single loan.

Here are some common mortgage fraud schemes:

✔ **Illegal property flipping:** After a property is purchased, it's fraudulently appraised at a higher value and then quickly sold. Kickbacks are provided to buyers, investors, brokers, appraisers, and title company employees to facilitate this scheme.

✔ **Silent second:** The seller provides the down payment to the buyer by issuing a mortgage that is not disclosed to the primary lender. The primary lender believes the buyer has invested his own money.

✔ **Nominee loans/straw buyers:** The identity of the borrower is concealed through the use of a nominee who allows the borrower to use the nominee's name and credit history to apply for a loan.

✔ **Fictitious/stolen identity:** Someone uses a fictitious or stolen identity on the loan application. The person's name, identifying information, and credit history are used without his or her knowledge.

✔ **Inflated appraisals:** An appraiser acts in collusion with a borrower and provides an inflated property value report to the lender.

✔ **Foreclosure schemes:** The fraudster identifies homeowners who are at risk of defaulting on loans or whose houses are foreclosed, and then misleads the homeowners into believing they can save their homes by transferring the deeds to the fraudster. The perpetrator profits by remortgaging the property.

Insurance fraud

Insurance fraud committed both by businesses and individuals is an investigative priority for the FBI's Financial Crimes Section, due in large part to the insurance industry's significant status in the U.S. economy. The U.S. insurance industry consists of thousands of companies and collects nearly $1 trillion in premiums each year.

The size of the industry makes it a prime target for criminal activity; the Coalition Against Insurance Fraud (CAIF) estimates that the cost of fraud in the insurance industry is as high as $80 billion each year. This cost is passed on to consumers in the form of higher premiums. The National Insurance Crime Bureau (NICB) calculates that insurance fraud raises the yearly cost of premiums by $300 for the average household.

In August 2005, Hurricane Katrina caused $100 billion in damages along the Gulf Coast. According to the CAIF, Katrina generated approximately 1.6 million insurance claims totaling $34.4 billion in insured losses. Over than $80 billion in government funds were allocated for reconstruction. With numbers this high, insurance fraud related to Hurricane Katrina alone is estimated to total $4 to $6 billion. With so much money at stake, the FBI created the Insurance Fraud Task Force (IFTF) to investigate insurance fraud related to Hurricane Katrina.

Mass marketing fraud

Mass marketing fraud is a general term for frauds that exploit mass-communication media, such as telemarketing fraud, Internet fraud, and identity theft. Since the 1930s, mass marketing has been an accepted and productive way of increasing a customer base. Advanced communications, including fax machines, computers, speed dialing, and automatic dialing, along with modern conveniences such as credit cards, electronic banking, and television, have led to tremendous growth in mass marketing. The growth of legitimate mass marketing has led to a substantial increase in fraudulent mass marketing.

Some of the common mass marketing frauds investigated by the FBI are as follows:

- **Foreign lotteries and sweepstakes:** In this scheme, victims are told that they have won a lottery or sweepstakes in a foreign drawing. To claim their prizes, victims are told to pay various taxes and fees.

- **Credit and loan scams:** Victims with poor or nonexistent credit are offered credit cards or loans for advance fees. Sometimes, victims with poor credit are told that their credit ratings can be improved by paying a fee in advance.

- **Overpayment scams:** The victim advertises an item for sale. The perpetrator, posing as the buyer, sends the seller a counterfeit check or money order for more than the cost of the item. The victim is asked to return the excess payment received. Since the payment is counterfeit, the victim is held responsible by the financial institution.

- **Charity scams:** Fraudsters solicit donations in the name of nonexistent or fraudulent charities.

Using RICO Laws to Prosecute Fraud

The government has many mechanisms at its disposal to prosecute an individual or organization for criminal activity. One of the statutes is the Racketeer Influenced and Corrupt Organizations Act (RICO), which provides for extended criminal penalties and a civil cause of action for acts performed as part of an ongoing criminal organization. Although RICO was originally intended to prosecute the Mafia and others engaged in organized crime, its application has been become more widespread over the years.

In addition to criminal charges, the RICO statute permits a private action on behalf of citizens harmed by the actions of such an enterprise. If successful, the individual can collect *treble damages* (three times the actual damages incurred) plus costs and attorney fees.

Here are some of the activities covered by RICO:

✔ Bribery, counterfeiting, theft, embezzlement, fraud, gambling, money laundering, and several other offenses covered under the federal criminal code

✔ Embezzlement of union funds

✔ Bankruptcy fraud or securities fraud

✔ Money laundering and related offenses

✔ Murder, kidnapping, extortion, arson, robbery, dealing in obscene matter, or dealing in a controlled substance

In 1989, a RICO case was brought against financier Michael Milken, who was indicted on 98 counts of racketeering and fraud relating to an investigation into insider trading and other offenses. Milken was accused of using a wide-ranging network of contacts to manipulate stock and bond prices. Milken pled guilty to six lesser offenses rather than face spending the rest of his life in prison. Milken's employer, Drexel Burnham Lambert, was also threatened with a RICO indictment because, as the employer of Milken, Drexel was responsible for its employees' crimes. Drexel avoided RICO charges by pleading no contest to lesser felonies.

Walking through a Federal Criminal Case

Federal criminal cases have a lifespan of many years. These cases are governed by a set of rules called the *Federal Rules of Criminal Procedure*. Each U.S. Attorney's office may also have its own set of procedures to process cases.

Some of the agents who assist in a federal criminal case have accounting or forensic accounting backgrounds. They assist the AUSAs by reviewing

documents, such as accounting records, and interviewing targets and subjects. Here is the sequence of proceedings in a federal criminal case:

✔ **Allegation:** A federal investigation begins with an allegation that a crime has been committed. Allegations can arise from virtually anywhere: a relative, a media report, a coworker, a classmate, an unsatisfied customer, or just a passerby noticing illegal activity. The actual source of an investigation is generally not made public.

✔ **Investigating the allegations:** Special Agents and support staff in the appropriate federal agency (or agencies) obtain facts and evidence to determine whether a crime has been committed. Two types of evidence exist:

• *Direct:* Evidence is direct when a person who has actual knowledge of the crime swears to it. (For example, a witness testifies that he has seen the defendant rob the victim.) Direct evidence may also take the form of admissions or confessions made in or out of court.

• *Indirect:* Also called *circumstantial* evidence, indirect evidence proves the existence of the principal fact by inference. You need to understand this type of evidence because it's the most common type of evidence available.

Evidence can be gathered administratively, without convening a grand jury. After the evidence is submitted to the appropriate U.S. Attorney's Office, a federal grand jury is convened. When this happens, the barriers for sharing information among federal agencies lessen; shared information then becomes grand jury material.

✔ **Convening a grand jury:** A federal grand jury consists of 16 to 23 people chosen from the general population in a judicial district. The grand jurors investigate accusations against people, businesses, and other entities. The role of the grand jury is that of a fact finder. The grand jury meets to gather information and documents, and to listen to witness testimony concerning alleged criminal violations.

A federal grand jury may hear from several different prosecutors and witnesses relating to many separate investigations during a single session. For example, a grand jury may receive an update on a major drug investigation, receive a second update on a public corruption case, and later be asked to decide if the owner of a corner deli should be indicted on tax evasion charges — all on the same day.

Normally a grand jury "sits," or deliberates, for a period of 18 months. The jurors meet a few days per month depending on the judicial district and the case load. Grand jury proceedings are held in secrecy; thus, only the jurors, federal prosecutors, witnesses, and a stenographer are present while the jury is in session.

To conduct its fact-finding role, the primary investigative tool available to the grand jury is a *subpoena.* By using its subpoena powers, the grand jury calls witnesses to provide testimony, issues orders requiring the production of records, and imposes legal sanctions to ensure compliance with its powers. Sometimes, it executes a search warrant to hunt down evidence.

✔ **Preparing an indictment or information:** When the prosecutor (the U.S. Attorney) believes that the grand jury has received sufficient information, an indictment is prepared. The indictment contains the names of the suspects, the statutes violated, and a listing of facts and reasons why the suspect should be charged. It is a formal accusation. The grand jury reviews the indictment and decides by voting whether to return a true bill of indictment. When the jury is deliberating or voting, only juror members are allowed in the jury room. A true bill of indictment is issued only on the concurrence of 12 or more jurors, no matter how many jurors are in attendance during a given session.

An *information* is an accusation in writing against a person named therein for some criminal offense. It waives the issuance of an indictment. This document is normally filed when a prosecutor negotiates with a defendant and reaches an agreement. The evidence is normally so overwhelming that a defendant believes that a trial by jury will not result in an acquittal. The filing of an *information* is normally followed by a guilty plea entered into court.

✔ **Arrest and arraignment:** Following an indictment, federal agents issue an arrest warrant, which authorizes them to apprehend the person(s) named in the indictment and escort the person(s) to a Federal District Court Judge. Upon arrest, the defendant is given Miranda warnings and normally taken to one of the investigative agency's offices to be fingerprinted, photographed, and further processed.

If the defendant has legal counsel, the attorney will be contacted to meet the defendant at the courthouse. If the defendant does not have legal counsel, one will be appointed. The defendant is given a copy of the formal indictment and discusses legal strategy with his counsel.

When the defendant initially appears before the court (during the *arraignment*), the judge formally reads the accusations in open court, unless the defendant waives the reading. At this stage, almost all defendants enter a guilty or not guilty plea, and bail is determined. Most defendants are given bail terms that can be posted. A status conference date is normally set to occur within a short period of time to discuss such items as discoverable material and possible trial dates.

✔ **Pretrial motions and discovery:** A variety of motions are usually filed prior to trial. Motions filed by the defense, such as motions for a change of venue or to disqualify a judge, are routinely responded to by an attorney for the government with minimal involvement from the Special Agent. Federal agents are involved in responding to other motions, such as those to return seized property or to suppress evidence. As part of discovery, the government and the defense have opportunities to examine evidence in the opposing party's possession, custody, or control.

✔ **Trial preparation:** Trial preparation is a tedious process for both the government and the defense. Original documents must be secured; official documents authenticated; expert witnesses located and prepared for trial; and documents labeled, organized, and copied for various parties to examine. Charts, graphs, and summary sheets are produced and organized. On both sides, potential witnesses are re-interviewed, sometimes several times as they prepare for their testimony. While this occurs, the attorneys take notes and prepare opening arguments to the jury.

✔ **Verdict:** During the course of trial preparation, plea negotiations may take place. As defendants see the evidence that the U.S. Attorney's office has gathered, some come to the realization that a trial may not end in a not guilty verdict. The two sides then may come to an agreement on terms. The document signed by the defendant is called a *plea agreement,* which is an agreement between the U.S. Attorney's office and the defendant. The terms of the agreement often include a reduced sentence in exchange for full cooperation and admission of the crime in court (a guilty plea). Keep in mind that the court is not a party to the agreement, and the judge is not required honor it. But in most cases, the court honors the agreement.

In a federal trial, there are 12 jurors who must unanimously agree on either a guilty or not guilty verdict. During the course of a trial, two to four alternates will sit in the juror's box. At the conclusion of a trial, the alternate jurors are dismissed, and the remaining jurors deliberate in secret proceedings. Several outcomes are possible:

- The jurors return a decision of not guilty.

- The jurors return a guilty verdict, in which case the defendant has the right of appeal.

- The jurors may not be able to come to a decision, in which case a *hung jury* exists. In that event, the government has the option to retry the case or dismiss the charges.

✔ **Appeal:** When a guilty verdict is returned, the defendant has ten days to file an appeal. If an appeal is filed, the Appellate court may affirm the decision or reverse it and send it back to the lower court for retrial.

✔ **Sentencing:** After a conviction, the sentencing phase begins. Sentences of financial crimes are based on the economic loss to the government. The sentencing guidelines take into account both the seriousness of the criminal conduct and the defendant's criminal record. Based on the severity of the offense, the guidelines assign most federal crimes to 1 of 43 offense levels. Each offender is also assigned to one of six criminal history categories based upon the extent and occurrence of his past misconduct.

Let's say Mary, a bookkeeper, rationalizes that her boss is not paying her enough. She devises a scheme and steals $5,000. Under the federal guidelines for embezzlement, the judge can issue a sentence of zero to six months probation. However, if she steals $10,001, she can be sentenced to 6 to 12 months of incarceration, and if she steals more than $70,000, she could face 15 to 21 months of incarceration.

The sentencing guidelines give a Federal District Court judge the authority to impose a sentence of probation or supervised release. *Probation* is a sentence in lieu of imprisonment where the convicted defendant will be supervised. *Supervised release* is a continuation of the imprisonment term with supervision.

What to Do If a Government Agency Knocks on Your Door

Should you ever work with a client facing a federal investigation for financial crimes, this section contains some crucial advice. If an individual, a company, or its officers or employees find themselves pulled into a federal investigation, here are a few important things to keep in mind:

✔ Retain attorneys who are highly competent and experienced in white-collar matters.

✔ Do not speak to a prosecutor or a case agent before conferring with counsel. When both the company and individual officers or employees are involved, it may be in each party's best interests to engage its own counsel.

✔ Arrange for an internal investigation to be conducted in cases where a company is being investigated.

✔ Retain consultants, including forensic accountants when an investigation is launched.

✔ Consider whether and how much to cooperate with the government. For example, the U.S. Attorney's office may ask the company to waive the attorney-client privilege and make certain privileged documents available to the government. In many instances, it may be in the company's interest to comply.

A company's cooperation with a U.S. Attorney's office during a criminal investigation may be to its benefit. Cooperation may persuade the government not to bring criminal charges. And even if a criminal charge is brought, the company's cooperation may bring leniency at the time of sentencing.

Part V
Preventing Occupational Fraud

The 5th Wave   By Rich Tennant

©RICHTENNANT

"I ran an evaluation of our last pie chart.
Apparently it's boysenberry."

In this part . . .

*W*hen a forensic accountant investigates an occupational fraud (one involving a business), the approach to the investigation is fairly standardized and involves a whole team of people. However, at times, an investigation may mushroom and take on a life of its own. We open this part with an overview of what the process generally looks like and who usually gets involved.

We move on to a discussion of how to track down fraud by following the money trail, and then to a chapter that's all about how to get your hands on relevant records that can help you prove that fraud has occurred.

Finally, we devote a chapter to the topic of technology in fraud investigations. The amount of data generated by a business — even a small one — is staggering. Part of your job as a forensic accountant is to figure out how to narrow your information searches, how to quickly find what you need, and how to analyze the information after you retrieve it. Software programs designed for these purposes are invaluable, and we walk you through the types of programs you need to get to know.

Chapter 20

Helping Small Businesses Prevent Fraud

In This Chapter

▶ Reviewing what internal controls are

▶ Recognizing frauds frequently affecting small businesses

▶ Putting internal controls in place

▶ Reacting after a small business client is victimized

*B*ig frauds that take place in big businesses are the stuff headlines are made of. (Enron, anyone?) But as horrid as those major frauds can be, they don't occur nearly as frequently as smaller frauds that chip away at the financial health and the integrity of a company of any size.

In the next chapter, we focus on how large businesses can steel themselves against fraud. Here, our focus is small businesses: those that bring in less than $250 million in revenue each year. We remind you what the all-important phrase *internal controls* refers to, and we show you the types of frauds that small businesses are most likely to face. We discuss specific fraud-deterrence techniques that forensic accountants can help small businesses establish to reduce the probability of fraud. Finally, we explain what you can do if a small business client is victimized.

Refresher: Defining Internal Controls

We know that you learned all about internal controls in your auditing class, so we won't bore you with details here. (If you're looking for the details, pick up a copy of *Auditing For Dummies*, by Maire Loughran [Wiley]). To help you prepare for what we talk about in this chapter (and the next one), we offer just the briefest refresher here.

Internal controls are policies and procedures that a business (or any other organization) establishes in order to

✓ Protect assets

✓ Assure correct financial reporting

✓ Assure compliance with all relevant laws, rules, and regulations

We want to clarify this definition a bit. When we talk about "policies and procedures," we mean that a business should have a set of appropriate policies and that those policies should be *implemented.* Frankly, a business could buy an internal control manual off the shelf. However, if the manual just sits on the shelf and gathers dust until the auditors come, it's meaningless.

What does the rest of the definition mean?

✓ When we say "protect assets," we mean all assets: tangible and non-tangible. Protecting assets also means guarding a business from excess liabilities.

✓ How about assuring *correct financial reporting*? Financial reporting is correct when the financial reports are relevant and reliable and they adhere to whatever standard of accounting the business is using (such as U.S. generally accepted accounting principles or international standards).

✓ *Compliance* refers to whatever federal, state, or local laws; union contracts; industry standards; or other regulations the business should adhere to.

Scouting for Signs of Fraud in a Small Business

Small businesses are very different than big businesses, principally in the management structure (or lack thereof). In this section, we introduce some of the most common small business frauds we've seen — and touch on some of the ways a company can try to prevent them.

Spotting inventory issues

We devote Chapter 6 to a detailed discussion of the ways people commit inventory fraud and the ways businesses should try to prevent it. In small businesses in particular, inventory may be the easiest place for fraud to be committed. That's because a small business may lack the resources to install proper inventory controls. Often, a small business may count its inventory only once a year. So if inventory is missing, that fact may not be noticed for quite a while. The owner may have a sense that something's not right but not really know until a proper count is done.

Of course, the nature of the business determines how big an issue inventory can be. If your client is running a small steel foundry, chances are the inventory won't spoil or walk away on its own. However, small consumer goods are another matter. One small bookstore owner told us that about 30 percent of her books were stolen.

Inventory can create a variety of fraud issues for a small business or for its customers. Here, we look at some common problems that can occur.

Missing inventory

Inventory may go missing for several reasons:

- ✔ Employees steal it.
- ✔ Customers steal it.
- ✔ Vendors send shipments that are *short* (meaning they don't include all the merchandise the business ordered).
- ✔ Abnormal amounts of the inventory are lost to spoilage.

Even though it takes time and money for a business to implement proper inventory controls, they may pay for themselves in reduced inventory loss. What types of controls work? That depends on the nature of the business and the inventory. Following are just a few examples.

We once had a client who was a small retail jeweler. He *bonded* all of his employees (which means he insured their honesty) to protect against theft. Bonding can be very expensive, but any one piece in his inventory could be worth upward of $100,000. That means even one theft could put him out of business, so it paid for him to go through the expense of bonding. He also did a partial inventory count every evening when the merchandise went back into the safe and a full-blown inventory count several times a year.

We've seen retailers who check all bags leaving the store: those carried by both customers and employees. Can security guards really catch a smart thief? Maybe not. But would you want to risk being caught — especially if the security guard looks like he's 300 pounds of pure muscle?

We also had a client who manufactured gold jewelry. It was a rather large operation with up to 1,000 employees in the factory during busy season. The company managers considered the operation a small business because it was owned by one person and managed by the owner and his two sons-in-law. Most of the bookkeeping systems were hand systems (not computerized), which made us wonder about the level of internal controls.

The first year we did this client's audit, we asked one son-in-law if he knew how much gold the company had on hand as of the balance sheet date. He gave us a number, expressed in ounces of gold. After the actual inventory count, we compared his estimate to the actual number, and there was very little difference. This became a game every year. We'd ask him and then compare his answer to the actual. He was always correct within 3 percent. What was going on? He kept a running total in his head of how much gold was coming in and how much was being shipped out. This system was crude but effective for management purposes. The company also had one bookkeeper who was dedicated to tracking gold. Her total for the amount of gold was always within 5 percent of the actual. Considering issues such as the creation of scrap during manufacturing and the use of many different methods of weighing and calculating gold purity by their vendors and customers, this percentage was a very tolerable margin of error.

At the factory, every exit was guarded by security guards with machine guns. They had orders to shoot anyone who passed through the metal detectors and caused the detectors to ring. (Keep in mind that this company was not located in the United States.) During the course of observing the inventory count, we took small samples to be sent to a laboratory to determine if the product was real gold and to find out the level of purity. The first year we did this, Frimette put the samples in her skirt pocket. When she left the factory at the end of the day, she set off the alarms. Immediately she was surrounded by angry guards with machine guns. The client's managers began shouting at the guards not to shoot, saying that Frimette was the only person allowed to take gold out of the factory outside of their normal shipping methods. (And you thought accounting was boring . . . *never!*)

Frimette has another story about being surrounded by U.S. federal marshals with drawn guns, but we'll leave that one for the next edition of this book.

Gray goods

Gray goods are goods that are manufactured for sale overseas and sold in the United States. This may create problems for the consumer because the goods may not be manufactured to the same standards and/or specifications required of U.S. manufacturers. Therefore, the items may not operate properly. This is very often a problem with small electronics sold at stores other than major chains.

Where does fraud come in? A small store that buys from a distributor may not even be aware that the merchandise is gray goods. Small stores are advised to check with the goods' manufacturers to make sure the distributor is on the up-and-up.

Also, sometimes what appear to be gray goods may actually be counterfeit goods. Some years back, people discovered that toothpaste being sold in discount stores was packaged and labeled to look like Colgate toothpaste manufactured in South Africa. The problem is that Colgate didn't have a factory in South Africa. Not only weren't the goods real tubes of Colgate, but they also did not contain fluoride and did contain DEG, a potentially lethal chemical. If you were a small store owner, would you know if your supplier were giving you real Colgate or counterfeit merchandise?

Used goods disguised as new

This is another common inventory problem that affects the consumer. Sometimes a store gets merchandise back from a customer, rewraps it, and puts it out on the selling floor again. This practice is not a problem if you return a shirt to Macy's in its original packaging. However, it can be a big problem with any item that comes with small parts or may be mechanical. The item may be broken or have parts missing.

We heard a story from a friend whose mother was sold a rewrapped VCR. (This was back when people actually purchased VCRs.) The machine couldn't be hooked up because parts were missing. When our friend took it back to the store, he was accused of stealing the parts, and the store refused to take the VCR back. A few threats later, the store finally relented and took the VCR back.

As a consumer, you should shop only at reputable stores and make sure an item's packaging looks like it is original. As a small business owner, you should make certain your return policies for mechanical items or other goods with small parts are stringent and clear so your employees don't accept returns that are incomplete. A good control system would also require that a supervisor or manager sign off on all returns of goods over a certain value. Some retailers keep lists of customers who excessively return goods and after a while deny them the privilege of returning — just in case the excessive returns are fraudulent.

Is the inventory for real?

As an auditor or forensic examiner, you may be called upon to determine if a company's inventory is what it's supposed to be. If your target (or client) were a jeweler, could you tell gold from brass or diamonds from glass? You may have to call in an expert to help with a case involving specialty inventory. We've used chemical engineers, gemologists, metallurgists, and jewelers to help us on forensic cases and audits.

We were engaged by a new client, a wholesale gem dealer, to do some general accounting work. In the process of our work we found that some of the accounts receivable looked very suspicious. A handful of large, old receivables didn't seem to change from month to month. When the client was confronted, we didn't get clear answers.

The client had been borrowing money from a bank with which we had a good relationship.

The loan was secured by inventory. The bulk of the value in the inventory was one large ruby. We didn't want to mess up our relationship with the bank because of this one new client. The accounting partner in charge of this account took one of the bank officers out to lunch one day. Because of the rules of confidentiality, the partner couldn't tell the banker about our suspicions. So the partner casually asked the banker when the bank would be doing a spot check of the inventory. (It's not uncommon for banks to do a spot check of inventory when they have a lien on the inventory.) The banker figured out that he ought to order an inventory check. The next week the bank surprised the client with an inventory audit. The bank came with a gemologist who determined that the ruby was really just red glass.

This situation can create problems for auditors as well. If your client has used goods in its inventory, your inventory valuation has to be for used goods, not new. When observing an inventory count of packaged goods, make sure that the packaging looks new. Also, ask to have a few boxes opened just to make sure that the inventory is real. We could write a whole book just on inventory frauds, but we had to settle for Chapter 6 — be sure to check it out.

Counterfeit goods

A large market exists for counterfeit goods: merchandise that appears to be manufactured by a well-known company but is actually manufactured by a fraudulent operation. To the untrained eye, counterfeit goods appear to be the real deal.

The Sunday *New York Times Magazine* recently ran a story about a manufacturing region in China that specializes in counterfeit shoes. If your store wants to sell Nike sneakers cheaper than your competitors, you just place your order with one of the counterfeit manufacturers in this region and voila! Nikes at a discount. How do the manufacturers do it? At one time they were stealing shoes from the real manufacturers and copying the designs. When the real manufacturers increased security, the counterfeiters just started buying real pairs of the designer shoes to use as models. They even counterfeit the shipping documents so that it appears the shoes are real.

How does counterfeiting impact an auditor or forensic accountant? If you're doing an inventory audit of merchandise that has a high probability of being counterfeit, you should take additional measures to verify the merchandise is the real deal. The inventory valuations for real Nikes and fake Nikes are very different. You want to do some intense document examination, send out confirmations to the real manufacturers to determine if they really shipped anything to your client, and possibly call in an expert.

Besides risking inventory valuation issues, any business that possesses or sells counterfeit goods may be subject to criminal prosecution for violation of copyrights, patents, and trademarks; civil litigation brought by the real manufacturers; and the confiscation of goods.

Keeping a close eye on cash

Cash is the most *fungible* asset (meaning it can easily be exchanged for something else), and, therefore, it's the most problematic. If someone takes a fancy piece of jewelry from a jeweler, that item can be identified by police. But money? Good luck figuring out which bills were yours! Also, of course, cash is the one commodity that *everybody* needs.

Here are some of the steps we recommend a small business take to protect itself from cash theft:

CASE FILE

Wite-out and erasable pens

Myrna Berg, CPA was retained by a client to perform monthly bank reconciliations. When the bank statement arrived, the bookkeeper would fax Myrna the statement and the cash receipts and disbursements journals. One month Myrna was not able to get the account to reconcile. She tried each of the various methods: forward, backward, and four-column. In exasperation she tried the ridiculous. She wondered if the bank added the statement correctly. This was a ridiculous thought since no accountant we know ever found an addition error by the bank's computer. Guess what? She found that the bank's statement did not add up. This raised all kinds of red flags.

Myrna went to the client's office and pulled the actual bank statement from the file cabinet. She found that many of the checks on the statement had their amounts covered with Wite-out. Myrna then went to look at the actual checks. She found they had erasure marks on them. Now she knew something was very wrong. She had the client call the bank and order a copy of the bank statement with photos of all the checks and had them sent directly to her office.

When Myrna compared the copies to the originals, of course she found differences.

Here's what Myrna figured out was going on: The bookkeeper would write checks using erasable pen. Originally the checks were made out to legitimate vendors and were backed by real invoices. After the boss signed the checks, the bookkeeper would erase the payee and amount and put in her own name or the names of her credit cards and other amounts. She would write up the cash disbursement journal so that it agreed with the actual vendor bills. When the statement came from the bank, she would erase the checks again and put in the names of the vendors and the original amounts of the checks. She knew that Myrna did a bank reconciliation. The bookkeeper thought that the reconciliation involved just a visual comparison of the cash journals to the bank statement. So she would use Wite-out to alter the bank statement so the amounts on the statement corresponded to the now re-altered checks.

It took about six weeks from the start of this fraud for Myrna to uncover it. In that time the bookkeeper stole about $36,000.

✔ Do a thorough background check on any employee who handles cash.

✔ *Bond* employees who handle cash (which means getting insurance policies on their honesty).

✔ Create physical barriers to the cash register. Design the cash register area so that it's not easy for a customer or thief to just reach over and take out money.

✔ Have a required daily reconciliation of cash. Allow for a certain small over/under amount and for a small number of times that this amount can occur before there are repercussions.

✔ Install cameras so that cash transactions can be recorded.

✔ Keep checkbooks in a secure place. Unauthorized persons should not be able to access the checkbooks.

✔ Perform bank reconciliations immediately upon receipt of the bank statement. The reconciliation should be performed by someone who does not write checks or prepare deposits.

✔ Consider having a *lock box*: a post office box where checks are received. The box is emptied by the bank, which prepares the deposit and sends the business a report of which checks have been received.

✔ Send bank statements directly to the owner's home or to the accountant assisting with the bookkeeping.

Establishing Effective Internal Controls

Regardless of size, every business should have control procedures. In this section we present some of the common control procedures that we think are most important. When advising a client on controls, you should always customize the plan for that particular client's needs. You should take into consideration

✔ The cost of particular controls and their potential benefits

✔ The nature of the business

✔ The simplicity or complexity of the client's industry

✔ The simplicity or complexity of the client's business

✔ The number of employees

Segregating duties

For proper controls, every business should separate the custody of an asset or liability from the record-keeping for that asset or liability. The bookkeeper who writes checks or makes deposits should not also be the one to reconcile the bank account. If the check writer or depositor also does the bank reconciliation, that person can adjust the books and records so as to conceal fraud.

On a related note, businesses should establish good anti-nepotism policies. *Nepotism* occurs when members of the same family work in the same place, and small businesses in particular are rife with nepotism. If one family member has custody of an asset and another is the record-keeper for that asset, the two people may *collude* (work together) to commit a fraud and cover it up. Collusion may be difficult to uncover, even for the most experienced forensic accountant.

Handling hiring issues

In this section, we present some key issues that employers face when making hiring decisions: running background checks, credit checks, and credential checks.

Background checks

Many small business owners believe that doing background checks on employees is expensive and time consuming. It can be, but background checks can also save a lot of money and aggravation in the long run. If your client's business sees a lot of turnover of low-paid employees who do not have access to a lot of assets, it may not pay to do background checks. But for employees who will have access to assets, we believe background and credit checks can be very important.

Consider the nature of the business when thinking about background checks. If your client is a fast food joint, and the employee won't have access to more than whatever cash is in the register, it may not pay to run a background check. If your client is a medical office, it may pay. In that situation, even a clerk or technician may have access to medical records and hence be able to access sensitive patient information. It wouldn't be hard for a clerk to steal information and sell it to an identity theft professional.

Running a background check need not be very expensive. Hiring a private investigator is the most expensive way to go and probably isn't necessary. Many online services run background checks for less than $100. If your client bonds employees, the *surety company* (the insurance company that issues the bonds) has a service that does the background checks.

State and federal laws govern background checks, so make sure your clients are in compliance. They may have to get permission from the prospective employee to do an investigation.

Credit checks

A commonly held belief is that employees who are in financial trouble are more likely to steal, and, therefore, it's wise to do a credit check and reject a job applicant with a poor credit rating. We have not seen any studies that actually prove this belief, but our gut instinct tells us it's valid. However, there are many reasons why employees steal and a need for cash is just one. (In Chapter 22, we outline a thorough list of motives for employee theft.) Also, a job applicant may be honest and responsible and still have a poor credit report. In fact, an honest worker who has had financial struggles in the past is likely to work very hard in order to keep the job. Bottom line: We recommend that checking credit be just one part of a system of vetting applicants. It certainly shouldn't be the primary criteria for making hiring decisions.

Credentialing

If your client's business requires any sort of licensing or other credentials, make sure all employees have the proper credentials and licenses. We've heard more than one story about phony doctors.

Advise your clients to start confirming credentials well before the employee's start date because the process may take quite a while. We were recently involved with a client who is a medical doctor. It took her employer almost three months to complete the credentialing process.

Knowing who has the keys

It may seem like common sense not to give office keys to people who shouldn't have them. However, our experience tells us that many times too many sets of keys are floating around.

Frimette once opened her office door to find another employee inside. He said he was just looking for a book. (He had a reputation for being a snoop.) The key to that office was given to him many years back for a reason that no one remembered, and he still had it. Nothing of value was taken or missing, but think about the possibilities!

Access to the business premises should always be secured. Advise your clients to keep a list of who has keys and to make sure that when an employee leaves or changes positions, keys are returned.

Electronic keys may offer an even better way to secure the premises. If an employee leaves or changes positions, her electronic key can be turned off or changed. Electronic keys are usually the same as employee ID cards with a magnetic strip or "magic middle" that can be swiped over a card reader. The better systems require a swipe and the entering of a code. Even better yet are biometric identification systems. An unscrupulous employee can "lend" his card to a thief, but a biometric system prevents that from happening because it requires an employee's finger or palm prints to identify the employee. More sophisticated systems use retinal scans. These systems were once very expensive but in recent years have become less so. As always, do a cost-benefit analysis and determine what kind of system best meets your client's needs.

The reverse of this issue is keeping people in. We've heard absolute horror stories of employers who keep their staffs locked inside so they'll get their work done. A century ago, the Triangle Shirtwaist Factory was the prime example of this problem. When a fire broke out at the factory in 1911, 146 lives were lost because the workers were locked in during work hours. You may want to believe that a similar situation couldn't happen today, but you'd be wrong. If you have even the slightest suspicion that a client is operating in such a manner, make your concerns loud and clear. A business should never consider violating fire and other safety rules. Any pennies the business is trying to save may lead to liabilities of unbelievable proportions.

Controlling who signs the checks

Access to the checkbook is a sticky issue in a small business. We've often seen the checkbook kept in an unlocked desk drawer. Obviously, we don't think this is a great idea. The checkbook, checks for the printer, and electronic signature machines should all be kept locked up until needed. We recommend that employees with access to these items be bonded.

The flip side of this situation is having only one person as a signatory on a check. What if that person takes a vacation or gets hit by a bus? Who will be able to sign checks so the business keeps going? Often in a small business, only the owner can sign checks. We recommend that signature authority be given to a trusted family member who can be reached to sign checks in the event of an emergency. (If your client is a small nonprofit organization, the better way to address this issue is to have three to five members of the board of trustees, as well as the executive director, be signatories and require at least two signatures for any check over a certain dollar amount.)

Banks don't check the signatures on checks clearing the account. Therefore, for a small business, we think it's a good idea for the bank statement to be mailed to the owner's home. Often in a small business it's hard to have someone besides the sole bookkeeper reconcile the bank account. For that reason, the business owner should at the very least peruse the statement and the check images to see if all the checks look like they are legitimate checks to real vendors and have the correct signature(s).

We had been working with a professional membership association. The executive director got a call from their bank one day. The bank had flagged some checks as being a bit odd. Three checks for exactly $10,000 each had been presented for payment. The executive director and controller ran down to the bank, and the bank officer gave them copies of the checks to examine. Neither of them knew the payee or could think of why these checks had been written. They did recognize the handwriting on the check as belonging to Eric, the assistant controller. The police were called in, and Eric was confronted. Apparently he owed his bookie $30,000 and did not have the means to pay. The bookie asked Eric if he could access his employer's checkbook. Because the checkbook was not locked up, access was available to anyone in the office. Eric was instructed, by the bookie, to make out the three checks. The bookie told Eric that no one would notice the difference; because Eric did the bank reconciliations, no one need ever know. The last we heard, Eric was in hiding and negotiating a reduced sentence for turning state's evidence against the bookie.

Limiting access to electronic systems

Clearly, computer systems should be kept secure — both physically and electronically. Computers should be in secure areas where the public does not have physical access. They should also be secured electronically with passwords, firewalls, and other tools.

Physical security

Many businesses leave computers in open areas so anyone can get at them. Have you been to a hospital lately? The medical profession is increasingly using electronic medical records (EMR). The computers are on carts and are left all over the halls. It would be relatively easy for a fraudster to get into the system and get patient information. Do you think that requiring passwords secures the computers? *Fuggedaboutit!* A smart hacker can break passwords quite easily. Some fraudsters have attached micro-cameras at ATMs to capture passwords; the same technology could work in any environment.

In any size business, computers should be locked down to the desk they are assigned to. These locks can be purchased at any office supply store. Rooms that hold the servers should be kept locked and only authorized personnel allowed to enter. If someone in a uniform shows up and says he's there to fix the printer, the business must make sure he is who he says he is. He could be there to access the system and get data with which to commit fraud. Or he could be there to crash the system.

Small businesses in particular tend to be much too lax with computer and server security. We were once invited to a holiday party at a client's site. Staff members were encouraged to bring their families. The server room was left open so the computer staff could walk in and out easily and attend the party while also watching the systems. We watched in horror as beautiful little tykes ran in and out of the server room playing hide and seek. Imagine if one would have tripped on a wire, tried to see what a switch did, or barfed on a machine?

Recent technological advances pose additional data security issues for small businesses. Data can be copied in a matter of seconds. This is especially true with the size of removable media. Employees can sneak information out on iPods, iPhones, Blackberrys, and the good old mp3 players.

Electronic security

A word about passwords: Don't get so password crazy that your staff gets password fatigue. If you ask staff to change passwords too often or have different criteria for the many different passwords, we *guarantee* that your staff will start writing down their passwords and keeping them under the keyboard. It's a balancing act to get a password system that works without going overboard.

We were once called in by a client and walked through the programming room. We noticed lots and lots of yellow sticky notes on the monitors and asked about them. Apparently, someone had suggested that passwords be changed monthly. Many of the staff members had logins for a variety of systems, each with its own password. Remembering passwords became so complicated that yellow stickies were the only way to deal with it. There was even a yellow sticky note with the entry code on the front door!

Here's a quick rundown of additional electronic security measures you may want your clients to consider. These are just quick snapshots, and you'll want to have your clients consult with their computer gurus and do a cost-benefit analysis to determine what is best for their particular situation:

- **Set access controls on data:** Various sections of data can be controlled to determine who has access. Even QuickBooks has built-in access controls.

- **Use synchronized logins:** This process uses a random number generator. The computer generates random numbers that change every minute or so. The employee also has a random number generator that is as small as a keychain, which is synchronized to the computer. Besides the usual passwords, the employee must also enter the randomly generated number at the right time. This step is particularly effective when employees log in from remote locations, such as when they're working from home.

- **Restrict downloading of files from the Internet and e-mail attachments:** Some fraudsters write programs that can get into a computer via e-mail or downloads and then harvest data about individuals or firms and e-mail the information back to the fraudster.

- **Secure servers:** These central computers that run *networks* (groups of computers that are all connected) should have firewall software to prevent outsiders from accessing data.

- **Invest in key simulation software:** This tool allows management to re-create what any one person on the network has been typing. This is crucial if the business suspects that data is being stolen by an insider. It helps management and investigators determine who the culprit is.

- **Use encryption software to store data in code.** If a fraudster gets his hands on the data, he sees only meaningless information.

- **Have a disaster recovery plan.** Every business should have one! If computers get stolen or data is corrupted, this plan allows the business to get up and running again quickly.

- **Password protect the printing of checks.** Many businesses are now electronically printing the signatures on checks, and should password protect who can print checks with the electronic signature.

Taking Action after a Small Business Gets Ripped Off

So your small business client has been the victim of a fraud. Now what? You need to consider several issues. In this section, we give you some pointers on what to discuss with your client. We also recommend that the client talk to its attorney. That's because if the situation isn't handled properly, the business can get into even more hot water, especially if the fraudster was an employee.

Weighing costs and benefits: To prosecute or not

Your client's knee-jerk reaction may be to call the police or district attorney and prosecute the offender. Advise them to hold their horses and consider the pros and cons of doing so.

Here are the crucial pros:

- ✔ To collect from its insurance company, the business may be required to prosecute.
- ✔ Prosecuting sets an example to other potential fraudsters that if they target your client and get caught they will face severe consequences.

And here are some cons to consider:

- ✔ Even if the fraud is only a small theft, if it goes on record it may cause your client's insurance premiums to rise.
- ✔ If the fraudster is found not guilty at trial, he may have a reason to sue for defamation or libel.
- ✔ The client, by association with the fraud, gets bad press.

If the fraudster is an employee, your client must make sure that any termination proceedings are in line with the company's written policies. Otherwise, the employee may be able to sue to get his job back, get lost compensation, or be eligible for unemployment benefits. Make sure your client dots all its *i*'s and crosses all its *t*'s.

Determining the company's weaknesses

The saying goes: When life gives you lemons, make lemonade. Being ripped off is horrible, but your client can turn the situation around and make some good of it. Use this opportunity to help your client take stock of its internal controls. Here are some questions you may want to ask:

- Are the internal control policies adequate and up-to-date?
- Have the internal control policies kept up with technology advances?
- Have the internal control policies kept up with legal issues and the business environment?
- Have the internal control policies kept up with the growth and maturation of the client?
- Are the internal controls being implemented properly?

Chapter 21

Assisting Larger Businesses with Fraud Prevention

. . . .

In This Chapter

▶ Probing the potential risk of fraud

▶ Setting up effective internal controls

▶ Reacting after a business gets ripped off

. . . .

*I*n Chapter 20, we discuss ways in which forensic accountants can help small businesses prevent fraud. Here, the topic is the same but the object of our attention is medium and large businesses. (We refer to them collectively as "larger businesses" in this chapter.) Although this chapter is focused on large businesses, these principles may also apply to small businesses, other entities, or businesses that are not publicly traded companies.

Before we go any further, let's define our terms. What exactly is a *medium* or *large* business? In Chapter 20, we explain that a small business generally brings in less than $250 million in revenue each year. We consider a medium-size business to be one that brings in between $250 million and $750 million in revenue each year. A large business, therefore, is one that has annual revenues in excess of $750 million.

Because larger businesses are faced with many of the fraud risks encountered by small businesses, many of the pearls of wisdom we offer for small businesses apply here as well. However, several types of frauds occur more often in larger businesses than in small ones, so larger businesses need even more pearls. For example, financial statement fraud, which we explain in Chapter 5, most often occurs in larger companies. The same is true of the violation of certain anticorruption laws, such as the Foreign Corrupt Practices Act, which we discuss in Chapter 3.

The size, geographic diversity, and organizational complexity of larger businesses create additional challenges for designing and implementing effective fraud prevention programs. In this chapter, we show you how to assist a larger business with that design and implementation so it can increase its fraud defenses.

Conducting a Fraud Risk Assessment

To help a larger business create an effective fraud prevention program, you have to start by researching what's happening at the business right now. This research is called a *fraud risk assessment analysis,* and it takes into account many variables. Some of the most crucial variables, which we discuss in detail in this section, include:

- ✔ The key players in the company
- ✔ The corporate culture that exists
- ✔ The nature of the industry in which the business operates
- ✔ The current state of the company's system of internal controls

Other variables to consider are the company's financial reporting requirements (which may differ for public companies and privately held businesses), any laws and regulations that the company is subject to, and the locations in which it operates. (You need to be aware of additional challenges for businesses that have an international presence, for example.)

As the company begins its fraud risk assessment analysis, you need to remind yourself (and company management) that fraud comes in many flavors. In larger businesses, employees (including managers) can commit fraud in a variety of ways:

- ✔ They may steal directly from the business.
- ✔ They may defraud customers, suppliers, or competitors.
- ✔ They may defraud investors, creditors, or other users of the company's financial statements and other financial information.
- ✔ They may defraud government agencies such as the U.S. Securities and Exchange Commission (SEC), the Internal Revenue Service (IRS), and state and local taxing authorities.

Meeting the key players

An effective fraud prevention program requires the active participation of the primary players in a larger business. Here, we briefly explain who they are and what they do.

Board of directors

This body of elected or appointed members oversees company activities. Typical duties performed by the board are:

✔ Governing the organization by establishing broad policies and objectives

✔ Selecting and appointing the chief executive, supporting her work, and reviewing her performance

✔ Ensuring the availability of adequate financial resources

✔ Approving annual budgets

✔ Accounting to the stakeholders for the organization's performance

Audit committee

An *audit committee* is an operating committee of the board of directors that oversees financial reporting and disclosure. Committee members are drawn from members of the company's board, and those members select a chairperson. The committee must be composed of independent outside directors (in other words, no staff members allowed), and at least one member must qualify as a financial expert. The audit committee typically oversees or monitors the following:

✔ The company's financial reporting and accounting

✔ The annual audit

✔ Compliance with regulations

✔ The internal control process (which we explain in the upcoming section "Assessing and Strengthening Internal Controls")

✔ *Risk management,* which refers to the company's efforts to reduce a broad range of risks, including competitive, environmental, financial, legal, operational, regulatory, strategic, and technological risks

Corporate executives

A company's corporate executives, or *senior management,* are the highest-level employees who have the day-to-day responsibilities of running the business. They hold specific executive powers conferred on them by the board of directors and/or the shareholders (who we introduce next).

The senior management team is responsible for establishing and maintaining the company's internal control process (see the upcoming section "Assessing and Strengthening Internal Controls"). Also, the Chief Executive Officer and Chief Financial Officer (known collectively as the company's *principal officers*) have a special responsibility: The Sarbanes-Oxley Act of 2002 (SOX) requires them to certify and approve the integrity of their company's financial reports quarterly.

With great responsibility comes great temptation. According to the Association of Certified Fraud Examiners (ACFE), corporate executives are more likely to engage in corruption and fraudulent financial statement schemes than any other employees.

Shareholders

A *shareholder* is an individual or a business that legally owns one or more shares of stock in a company. A company's shareholders collectively own that company. The goal of such companies is to maximize shareholder value.

Shareholders are granted special privileges depending on the class of stock they own. These rights may include:

- The right to vote on matters such as elections to the board of directors
- The right to receive dividends
- The right to purchase new shares issued by the company
- The right to a company's assets during a liquidation of the company

A shareholder's rights to a company's assets are subordinate to the rights of the company's creditors. This means that stockholders typically receive nothing if a company is liquidated after bankruptcy. Although a company's directors and officers have duties to act in the best interest of the shareholders, the shareholders themselves normally do not have such duties toward each other. (In other words, each shareholder can make decisions based on self-interest rather than on the interests of the entire group of shareholders.)

Becoming familiar with corporate culture

In this section, we examine the role that an entity's corporate culture plays in the fraud prevention process. *Corporate culture* is the total sum of the values, customs, beliefs, and traditions that make a company unique. It's the glue that holds the company together. Corporate culture is often called the *character* of an organization and (depending on how long the company has been in business and how successfully it has been managed) may or may not reflect the founders' intentions.

The values of a corporate culture influence the ethical standards within a company, as well as managerial behavior. A board of directors and/or senior managers may try to determine a corporate culture; they may want to impose corporate values and standards of behavior that specifically reflect the objectives of the organization. In this section, we explain how you assess a company's corporate culture and what the hallmarks of a risky corporate culture are.

Doing your research

When you're conducting a fraud risk assessment, you need to know what the *tone at the top* of the company is. In other words, you need to find out what message the company's leaders (the board of directors and senior management) are sending about the necessity of ethical behavior or the tolerance for unethical behavior. Employees generally follow the ethics and values that are laid out by their leaders.

How do you start assessing the tone at the top? Here are two key methods:

- ✔ **Interview management and employees:** Conducting interviews is a great way to get familiar with what's happening in the company. Ask both managers and lower-level employees about their knowledge of any fraud occurring in the company or their suspicions about fraud.

  Employees are generally aware of potential fraud risks and faulty internal controls, and they're your best resource for information about whether such risks and faulty controls are the result of poor management or intentional business practices.

  You also want to find out whether management has reported to the audit committee what they know about existing fraud risks and the need for additional internal controls to detect, deter, or prevent fraud.

- ✔ **Administer fraud risk questionnaires to employees:** A fraud risk or ethics questionnaire can also help you evaluate the ethical culture of the organization. It can help you identify how ethics are handled on a day-to-day basis. For example:

  - Are employees informed appropriately on the actions the board or senior management is taking to prevent and deter fraud?

  - How well do employees embrace management's attempts to create an ethical environment? Do they respect those efforts and take them seriously? Or do they consider the efforts to be a joke because they don't fear any consequences?

  - Do employees know how to report inappropriate behavior they witness? For example, does the company have a whistleblower hotline?

  - Are processes in place to ensure that allegations of misconduct are investigated and findings reported properly?

Identifying a poor tone at the top

As we note in Chapter 1, occupational fraud occurs when three conditions are present:

- ✔ Management or employees have an incentive or *motive* to commit fraud. (For example, they're under some kind of financial pressure.)

- ✔ Circumstances exist that create an *opportunity* for fraud to occur.

- ✔ The individuals involved are able to *rationalize* committing fraud.

A poor corporate culture can influence all three conditions. It can determine whether an individual feels motivated to commit fraud; it can create the opportunity by neglecting internal controls; and it can help the fraudster rationalize the act by saying, for example, "I had no choice — the company share price would have dropped if I didn't dress up the financial reports."

What are some of the indicators of a poor tone at the top of an organization?

✔ Poor communication, implementation, support, or enforcement of the company's values or ethical standards; or, conversely, the communication of *inappropriate* values or ethical standards.

✔ Non-financial managers' excessive participation in (or preoccupation with) selecting the accounting principles the company follows when creating its financial statements. (Note that publicly held companies must follow generally accepted accounting principles, or GAAP.)

✔ Non-financial managers' excessive participation in determining significant estimates that appear on the company's financial statements.

✔ Excessive interest by management in maintaining or increasing the company's stock price. (Keep in mind that all managers feel some pressure to maintain and increase the stock price, so you need to determine what *excessive* looks like.)

✔ A practice by management of committing to analysts, creditors, and other third parties to achieve aggressive or unrealistic revenue or earnings forecasts.

Another huge indicator of poor tone at the top is a lack of sufficient internal controls. That subject is so big that we deal with it at length in the upcoming section, "Assessing and Strengthening Internal Controls."

Knowing the nature of the industry

Sometimes, the industry that the business is situated in presents opportunities to commit fraud, so you need to become familiar with the industry itself during your fraud risk assessment. For example, many of the leading producers in the oil and gas industry are located in the Middle East and Sub-Saharan Africa, and bribery is rampant in many of these countries. If your client is a business in the oil or gas industry, you would want to pay close attention to

✔ Assets, liabilities, revenues, or expenses based on significant estimates that involve subjective judgments.

✔ Significant, unusual, or highly complex transactions, especially those that occur close to the end of the accounting period.

No matter what your client does to earn revenue, you want to be aware of how its industry as a whole is performing in the current economy. If an industry is struggling in a given year, you need to realize that your client is struggling as well. That means the pressure is on, and individual employees or managers may feel increased motivation to commit fraud. If the financial reports show that your client experienced growth or high profits that don't jibe with the performance of its industry as a whole, know that you're looking at red flags for fraud.

Fred needs money

Here's a study in the importance of proper fraud prevention controls and what can happen if a company underestimates its level of fraud risk and overestimates the integrity of its managers. It also illustrates how one type of fraud (embezzlement) can lead to another type of fraud (financial reporting fraud). Some of Vijay's former colleagues worked on investigating this case.

Fred was a vice president of finance. He worked hard to get to where he was. In college, he had to work two jobs to pay for his tuition; nobody ever gave Fred anything. When he landed his job as a vice president of finance he felt that he truly made it. But after a few years in his position, he noticed that other employees were getting raises and promotions and he wasn't. He felt that he wasn't getting the proper respect from his employer or from the local business community.

Fred decided to search for other ways to make money, and his workplace seemed a logical place to look. Fred was able to write checks for any amount without approval from the chief financial officer (CFO) or chief executive officer (CEO). In fact, the CEO was happy to sign blank checks for Fred to make his life easier. Fred also was able to enter journal entries in the general ledger without review or approval. Needless to say, such lax controls made Fred's decision to skim money from the company pretty easy.

One day he received an offer from a newly formed bank to be its chief financial officer. Fred was plagued by a guilty conscience because of the fraud he was committing. Plus, he was truly happy about the success of landing a new great job. So he quit his old job and vowed he would start anew. Fred left the company in April 2006, and his assistant left shortly thereafter. When Fred left he took his company laptop, promising to complete the bookkeeping for the company's employee benefit plan. As he said, "This is the least I can do for you." He figured that his misappropriations would never be discovered. He had covered them up well and had been through several external audits without discovery.

The company closed its books on June 30, 2006. The external auditors arrived to perform fieldwork in late August. In September, the auditors withdrew from the audit, and the company notified its lenders that it would not be able to deliver audited financial statements within a specified period of time. The auditors had noted that various key accounts didn't appear to reconcile properly and there were some large, unexplained journal entries. The company performed an initial review of the accounting records but couldn't ascertain the reason for the discrepancies.

The company's major lender contacted fraud investigators, who started their investigation in November 2006. The investigators scanned ledgers and reconciliations, inquired regarding the origins of documents, and had discussions with accounting staff and management regarding policies and procedures.

Most financial data was retained on Fred's laptop, which he still had in his possession. The investigators contacted the bank to get copies of canceled checks. These showed in many cases that the payee was the "VP Finance" or his wife's business. When investigators analyzed the manual summary schedules, they saw that the check descriptions differed and certain checks didn't appear on the schedules. The investigators presented to the CEO suspicious checks totaling more than $1 million for the prior four years.

Subsequently, the investigators obtained Fred's laptop and had interviews (with attorneys present) with him and his assistant. The investigators also helped the FBI prosecute Fred. Fred was ultimately sentenced to ten years and one day in a state penitentiary. No charges were brought against his assistant.

Assessing and Strengthening Internal Controls

If you've read the preceding sections in this chapter, you already know that internal controls are at the core of any company's efforts to prevent fraud. Strong internal controls can keep fraud at bay. Weak internal controls invite fraud in the front door of the office. A corporate culture that promotes ethical behavior goes hand-in-hand with strong internal controls. A poor tone at the top of the organization often results in lax, ineffective controls.

A crucial piece of conducting a fraud risk assessment is assessing existing internal controls. After that assessment has taken place, company management should react to any control deficiencies by taking steps to plug the gaps. In this section, we cover both topics so you know how to work with management to assess internal controls and make them stronger.

Performing an internal control assessment

What exactly is an *internal control*? Let's focus on the word *control* first. A control is any action taken by management, the board, or any other party to manage a company's risk and increase the likelihood that its established objectives and goals will be achieved.

An internal control is a bit more specific. It's any process designed to help a company achieve its objectives related to making the business operate effectively and efficiently; creating reliable financial reports; and achieving compliance with applicable laws and regulations.

An internal control assessment focuses on determining whether internal controls are working as they were intended to. As an auditor, your job is to get to know the business better and to review all its significant processes. Sound simple? It isn't. This type of assessment takes time and involves lots of detail work. (Translation: It's tedious.) But doing a thorough job can give your client vital information for building stronger fraud defenses.

Understanding the business

As part of your fraud risk assessment, you're already getting to know the business by studying its corporate culture, its players, and the industry in which it operates. To understand its internal controls, you need to analyze the company's overall organization and processes. Here are the tasks involved:

✔ Interview management and key personnel to develop an understanding of the control environment.

✔ Identify other people who are the most involved in specific processes, and interview them as well. This is to make sure that the company actually has the processes in place that you have previously developed an understanding of.

✔ Review the relevant company policies and procedures that contain management and employees' responsibilities. For example, analyze any internal audit examinations that have been performed, review the company's ethics policy, and study its whistleblower hotline system (if it exists).

Reviewing significant processes

After doing the tasks outlined in the previous section, you should have a list of various processes that take place within the company. Your next step is to analyze and assess those processes.

First, identify the significant process areas in the company, such as shipping and receiving; purchasing and accounts payable; revenues and accounts receivable; human resources; and investments, debt, and equity financing.

To assess key internal controls in each process area, do the following:

✔ Identify and document the significant processes that occur within that area.

✔ Perform an in-depth review of all relevant policies and procedures that establish internal controls for that area.

✔ Conduct in-depth interviews with the employees who "own" the various processes to fully understand the flows of transactions and data.

✔ Document each process. The documentation can take many forms, such as a narrative or a flowchart:

 • A *narrative* is a map that provides a step-by-step picture of a process in a single document without the use of detailed symbols or keys. It basically explains the process and describes all activities performed in the process with words.

 • A *flowchart* is perhaps the easiest depiction to understand a process. It is a graphical presentation of the actual or ideal path followed by any service or product. It provides a visual sequence of the steps in a process and identifies what a process does. A flowchart shows the process and how data and documents flow, as well as which internal controls are built into the process.

✔ Perform walkthroughs of the processes. Your goal is to observe each process from start to finish to see whether it works the way your narrative or flowchart document indicates. During the walkthrough, you collect evidence that shows how the process is functioning, such as copies of forms or documents. Walkthroughs also help you identify what controls actually exist. A control may look good on paper, but if it isn't performed in the workplace, it's worthless.

✔ Identify key internal controls, as well as risks that are not addressed by existing controls, and evaluate their significance.

✔ Assess the design effectiveness and operating effectiveness of controls by testing sample transactions of the key processes identified. For example, test the evidence you've collected. If a payment has to be approved prior to being issued, take a sample of payments and look for signs of approval, such as signatures or initials.

✔ Classify any internal control deficiencies you identify by breaking them into these three categories (watch out — these definitions get pretty technical):

- *Control deficiencies:* Control deficiencies are defined by the Public Company Accounting Oversight Board (PCAOB) as design or operational deficiencies. *Design deficiencies* occur when either a necessary control is missing or is designed in such a way that it doesn't necessarily meet the control objective. An *operational deficiency* occurs when a properly designed control doesn't operate as designed or when a person performing a control does not possess the necessary authority or qualifications to perform the control.

  In general, a control deficiency exists if "in the normal course of doing their assigned jobs, to prevent, or detect and correct misstatements on a timely basis."

- *Significant deficiencies:* A significant deficiency is a deficiency, or a combination of deficiencies, in internal control that is less severe than a material weakness, yet important enough to merit attention by those charged with governance.

- *Material weaknesses:* A material weakness is a deficiency or combination of deficiencies in internal control, such that there is a reasonable possibility that a material misstatement of the entity's financial statements will not be prevented, or detected and corrected on a timely basis.

✔ Document possible remediation steps for internal controls that you have deemed inefficient. Draft summaries for each issue for all key controls determined not to be operating or designed effectively. Each summary evaluates the impact and risk for the specific process. It also presents a possible solution to the root cause of the deficiency or weakness, which management may choose to adopt.

Your job is to help identify the control weaknesses. Company management is the decision maker in this case; it can decide whether to assume the risk of not remediating or reacting to the deficient controls.

Working together with management

The auditor never bears sole responsibility for assessing a company's internal controls. Company management is ultimately responsible for the accuracy of its financial statements. Therefore, management is also ultimately responsible for assessing the effectiveness of its internal control structure and procedures. It must perform its own risk assessment to identify and measure the risks associated with existing controls. Then, management must *prioritize risk* by identifying which risks are more significant than others.

Management determines the scale of its risk assessment based on the size and complexity of the company. Ideally, it relies on individual managers' work to complete the assessment, but it has to evaluate those managers' competency and objectivity before doing so.

During its risk assessment, management does the following tasks:

- Assesses both the design and operating effectiveness of selected internal controls related to significant accounts. The context is always this: Does this control effectively reduce the risk that the financial statements may be materially misstated?

- Understands the flow of transactions, including information technology aspects, sufficiently enough to identify points at which a misstatement could arise.

- Evaluates company-level controls, which correspond to the components of the Committee of Sponsoring Organizations framework we discuss in the next section.

- Performs a fraud risk assessment (such as the one we describe earlier in the chapter).

- Evaluates controls designed to prevent or detect fraud, including management override of controls.

- Evaluates controls over the period-end financial reporting process.

- Draws a conclusion about the adequacy of internal control over financial reporting.

Improving internal controls

After you and company management have spent lots of quality time reviewing the company's internal controls, management's next step is to determine which control improvements to make. The possibilities are truly endless, so we won't try to get into specifics here. But knowing the guidelines of the Committee of Sponsoring Organizations of the Treadway Commission (COSO) can help.

What is COSO? It's a private-sector organization with the mission of helping boards and company executives establish "more effective, efficient, and ethical business operations." (Check out www.coso.org to find out more.) And it has published a framework that many managers and auditors use to evaluate internal controls. COSO guidelines state that effective internal controls rely on five interrelated components:

✔ **A strong control environment:** Here, we're looking back at the company's corporate culture — the tone at the top. Effective internal controls demand a written code of conduct, employee guidelines, an oversight committee, and proper (prompt) handling of investigations or remediations.

Another crucial piece of the puzzle is a well-established and functioning whistleblower hotline combined with a nonretaliation policy and an incentive system. Whistleblower hotlines should be set up so they are accessible all the time. In addition, their existence should be communicated in a way that also states to the employees how confidentiality and anonymity will be handled. It often makes sense to have these hotlines contracted out to third-party vendors.

✔ **Regular, periodic risk assessments:** The company must regularly identify and analyze relevant risks, and it must assess whether it maintains a sufficient segregation of duties.

✔ **Control activities:** Here's the meat of the matter. These management actions ensure that directives are carried out and objectives are achieved. Controls consist of policies and procedures that address risks. One such control is the process of confirming that employees fully understand these policies and procedures!

Companies must provide clear instructions to employees on the do's and don'ts in the business. An ethics policy and a code of conduct pointing out how violations are handled are a good start. If employees know from the beginning the repercussions of their actions, they may think twice before acting in a fraudulent manner.

✔ **Information and communication:** Information that helps the company carry out its activities must be effectively identified, collected, and exchanged. An example of this component is training.

✔ **Monitoring:** Monitoring is a process to assess the quality of internal control performance over time. Management needs to monitor controls in order to know whether they are operating as intended. Monitoring can be accomplished either through ongoing activities or through separate evaluations. Ongoing monitoring activities are mostly performed on a real-time basis during the regular course of business. They can even be performed through software programs included in the regular software applications of a company.

Are any internal controls dictated to a company by outside regulations? That depends on the company. For publicly held corporations, the Sarbanes-Oxley Act of 2002 (SOX) comes into play. For public companies registered with the U.S. Securities and Exchange Commission (SEC), the Foreign Corrupt Practices Act (FCPA) is relevant.

Here are the few internal controls mandated by SOX:

- An independent audit committee
- Management certification of financial statements
- An external audit of internal controls
- A whistleblower hotline
- Management review of internal controls

The FCPA requires the implementation of an internal control system that is able to assure that

- All transactions and expenditures are conducted with the proper management authorization.
- All transactions are recorded properly to ensure adequate preparation of financial statements conforming with GAAP and to maintain accountability for all company assets.
- All access to company assets is conducted with proper management authorization.
- Actual company assets are audited compared with books and records, and differences are investigated and corrected.

Taking Action after a Larger Business Gets Ripped Off

According to the 2008 Association of Certified Fraud Examiners (ACFE) *Report to the Nation,* here are the ways that fraud was most often detected within public companies:

- 54 percent: Employee tips
- 27 percent: Internal controls
- 21 percent: Internal audit
- 12 percent: By accident
- 4 percent: External audit
- 2.5 percent: Law enforcement

What do these numbers tell us? Even effective internal controls won't catch every instance of fraud. So when fraud does happen in a larger company, what steps should it take? Read on to find out.

Launching fraud investigations

The obvious thing to do after a fraud has occurred is to start a fraud investigation. Most fraud investigations begin with a meeting between the investigators and the client. The person launching the investigation explains to the investigators why he suspects fraud has taken place and hands over any evidence.

A fraud investigator may use surveillance, asset searches, background checks, employee investigations, business investigations, and other types of methods to get to the bottom of a case. In most cases, fraud investigations are investigations of white collar crime, which involves surveillance and careful consideration of complicated financial records.

Conducting surprise audits

Surprise audits incorporate a number of different accounting procedures to detect malfeasance at all levels in an organization. In many fraud cases, a surprise audit could have led to early detection of the fraud. (The red flags existed, but no one was looking for them.)

Traditionally, large financial statement frauds revolve around inventory, sales, and accounts receivable. Examining certain accounts without warning prevents upper management from artificially inflating assets or revenue. If a company has multiple inventory locations, and management knows when and where auditors will conduct test counts, they have a chance to conceal shortages at places not scheduled for a visit. Going to locations and counting inventory without prior notification is a longstanding and effective audit technique.

Surprise audits can both detect and deter fraud. Seeing other employees get caught through surprise audits may deter employees from committing frauds.

Rotating jobs and requiring vacations

In many cases fraudsters take advantage of a loophole in the company's control environment or of the ability to override controls. An employee who finds an effective way to defraud the company always leaves some kind of trail. However, if this employee is solely responsible for the area in which the fraud occurs, the wrongdoing may never be detected because the perpetrator finds ways to cover that trail.

How to overcome this situation? Companies should force their employees to take vacations or to rotate jobs periodically. Doing so ensures that fresh eyes will be looking at the area under the purview of the perpetrator. This advice is universal, no matter the size of the company. Large or small, a business must make sure that no employee has constant, uninterrupted control of any significant work process.

Setting up an internal audit department

Internal auditing is an independent, objective assurance and consulting activity designed to add value and improve an organization's operations. The internal audit department can be seen as the organization's corporate conscience. The department determines whether proper controls are in place and functioning properly. In addition, the department makes recommendations to company management for improving controls.

Establishing a code of conduct

A code of conduct aims to govern acceptable employee behavior. The code should clearly state what kind of behavior an organization expects from its employees in certain situations. Here are the most important areas to cover in a code of conduct:

- Conflicts of interest
- Confidentiality
- The proper use of the organization's assets
- Rules for accepting and giving gifts and gratuities
- Compliance with laws and regulations
- How to report illegal or unethical behavior

The code should specifically define each potential wrongdoing, state the expected behavior in a clear and easy to understand manner, and include what repercussions the employee should expect for violating the code.

Training employees

Employees should attend frequent training courses in fraud education and internal controls. The training sessions should include discussions of the following subjects:

- ✔ Laws and regulations employees must follow
- ✔ Company policies and procedures employees must follow
- ✔ The company's financial and personnel procedures
- ✔ The company's information-processing procedures
- ✔ What's expected from employees when they use the company's physical property and assets
- ✔ The roles and responsibilities of all employees

Chapter 22

Keeping Employees Honest (And Happy)

. . . .

In This Chapter

▶ Pinpointing the causes of employee theft

▶ Understanding how management's ethics affects employee theft

▶ Measuring employee happiness

. . . .

*I*n this chapter, we connect the dots between employee job satisfaction and employee loyalty. Based on our experience (and good old common sense), satisfied employees are less likely to steal from a company.

Why is employee satisfaction the concern of an accountant? Isn't this subject more the concern of human resource professionals or psychologists? As we note in several other chapters in this book, employee theft is a form of fraud that seriously drains the resources of businesses large and small. But business owners and managers can't always see the wart on the end of their nose, or maybe they don't know how to identify and address the sources of the problem.

Always remember that accountants are trusted business advisors. Business owners respect and listen to their accountants. We are in a unique position to serve as advisors and counselors to our clients.

Also, we have the benefit of not being at the client site every day; we come intermittently. We get to see the workplace through a different lens than the business owner who is there every day. Your audit training teaches you to look at each business with a critical eye. While you're looking for internal control issues and financial statement problems, you can't help but notice other things going on in the workplace. If you're serious about helping your clients prevent fraud (and you will be), you'll learn to spot signs that employees are taking their employers to the cleaners. And with help from this chapter, you can explain to the business owners and managers why the problem may exist and how to deal with it.

Identifying Common Causes of Employee Theft

Keeping employees happy won't necessarily prevent them from embezzling. However, if employees are unhappy, a business is most certainly at greater risk for employee embezzlement. Their dissatisfaction may cause them to rationalize or justify this form of fraud. In this section, we cover four common scenarios that are red flags for potential theft.

"They owe it to me"

Imagine that you go shopping, and at the checkout line you pay the bill in cash. You're owed 78 cents in change, but the store employee hands you back only 58 cents. Do you ignore the 20-cent difference? Probably not. Assuming you notice the problem, we're guessing you'll speak up and ask for the correct change. That's because you'll probably feel cheated and maybe even angry. You will demand more change because the store owes it to you.

Now imagine that you work for a company that (you believe) short-changes you every day — and not just by 20 cents. How angry would that situation make you feel? Here are some likely reasons that employees feel this way:

- They're getting paid substantially below the going rate for the type of work they do.

- They're required to work overtime regardless of their need to get home to family.

- Someone else in the organization is getting paid more for the same work because that person is the boss' pet.

- Men in the organization are getting paid more for the same work than women (or vice versa).

- White people in the organization are getting paid more for the same work than people with other ethnic backgrounds (or vice versa).

- Employees don't have benefit plans that are similar to the industry or region standards.

- The work environment itself is problematic. For example, maybe employees have to use dirty bathrooms, work in unsafe conditions, or feel a lack of security for their person or belongings.

- Other people get promotions that the employees truly deserve.

We've been to work sites where these conditions exist, and we always feel like our skin is crawling and want to get out. Imagine how an employee who lives with this reality day in and day out feels.

Cynthia Shapiro, author of *What Does Somebody Have to Do to Get a Job Around Here!* and *Corporate Confidential* (both published by St. Martin's Griffin), says that employees who are treated poorly feel bitter, and bitterness leads to theft. Our experience confirms that fact.

Employees who work under these types of adverse conditions sometimes feel like the business owes them more and, therefore, stealing from the business isn't really stealing. Because they're just taking what they believe is owed to them, it's as if they're creating justice for themselves (because the company won't create it for them).

"I'm just borrowing it"

Sometimes employees have temporary financial needs that inspire theft. For example, we know of a case of a bookkeeper who was embezzling because a family member had medical bills. The bookkeeper had every intention of paying the money back. But she got caught before she had a chance to do so. In her mind she wasn't stealing; she was just borrowing. This scenario is very common.

And money isn't the only thing that employees may borrow from the company. We've heard numerous stories of cars going missing from dealerships and mechanics' garages — just for the night. It may not sound like a big deal, but think about the potential for liability if the borrower got into an accident!

"I need it more than they do"

Employees have needs. They need to feed their families and provide clothing, shelter, and education. Imagine the (very common) scenario where an employee is having a tough time making ends meet and sees the higher-ups in the company spending money on seemingly frivolous items. The employee may become convinced that he could find better uses for the money and, therefore, would be justified in taking it.

Dennis Kozlowski, the former CEO of Tyco International, was convicted in 2005 on various counts including taking unauthorized bonuses from Tyco. The frenzied pretrial publicity included many stories of Kozlowski's extravagant spending and luxurious lifestyle. It was reported that he had a shower curtain in his apartment that Tyco paid for, and the shower curtain cost $6,000. We think that's a bit extravagant! Imagine a Tyco employee at the time who was having trouble paying his daily bills and couldn't afford to send his kids to college. When he heard about the shower curtain, could you blame him if his first thought was "I need it more than Kozlowski — I can spend it on better and more important things." That's a situation that's rife with the potential for fraud. We don't know whether any Tyco employees actually went the route of employee theft based on the revelations about Kozlowski. But our experience tells us that some employees very likely did.

Opportunity: Weak controls and the thrill of theft

Some employees steal for reasons that generate less sympathy than the ones we've described so far. Some just like the thrill of stealing; they get a high like being on drugs. They look for the tiniest weaknesses in internal controls and try to exploit them just to see if they can get away with it. (This is a good reason to make sure a company has proper controls, such as those we discuss in Chapters 20 and 21.)

Other people steal or attempt to steal repeatedly and may have a psychological disorder called *kleptomania.* You've undoubtedly heard of it, but maybe you didn't realize it's a true disease. Dealing with an employee with this disorder is best left to the professionals. If the business has a mental health program, the employee should be referred to that program. If business owners or managers are considering severing the relationship with an employee who suffers from this disorder, advise them to talk to their attorneys first. You want them to make sure they're not violating any laws protecting disabled employees.

We knew a volunteer emergency medical technician who took supplies out of emergency rooms every time he brought in a patient. It's customary for the ERs to replace items that are used on the ambulance, but this guy took replacements and then some. He had large pockets sewn into the lining of his jacket to be able to hide the supplies on the way out. He really had no need for these supplies; he just stored them until he had no room anymore. Then he distributed the items to his EMT friends to keep in their cars in case they came across an accident. The stories about his thievery became so legendary that we even heard a story that he stole a light bar off of a police car one night just to see if he could. (We suspect that one's just a tall tale.)

How Do Employees Steal?

Let us count the ways . . .

In many places in this book, we discuss methods of employee theft. Sometimes people just walk out of their company with inventory or supplies. (Usually they take small items that can be hidden in a purse or bag, but sometimes they boldly walk out with items as large as computers!) Other times, employees concoct schemes to steal cash — and their creativity is limitless.

If you read stories about employee theft in Las Vegas, you'd be truly amazed at how many ways there are for a dealer to steal cash or chips! We read one story about a dealer who was constantly straightening out his tie. Management was curious about his habit and why his tie looked heavy and droopy at the end of the day. They found that this dealer was *palming* chips (hiding chips in his hand). When he straightened out his tie, he was sliding the chips into the innards of his tie. He had opened the seam to make this possible.

One of the more common ways to steal funds is by fudging travel expense reports, which can be really easy to do. To inflate the expense report, an employee just tacks on cash expenses that don't always get a receipt (such as bus fares, cab fares, and tips) or claims that she lost certain receipts.

Sometimes an employee will take a spouse along on a business trip, which is also a form of employee theft. As long as the boss is paying for the hotel room, it seems like a great way for the spouse to travel and see another city cheaply. When the employee goes out to dinner, she takes her hubby along and writes up the receipt on her expense report as if she were entertaining a business contact.

We heard of one story where the employee was supposed to go to a conference for a week. He bought an airline ticket on his own credit card and requested reimbursement. He then cashed in the ticket and stayed home to watch TV. The accounting department at his workplace became suspicious when they didn't see requests for reimbursements of other travel-related expenses like hotels, meals, and cabs.

That's bold: Stealing an entire business

One form of employee theft is outright stealing the business! How does this happen? We personally know of two cases.

In one instance a senior manager stole inventory from a retail electronics chain. There were weak controls, and the manager happened to be related to the boss. He just had goods shipped to another warehouse, which was his. After he had enough goods to start his own business, he "dropped a dime" on the boss to the IRS. When the boss had to sell off the assets of the business to pay back taxes (and went to jail for tax fraud), the manager opened his own store. Talk about a good argument for increasing internal controls!

The other story centers on a personal training salon: a gym where clients work only with personal trainers. One trainer endeared himself to young single women. He would steer things so that he was the one working with these clients. He offered them diet information even though he was not qualified to do so. There were even rumors of sexual liaisons. One day he told the boss that he quit and wasn't coming back. The next day, many of these young women also cancelled their memberships. A few days later, the boss heard that the trainer opened his own salon "for women only." The original business almost collapsed. If the boss had been more mindful of some strange behavior patterns, that would have saved the day.

Does Barbie count as motive?

Here's an example of just how creative employees can get when they have the motive and opportunity to steal.

Zeke was an attorney with a large firm that had offices in many cities. He went to the New York City office for a client meeting. The New York office housed the payroll function for the entire firm. One day, Zeke just happened to walk by the office of Peter, the person in charge of payroll. As Zeke passed by, Peter was running down a list of the paychecks for that period with a subordinate, and Zeke overheard the conversation. What Zeke overheard was Peter calling the name of an attorney from Zeke's home office who had not been with the firm for a few years. Zeke immediately notified the firm's managing partner, who called in forensic accountants to investigate. The investigators found that when the attorney left the firm, Peter did not take him off the payroll; he kept cutting checks as usual. When paychecks needed to be signed, Peter just put a large stack of checks on the desk of the managing partner. Because the managing partner was very busy, he didn't look at the checks he was signing. Besides, he didn't know everyone in all the satellite offices anyway. Before the checks were shipped out to the various offices to be disbursed to employees, Peter would pull out the check made out to the long-gone attorney. He cashed the check and took the proceeds for himself.

When the firm's forensic accountants confirmed the fraud, the managing partner turned over the findings to the district attorney for prosecution. When the district attorney's investigators executed a search warrant at Peter's home, they found a collection of Barbie dolls worth about $12 million.

To prevent employee theft of any kind requires a combination of good internal controls and a good environment for employees. In the case of expense reports, if a company sees that employees are trying to be reimbursed for illegitimate expenses, one step would be to tighten controls (by, for example, requiring that employees get receipts for cab rides or setting a limit on the amount of money that person can spend on meals). At the same time, the company owners and managers should consider whether their travel policies are *too* strict. If they are, perhaps employees aren't getting reimbursed for legitimate expenses. To make up for this fact, they're padding their expense reports in other areas.

The key here is that, no matter what form the theft is taking, the company needs to look at it from as many angles as possible. Only then can it hope to identify the issues at the root of the problem.

Setting the Right Tone from the Top

The tone at the top of a company is management's attitude, which creates the company atmosphere. The tone can be one of respect and honesty, or it can be secretive and suspicious. Some company atmospheres are warm and welcoming, and others are downright toxic. Employees know what the tone of their company is; they pick up on management's attitude and respond accordingly. If management values ethics, the employees (by and large) will behave ethically. If management itself is unethical, you can guess the results.

Connecting management fraud and employee fraud

In our experience, if a company's management commits fraud, the employees are very likely to commit fraud as well. This connection is especially evident in small businesses because employees tend to know more about management's actions. (In large businesses, employees are more easily shielded from management's misdeeds — consider how blindsided most employees of Enron were by the actions of a few top managers.) If a small-business owner cheats on the company taxes to save some money, chances are good that his employees will cheat and steal also. Maybe they'll take home paper and staples, or they'll steal from customers. The thinking goes like this: "If it's okay for the boss to do it, it's okay for me to do it. Besides, it only costs the boss half of what I steal because he gets a tax break for the other half." We've seen this happen time and time again.

Responding to employee fraud when it's found

When company managers discover employee theft, their response should be quick, just, and tough. Obviously, they need to do adequate research to make sure they have the right employee and make sure the theft really occurred. But when the facts are clear, they need to do something!

The nature of that "something" depends on the circumstances. If the theft is relatively small, the company may not want to call the police or the insurance company. That's because its insurance rates may skyrocket in response to a single instance of reported theft.

The company managers also have to be careful when firing employees because the employee may retaliate with a lawsuit for defamation, for example. With advice from their lawyers, company managers should take every appropriate step before firing someone for theft.

But the bottom line is that the company needs to act, and act swiftly. If nothing is done to the thief, other employees get the message that stealing is not a big deal. If they're worried about being punished (and possibly even fired), stealing becomes a very big deal — and much less worth the risk.

Using the tone from the top to boost business

If your business client has a poor tone from the top, and you're having trouble convincing managers to correct it, consider this approach: Try to convince them that the right tone from the top will boost their bottom line. Here's the link: a positive work atmosphere improves the level of employee satisfaction, and increased employee satisfaction translates into higher customer satisfaction. Therefore, treating employees well and promoting an ethical environment not only fend off the threat of theft but also can increase the company's sales.

As a forensic accountant, you may be called in to a client's workplace to help the company figure out why it isn't making money. Of course, you're going to search for signs of fraud. But while you do, be sure to consider more than just the books. Consider the following example:

A private ambulance service in our area seemed to sprout all kinds of stories of management fraud. Its primary business was transporting patients between facilities: hospitals, nursing homes, and back home again. Multiple stories emerged about the owner filing false Medicaid claims and charging personal expenses to the business.

The service also seemed to have a high employee turnover rate. Employees were asked to work overtime without being paid the proper rate, and they were not reimbursed for out-of-pocket expenses. We even heard one story of how the boss (who was often irate and irrational) fired an employee over the radio while this person was driving the ambulance!

But what bothered us the most was hearing stories from patients who complained about being treated very poorly by the EMTs working for this service. The patients were bumped and jostled regardless of their health issues or injuries. Sometimes, when the stretchers were removed from the ambulances, the EMTs let them drop down hard onto the ground, which really frightened the patients. It got so bad that when patients needed transport, they asked the hospitals specifically *not* to call that particular ambulance service. This started to put a serious dent in the company's business.

Eventually, we heard that the owner was indicted on a tax evasion charge. We could only imagine his employees cheering at the thought of him going to jail.

Gauging Employee Satisfaction (Or Lack Thereof)

In this chapter, we make the case that employees who are happy and well treated are less likely to steal. But how do you know whether employees are happy? In this section, we introduce some ways to measure employee job satisfaction.

Doing some informal testing

Over the years we've been in and out of hundreds of workplaces. Along the way, we've discovered a few informal ways of figuring out the level of employee satisfaction or dissatisfaction. (As you gain experience in the field, you'll undoubtedly discover ways to do the same.)

Our friend May uses the "bathroom test." As silly as it may seem, whenever she would go on a job interview, she would ask to use the ladies' room. If the ladies' room was clean and well kept, that was a sign to her that the management was considerate of employees.

The "water cooler test" can also be helpful. If you walk into a workplace and lots of people spend time standing around the water cooler with grim looks on their faces, you can bet they're grousing about their unhappiness on the job. If, instead, employees are at their desks working, that may be a sign that they are happy at their jobs.

Obviously, the water cooler test is not foolproof. Sometimes employees are virtually chained to their desks, which certainly isn't a good thing! We once went to a workplace where the bookkeeping office reminded us of slave ships. The bookkeeper-in-charge's desk was higher than the others. He watched over the assistant bookkeepers to make sure that they were all working all the time. They were never allowed to talk to each other. To go to the bathroom, they had to ask permission as if they were in first grade. Plus, their bathroom outings were timed to make sure they weren't out too long. We were asked to figure out why this company had a high turnover of bookkeepers and why the error rate of bookkeepers was also high. It didn't require high-level forensic accounting skills to figure out this one.

The water cooler test is also not accurate on Mondays after big football games, for obvious reasons.

Testing more formally for employee satisfaction

Companies can also use formal methods of testing employee satisfaction and correlate the results of these tests to issues in the workplace. This step usually occurs when management has specific concerns and is serious about finding solutions.

These days, the most popular tool being used to test for employee satisfaction is a survey called the "Job Descriptive Index" published by Bowling Green State University. (Visit www.bgsu.edu/departments/psych/io/jdi/ to find out details about it.) Questionnaires like this one are usually administered and analyzed by industrial or organizational psychologists.

Using psychological tools to turn things around

We've always thought that accounting majors should minor in psychology because accounting isn't just about numbers; it's about dealing with people. (That's true of many fields, of course.) Here's a true story about how a business used psychology to stop a huge amount of employee theft.

Renowned researcher Gary Latham was called in by a mill that was experiencing huge amounts of theft, about $1 million a year. In one case a 2,000-pound piece of equipment was stolen. Management was powerless to stop the thievery. Once, a supervisor caught an employee leaving with a very heavy tool box. He stopped the employee. In retaliation, the union flooded management with grievances. The flood of grievances paralyzed the administration. They had to ask the supervisor to back off his accusation of employee theft. After that, there was nothing management could do. Because almost everything being stolen had to do with heavy equipment, they knew the employees were stealing for the thrill and not for personal use. That's when they called in Latham.

Latham devised a plan to take the thrill out of the stealing. He developed a two-pronged approach. First, he developed what the company called the "library." Any worker who needed a piece of equipment for personal use was permitted to borrow equipment at any time just by "checking it out." This removed the thrill of stealing.

Second, management sought to recover some if its losses. To do this, they created an amnesty day. Big cities have had successful amnesty days for people to turn in firearms. Several states have had successful amnesty periods for citizens to file and/or pay late taxes without penalty. For the mill, their amnesty day was successful beyond their wildest dreams. So many truckloads of materials showed up at the mill that they couldn't handle the load. They had to extend the amnesty until all the materials could be accommodated. They later found out that the materials were not returned out of guilt or benevolence. The wives of the mill workers were the motivation. As long as there was someplace to take all the stuff that had accumulated in their garages, backyards, and sheds, they wanted the stuff to go.

Chapter 23

Applying Technology to Fraud Prevention

● ●

In This Chapter

▶ Understanding information security and risks

▶ Establishing solid controls

▶ Recognizing social engineering schemes

▶ Learning about specific Internet and e-mail scams

▶ Helping companies recognize and avoid scams

● ●

*A*ccording to the Internet Software Consortium, as of July 2010, the Internet connected an estimated 769 million computers in more than 250 countries on every continent, even Antarctica. The Internet is a collection of loosely connected networks that are accessible to anyone with a computer and a network connection. Individuals and organizations anywhere in the world can reach any point on the Internet at any time of day.

Along with the convenience and easy access to information come risks. Among them are the risks that valuable information will be lost, stolen, changed, or misused. If information is recorded electronically and is available on networked computers, it is more vulnerable than if the same information is printed on paper and locked in a file cabinet. Electronic intruders don't need to enter an office or home; they may not even be in the same country. They can steal or tamper with information without touching a piece of paper or a photocopier. They can also create new electronic files, run their own programs, and hide evidence of their unauthorized activity.

The information stored, managed, and used within a business is an extremely valuable asset. This is true of any type of information, regardless of whether you use computer systems or rely mainly on paper records. Consider for the moment what would happen if a fire occurred in an office. If the fire destroyed paper files and PCs, the company could replace all the equipment pretty easily. But unless it had good information security, the company may never be able to replace the lost information, and the business could fail.

In this chapter, we show you how to help your clients understand the importance of information security, take steps to make their IT systems less prone, and be on high alert for electronic scams.

What Is Information Security?

A company's information must be secure against outside threats. With good security comes the ability to trust that a company's records haven't been tampered with. If a business owner wants to sleep well at night, she has to feel that trust. She needs to know that she has control over who can see and use the company's records.

Information security means preserving three crucial things:

- **Confidentiality:** A company's information should be accessible only to authorized users. When information is read or copied by someone not authorized to do so, the result is known as *loss of confidentiality*.

  Confidentiality is extremely important when it comes to research data, medical and insurance records, new product specifications, and corporate investment strategies. In some cases, confidentiality may even be a legal obligation to protect individuals — think about banks and loan companies, debt collectors, businesses that extend credit to their customers or issue credit cards, hospitals, doctors' offices, and medical testing laboratories. People or agencies that offer psychological counseling or drug treatment, as well as agencies that collect taxes, must also keep clients' information confidential.

- **Integrity:** A business has to safeguard the accuracy and completeness of its information. Information can be corrupted when it's available on an insecure network. When information is modified in unexpected ways, the result is known as *loss of integrity*. Unauthorized changes can be made to information either by human error or intentional tampering. Integrity is especially important for financial data, such as electronic funds transfers and financial accounting.

- **Availability:** Authorized users must have access to information and associated assets when required. If information is erased or becomes inaccessible, the result is a *loss of availability*. This means that people who are authorized to get information cannot do so when they need it. Availability is often the most important attribute in service-oriented businesses that depend on information (for example, airline schedules and online inventory systems).

Managing Information Risks

Good information security is based on understanding the risks that a particular business faces. The process of determining what those risks are and deciding what to do about them is known as *risk management*.

To manage risks you first need to identify threats. Typical threats include:

- ✔ Fraud, including identity theft
- ✔ Fire, flood, and other natural disasters
- ✔ Industrial espionage
- ✔ Computer viruses
- ✔ Data loss
- ✔ Loss of service

You should consider your clients' vulnerability to each of these types of threat. You should also consider the likelihood of each particular risk actually happening.

Given your analysis of the risks that are serious for your client, you should consider how to mitigate or reduce those risks. The objective of risk management is to reduce risks to a level that is acceptable to the business at an economically sensible cost.

For example, assume that your client has developed a Web site that it runs on one of its internal servers. The Web site can be used by customers to place orders that are then automatically processed. Your client must make sure that the Web site is securely designed; otherwise, hackers may be able to change the prices on its products, resulting in a flood of orders at prices that will cause the business a severe loss. In this case, the business is potentially vulnerable to fraud, theft, data loss, and loss of service.

Securing IT Resources and the Network

In this section, we show you how a company can protect itself by establishing good controls related to information technology and using passwords, encryption, and firewalls.

Creating a strong IT department

The way a company operates its information technology (IT) department largely determines the strength or weakness of its information security. Here are some ways to make sure an IT department is in good shape:

- ✔ **Separate duties:** No single person should have the authority to develop and/or install new software. Any changes to the company's network or computers should always involve at least two people.

- ✔ **Establish controls regarding new software:** New software potentially brings new risks to the business. If controls are very weak, someone in IT could install unchecked software from the Internet that imports a virus. All businesses should have strict controls over what software can be installed.

- ✔ **Establish solid backup routines:** Anyone who uses a computer knows that information can be lost if the hardware on which it's stored develops a problem. Although it's a pain for an individual to lose information when a hard drive crashes, the same scenario occurring in a business can spell disaster. That's why every company must have an effective backup routine that involves making copies of data to external media such as tapes or portable hard disks. Ideally, some of the backups should be stored offsite (in case of fire or flood, for example).

- ✔ **Limit access:** A business must control who can use each software application and what that person can do with the associated data. This access control is a necessary part of information management. For example, Michael in accounts can see the payroll but not change it, and all members of the human resources department can have access to personnel records.

Making the case for passwords

Passwords are often the only barrier between a user and a company's information. Hackers use several programs to help crack passwords, but by choosing good passwords and keeping them confidential, a company can make it more difficult for an unauthorized person to access information.

Most people use passwords that are based on personal information and are easy to remember. Unfortunately, that fact makes it easier for an attacker to crack them. In your personal life, if you need a four-digit PIN to access your bank account, do you think it's wise to combine the month, day, and/or year of your birthday? Or to use the last four digits of your Social Security number? Or part of your phone number? Think about how easy it is for someone to find this information. (Even your Social Security number isn't sacred.) What about your e-mail password — is it an English word? If so, it may be susceptible to *dictionary attacks,* which attempt to guess passwords based on words in the dictionary.

Here are some ideas for a company to use when selecting passwords — and when instructing employees on how to select them:

✔ Always use a password that is at least 8 characters long; 14 characters is recommended.

✔ Don't use sequences or repeated characters like 123456 or ZZZZZZ.

✔ Don't use any part of your name.

✔ Rely on a series of words and use memory techniques, or *mnemonics,* to help remember how to decode the password. For example, *AsSpTU* stands for "[A] [S]omewhat [S]afer [P]assword [T]o [U]se."

✔ Use both lowercase and capital letters to add another layer of obscurity.

✔ Combine numbers, special characters (such as !@#$%^&*,;"), and both lowercase and capital letters. This is your best defense. If you change "AsSpTU" to "A55p7U!", the password becomes much more complicated.

✔ Consider using a phrase instead of a single word. Longer passwords are more secure than shorter ones because there are more characters to guess. For example, "The Dr3ss C0l0r 15 turquoise!" would be a strong password because it has many characters and includes lowercase and capital letters, numbers, and special characters. You may need to try different variations of a passphrase — many applications limit the length of passwords, and some do not accept spaces. Avoid common phrases, famous quotations, and song lyrics.

Employees should use different passwords for different accounts and change their passwords every 30 days using a good selection of new characters. They should never write down their passwords in a place someone else can see (in a desk, next to a computer, or — worse — taped to the computer!). The company should remind them not to share their passwords with anyone and to watch out for attackers trying to trick them through phone calls or e-mail messages requesting that they reveal their passwords. (We talk about such tricksters in the upcoming section, "Protecting a Company from Social Engineering.")

Encrypting data

Your client may want to invest in encryption software. *Encryption* means converting information using a scheme that prevents it being understood by anyone who isn't authorized to read it. Files, e-mails, and even whole hard disks can be encrypted. When e-mails are encrypted, you get the additional benefit of being able to validate who sent the message and check that it hasn't been tampered with en route. Encryption is also used for electronic commerce (such as making purchases on Amazon.com or eBay), wireless networking security, and remote access (to prevent eavesdropping).

Setting up firewalls

Firewalls provide protection against outside attackers by shielding a computer or network from malicious or unnecessary Internet traffic. Firewalls can be configured to block data from certain locations while allowing the relevant and necessary data through. Firewalls are offered in two forms: hardware (external) and software (internal). Both have their advantages and disadvantages, but the decision to use a firewall is far more important than deciding which type is used.

Guarding against spyware

Spyware is the name given to hidden programs running on a computer without the owner's knowledge or consent. The programs track and communicate all online activity to a third party. More malicious spyware programs are able to log everything you type — which may include credit card details, important client data, and online banking passwords — before sending it back to the creator. If a company's computer system runs slowly or becomes less stable, that could be a sign that spyware is active.

Here's what you can advise your client to do:

✔ Ensure that in addition to antivirus software, the computers also have antispyware capabilities. Newer versions of antivirus software include antispyware.

✔ Caution employees to be cautious when clicking on Web sites or downloading or opening e-mails. Make sure they know not to open attachments on e-mails unless they know the senders.

Avoiding viruses and worms

A computer *virus* is software written for the sole purpose of infecting a computer. Viruses are most commonly spread via e-mail, but they are equally dangerous if spread using pictures, screensavers, computer disks, and memory storage devices. An e-mail-based virus can scan your address book, forwarding the virus to your friends, clients, and colleagues. That's why a virus can circle the globe in a matter of hours.

A *worm* is an advanced virus that self-replicates and spreads via the Internet. In theory, a worm can spread to all computers connected to the Internet.

No company wants to deal with viruses and worms. Here's how to shield against these threats:

✔ Every computer in the company's network should be protected with antivirus software. The software must have the ability to receive updates to keep up with the virus writers. Each computer should be set up so that antivirus updates are received automatically every day.

✔ Employees must exercise caution when opening all e-mails and attachments. Viruses use social engineering tricks to tempt users into opening them.

✔ The IT department must keep up-to-date with software updates and *patches*: pieces of software used to fix problems.

Protecting a Company from Social Engineering

Human beings are often the weakest link in the security chain. Criminals and con artists know this fact and exploit it. In a *social engineering* attack, an attacker uses human interaction (social skills) to obtain or compromise information about an organization or its computer systems. An attacker may seem unassuming and respectable, possibly claiming to be a new employee, repairman, or researcher — even offering credentials to support that identity. By asking questions, he may be able to piece together enough information to infiltrate an organization's network.

Fraudsters use the Internet to find out about their victims, and sometimes they even go through their garbage to add to their information. They can build up a detailed picture by accumulating small bits of data. Here, we show you how to help companies spot social engineering and protect against it, and we explain what phishing is and how to combat it.

Spotting and preventing social engineering

Social engineering takes many forms, some subtle, some much more blatant. For example:

✔ A stranger tries to get into your good graces or asks for information such as PIN numbers, passwords, and credit card numbers or asks you to do something on your computer such as installing a program or opening a file.

✔ Your trash is taken away before the normal garbage day or is otherwise disturbed.

✔ You get an unexpected call, e-mail, or visit from a repairman, technical support person, or fellow employee. (If you work for a large company, you likely don't know everyone who works there.)

Here are the fundamental steps to take to protect against social engineering schemes:

- ✓ Trust your instincts. If you think someone is trying to con you, stand back from the situation and take stock. Buy yourself some time if you can; for example, ask for the person's telephone number and promise to call back. Contact your manager or someone else within the company as soon as possible.

- ✓ Shred any documents with personal information or confidential company information before throwing them out.

  Be conscious of what is personal information: bank details, credit card numbers, and passwords are obvious. But a fraudster can also make use of trivial information such as where someone works, or information about that person's friends and family.

- ✓ Take steps to protect your privacy online, whether you're using a work computer or home computer.

- ✓ Be careful what you publish on social networking sites. Not only is it dangerous to write too much personal information, but information about the goings-on in your company can be fodder for a fraudster as well.

- ✓ Check credentials carefully. For example, if someone claims to be working for a computer repair company, call the company and check with your IT department to see if it hired this individual.

- ✓ Be firm. Con men can be very persistent and persuasive; they play on human emotions such as guilt, greed, and the desire to be liked. Stick to your guns.

- ✓ Discuss the problem with your coworkers, and set ground rules for how to respond.

Avoiding phishing attacks

Phishing is a form of social engineering. Phishing attackers use e-mail or malicious Web sites to solicit personal information by posing as trustworthy organizations. For example, an attacker may send an e-mail that seems to be from a reputable credit card company or financial institution. The e-mail requests account information, often suggesting that there is a problem. The e-mail may appear credible, but its aim is to steal your data and money. When users respond with the requested information, attackers can use it to gain access to the accounts.

Here's how you protect your company and avoid being a victim of phishing:

✔ Be suspicious of unsolicited phone calls, visits, or e-mail messages from individuals asking about employees or other internal information. If an unknown individual claims to be from a legitimate organization, try to verify the person's identity directly with the organization.

✔ Do not provide personal information or information about your organization, including its structure or networks.

✔ Do not reveal personal or financial information in e-mails, and do not respond to e-mail solicitations for this information. This includes following links sent in e-mail.

✔ Don't send sensitive information over the Internet before checking a Web site's security.

✔ Pay attention to the URL of a Web site (its Web address). A malicious Web site may look identical to a legitimate site, but the URL may use a variation in spelling or a different domain (such as *.com* instead of *.net*).

✔ If you are unsure whether an e-mail request is legitimate, try to verify it by contacting the company directly. Do not use contact information provided on a Web site connected to the request; instead, check previous statements for contact information. Information about known phishing attacks is also available online from groups such as the Anti-Phishing Working Group (http://www.antiphishing.org).

✔ Install and maintain antivirus software, firewalls, and e-mail filters to reduce some of this traffic.

✔ Take advantage of any antiphishing features offered by your e-mail client and Web browser.

✔ Trust that it's highly unlikely for a reputable company to lose account information and, if it does, it wouldn't request the information via e-mail.

✔ Regularly check financial accounts for unusual activity.

✔ Keep an eye out for grammatical or spelling errors; phishing e-mails are often full of them.

Identifying Common Electronic Scams

E-mail has changed the game for scammers. The convenience and anonymity of e-mail, along with the capability it provides for easily contacting thousands of people at once, enables scammers to work efficiently. Scammers need to fool only a small percentage of the tens of thousands of people they e-mail for their ruse to pay off.

The following sections provide information to help your clients spot an e-mail scam when it lands in their mailbox. Armed with this information, your clients can better recognize scams and avoid getting entangled in them.

Old-fashioned e-mail schemes

Many Internet and e-mail scams have existed for a long time. In fact, a number of them are merely "recycled" scams that predate the use of e-mail. The Federal Trade Commission has a list of the most common, which include:

- Bogus business opportunities
- Chain letters
- Work-at-home schemes
- Health and diet scams
- "Free" goods
- Investment opportunities
- Bulk (spam) e-mail schemes
- Cable descrambler kits
- "Guaranteed" loans or credit
- Easy money

Trojan horse e-mails

A *Trojan horse e-mail* offers the promise of something you may be interested in — such as an attachment containing a joke, a photograph, or a patch for a software problem. When opened, the attachment may do any or all of the following:

- Create vulnerability on your computer.
- Open a secret "back door" to allow an attacker future illicit access to your computer.
- Install software that logs your keystrokes and sends the logs to an attacker, allowing the attacker to ferret out your passwords and other important information.
- Install software that monitors your online transactions and activities and provides an attacker with access to your files.

Advanced fee or 419 fraud

Would you like to win a lottery? Get a share of a dead rich person's bank account? Of course. Would you be prepared to pay a little up front to facilitate the process? Perhaps. That's just what fraudsters want you to do.

Advance fee fraud occurs when someone promises wealth (often very large sums) or employment in exchange for a payment made up front. The fraudster contacts targets by mail, phone, fax, or e-mail.

These schemes are quite elaborate and manage to hook a surprising number of victims. Essentially, they attempt to entice the victim into a bogus plot to acquire and split a large sum of cash. This type of scam, originally known as the "Spanish Prisoner Letter," has been carried out since at least the sixteenth century via ordinary postal mail. Many perpetrators of this kind of fraud have been Nigerian citizens. Consequently, the name "419 scheme" is taken from the section of the Nigerian penal code that addresses fraud.

Many of these scams involve stories of former dictators and Swiss bank accounts. Seemingly plausible (but often unverifiable) details like names and dates or elaborate technical descriptions are given. Often the initial contact includes a phone number or a request for your bank details (on the pretence that someone is going to wire you some money). The e-mails may be addressed to the "CEO" or "Managing Director" rather than to a named individual. These messages may be marked "urgent" or "confidential." Spelling and grammar mistakes are common and may be included deliberately to make you feel superior or sympathetic.

If your clients' employees receive these types of e-mails, they should be reminded not to send payments to anyone requesting money in this way, to guard their bank account information carefully, and to contact police immediately if they make the mistake of sending money. They shouldn't even respond at all via e-mail. In case you do, that would let the scammers know that they've hit a legitimate e-mail.

Reacting smartly

We all get e-mails that resemble those we just described. If you react appropriately, they can be harmless. Here's what you want your clients to do so a nasty e-mail can't wreak havoc:

- ✔ **Filter spam:** Because most e-mail scams begin with unsolicited commercial e-mail, your clients should take measures to prevent spam from getting into employees' mailboxes. Most e-mail applications and Web mail services include spam-filtering features, or ways in which you can configure your e-mail applications to filter spam.

  You may not be able to eliminate *all* spam, but filtering will keep a great deal of it from reaching employees' mailboxes. You should be aware that spammers monitor spam filtering tools and software, and take measures to elude them.

✔ **Teach employees to regard unsolicited e-mails with suspicion:** No one should automatically trust an e-mail sent by an unknown individual or organization. And employees shouldn't open attachments or click on links sent in an unsolicited e-mail. Cleverly crafted links can take the reader to Web sites set up to trick him into divulging private information or downloading viruses, spyware, and other malicious software.

Remember that even e-mail sent from a familiar address may create problems. Many viruses spread themselves by scanning the victim's computer for e-mail addresses and sending themselves to these addresses in the guise of an e-mail from the owner of the infected computer.

✔ **Lobby for common sense:** Employees need to be reminded that when e-mails arrive promising them big money for little effort, accusing them of violating the Patriot Act, or inviting them to join a plot to grab unclaimed funds involving persons they don't know in a country on the other side of the world, they should take a moment to consider the likelihood that the e-mail is fraudulent.

Putting Technology to Good Use

As we note in other chapters, occupational fraud is a huge and ever-growing problem. A timely detection of fraud directly impacts a company's bottom line, reducing its losses. Effective detection techniques also serve as a deterrent to potential fraudsters, such as employees who know that experts are looking for fraud or that employee actions are being continuously monitored.

Several issues make effective fraud management a particularly challenging task. These include:

✔ The enormous and ever-expanding volumes of data created within a business

✔ The growing complexity of business systems

✔ Changes in business processes and activities

✔ The continuous evolution of fraud schemes to bypass existing detection techniques

✔ Regulatory issues related to employee privacy and discrimination

To maximize the efficiency and effectiveness of a fraud detection and prevention program, a business simply must use technology. See Chapter 15 for a detailed discussion of how technology comes into play during a fraud investigation. The same types of tools can help a business prevent fraud in the first place.

One category of technological tools commonly used by auditors and examiners is known as *Computer-Assisted Audit Tools and Techniques* (CAATTs). CAATTs are used in a wide array of accounting settings. Here are three such programs you may encounter:

✔ **ACL:** This advanced data analysis software is geared toward audit and fraud analysis. ACL technology can be used to access and analyze very large volumes of data from virtually any enterprise application. By doing so, organizations can quickly identify suspicious transactions that may represent frauds and errors, and they can close internal control deficiencies before the fraud escalates.

Through a unique and powerful combination of data access, analysis, and reporting capabilities, ACL software reaches data from virtually any source, across any system, through a consistent user interface. By independently comparing and analyzing data from different computer systems, ACL technology provides insight into the transactional data underlying business processes and financial reporting.

✔ **ActiveData for Excel or Office:** ActiveData for Excel is an add-in for Microsoft Excel. For smaller data sets, the add-in adds a number of audit and analysis functions. For larger datasets, another tool is available: ActiveData for Office. It enables the analysis and manipulation of up to 2 billion rows of data. The whole analysis and reporting is done within the familiar Microsoft Office environment.

✔ **Caseware IDEA:** IDEA is also an advanced data analysis software. It can import data from a large number of formats and includes a collection of basic audit tests and reports that can be run by any auditor or forensic accountant with a minimum amount of training. IDEA can process and examine large amounts of transactions, which helps greatly in fraud analysis.

Technology makes it easier to investigate frauds but is not a substitute for experienced fraud investigators. These tools work wonderfully when used by skilled investigators. So study hard, keep up with the latest forensic accounting technology, and share what you know with your clients.

Part VI
The Part of Tens

The 5th Wave   By Rich Tennant

"Lucky for us—our Net Income column ended directly over a 'Triple Word Score' square."

In this part . . .

Fraud is a serious problem, but sometimes stories about fraud can be seriously entertaining. In this part, we supply three chapters that offer quick info to go: ten portrayals of fraud on TV and in the movies, ten frauds that are fairly common but often unsuspected, and ten truly strange fraud stories that make you wonder what the perpetrators could possibly have been thinking.

Chapter 24

Ten Entertaining Portrayals
of Fraud

- -

- -

*F*or all the negative adjectives that apply to fraud, we can think of at least one positive adjective: entertaining. Fraudsters can be larger-than-life characters, and their antics, as despicable as they may be, often prove fascinating. That's probably why so many books, movies, and TV shows derive their plots from fraud cases.

In this chapter, we offer just a sampling of the choices you have if you're looking for a break from your forensic accounting studies but don't want to stray too far from the subject matter.

The Fly on the Wall

This novel by Tony Hillerman was first published in 1971. Reporter John Cotton learns of something fishy going on at the state highway and parks commissions. A colleague was murdered for starting this investigation. To dig up the abuses, Cotton uses forensic accounting techniques. First, he researches all the corporations involved. Some of his searches lead to familiar names, such as the business owners, who happen also to be politicians and others working for the government. Cotton then goes through all the paperwork on some contracts for building highways and concessions at the parks. He compares amounts of cement mixture shipped, shipping costs from the cement plants to the work sites, amount of cement ordered, and amount of cement needed.

We won't tell you exactly what Cotton discovers because that will ruin the ending for you. Let's just say that careful working of the numbers leads him to a large discrepancy and a major fraud.

This book is an easy read. It demonstrates how a pencil, a pad of accounting paper, an adding machine, and the mind of a forensic accountant can uncover the largest of frauds.

The Big Shakedown

Okay, so maybe it wasn't the best movie ever made, but if you're a Bette Davis fan, this 1934 film may interest you. And the subject matter is still timely after all these years.

A former bootlegger approaches a small-time pharmacist, Jimmy (played by Charles Farrell), about counterfeiting name-brand toothpaste and cosmetics and selling them at the name-brand prices. The pharmacist eventually agrees because he's cash-strapped and wants enough money to get married to Norma (played by Davis). He ends up bullied into counterfeiting more products, including pharmaceuticals, and his own wife miscarries their child after being given one of them in the hospital.

Melodramatic? A touch. An interesting conversation starter about the enduring role of counterfeiting in the U.S. economy? You betcha.

The Sting

Old-time con men were the quintessential fraudsters, long before anyone had heard of the term *white-collar crime*. Robert Redford and Paul Newman played some truly entertaining con men in this 1973 movie that won seven Academy Awards, including best picture and best director.

The action is set in the 1930s. Redford and Newman are grifters who attempt to con a mob boss in revenge for the murder of Redford's former partner. The grifters are out to get every dime from the mobster, but the FBI gets involved and convinces one grifter to help them catch the other. The cons and double-crosses continue until the very end.

The Sting was inspired by real-life brothers Fred and Charley Gondorff, whose story (along with the stories of lots of other grifters) was featured in the book *The Big Con: The Story of the Confidence Man* by David Maurer, published in 1940. After the movie was made, Maurer filed a $10 million lawsuit claiming it had used parts of his book. The lawsuit was settled out of court.

Trading Places

Starring Dan Aykroyd as a commodity broker and Eddie Murphy as a homeless street con, this 1983 comedy is a modern take on Mark Twain's novel *The Prince and the Pauper*. Unbeknownst to them, the two main characters' lives are switched as part of an elaborate bet between the owners of the brokerage firm. Murphy's character is given the chance to become a businessman, and Aykroyd's character loses everything.

After hitting rock bottom, Aykroyd's character decides to take revenge against the brokerage owners. He learns that they're part of a fraudulent effort to corner the frozen orange juice market and commits a fraud of his own to lead to their financial ruin.

Small-time cons, big-time commodities fraud, Eddie Murphy, Dan Aykroyd . . . what more could you want from a movie?

Wall Street

Oliver Stone directed this 1987 classic about a young, ambitious stockbroker named Bud Fox (played by Charlie Sheen) in New York in the early 1980s. Fox convinces high-powered stock speculator Gordon Gekko (Michael Douglas) to take him under his wing, and Fox buys into Gekko's philosophy that "greed is good."

Using insider information, Gekko manipulates the stock market to his advantage, and Fox quickly learns that he's valuable to Gekko only if he can provide such information. But when the target of their market sabotage is the airline where Fox's father works, the waters get muddy.

Stone also directed the 2010 sequel *Wall Street: Money Never Sleeps*, in which Douglas reprises his Gekko role (and Sheen makes a cameo as Bud Fox). This film's plot centers around the 2008 financial crisis.

Working Girl

The hair was big, and so were the fraud and deception! This 1988 movie starred Melanie Griffith as Tess McGill, a New York secretary working for a Wall Street investment bank and longing to become an executive. Her boss, Katharine Parker (played by Sigourney Weaver), encourages Tess to share her business ideas, which seems great at first. But when Parker breaks her leg in a skiing accident, Tess discovers that her boss was planning to steal Tess's idea for helping a client business improve its market hold and fend off a foreign takeover.

Steamed at her boss, Tess decides to promote the idea herself. To do so, she temporarily takes over Parker's apartment and wardrobe, and she uses Parker's contacts to get a foot in the client's door. When her boss returns, Tess is fired for her deception, but in the end Parker's own deception costs her the account. (It's a comedy; there has to be a happy ending, right?)

Quiz Show

Produced and directed by Robert Redford, this 1994 film tells the true story of a 1950s scandal centering on a TV quiz show called *Twenty One*. When the show first went on the air, its contestants performed dismally, not knowing the answers to most of the questions. The show's sponsor was livid and demanded change.

The show's producers found the secret to a successful broadcast by feeding answers to contestants they wanted to win. The show was essentially scripted this way, but it was presented to the American public as if each contestant had equal opportunity to win.

The film demonstrates that the beginning of the show's end comes when the producers ask a long-winning contestant, Herbert Stempel (played by John Turturro), to lose because ratings are dropping. Stempel agrees to lose to Charles Van Doren (played by Ralph Fiennes), who rises to national stardom and brings the ratings back up.

But having lost his winnings and fuming from the way he was treated, Stempel tries to blow the show's cover. He eventually testifies to the U.S. Congress about the deceit, and Van Doren follows suit.

Fargo

The Coen brothers — Joel and Ethan — wrote and directed this acclaimed 1996 movie that starred William H. Macy as Jerry Lundegaard, a car salesman who hires two goons (played by Steve Buscemi and Peter Stormare) to kidnap his wife. Jerry is in a heap of financial trouble and tries (but fails) to scheme his way out of it. The kidnapping plot is designed to bring Jerry a pretty penny in ransom from his father-in-law, who owns the car dealership. No one is supposed to get hurt.

But (of course) the plot goes seriously awry, and lots of folks get killed. Frances McDormand is wonderful as a pregnant police chief who pieces together the clues.

Oh, and did we mention it's a comedy?

Telling Lies in America

A semi-autobiographical story written by Joe Eszterhas (who is famous for writing *Basic Instinct* and infamous for writing *Showgirls*), this 1997 movie tells the story of a 17-year-old boy named Karchy Jonas, played by Brad Renfro. Jonas is a Hungarian immigrant struggling at school and trying to figure out American culture. In an effort to boost his popularity, he cheats to win a contest to become an assistant for a radio personality, Billy Magic, played by Kevin Bacon.

Billy Magic seems to have everything a young man could want: money, women, and fame. But his life is built on lies, including those told to hide the fact that he accepts record company bribes (*payola*) to play certain songs.

Enron: The Smartest Guys in the Room

Warning: This film isn't entertaining in the same way that, say, *Trading Places* or *Working Girl* are. In fact, it may leave you shaking your head in disgust and disbelief.

This 2005 documentary was based on a best-selling book written by *Fortune* reporters Bethany McLean and Peter Elkind. In case you lived in a cave around the turn of the 21st century, Enron was the Houston-based company that went from being the seventh largest business in the United States to being bankrupt within the course of a single year. Why? Because its business model was built on fraud. While its top executives pocketed more than $1 billion, Enron's investors and employees were devastated.

The movie features interviews with former Enron executives and employees, reporters, and stock analysts. It homes in on the human drama behind the headlines, telling the stories of some of the 20,000 people who lost their jobs, as well as the stories of the executives who crafted the fraud.

Chapter 25

Ten Fairly Common – and Unsuspected – Frauds

. . . .

In This Chapter

▶ Seeing how fraud can be committed right under your nose

▶ Trying to spot such frauds

. . . .

As we note throughout this book, frauds are commonplace in businesses today. Volumes could be written to catalogue the frauds that are perpetrated every year. Fraudsters generally operate in two ways: They gain the trust of others before committing fraud, and/or they use the ignorance of others (such as someone's unfamiliarity with using the Internet) for their benefit.

In this chapter, we provide ten examples of fraud that are common yet unsuspected: *common* because they occur frequently or the method used is typically used by many fraudsters; *unsuspected* because the victims generally do not have any inkling that they are being defrauded. The only way to protect yourself or a client is to know about them, so keep reading!

Doctoring a Résumé

Organizations often overlook pre-employment screenings when hiring employees. That oversight can prove disastrous. Screenings provide valuable information about a prospective employee's character, integrity, and instances of prior fraud.

Here's a high profile example of a very common problem: Do you happen to remember the nickname *Chainsaw Al* from back in the 1990s? Sunbeam Corporation hired Al Dunlap as its CEO in 1996 to restructure the financially ailing company. (He had a reputation for ruthlessly downsizing companies; hence his nickname.) Sunbeam fired him 23 months later for allegations of fraud.

Dunlap's actions forced Sunbeam into bankruptcy. He is alleged to have engineered massive accounting fraud at Sunbeam, including the following two types of fraud:

✔ **Bill and hold:** Sunbeam sold certain seasonal items at higher volume than normal for the time of year. For instance, large numbers of barbecue grills were sold during winter, which corresponded to the fourth quarter for the company. Dunlap sold products to retailers at large discounts and booked the sales immediately. However, he did not deliver the products; he stored them in third-party warehouses to be delivered at later dates.

✔ **Channel stuffing:** Dunlap offered incentives to retailers to sell products that would have otherwise been sold later in the year.

Sunbeam's board of directors had failed to do its homework before hiring Dunlap. Had it checked into Dunlap's background, it would have found that in the 1970s he was accused of similar fraud charges as president of Nitec Paper. Dunlap omitted all references to Nitec in the résumé he submitted to Sunbeam. Sunbeam could have found reports of his prior misconduct on public electronic media archives.

Selling Art That Is Not Authentic

Selling and buying art is a multibillion dollar business. Art collecting takes place in art galleries, auction houses, and estate sales, and also via the Internet. According to some estimates, *40 percent* of the art for sale is either forged or of questionable authenticity.

Ely Sakhia owned an art gallery in Manhattan for 15 years. He purchased original Impressionist and Post-Impressionist works and hired artists to reproduce them. He then sold the fakes to private clients with copies of certificates of authenticity. He sold the original artworks (with the genuine certificates of authenticity) to art galleries in New York and London.

Sakhia was caught when a past buyer of a fake tried to sell his forged piece to an auction house while Sakhia attempted to sell the original to another auction house — what perfect timing! Both auction houses brought in an expert who stated that the past buyer's work was a fake. In July 2005, Sakhia was sentenced to 41 months in prison, fined $12.5 million, and ordered to forfeit 11 pieces.

Using Spreadsheets Fraudulently

Spreadsheets have become ubiquitous, and the danger in using spreadsheets is that they are error-prone; some estimates indicate that more than 90 percent of corporate spreadsheets have *material* (financially significant) errors in them. Sadly, spreadsheets can be — and have been — used to commit fraud. Because a spreadsheet on average contains thousands of lines of data, spreadsheet fraud is difficult to detect.

The U.S. Securities and Exchange Commission (SEC) charged Scott Hirth, the former CFO of ProQuest Company, with using spreadsheet aids to make fraudulent monthly and quarterly accounting entries for more than five years. As part of the scheme, Hirth created false documentation to back up the balances in accounts he allegedly manipulated. His account-reconciliation spreadsheets contained *hidden rows* so that false account entries didn't show up when they were printed in hard copy. (Spreadsheets have a feature to hide rows and columns from a user without affecting the underlying calculations in any way.)

Hirth settled with the SEC. He was ordered to pay $233,676 in disgorgement of ill-gotten gains, $54,474 in prejudgment interest, and a $130,000 civil money penalty. He was also prohibited from ever serving as an officer or director of a public company again.

Selling Counterfeit Tickets

The FBI named *document fraud,* which includes the counterfeiting of tickets, as the top crime of the 1990s. This type of fraud is still flourishing today. The proliferation of home computers, scanners, color copiers, and desktop publishing has led to an increase in counterfeiting. As the problem has dramatically increased, ticket companies have taken steps to combat the threat, including using holograms and no-copy inks. (Holograms create a three-dimensional image that is difficult to counterfeit.)

Online ticket brokers guarantee the validity of tickets sold by re-sellers. Cindy, a music fan, purchased a pair of tickets from one such re-seller. She was skeptical about the tickets because they were priced 300 percent below others for the same event. Nevertheless, Cindy bought the tickets knowing that the broker guaranteed her purchase. Upon inspecting the tickets a few days later, she found several red flags:

- ✔ The tickets were electronic tickets that had been printed out (rather than hard tickets that would have been mailed to her).
- ✔ The *Purchased By* name was spelled differently on each ticket.
- ✔ The seat numbers for each ticket exceeded the total number of seats in the indicated row.
- ✔ The entrance gate did not match the section according to a seat map of the venue.

After receiving copies of the tickets from Cindy, the broker confirmed that they were counterfeit and sent replacement tickets.

Staging Accidents to Bilk Insurance Companies

In Chapter 19, we explain that insurance fraud costs the insurance industry about $80 billion annually. One of the common schemes carried out by some healthcare providers is to bill insurance companies for services to accident victims that are not medically necessary. These providers tend to be in close touch with ambulance chasers who bring them patients. In some cases, there's an added fraudulent twist: The patients are "injured" in staged accidents.

In 2009, two chiropractors in Miami were sentenced for their roles in a health-care and insurance fraud scheme. To execute the scheme, the defendants solicited real victims of automobile accidents, as well as individuals willing to participate in staged accidents, to visit their chiropractic clinics and seek treatments that were not medically necessary. The defendants then filed fraudulent insurance claims for nonexistent and inflated personal injuries on behalf of the participants. The defendants submitted false claims in excess of $3 million to insurance companies.

Inflating Tax Refunds

The Internal Revenue Service (IRS) cautions taxpayers to carefully select tax preparers because taxpayers are ultimately responsible for their own tax returns. Tax preparers can commit fraud by preparing and filing false income tax returns by claiming inflated personal or business expenses, false deductions, unallowable credits, or excessive exemptions on returns prepared for their clients.

In one instance, a tax preparer would provide his clients with correct copies of their state and federal income tax returns. Then he would alter the returns prior to actually sending them to the IRS and the Franchise Tax Board (FTB — the department that collects state personal income taxes and bank and corporation taxes for the State of California). The returns included bogus deductions to reduce the taxpayers' state and federal tax liability, which in turn caused the issuance of larger refunds than were actually due. The preparer directed the IRS and FTB to mail the checks directly to him.

Upon receipt of the refund checks, he would forge his clients' signatures and personally deposit or cash the refund checks. The preparer then issued new checks to his clients for the amount of the refund they were led to believe they were getting. He pleaded guilty to mail fraud, aiding and assisting in the preparation of false income tax returns, and forging endorsements on treasury checks.

Committing Credit/Debit Card Fraud

Bank robberies get a lot of media attention and account for $65 million in losses annually. Meanwhile, check fraud, which gets fairly little media attention, costs over $800 million annually. It is estimated that a bank robber normally steals $700 and gets caught within 24 hours. On the other hand, check frauds can go undetected, especially when the amount involved is relatively small.

Here's a hypothetical example of how this fraud works: Two college roommates, Adam and Steve, in dire need for cash, decide to commit bank fraud. Adam orders a new debit card for himself from the bank where he holds an account. Upon receipt of the card, Steve signs the card on behalf of Adam and goes to the bank to withdraw money. Knowing that for withdrawals exceeding $2,000 the bank would require multiple forms of identity, Steve makes out a withdrawal slip for $1,500. After matching the signatures on the withdrawal slip and the debit card, the teller dispenses the funds.

Upon Steve's return to the college dormitory, Adam calls the bank and notifies that his wallet, which contained his debit card, was stolen. When asked by the bank to confirm the last known transaction, Adam omits mentioning the $1,500 withdrawal. After identifying the transactions as fraudulent, the bank reimburses Adam's account for $1,500. Had the teller been more vigilant and asked Steve for his government-issued photo ID as proof of identity, it is likely that Steve would have been caught.

Perpetrating Adoption Subsidy Schemes

The federal, state, and local governments provide assistance in the hundreds of billions of dollars every year. Government programs, including those that support families with adopted children, are a ripe ground for fraud.

Here's how adoption subsidy fraud may work: Say that a supervisor of a city adoption agency is friends with his neighbors, who adopt children and apply for adoption subsidy. Everything is legit so far. To support his lavish way of life, the supervisor devises an elaborate scheme. The supervisor asks his neighbors to add several fictitious children in the subsidy application. He convinces the adoptive family to share in the increased portion of monthly adoption subsidy payments. It's an ingenious way for the supervisor to make money, until he gets caught!

Creating Fake Bank Confirmations

In the opening paragraphs of Chapter 13, we mention a $4.9 billion fake bank confirmation that the management at a company called Parmalat provided to its auditors. Although the scale of that example is huge, it's not uncommon for auditors to receive phony bank confirmations. Imagine a large company where the auditors have to confirm bank balances maintained in literally hundreds of banks. Audit time is extremely busy, and it's fairly easy for fraudsters to slip in one or two fake confirmations.

A finance director of a publishing company concocted a scheme to defraud his employer that involved creating fictitious confirmations of bank balances. This is how he went about doing it: He captured a screenshot of the bank's online access portal and printed the image. He taped over the actual balance figure, inserting a fictitious balance that he printed from his computer. He cut out the fictitious balance with scissors and literally cut and pasted it on the bank balance. The falsified balance confirmation was reproduced on a photocopier in an attempt to hide the physical manipulation of the document.

The final product was produced to the company's auditors in support of the fictitious account balance. Here is a teaching moment for auditors: Seek bank account balance confirmations directly from the bank, not from company employees. If for some reason the bank confirmation does not arrive before the completion of the audit, observe the client logon to the bank's Web site to verify the account balance. Make sure to look at the subsequent bank activity as well.

Carrying Out Commodity Fraud

This type of fraud is common in times of economic downturns. When the stock markets decline, some investors turn to commodities hoping to make profits. Their beliefs are premised on the notion that a large amount of the commodity is available at a significant discount to its market price. A common red flag to look for is the amount of the commodity involved, which is often unrealistically large.

A colleague of Vijay was once consulted about a deal involving platinum. All other aspects of the deal appeared to be legitimate except for the quantity. Upon investigation, it turned out that the platinum involved in the deal was more than half of the platinum known to exist in the entire world!

Chapter 26

Ten Truly Strange Fraud Stories

In This Chapter

▶ Seeing how creative some fraudsters can be

▶ Watching these creative fraudsters get caught

Sometime during your career as an accountant or auditor, you're bound to come across a truly unusual fraud — or at least hear a great fraud story. In this chapter, we tell you some of the wacky stories that we have come across over the years. If you have a wacky fraud story of your own, we'd love to hear it; e-mail us at frimette@brooklyn.cuny.edu.

Fraudsters can be caught because of good internal controls or good auditing. Sometimes they get caught just because the good guys get lucky. Sometimes they get lucky and don't get caught at all. We hope you get a chuckle and a lesson from reading some of our stories.

The Paper Behind the Wallpaper

An accountant friend of ours was called in by an attorney who specialized in white-collar criminals. The attorney had just finished working a plea deal for a client who was investigated for being a bookmaker. As part of the plea deal, the client agreed to pay about $5 million in back taxes on previously unreported income.

The client said he did not have $5 million handy and wanted our friend to work out a payout agreement with the Internal Revenue Service. Normally when working out a payout agreement, the IRS requires that the taxpayer file statements of net worth and income (Forms 433-A and 433-B). Filing statements with inaccurate information is a fraud. The client did not want to let the IRS know about assets that he had overseas. Our accountant friend, therefore, could not file these forms with the IRS because he wouldn't intentionally leave out assets. Somehow, via miracles, our friend convinced the IRS to accept a plan where the $5 million would be paid out over a ten-year period and the IRS didn't ask for the requisite statements to be filed.

While sitting in his office one day, our friend got a call from the client. He didn't like the agreement. He thought that if he called the IRS directly he would be able to get himself a better deal. Our friend called the lawyer to let him know what was going on. The lawyer said he would try to talk some sense into the client and call back.

Later that afternoon, the lawyer called with this story: He'd been on the phone with the client trying to convince him to take the deal our friend worked out. While they were talking, the lawyer heard a loud banging noise in the background. IRS special agents were at the client's door with a search warrant. When the agents entered the apartment, they proceeded to peel back the wallpaper. In the walls they found wads and wads of cash.

The client ended up in jail for the original charges plus tax evasion. He also forfeited most of his assets to the government.

Winning in Las Vegas . . . or Not

Our friend Julius was performing an audit of a large company that provided supplies to the garment industry. He was working on the audit of a division that made plastic hangers. Somehow Julius got word that the chairman of this division was going to Las Vegas on a regular basis and that he always won at the tables. This information set off all kinds of bells and whistles. *No one* wins consistently in Las Vegas. (Even casinos have losing streaks sometimes.) Julius started asking around to see if he could gather any more information. He found out that this chairman was going to Las Vegas with a salesman from the company that supplied the plastic pellets used to make the hangers. He also managed to make a connection with the staff of the Big Eight firm that was auditing the supplier.

An examination of the relevant documents showed that the hanger manufacturer was buying high-grade plastic pellets from the plastic supplier. Julius confirmed with the Big Eight auditor that the supplier's documents also showed sales of the high-quality plastic pellets. The Big Eight auditor also told him that one of the salesmen was supposedly going to Las Vegas regularly and always losing. As part of the investigation, our friend interviewed some of the people who worked in the factory. They all complained that the plastic they were receiving was a low quality and was causing all kinds of production problems. Julius then sent some of the plastic material to a lab for analysis. When the reports came back that the plastic was indeed low grade, he knew there was a fraud going on.

When the chairman and the salesman were confronted, the whole story came out. This was a kickback scheme. The supplier was sending low-quality plastic and billing for the high quality. Once a month the salesman and the chairman would take a trip to Las Vegas. The salesman would buy chips at a table and pass them to the chairman. The chairman would cash them in. The salesman would come home saying he lost all his money, and the chairman came back a "winner."

We wonder if they used their gambling skills in jail.

It's Curtains for the Thief

Jake was manager at a midsize CPA firm. One of his friends was auditing a curtain and drape manufacturer. The friend was traveling to Georgia to observe inventory at the main plant. He asked Jake to help out and observe the inventory at the plant just outside New York City.

Jake took his team to the plant bright and early on a Saturday morning to do the inventory observation. While walking around the plant, he noticed an area with empty steel shelving. Jake engaged the maintenance man in casual conversation. During the conversation he casually asked about the empty shelves. The maintenance man said that the shelves were used to hold remnants and scrap fabric. Every Saturday morning the plant manager would open his doors to the women in the neighborhood and sell them the remnants and scrap.

Jake then trotted up to the plant office and started asking the bookkeeper about the remnant sales and how she handled the bookkeeping. She said that she would generate invoices for cash sales. She would then put the cash and the invoices in a package. When the plant manager traveled to the home office in Georgia, he would take the package with him so they could deposit the money and add the cash sales into the accounting records. She also said that the sales ran about $1,000 to $1,200 a week.

Jake immediately called his friend who was observing the inventory in the Georgia plant. He went to the bookkeeping office to pore over the general ledger but couldn't find any account for "Cash Sales," and the bookkeeping staff didn't know what he was talking about.

Jake and his friend immediately called the CPA partner in charge of the account and told their story of this suspected fraud. The partner hurriedly called for a meeting with the owner of the company and laid out their suspicions and the evidence they had uncovered.

The owner told them that the plant manager was his brother-in-law who he hired as a favor to his wife's family. He had wondered how his brother-in-law was living as nicely as he did on the salary he was paid. The brother-in-law lost his job but was still lucky because the owner didn't pursue criminal charges.

Rolling the Car Downhill

Jeffrey was a senior partner at a midsize accounting firm. One of the firm's clients was in the process of buying a group of auto dealerships in and around Glens Falls, New York, a beautiful upstate resort area. Jeffrey was asked to go up to Glens Falls and perform an audit on the dealership that was being purchased. Besides the auto showrooms, the dealership would set up kiosks near the tourist attractions (during tourist season, of course) and do short-term auto rentals for cash.

One of the first things that Jeffrey did was leaf through the general ledger. He noticed some strange-looking entries. He traced these entries to the general journal, where he found a whole lot of simple entries with a debit to an expense account and a credit to sales. Entries like this were very strange.

Jeffrey called the partner in charge of the engagement, who flew right up to Glens Falls for a meeting with the 80-year-old owner of the business. The partner explained that the accounting firm thought someone was stealing money from sales. The sales portion of the transaction was being booked, but the cash side of the transaction was being fudged. The firm estimated that about $100,000 was being stolen each year.

The owner was very, very agitated because the company's controller had made these entries. The controller had been with the business for 30 years and had been treated like a son. Why would the controller do something like this? Because the company had a *fidelity policy* (an insurance policy that makes the company whole in the event that an employee steals from it), Jeffrey and his partner recommended that the owner file a claim with the fidelity insurance company. They knew that this fidelity insurer employed very experienced ex-FBI agents and would come in and do a thorough forensic audit.

The owner was loathe to have his "son" investigated and possibly go to jail, but he happened to be friendly with the fidelity insurance company, which owed him a few favors. The insurance company agreed to help. It sent in some of its investigators who presented the controller with Jeffrey's findings. When presented with the facts, the controller agreed to restitution of $300,000 and resigned from his job. He also explained that he had been taking all the cash from the rentals at the kiosks.

Scraps for Sale

When Jeffrey left public accounting, he got a position as a controller at a company that manufactured electric cables. Electric cables are made out of copper, and there is quite a bit of scrap copper as a result of the manufacturing process. Jeffrey knew that any company with scrap metal tries to sell the scraps for some extra cash.

To acclimate himself to the new job, Jeffrey started going through accounting documents. He noticed the receipt from the scrap metal dealer that bought the excess copper. Jeffrey thought it was strange that all the receipts took the form of a business name rubber-stamped at the top of a piece of paper from a plain legal pad. He also thought it strange that every receipt showed copper being purchased for the exact same amount of money per pound. Jeffrey knew that copper was traded on the commodities markets with fluctuating prices.

Jeffrey's first step was to check out the scrap dealer. He called Dun & Bradstreet (a seller of credit and other information about corporations) and ordered a D&B report on the dealer. D&B couldn't find this company in its database. Curiouser and curiouser! Because this was pre-Internet, Jeffrey then hired a private investigator to look at the dealer. While waiting for the investigator's report, Jeffrey started interviewing some of the guys who worked in the warehouse. They told him that a different company was picking up the scrap than the one shown on the receipts. Jeffrey also got a subscription to an industry publication that showed the fluctuating price of copper. Apparently copper was actually trading for a price much higher than the price on the suspect receipts. Eventually the investigator got back to Jeffrey that the corporation was formed by the brother-in-law of the electric cable plant manager.

When the whole story unraveled, it became known that the plant manager was actually selling the scrap to the company that picked up the copper. The brother-in-law's company was simultaneously pretending to buy the scrap from the plant at a much lower price. The plant manager and his brother-in-law were pocketing the difference between those two amounts. We wonder if their knowledge of metals came in handy with those metal prison bars!

Cleanup in Aisle 3, Please!

A certain regional supermarket chain did extensive marketing research and had projections of sales before any of its stores were opened. It bothered management terribly that one store was consistently underperforming. They suspected theft, so they sent investigators to surreptitiously watch what was going on in the store. The investigators were never able to find anything wrong. At the end of the fiscal year, management submitted the financial statements for audit.

Geraldine was a junior auditor at the audit firm. She remembered her auditing professor saying that nothing should be taken for granted on an audit and that every little thing should be examined. Geraldine was assigned to audit certain aspects of revenue. She noticed that there were sales logs from 15 cash registers. Taking her professor's words to heart, Geraldine went down to the store to see for herself how the manager was gathering information from the 15 registers for submission to headquarters. Not taking anything for granted, she counted the number of registers. When she realized there were 16 registers, she counted again and again. Now she was onto something!

The next set of investigators went in and watched register number 16 very, very carefully. They found that the manager himself was working this register for a few hours each afternoon. When confronted, the manager spilled the beans on his fraud.

While the store was being built, he was onsite supervising the construction. He realized that there was some extra room in the checkout area, so he asked the contractor to put in an extra cash register station. That register was not linked to any of the supermarket systems. Each day he would reward one of his cashiers with an extra long break. To make up for the missing manpower, he would step up and man register number 16. All the revenues from number 16 were going to his personal cookie jar.

Let's Count What's in the Piggy Bank

Gail was a junior auditor assigned to a bank audit. The senior member on the audit team assigned Gail to do an audit of the change in the vault. Gail met with a senior vice president of the bank, and together they went to the vault to count the change. The vault contained neat rows of change rolls stacked wall to wall, floor to ceiling, and about six rolls deep. Gail dutifully counted the layers and columns, multiplied them by six, and then multiplied them by the various denominations. She came up with an amount of change that was equal to the amount in the general ledger. All well and good!

Gail then asked the senior VP to pull out a roll of coins so she could actually count the roll. She remembered her auditing professor saying that when observing packaged inventory, an auditor should test some of the packages. The senior VP started to pull out one of the rolls from up front and unroll it for Gail to see. Gail then asked to have one of the rolls from deeper inside unwrapped. The senior VP refused Gail's request. Gail remembered the many fraud stories her professor told about clients trying to steer auditors to look at the particular inventory they wanted the auditor to see. She knew it was best to force the client to show her what *she* wanted to see.

The senior VP was adamant, but Gail stuck to her guns. She called the partner in charge of the account to come down to the vault. When he arrived, the senior VP gave the partner a hard time over pulling out an inside roll of coins. It struck the partner as strange that the VP should get so agitated over such an innocuous request. The partner supported Gail and forced the issue. When they finally got to examine an inside roll, they found a quarter at each end and a wooden dowel in the middle. The partner then called in the whole team and did a detailed count of the coins.

In the end, they found that over $300,000 in coins was missing. Apparently, over the years, every time the VP needed some extra cash, he would go down to the vault and take a roll of coins, replacing them with the wooden dowel so no one would suspect.

(Mind you, this is an old story from when coins were worth something!)

Baby, It's Cold Outside!

Barney was a manager at a midsize accounting firm. The firm was engaged by a bank to examine inventory at a small department store. The department store had applied to the bank for an operating loan. As part of the loan agreement, the store was pledging its inventory, including the furs in the vault.

Barney was sent down to the store with a team of fur experts to examine the furs. Barney and the experts were placed in a room near the fur vault. The store's staff would wheel in a coat rack with fur coats. The experts would examine each garment and make notes about the coat and its approximate value. After a few hours of this, one of the experts jumped up and asked Barney to come outside with him. Over a coffee, the expert said that something was amiss. He thought they were seeing the same garments more than once. Barney asked how he knew this. The expert exclaimed that there was one particularly unusual lamb's wool coat that was hanging next to a particular mink. Because the lamb's coat was unusual and there was a stark contrast to that particular mink, he took note of it. And he had seen this combination come through a second time.

Barney went back in and declared to all that he had a new plan. He made the store staff take all the racks out of the vault. He then organized his experts at the entrance to the vault and told the store employee's to bring the racks to them one by one. After each rack was examined the rack would go into the vault and stay there. When they completed this process, the total fur inventory came out much lower than the store record and the first round of counting showed.

When Barney started interviewing the store's staff, they told Barney that they were instructed to recycle the racks they were presenting to the auditors. Each time a rack was recycled, they were supposed to mix up the order of the coats. After several hours of doing this, they got tired and lazy and stopped reordering the coats. That's why the expert was able to notice the mink and lamb combination.

The Answer Is Blowing in the Wind

Our friend Moe told us this story that occurred when he first started in public accounting many, many years ago. The systems that are described in this story don't exist in today's business world, but there are still important lessons to be learned.

Moe's firm had a client that was a midsize department store in Manhattan. In those days most customers paid in cash. To control the monies at each register there were a set of prenumbered invoices. At the end of the day, all the invoices had to be accounted for. Also, the floor personnel did not have cash. When they made a sale they wrote up an invoice, with a myriad of carbon copies. They would put the customer's cash and the invoice into a capsule and send it, via a pneumatic tube system, to the cashier. (If you don't know what this system is, you can still see it in some hospitals where it's used to send blood samples to the lab. Some Costco stores also use it to send cash from the registers to the office.) The cashier would make the change and send it back down to the sales floor with a copy of the invoice for the customer. She would also send the carbon copies of the invoice to the various departments that were supposed to receive them.

The store was always considered an underachiever. It never seemed to show the profits that were expected by management. Management brought in security personnel to watch the goings on in the store, but they were never able to detect any fraud. Finally, management called in the accountants and asked for their recommendations.

The accountants took the approach of shoring up the internal controls. They found that the store did not have a required vacation policy, so they instituted one. As the various employees took their required vacations, the accountants tried to analyze the numbers to see if there were any changes in sales or profits. For a long time they didn't see any changes.

Most employees did not argue with the new vacation policy. But there was one holdout — John the janitor, who insisted he couldn't comply with the policy because he just couldn't afford to take a vacation. After much argument John was forced to abandon his "office" for a week and take a vacation.

John was very proud of having his own office. The office was actually a largish broom closet. John had found an old desk and chair, which he used decorate his office. While John was out on vacation the accountants noticed that the profit numbers started to rise. They went to the office to see if they could find any documents that would indicate that John was stealing. They didn't find any documents in the office at all. But while combing through the office, one of the accountants noticed that one of the floor boards was loose.

When they pried open the floorboard, they found a junction for the pneumatic tube system. There seemed to be a makeshift opening and door cover in the system. On further investigation they found a "paid" stamp in one of the drawers of John's desk.

John had made a cut into the pneumatic tube system. He also stole a "paid" stamp from one of the offices. Every so often he would open his door to the pneumatic tube system and take a capsule that was on its way from the sales floor to the cashier. He would take out the invoice and cash. He would do the cashier's job of making change and sending a copy of the invoice back to the sales floor stamped "paid." He would then send the copies of the invoice to the various offices. At the end of every day, therefore, every invoice was accounted for.

When John made restitution, it was in excess of $1 million.

"Grand" Theft

We heard of a local television station manager whose job was on the chopping block. One Saturday afternoon, he concocted a story about why he had to move one of the two Steinways grand pianos from the station to his home. He conned several station engineers into loading the piano into a rented truck, going to his home with him, and carrying the thing into his living room. A month went by, and the manager was fired from the station. He never did return that piano, and the engineers never did "tattle" on him because they were scared they'd lose their jobs for unwittingly being part of this theft.

Index